Y0-CSF-470

TELECOMMUNICATIONS

TELECOMMUNICATIONS

Advisory Editor

Christopher H. Sterling

Editorial Board

John M. Kittross
George Shiers
Elliot Sivowitch

FESSENDEN

BUILDER OF TOMORROWS

BY HELEN M. FESSENDEN

Index
By
Ormond Raby

ARNO PRESS
A New York Times Company
New York • 1974

Reprint Edition 1974 by Arno Press Inc.

Index Copyright © 1974 by Ormond Raby

TELECOMMUNICATIONS
ISBN for complete set: 0-405-06030-0
See last pages of this volume for titles.

Manufactured in the United States of America

Library of Congress Cataloging in Publication Data

  Fessenden, Helen May Trott.
    Fessenden, builder of tomorrows.

    (Telecommunications)
    Reprint of the ed. published by Coward-McCann, New York.
    Bibliography: p.
    1. Fessenden, Reginald Aubrey, 1866-1932.
I. Title. II. Series: Telecommunications (New York, 1974-
TK6545.F4F4 1974   621.3841'092'4 [B]   74-4681
ISBN 0-405-06047-5

FESSENDEN

BUILDER OF TOMORROWS

BY HIS GENIUS DISTANT LANDS CONVERSE
AND MEN SAIL UNAFRAID UPON THE DEEP.
R. K. F.

FESSENDEN
BUILDER OF TOMORROWS

BY HELEN M. FESSENDEN

COWARD-McCANN, INC. · NEW YORK

1940

COPYRIGHT, 1940, BY
HELEN M. FESSENDEN

All rights reserved. This book, or parts thereof, must not be reproduced in any form without written permission.

MANUFACTURED IN THE UNITED STATES OF AMERICA

FOREWORD

To the World of Today and the World of Tomorrow, worlds alike benefited and enriched by the life of Reginald A. Fessenden, I give the man himself. That the mind which conceived the correct theory of wireless transmission, which invented the Wireless Telephone and with it accomplished the first Broadcasting, which invented and developed the Fathometer and all it implied, that this mind failed to defend itself against commercial assault, whether financial or scientific, is an inescapable fact. For this fact I make no apology. Mine is the setting forth of factual data, an indication of trends, not the indictment of any man or group of men. Without a straightforward account of certain legal encounters, the life of my husband would be but partly told. The outcome of these encounters is a matter of court record which "he who runs may read." It is however not by court decisions but by his work that the man will be remembered.

Helen M. Fessenden

"It is a pet idea of mine that one gets more real truth out of one avowed partisan than out of a dozen of your sham impartialists—wolves in sheep's clothing—simpering honesty as they suppress documents. After all, what one wants to know is not what people did, but why they did it—or rather why they *thought* they did it; and to learn that you should go to the men themselves, their very falsehood is often more than another man's truth."

LETTERS OF ROBERT LOUIS STEVENSON.
"Student Days at Edinburgh," p. 27

CONTENTS

I.	FOREBEARS AND CHILDHOOD	3
II.	SCHOOL AND COLLEGE	13
III.	BERMUDA	23
IV.	NEW YORK	27
V.	A YANKEE BOY AND A CHINA MUG	31
VI.	FESSENDEN FINDS HIMSELF	39
VII.	NEWARK, PITTSFIELD AND PURDUE	47
VIII.	PITTSBURGH DAYS	64
IX.	A MOMENTOUS DECISION	73
X.	WIRELESS AT ROANOKE ISLAND	86
XI.	NATIONAL ELECTRIC SIGNALING COMPANY	105
XII.	WIRELESS AS A BUSINESS ENTERPRISE AND TRANS-ATLANTIC STATIONS	119
XIII.	TRANS-ATLANTIC WORKING	131
XIV.	DASHED HOPES	140
XV.	WIRELESS TELEPHONY AND THE HIGH-FREQUENCY ALTERNATOR	147
XVI.	DIFFICULTIES—LEGISLATIVE AND COMPANY	157
XVII.	SERVICE ABROAD	169
XVIII.	DESTRUCTION AT HOME	182

vi CONTENTS

XIX.	DUST AND ASHES	188
XX.	POWER AND POWER STORAGE	194
XXI.	TURBO-ELECTRIC DRIVE. THE FESSENDEN COMBUSTION ENGINE	204
XXII.	SUBMARINE SIGNALING AND THE FESSENDEN OSCILLATOR	214
XXIII.	THE WORLD WAR	224
XXIV.	SUBMARINE SIGNALING IN WAR TIME AND CIVILIAN WAR BOARDS	235
XXV.	OTHER EVENTS OF WAR YEARS	255
XXVI.	INVENTION	261
XXVII.	GREAT AGES	275
XXVIII.	LOOKING FAR BACKWARDS — THE DELUGED CIVILIZATION	286
XXIX.	THE FESSENDEN FATHOMETER	297
XXX.	OTHER DEVICES	304
XXXI.	"GOD ALMIGHTY HATES A QUITTER"	312
XXXII.	SANCTUARY	335

ADDENDA

I.	SUMMARY. THE SCIENTIFIC WORK OF REGINALD A. FESSENDEN	347
II.	FESSENDEN'S DISCOVERY OF THE ELECTROSTATIC DOUBLET THEORY AND OF THE NATURE OF COHESION AND ELASTICITY—as told by himself	348
III.	BIBLIOGRAPHY	353
IV.	INDEX	365

FESSENDEN

Builder of Tomorrows

CHAPTER I

FOREBEARS AND CHILDHOOD

REGINALD AUBREY FESSENDEN was born on October 6, 1866 in the rectory of the small parish of East Bolton on a bay of Lake Memphremagog, Lower Canada.

The tapestry of commingled lives that forms the background of an individual is always revealing. The pattern never exactly repeats itself, but dominant characteristics recur again and again. Fortunate is the man whose birthright is a fabric, close knit, clean and strong; such a one is indeed well born. From Kent, from Yorkshire, from Northumberland came the warp threads of the fabric forming the background of this rectory baby. Fessenden, Tibbits, Trenholme and Ridley were the names of the four grandparents whose lives were the woof, bright threads spun strong on the wheel of American pioneer living.

The Fessendens were "men of Kent" from very early times, the name being traceable in that English county to the 13th century. They were of the minor gentry, an ancient, respectable and cultivated race. But, like many another family of the kind, the sons left England for the American colonies and it is in the New World that we must look for the rise of this old race. One John Fessenden was the first to pioneer, being settled in Cambridge, Massachusetts before 1640. He was a glover and tradition says that his vats and tan yard were on the site of what is now part of Harvard College.

Nicholas Fessenden, nephew and heir of John, came over while young and lived and carried on the family business and died on the property of his uncle. From him almost certainly are descended all of the name of Fessenden in the United States and Canada. The family increased, but lost nothing of its tradition of cultivated minds. The boys of each generation reached out as a matter of course after scholarship, fitting themselves to become teachers, lawyers, preachers and statesmen; and this without neglecting the various crafts that dwellers in a newly settled land must of necessity practice. They were leaders in their communities, shaping public thought, forming their own opinions and sticking to them.

William Pitt Fessenden, Senator from Maine and Secretary of the Treasury under Lincoln, is a shining example of the stalwart uprightness and independence that mark the family. In a home letter from Washington he wrote concerning negroes in the Army:

> "I see that Philip Douglas, the Tribune and the whole tribe of dogs have been barking at me for my action touching negro soldiers. Well, they are wrong and I am right. So they may bark and howl as suits them best and I shall stick to my text."

Again, during the grueling days of the trial for the impeachment of President Johnson:

> "Whatever may be the consequences to myself personally I will not decide the question against my own judgment. —The President has nothing to give, even if there were anything that I desired. What then could induce me to vote for his acquittal but an imperative sense of what was due, not so much to him, as to the great office he holds, and above all to myself as a judge sworn in all things 'to do impartial duty.'"

In the face of anonymous threats and of the still more insidious letters from friends, he nailed his colors to the mast, thinking to go down in the storm that raged against the small group who voted the decisive "Not Guilty." Fortunately, the grave charges could not be maintained, even by a biased House of Representatives still rankling with bitter war memories. Fessenden and all other supporters were spared the sacrifice of their careers but the episode is an outstanding example of the dominant family characteristic.

With Peter Fessenden, the grandson of Nicholas, there began a drifting away from Cambridge, for he became one of the city fathers of Barre. Ebenezer, the son of Peter, moved to New Hampshire and then to Lower Canada. His son, Elisha Moss, settled in Armada, Michigan and there Elisha Joseph, the father of Reginald Aubrey Fessenden, was born.

Of the personalities of Elisha Moss Fessenden and his wife, Elsie Tibbits, only a faint impression remains, but though faint, it is of people scholarly and austere. They moved with their family of five sons and one daughter to Canada. Later, in the Civil War, one of their sons, a captain in the Union Army fell at the battle of the Crater, Petersburg.

In 1820 William Trenholme with Ann Winn, his wife, and their family came from North Cave, Yorkshire and settled in Lower Canada on the St. Francis River. There they bought a large tract of land, enough that each of their sons might inherit three hundred acres of choice farm and timber land. They named the place Trenholme and were very thoroughgoing in their colonization, building their own mills for grain and lumber, their own school and their own church.

Edward Trenholme, a son of William and the maternal grandfather of Reginald is the figure of greatest portent, since the similarity between him and his grandson is very marked. He was quick to wrath, hating mean and devious traits and lashing out at people because of them and the acts they fostered, but with the storm quickly over and no lingering rancor. The possessor of a constructive mind and always foremost in progressive movements, he counted as gain a loss in the cause of Progress. A man of vision, he was capable of foreseeing the future needs and developments of the region in which he lived.

He married Marian Ridley and they had a large family—three sons and seven daughters. They owned a three-hundred-acre farm, a grist mill and a lumber mill and for years they prospered. Then, when Edward Trenholme was in his forties, the grist mill burned to the ground. A new mill was immediately begun and an order sent to France for the best millstone that could be procured. Soon the new building neared completion and grain came in so quickly that operation was started before the debris of building was entirely cleared away. Again the mill caught fire, possibly from the smoldering pipe of an overtired watchman. There had been insurance to cover the first loss but this time no insurance had been placed and the blow was staggering.

Again the mill was rebuilt, but this time with borrowed capital, much of it taken up at usurious rates. Something quickly productive of money had to be found and Edward Trenholme turned his attention to the solution of several problems that were of vast importance to this new land and which for some time had interested him. The answers that he found to these problems were three pioneer and basic inventions,—the grain elevator, the grain cooler and the snow plough. One of his children recalls an adorable little model of the grain elevator, placed on top of a high wardrobe to be safe from childish hands, but watched with longing by childish eyes.

With the financial aid of the Hon. John Young of Montreal, Edward Trenholme took out patents on these inventions; going on one occasion to Washington he met and talked with Lincoln and brought from the interview an enduring impression of the greatness of the man. Both the grain elevator and the grain cooler came into general use in practically unchanged form, but not till after the death of Trenholme and from them his family reaped no benefit.

This unusual family, before its circle was broken and the group scattered, merits special consideration. Three boys and seven girls—not a mental or moral weakling amongst them—all eager to try a lance with life for some high cause—threshing out in the home forum the pros and cons of every bit of knowledge that came their way—seeking education at any cost. A happy solution of the problem of schooling came while two of the boys were at McGill, one preparing for the law, the other for medicine. With one or two of their fellow students to share expenses, the boys took a house in Montreal and some of their sisters came up from Trenholme to keep house and at the same time to attend a seminary for young ladies.

It is easy to imagine this group of young people of the late 1850's, their bright visions, their long thoughts of the future, the gay good times and hard work they all shared. The fact that they were living under unconventional conditions seems never to have entered the heads of the group; if they were criticized, they were too busy to be aware of it.

As was wholly natural, romance entered the circle and Clementina Trenholme became engaged to Elisha Joseph Fessenden who was preparing for the ministry, a friend of her brothers and a member of the group. Other weddings had taken place in the Trenholme family, but when Edward Trenholme heard of Clementina's engagement, he said, "the light of the house will be gone."

The young couple were married at Trenholme on January 4, 1865. Three weeks later the shadow fell on them as well as on the rest of the Trenholme family, for on January 25 Edward Trenholme died. This loss coming to his favorite daughter in the first days of her married life, would it be surprising if she idealized all that was best in her father and desired for a child of hers the qualities of his greatness?

Of the last Sunday night in the home before this untimely end, a vivid picture has been handed down; a shabby parlor, a round table on which rested the family Bible, the father seated beside the table with his little wife on his knee, she reading aloud from the Sacred Book while he, with one arm around her, held the lamp so that its light might shine more clearly on the printed page.

His latest invention, the railroad snow plough, had reached the stage of full-sized construction and in January of his 55th year Edward Trenholme went to Sherbrook to witness a trial run. He was at breakfast when somebody told him that the new snow plough was being taken out. Anxious to be on the spot to watch the performance of his creation, Trenholme ran out of the house and to the railroad. Excitement and exertion brought on an attack of apoplexy or heart failure and he was fatally stricken.

In the dead of Tuesday night Mrs. Trenholme received news of her husband's illness. She called a farm hand and bade him hitch a horse to a sleigh, then drove the thirty long miles through the snow and the cold, reaching her husband many hours before she could have done had she waited for a train. Edward Trenholme lingered three days after his first stroke and his last words were "Tell them (the children) to serve God with all sincerity and truth".

And what of the mother on whom the mantle of family guidance fell? In the years following the heavy losses by fire and the subsequent neglect of farming in favor of the great inventions taking shape in the mind of Edward Trenholme, his affairs had become sadly involved—his land heritage had diminished—there were debts. A large family eager for the best education within reach could not be reared on nothing, even in those times. The tiny woman who had been Marian Ridley faced her children in solemn conclave. Debt stared them in the face and was intolerable to them all.

The debts must be paid and to do that Marian Trenholme willingly sacrificed the whole of her widow's third of the estate. "We will take care of you, Mother", her children promised, and in the meager years that followed, she practiced simple living until it became an art and the burden of their promise fell but lightly on her children. Mills and broad acres were forfeited but kindness and hospitality dwelt ever beneath her roof. She had married a strong man, shared the storms of his career, borne a family of children all showing the dominant Trenholme strain of progressiveness and aggressiveness. But even against this background of strength, she stands out, possessed of a sturdy personality of her own which hardships and misfortune never warped—a blend of the simplicity of essentials, the kindness of understanding and unselfish endurance.

Endurance Marian Ridley inherited as a tradition. Her father, a Ridley of a family "long seated in Northumberland", had moved from England to Ireland to take up a property on which the terms of lease were "as long as grass grows and water flows". It was evidently a considerable estate with the concomitants of a squire's duties and privileges—hunting and riding for sport—stock raising and farming and added to other duties, the obligations of a millwright.

But to them as to many others there applied the familiar phrase "these were troublous days in Ireland." Mutual religious intolerance was at its ghastly work and persecutions were rife. There was a round-up of Protestants in the neighborhood and Mr. Ridley and his brothers were caught in the net. All were imprisoned in a barn which was to be set on fire; however, it chanced that a Roman Catholic priest of the district had come to know and like Mr. Ridley. "One man in that building must be saved," said the priest, and by some means he effected the rescue. With Ireland no longer a safe home, the Ridley family moved to Canada and settled in the Eastern Townships. The youngest of the ten children—a girl of seven—was Marian, afterwards the wife of Edward Trenholme.

Marian Trenholme's children adored her and to her grandchildren she was a beloved character. Little Reginald, standing one day beside her said, "I'm going to marry you, Grandma, when I grow up." His father told him the prayer book said that a man may not marry his grandmother. "My prayer book says a man *may* marry his grandmother", answered Reginald stoutly, then as always undaunted by high authority if he believed himself right.

The early years were very quiet. His father, after a short period at the East Bolton living, was transferred to Bolton Centre and there two more sons were born, Kenneth Harcourt in 1869 and Cortez Ridley Trenholme in 1871. The fourth and last child of this marriage, Lionel Victor, was born at Fergus in 1873. This was the third parish to which Mr. Fessenden had been appointed.

Life at the Rectory was on a very simple scale as far as material things went and 'passing rich on forty pounds a year' would have been no gross exaggeration for country livings in Canada in the seventies. Every penny of income needed to be budgeted and husbanded. But Mr. Fessenden was a lovable and saintly spirit, instinct with charity, and he could deny no appeal for help if he had the means at hand to satisfy it. Often much needed funds were disbursed in charity instead of being used to replenish the family exchequer. The courageous, practical ability of his wife accepted these conditions and overcame them. Life could be a great Adventure and Nature an inexhaustible treasure house, and that is what they made it.

Two special characteristics marked little Reginald's nature; prompt obedience and untiring industry. When but three years old and just running around, an instinct for helpfulness was evident; small hands struggled with sticks of wood to keep the kitchen wood box filled and tiny feet toiled up and down a slope to carry little pails of water to the large kitchen bucket. His obedience was such that never once in his childhood was a punishment administered or needed. "The lad is of finer clay" was the private and pardonable family estimate of this boy.

Nature held great marvels for the child. Big trees or high winds roused his imagination. Once when a wind storm swept the place the little fellow was found leaping for joy, clapping his hands and shouting "Wind-a-blowing, Wind-a-blowing", his small body a vibrating part of the storm. He was always resourceful; on being told that he must not scratch with his hands where the mosquitoes bit him he gravely pondered the ruling and was next seen whittling busily with a dull knife at some 'scratching sticks' to keep within the law and yet be comfortable.

From the first he was observant and a seeker after the cause and reason of things. On the occasion of his first church attendance he heard for the first time a musical instrument. Like a magnet the wonder of it drew him and during an intermission of prayer when adult eyes were not upon him, he wandered up to the big box and, unmindful of the silence of the church, remarked very earnestly and distinctly to the young lady at the harmonium, "That's a pleasant noise."

Nothing was meaningless or without import to him. It is recalled that he had learned a nursery rhyme about Jenny Wren who in illness was succored by Cock Robin with wine and sops. She promised to wed him but with restored health forgot her promise. This broken faith stirred the child strongly and "Fie upon you, fie upon you, Bold Faced Jig" burst forth in tones of condemnation accompanied by the winged jerk of the arms that, to the end, was always a gesture of disturbance.

The world of books opened to him with almost magic touch and at a very early age. In his unfinished autobiography, begun in Radio News in 1924, he says:

"When I learned to read I cannot remember, for my next (second) recollection is of a copy in fine print, of the Arabian Nights. In those days children learned to read earlier than they do now. My mother could read when she was five and she told me I learned slightly earlier. The present method of delaying until seven or eight would seem to be a mistake. The great character-forming influences are those received before the age of seven; what a man is at seven he will probably be for the rest of his life. The Jesuits used to say that if they had the training of a child until he was seven they did not care who had charge of his training afterwards.

Now in our present civilization by far the greater number of the intellectual impulses which reach us come from what has been written; and what seem to be the more important impulses can only be received in this way. If, then, we do not learn to read some years before we are seven, these extremely important impulses are lacking during the age when the character is forming. I think that what is called 'vision' is largely influenced by the ability to read at an early age. And 'without vision the people perisheth', the prophet says.

Certainly it gives increased facility in acquiring Knowledge. Many young people now, I notice, read what would have been considered rather slowly. One soon learns to read words as words and not combinations of letters, but it is possible to read lines and even short paragraphs as units and not as groups of words, so that one may read a scientific book while turning over the pages somewhat slowly. This is a great help to one engaged in investigation and as it is purely a matter of practice it is doubtful if it can be acquired without an early start."

His mother was Reginald's first teacher; later a governess, Miss Ardagh, took a hand in training the boy. But the important factor was his unusual desire for information and his capacity to absorb it; learning was a game; knowing things a glowing objective.

Four boys together can generally find amusement and the young Fessendens' diversions were simple and wholesome, chief among them swimming and skating according to season. Pets were numerous, cats especially favored; but all the live stock were humored to the point of developing temperament in them. Daffy the cow when bored at life in the field clumped into the kitchen shed. The horse would permit one brother to ride and not another, promptly depositing an unapproved rider on the ground. The ducks habitually waddled noisily after the boys to the creek and once in their own element proceeded industriously to nip at forty toes if and as they got the chance.

The season's round of fruits in Canada's lavish abundance was a happy memory of Reginald's childhood. Fruit in such unstinted plenty that the well-known quip designed to bewilder the Englishman—"we eat what we can and can what we can't" was literally true. Big, two-quart jars of every variety of berry and stone fruit filled the pantry shelves; apples and pears that would keep were stored for winter consumption and, best of all perhaps, were the fall nutting expeditions from which the boys would return with bursting bags which were dumped in luxurious waves on the floor of a small sun room.

Here, with a book, with his white cat on his lap, and with a sea of nuts around him is how I like best to picture this **boy's childhood.**

CHAPTER II

SCHOOL AND COLLEGE

BY THE TIME Reginald was nine years old the family had moved to Niagara Falls. At De Veaux Military College on the U. S. side of the river, a scholarship was vacant. Though the lad was hardly old enough to attend and it was impossible to send him as a boarder as that would cost too much, the opportunity was too good to be lost.

Here is Reginald's own recollection of this experience.

"The walk was rather long and the work started early so I got my own breakfast. In the fall and spring terms the sun would just be coming up as I got to a place called Mount Eagle and it was a lovely sight and a lovely walk from there on, for the school was in the extensive and wooded grounds just at the Whirlpool Rapids. But in winter it was different. Those were bitter struggles across the old Suspension Bridge, forcing my way into and across the heavy winds blowing down the Niagara Gorge, and holding every now and then with both hands to the railing of the footway. But it was always a good fight and I enjoyed it. Only once the experience was not so pleasant. My clock had gone wrong and I started off at one in the morning, reached the school about two, could not waken anyone and had to roost in the gymnasium until five. And it was one of those below zero nights."

In connection with this episode, it was not long before it was realized at the rectory that something was amiss. The knowledge of a warm breakfast made ready the night before and a bright moon on snow which gave the effect of early morning, reassured the mother as she heard sounds of departure, but wakening after a nap and finding it now quite dark, she roused her husband with the cry "Oh Fess, Fess, what have I done. I've sent Reggie off to school in the dead of the night. You must go at once to De Veaux to find out what has happened to him."

As quickly as possible Mr. Fessenden reached the school to find all well. The Principal, Mr. Patterson, had by this time heard a bell, had gone in person to the door and promptly put the little fellow to bed. But a school saga was launched for all time of a zeal for learning that sent a boy off to school at 1 A.M.

As regards the school itself, Reginald writes further in his autobiography:

"It was then not so very long after the close of the Civil War, the military discipline was very strict and our inspectors of the regular service were martinets. So there was nothing slovenly about our drill and the smartness permeated to the class rooms. But we were worked too continuously; it was always a rush at the end of a class to fall in on the drill ground or to get to another class. I never played for one minute at that school, coming as I did, and leaving immediately after classes or at noon on Saturdays."

Young as he was, at the end of his year there his name was on the honor roll of the school and he won so many prizes that a young friend said, "Well, Fess, you must have had a good teacher." "Yes," he said, "I had my mother."

In 1877 came the first extended absence from home. He was sent to Trinity College School at Port Hope, Ontario, then as now one of Canada's outstanding public schools.

A bundle of old letters, faded ink and careful, childish script, gives a flickering picture of these years.

1877

(Trinity College School) "How is it I received no letters from home? I wrote a long letter to you Mama and a letter to Tren and Vic. It seems so lonely to get no letters from home for two weeks. I am head in everything except 'repetitions' and that is because I can't say it as naturally as another boy. The masters are very kind to me because when the whole form misses a question I always know it. . . .

In four weeks there will be an examination and I hope to distinguish myself in it. At Midsummer the marks of the last and Midsummer examinations will be added together and the prizes then given. I have the best hopes a boy could have and no fears. In honor of my being head in my form I went and had a splendid skate on the rink Wednesday as it was a half holiday. I have everything a boy could have and am very happy. They don't make me 'brace up' here.

T.C.S. "I meant to have written on Saturday but I heard that the half term marks were to be given out today so I waited. The following is my list of marks. No. 1 is head of your class in that lesson. 1 in Divinity, Eng. Gram. Tables, Phy. Geo., Geography, Dictation; 2 in Latin and Reading; 3 in History; 4 in Arithmetic and Repetitions; 6 in writing; total 27.

If I go on like this I will be likely to get out of college when I am fifteen years old. I got a valentine on Saturday representing me kicked out of the college backdoor but I hope I will not be kicked out of college but take my hat, brush my hair and clothes so that I may be more decent than my portrait and walk out of the college front door. And moreover I hope to walk out without a whisker on my chin.—I think as God has made me beat boys of 18 in my studies he means me to be of use in the way of learning. But I must bid you good by with my best wishes."

T.C.S. "Feb. In my half term I found I was head of my class so far. I got six 1-s, which the boys tell me is more than anybody in our form ever had before. Tell Papa I am doing as well as I ever thought of doing. The boys said to me after the marks had been read, "You're a queer fellow but you'll win the Form Prize yet." That night about 30 of the boys said "You'll win the Form Prize yet." I carved a stick for a boy for a set of checkers but without the board. I thought I could give it to Ken on his birthday. Don't tell him. I picked up 2 bits of iron with holes in them and while looking through one of the holes I discovered something. By arranging the bits of iron and looking through one of the holes I can find the exact distance of anything from me.——"

(Here already is a glimpse of his ability to observe facts and to coordinate them to a purpose.)

> T.C.S. "Feb. All the boys are getting expresses, that is packages with something in them. You know how miserable it is to have other people giving you things and you not able to give them anything in return. Would you mind sending me one in the summer. Several nicknames at our school. 'Pheasant' or 'Soldier Boy' is me, for all the boys saw me the first night I was here." (In his De Veaux cadet uniform.)
>
> T.C.S. "Feb.—The cakes and apples were very nice and the boys liked the apples very much."
>
> T.C.S. "March. In about three weeks Lent will be ended and my first examination at Trin. Coll. will begin. If I am successful in that it will throw a good deal in my favor at the Midsummer examinations. I am getting on as well as ever in my lessons and am head in either 4 or 5 things every day."

A letter from his mother reveals the home atmosphere and her understanding of her industrious small son.

> The Rectory. "My dear Boy, I am very glad to know that you are still ahead—keep at it as Captain Cuttle says, all the days of your life and prosper. Papa will send you change in this for a cap, two dollars will buy you a good one I think. I hope to see you home soon, well and rosy, mind. Your chance seems good for promotion at least and whether you succeed or fail the consciousness that you have done your level best will be a comfort to us all.
>
> We have a regular cattery, (did you ever hear that word before?), some five now take refuge under the Rectory rafters and shed-beams. The chickens are disappearing in appetizing stews. Nuts, grapes and wine still hold out for my great man's return. We had nice sleighing Monday. Tren is great on snow ploughs, using a pound of nails to make one. Ken is passing exams for upper school. All well and send love. Tina." (Mother).
>
> T.C.S. "May. I am promoted into the lower second this term and will have to work very hard, for I have to do two

terms work in one term and that term is only ten weeks, that is 23 weeks work in 10.—It will not be long now till I'm back to my old cat and everybody else there."

1878

T.C.S. "March. We had a concert and theatre combined the same night as you had the Indian Concert. I went to it. I wish we had a powerful telephone between here and Clifton and we could go to a double concert for 25 cents."

Years later this childish wish was gloriously realized when he gave the world its first Broadcast.

1879

(From his father). "Oct. 30. Was as we ever are very glad to get your letter on Tuesday and to hear so gratifying news of your success in your studies. We shall get the half-term's report soon now and it will I am sure be a pleasant one to have.—On Friday being at a Committee Meeting at Hamilton I went on to Brampton and was at the baptism of your little cousin, Uncle Corte's eldest son. It will be some time before he will be at Port Hope. I hope he will do as well there as my Reggie has done and is doing.—"

(From his mother—same letter). "My dear Boy—Seems to me I am always in a hurry but do not think I don't find time to hold you in my thoughts. We got some nice cider the other day. I wish I could send you a bottle. The white cat is well and growling as usual; she caught a mouse and was terrible to hear for a long time after. Winter will soon be on us. I hope you are warm and comfortable—tell me how your clothes do. B.M. and J.C. were married here yesterday. I got the fee, $5., which just paid a bill for me— wish some one else would get married. I wish you'd play and not read during the holiday time, as the mind needs rest as well as the body. Goodbye with love and kisses.

Your Mother

T.C.S. "Nov. I got your letter and intend to get a good knife with the dollar Papa sent me and you can give him a kiss for me and for his half of the letter and he can give you one for your half of it, I send both enclosed in the envelope. I have got some envelopes and a few more stamps and will manage very well the rest of the term. Tell me how that cricket match came off, which beat and who played. How does Ken manage with the horse and does Daff give as much milk as she used to. I am head in the greater part of my studies or near it. How is my old cat getting on?"

T.C.S. "Nov. In my report he who has the least marks when added together is head of the form, so I am head as you see. I have only 39 marks while Schofield who has the next least has 56, so as I said before, a great deal ahead of him. I will explain this when I get home which will be in a month as it is rather long for a letter. The one Prize at Christmas will be as hard to get as the six at Midsummer and hence if I take it, it will really be as much honor."

(From his father). "Nov. My dear Reggie—Three cheers for you—you did splendidly the last half term I think. I enclose the report you ask for and only hope the Xmas one may be as good and I have no doubt it will be.——"

1880

T.C.S. "Feb.—Sometimes I take one sentence in English and turn it first into French then into Latin and last into Greek and I think I learn a great many new words that way.——"

Reginald was confirmed on Sunday, March 21, 1880 and received Holy Communion for the first time on Easter Day, March 28, 1880.

T.C.S. "March 21 (the day he was confirmed) I got your letter with that pretty card and the prayer which I have used several times, but though I should have liked to, I had no opportunity of using it in the service though I repeated such parts as I remembered during the pause. I am thinking so much tonight that I shall not be able to write you a very long letter."

Dr. Bethune, head master of Port Hope said that Fessenden was one of the most industrious boys ever at the school. One year he carried off all prizes in his Form and wrote quite impersonally to his mother that 'she ought to be proud of such a son', also that he hoped some day to be worth $10,-000.00.

He shared in sports but they were incidental to the main purpose—study—and yet this did not as might have been expected, result in hazing and teasing. School boys are apt to make life miserable for the prodigy, but in this case, the lad's healthy interest and enjoyment of all that went on around him was so obvious that his fellows appear to have accepted him as a jolly good chap whose scholastic attainments were in the nature of a harmless idiosyncrasy.

1881

Defective vision made glasses necessary from his early years. He wrote from school:

> T.C.S. "My eyes are beginning to be very sore and every night I tie a wet handkerchief round them and sleep as soon as I can which is not hard to do."

During 1881 there was an illness and an operation on his eyes and a subsequent period of following his own devices. He could well afford the interlude, being advanced beyond his years.

As time went on he sought for greater accuracy of lens to reduce eyestrain, and of course different kinds for different needs, but not till middle life did he obtain maximum relief when, through the kindness of Dr. Max Poser, the facilities of the Bausch & Lomb optical department were placed at his service.

The complete charting of the eye that was possible with the splendid apparatus of the Laboratory resulted in a lens which, for him, was a revelation in improved vision and lightness. His eyes had a magnifying power and for minute, close-up or delicate adjustments, off came the glasses and one eye was brought to bear, like a microscope, upon the thing to be investigated. Mr. Wolf, head instrument maker for a Boston optical company, described in after years his first impressions of Professor Fessenden. Fine physique and imposing presence were naturally first noted, but Mr. Wolf's trained eyes at once detected something unusual about his glasses. "That man has a microscopic eye" he said to himself. Then discussion of the work engrossed his attention but days later when the work was completed, he again said to himself "that man has a microscopic eye" and proceeded to examine his own work under a microscope so as to be sure of the effect it would produce.

Meantime, sixteen was the minimum age of admission to college and, with the lad only fourteen and practically ready for college, what was to be done in the interim?

He found a job with the Imperial Bank at Woodstock, advanced there very rapidly and was beginning to think complacently of a future as a banker when he learned the bank's policy in regard to promotion to positions that really counted. This would have been 'time on leaden wings' indeed. So he returned to Trinity School for two terms to prepare for and to take honor examinations—winning only second or third place.

Not up to past performance, was his opinion of that.

During the summer vacation an unexpected offer came from his father's old University, Bishop's College and Bishop's College School. This was a mathematical mastership in the School with privilege of being credited with the year's college work without attendance, provided he passed the college examinations on the subjects. This automatically lightened the family budget of the cost of one boy's schooling and was gladly accepted.

The College is at Lennoxville, Province of Quebec, and on the St. Francis River—the river of happy memories in the Trenholme family. The School Catalog described Fessenden as senior mathematical master but at no time was the work difficult and he even added junior classes in Greek and French to his duties. Perhaps it was not thought wise, he said, to put too much responsibility on a master who was younger than some of his pupils.

Above all else, the quality of scholarly leisure which he found at Bishop's College appealed to him; he sensed its importance, it gave one time to think and to get the real beauty of the books they read. Years later in talk with A. L. Smith, late Master of Balliol and successor to Jowett who had trained so many of England's great men, he sought his views on this matter and learned that Jowett's dictum was: "Six hours gets the best out of a man."

But to point the pitfalls of too keen appreciation, Reg told of a happening which was for many years a mortifying recollection to him. Under Lobley, the President, a class was reading a play of Euripides and Fessenden was translating. In the middle of his turn along with the feeling that he was getting it into pretty good English, he found to his disgust that the tears were beginning to come. Lobley was supposed to give the signal to stop and several times Reg gave him a chance which Lobley ignored, so the reading had to go on to the end. Said Fessenden, "I must have been a funny sight with the tears streaming down and furious with shame, but no one laughed for they knew I would have licked them good."

Another fine thing about the College was that it had no secret societies with their petty politics, nor did sports play a dominant role and the community was too small for much social distraction so study had undisputed right of way. Reg took up the regular work in Hebrew as an extra, also some Arabic and did enough Sanscrit to read a part of the Mahabharata, all of which curiously enough proved of immense value long after.

Lobley thought Fessenden should go to England on the chance of a scholarship and his father also wished him to do this but the College wove a spell to shape his future to a different destiny and it was the Library that did it. Such a friendly, welcoming place as it was, with comfortable chairs and sturdy tables and walls lined round with book shelves; high up were fine examples of the early printers, lower down, more modern works. Evening after evening when preparation for the next day's work was finished, came hours of sheer content exploring new paths of learning.

A weekly scientific publication, Nature, lay always on the Library table and Reg became deeply interested, passing from it to the practical Scientific American, from that to some experiments with electric batteries and so to his first very minor invention.

This had to do with a tractor which progressed by the lifting, moving forward and setting down again of its supports, by means of a four-bar-link motion which gave very closely the required straight line motion. The editorial comment was that a true straight line motion could not be produced except by using another straight line in some fashion. The young mathematical master built a small model applying the principle of the elementary theorem that if a circle rolls round inside on the circumference of another circle of twice its diameter, every point on the circumference of the smaller circle will describe a straight line, and he incorporated with it some form of link motion.

No acknowledgment of his communication describing this was received but a sense of shared effort came to him long after when reading of the difficulty Watt ran up against owing to the crank motion being covered by the patent of another inventor, so that he had to invent the wheel and planet motion based on the same principle. It showed how rapidly mechanics advanced that as early as 1780 the crank motion had already been patented.

Close of the College year brought another change. The yeast of these new studies was working in the young man, making him restless at the thought of continued classical specialization. All necessary work for a degree had been completed and an increase of salary was much needed so when an offer of the principalship of the Whitney Institute in Bermuda was made, it was at once accepted.

CHAPTER III

BERMUDA

ARRIVED IN BERMUDA, he found life set to a different rhythm from any he had yet known—the sun shone brighter—the blue of sea and sky revealed an intensity hitherto undreamed —the air was soft and caressing and the people friendly and hospitable.

In appearance he was tall and well proportioned and with the slimness of youth. He had small hands and feet, a fair complexion made more noticeable by a student's pallor—a broad, high forehead, blue eyes behind indispensable eyeglasses and a mop of flaxen hair that was always rumpled.

He was shy and quiet and naturally retiring with strangers. But fortunately, he was met at the dock by our uncle, Scott Pearman, one of the trustees of the Whitney Institute, a man of wide public interests and a charming host. One of my sisters was invited to drive to Hamilton to meet the new school teacher. On her return she announced that the young man spoke in such a low voice that she could not understand anything he had said.

Board and lodging for the school teacher had been arranged at Frascati, one of the old houses of the parish at that time being run as a boarding house. Scott Pearman did not, however, leave the stranger to face his first afternoon and evening at his lodgings, but insisted on taking him first to "Mount Hope" the Pearman home, and then, on the way back, to our home "Rockmore."

We were a family of nine sisters and one brother, our parents still living and all of us at home at that time. Because of the early bulletin of the afternoon I was given the responsibility of playing hostess and did not find the job as difficult as anticipated.

Scott Pearman took young Fessenden under his friendly wing, and week-ending at Mount Hope became for him an established habit. The friendship thus begun grew and ripened through the years and the young man was quickly at ease in the family circle.

At Frascati, his boarding house, Reginald was the object of constant and kind attention from his hosts; from time to time there were interesting visitors there, among them Doctor and Mrs. Evans, the Evans who was a fashionable American dentist in Paris during the second Empire and who, after the débâcle of Sedan, helped Empress Eugenie to escape from Paris and out of France. The friendship between the Empress and her dentist and his wife no doubt was cemented by Eugenie's childhood memories and instinctive loyalties, for her mother was the daughter of an American Consul at Malaga—a Scotchman by birth, but a naturalized American citizen. The reminiscences of the Evanses were thrilling and well told. In them Court life of the Second Empire lived again.

There was also an American missionary who for many years had lived in Turkey. This man grounded Reginald in Aramaic, a tongue which in later years was to prove a key that helped unlock the Tower of Babel when Fessenden undertook his archeological researches.

Then too, there was a highly intelligent New York lawyer who preached the doctrines of Henry George and stirred the enthusiasm of the young student for his new economic theory.

As for his school position, there was a simple omnipotence about it, for it was a one-man job. He was the Principal and the entire teaching staff. The work was difficult in that he had to juggle three or four classes adroitly so as to keep all grades occupied and all subjects taught, but it was attractive in that he was free to use his own methods of teaching.

As might be expected these methods embodied innovations, the result of youthful theories and enthusiasms. But in after years he wrote—"I think I can congratulate myself on the results though the means employed did not always fit with the ideas of the school inspector of the Islands, a conscientious but not very liberally educated product of the Board Schools."

Then, as later, he believed in teaching people how to find out things for themselves. Even then he was deeply conscious of responsibility to Youth, believing that in the training of the young of a community or a country lies the opportunity of building the future on a sound basis. This sense of responsibility deepened with the years and we can be certain that his two years of teaching at the Whitney Institute were taken seriously by the young principal and that they shaped to more progressive ends the lives and characters of his pupils.

It was a happy time and always thereafter Bermuda was in memory, and—in later years—in fact—sanctuary. Of that time he wrote:

> "Coming direct from Bishop's College, life in Bermuda appeared to me to be what Alfred Henry Lewis has called 'One continuous round of flour doin's and chicken fixin's' —what with all the picnics, fishing trips, dances, amateur theatricals, dinners and swimming parties. Up to that time I was rather bashful and had had very little to do with girls, so it was about the right time and the right place for me to fall in love; which I promptly did, with Miss Helen Trott, niece of my friend Pearman and the daughter of one of the old island planters and who had just finished her school days in England and on the Continent. One could miss a great deal out of one's life and still be happy remembering those drives back after a dance, along the shores of Harrington Sound, and the moonlight, the semi-tropical air and the smell of the jasmine flowers."

Saturdays always brought their quota of excitement and adventure. The *Sally Ann*, a cranky dinghy, owned by his friend Scott Pearman and placed at Reginald's disposal, was sooner or later sure to upset, leaving her crew of one swimming desperately around, collecting floating parts. Land adventures might mean exploration of caves with rope ladders catching fire, or Roman candles, set off for illuminating far corners, sending out drifting clouds of fumes, which in the unventilated confines of the caves, almost asphyxiated the young explorers. There were long tramps too, often as much as twenty-five miles covered in a day, but always ending in time so that he could be my escort to evening choir practice.

They were halcyon days that lasted for two years. Then the magic spell ended, for though Reg knew that he could go on indefinitely as he was doing, his position at the Whitney Institute was only a blind alley for the ambitions that stirred within him.

But what next? His father, writing from England, told him that his name had been entered at Keble College, Oxford, in case he could get a scholarship. This meant the completion of his classical education, with a teaching career to follow— or possibly the ministry. But another line of work had begun to exert a strong pull; beginning with his reading of scientific periodicals and books at Bishop's College, the urge heightened rather than depressed by the lack of interest shown in his first invention, Reg had centered his desires on the science of Electricity for his career.

He wrote his father that he intended to return to Bishop's College to teach a certain number of hours a day, complete his classics and "get some insight into really higher Mathematics."

However, this plan was quickly cancelled in favor of making an immediate start in New York. Armed with a few letters of introduction, he set out, determined to try writing for papers and magazines and in odd hours to get sufficient experience in practical electricity to fit himself for employment under Edison.

CHAPTER IV

NEW YORK

FOR THE FIRST MONTHS the outlook was uncertain and precarious. There was cold comfort in his mathematical philosophy that there is a definite ratio of failure to success and that the sooner the quota of failures is exhausted, the sooner the plums of success are reached. He was given a chance to write for the Henry George publications but found on closer study that in spite of his earlier sympathies, he could not accept the Land Tax theory. So he had to relinquish that certain job and other editorial doors did not swing open to him; he decided therefore to try his luck with Edison without further delay. Of this experience he wrote:

"At the New York office they told me that he was spending most of his time at the Lamp works at Harrison N. J. Arrived there, my card went in to him with the slip of paper given me to state my business on, and the slip came back endorsed—"Am very busy. What do you know about electricity?" This was a facer. I was a pretty fair mathematician and knew something about electrical theory and if I had had the sense to say that, would probably have been engaged. But the idea that mathematics was of value in electrical work had hardly been born. Edison himself was perhaps the first to realize it when he engaged Hopkinson to improve the design of his dynamos.

In desperation at last I wrote—"Do not know anything about electricity, but can learn pretty quick." The 'old Man' must have been in a bad humor that day, for back came the slip—"Have enough men now who do not know anything about electricity," and back I went to New York. A few years after that looking through some papers, I ran across the slip and handed it to him. He grinned and said "Things must have been going pretty badly that day." And that was the fact, for he was normally the most considerate of men and I was told that just then they were having some extremely difficult situations to handle in connection with the incandescent lamps."

So back to New York he went, to writing, to an occasional lucky acceptance of some special article. In this he prospered to the point of being made assistant editor of Social Science, and enjoyed pleasant association with Weaverson, the editor and through him made many interesting contacts.

But always there was a weekly call at the Edison Machine Works on the chance of a possible opening. This company was at the time laying mains in the 14th to 52nd Street district. At last on one of his weekly calls, Mr. Kreussi, head of the Edison Machine Works at Schenectady, told him that he seemed pretty persevering and he thought he would have to give him a job as assistant tester.

"Practically" Reg wrote, "this meant scraping the conductors sticking out of the ends of the iron pipes of the mains and feeders while the tester put the galvanometer on them for grounds which had developed in mains already laid. It was harder work than it sounds, but I had got a start and was putting in my lunch hour in working at electrical theory and analytical mechanics, which we had not had at college.

Acting on the principle that one should always leave one's chief free to go away at any time with the knowledge that his work will be taken care of during his absence, I managed to simplify operations and lay out the work so that our section was always ahead of schedule. So my chief got his promotion to chief tester and I succeeded him. Then he went to Schenectady and I became chief tester and before the end of the year inspecting engineer for the third section of the work.

They were putting down the telephone conduits in the same trenches. Crimmins, a well known New York Contractor and a fine man was in charge of that work. There were about 3000 men employed and, occasionally at first and more often later, it fell to me to take charge of a portion of the telephone conduit work as well, which gave useful experience in handling men. The sum of my experience in this line, obtained then and later, is that the one thing which the men working under one appreciate above all else, and substantially the only thing, is that the "boss" is not influenced by prejudice or favor and that under all circumstances they will have a "square deal."

The only exciting part of the work was getting up defective mains without permits. Once the street was closed there was a heavy fine for opening without a permit, which was hard to get, took much time and generally a money payment. It was a matter of high strategy to open a street, replace a dozen lengths of main and get the street into innocent looking shape again between police patrols.

Much of the laying was on Madison Avenue and Fifth Avenue, which were the fashionable residence districts, and many, perhaps most of the residents walked to and back from their offices and would stop and chat about the new lighting system; a number of acquaintances were made in this way.

It was meeting Mr. J. P. Morgan in this way that led to what perhaps might be called my second invention. He, and some others in this section had private lighting plants, and it was my unwarranted use, when testing the mains, to send an assistant to shut down any private plants which might be running near-by, as they threw out the galvanometer reading. Mr. Morgan happened to be the one on this occasion whose light had been shut off while he was reading and he had come out to see me about it in a not entirely amiable temper. I explained that I would be through in a very short time and he asked if I would come in and advise him about insulating his house circuits as he was having considerable trouble, and no one seemed able to tell him what to do.

Mr. Morgan and his charming daughter showed me all over the house and explained that they had had their wiring renewed a number of times, necessitating re-plastering each time, and had had several small fires and could I tell them how to fix things permanently. They had been using heavy rubber covered wire embedded directly in the plaster, as was the practice at that time. I suggested using galvanized pipe, lined with waterproof paper tubing, and drawing the rubber covered wire into that. Some objections suggested themselves but were solved satisfactorily, sketches were made and dimensioned, and before long this system of interior conduits was installed. In after years Mr. Morgan helped me very materially in several matters I wished to put through."

The Edison Machine Company had feared delay in the work, but the fear was groundless. To the great satisfaction of the company, on the day before Christmas, 1886, Reg reported that his section of the work was complete, tested and ready to connect. He was offered a position with the company in Schenectady, but knowing of his desire to work under Edison, he was given the choice between the Schenectady job and becoming one of Edison's assistants at the Llewellyn Park Laboratory to carry out some experiments on dynamo development which Edison was making for the Machine Company.

It is not necessary to say that Reg chose to work under Edison.

CHAPTER V

A YANKEE BOY AND A CHINA MUG

WITH EDISON DAWNED the Golden Age of Invention—the Laboratory was its Shrine and Edison its High Priest.

This was Fessenden's early reaction to this remarkable center of creative work and his loyalty to its influence and to its traditions never wavered. He believed that the atmosphere of such a place and period, the methods and technique evolved there, should be an inheritance and his own recollections of it were given in considerable detail in his unfinished autobiography.

The comprehensiveness of the Laboratory equipment amazed him. A most complete technical library on electricity, chemistry, mechanics, engineering, mining and physics filled the Library shelves; other subjects were well represented with the exception of mathematics but the weakness in this subject was made up for by complete sets of proceedings of the various mathematical societies.

In the galleries of the building were cases containing specimens of every known mineral, many of them rare and beautiful. The work of collecting these lasted several years and was carried out by Dr. Kunz the famous Tiffany expert.

The store room held samples of all known organic and inorganic substances. It was Edison's habit to browse through technical dictionaries and encyclopedias of chemistry making lists of substances to be ordered. Such as could not be supplied by usual trade channels he assigned to his special agents to obtain. He employed many agents, also missions, and for many purposes; there is the story of the man sent around the world to obtain every known species of bamboo. One of Fessenden's own memories of the plenitude of this store room was connected with the great blizzard of 1888 when he and Mr. Aylesworth (later the inventor of condensite) were marooned in the Laboratory and fared extremely well on buckwheat cakes and maple syrup, stews of dried beef and pemmican, macaroni with olive oil, dried fruits, zweiback, coffee which they roasted and flavored with vanilla bean, and condensed milk.

On reporting for work at the Laboratory, Fessenden met with some disappointment. The dynamo development work had not started and the engine room and electrical building were not even wired. The first assignment given him by Batchelor, Edison's partner, was to wire up the electrical building. This was not exactly Fessenden's idea of scientific experimenting but he tackled the job and Kennelly, then chief electrician, joined him and together they did a good piece of work.

When this was finished Batchelor had nothing else for him to do and suggested that he report for work at Schenectady. But Fessenden had no intention of abandoning the opportunity he had sought so earnestly if he could help it, and saw Edison next morning at his house and explained the situation. Again Edison's probing formula—"Do you know anything about chemistry?" "No," said Fessenden. "Then I want you to be a chemist. I have had a lot of chemists. I had one whose name was all through Watt's Dictionary. But none of them got results. I want you to take it up. You can start in helping Cousins."

This time the answer had been right and Fessenden had his real start.

To Cousins, Edison said, "We are having trouble with fires from electric light wires and the Machine Works wants a fireproof insulation. What they want is something which is as good an insulator as glass but as flexible as Indiarubber, not affected by acids or alkalies or oils, and fireproof, and" his face relaxed for an instant "it must not cost more than 15 cents a pound."

His instructions were to start mixing some of every chemical, in alphabetical order, which was on the shelves of the chemical building, with linseed oil, and record in their note books how it stood a Bunsen flame.

Upon reaching antimony trichloride, Fessenden found that mixture did not burn. He reported it to Cousins who thought that traces of water in the oil had decomposed the chlorides and that the hydrochloric acid had smothered the flame.

But that night Fessenden read up on combustion and on oils and elementary organic chemistry and came to the conclusion that combustion started first with the hydrogen atoms of the oil. Reasoning from that he assumed that if some other atom could be substituted for the hydrogen and one which had a very slight affinity for oxygen, a non-inflammable substitution compound would result which physically would be very much like the original inflammable hydrocarbon. He decided that this was what had happened with the antimony trichloride, i.e., that a chlorine substitution had been formed.

Cousins did not agree with this theory but, when reporting to Edison that morning, after stating his own view, he said "but Fessenden here has a theory that the chlorine has gone in and taken the place of hydrogen in the oil and that that is why it will not burn."

Edison considered the matter, then said to continue working along the line laid down but to try out the substitution theory. This was characteristic; he would never be led away from any line he had laid down, because of apparent success in a side line, until he had followed the original line to the end.

But Cousins had another suggestion. "You know I want to get into the telegraphy work. Why don't you let Fessenden handle this job and let me work at the high speed system?"

To this Edison consented and Fessenden climbed another rung of the ladder.

For a time thereafter the chemical laboratory must have been a place to avoid, filled always with yellow fog from the thousands of experiments with chlorine substituted organic compounds. This so impressed visitors that a New York

Herald reporter printed a sketch of Mr. Edison introducing Fessenden as "the man with the platinum lungs." He noticed that the men in the chemical building never suffered from influenza during epidemics and ascribed it to the chlorine gas. Even letters to distant Bermuda were steeped in the fumes and stains of this intensive research.

The outcome of it all was a compound which was noninflammable, a good insulator, not attacked by acids or alkalies and not at all by oils; slightly but sufficiently elastic, and reasonably cheap. In addition to this were the valuable by-products, later known as the halo-waxes and the use of tetrachloride, 'Pyrene' for extinguishing fires where water could not be used.

Developments in other lines which Fessenden worked out were a coating for iron armature laminations, also a method of making rail bonds where good joints were essential, and on one occasion Edison came in and said "Fessenden, we have just two weeks to get out a structureless carbon filament. They have obtained an injunction in Pennsylvania against our using the bamboo filament on the claim that it infringes the old Sawyer-Mann filament."

The line to be tried was laid down and since the matter was urgent Edison worked along with Fessenden. They had been experimenting continuously for three or four days with barely time out for a cup of coffee and a sandwich. The new organic compound, which was to be used, dissolved in chloroform but this evaporated when the filaments were squirted leaving them in powder form which could not be carbonized. The thing was to find some other solvent which didn't evaporate.

So, many small tumblers each with small quantities of different fluids and some of the substance to be dissolved were under observation. Only one thing dissolved it—oil of birch. Fessenden told Edison of this and speculated a little on the reason why this particular oil should be the solvent. Edison listened, chewing his cigar. "Well Fezzy," and tired as both men must have been, his eyes twinkled, "I guess what we need is more tumblers." As Fessenden wrote—"Of course he was right. It was what Pythagoras might have said if he had been an inventor."

Such concentrated day and night attack on any given problem was by no means infrequent. Fessenden estimated that Edison and three or four of his assistants did this 25% of the time. It was indicative of course of outside pressure but far more of the tremendous enthusiasm inspired by this new form of adventure—this coming 'to grips' with the unknown and wrestling through to success.

Sleep was a minor consideration, almost a disgrace to feel the need of it. One machinist disappeared in the middle of a job and was finally located asleep on top of a crane where, if he had moved, he would have been killed. A few cat-naps were permissible while waiting for some chemical reaction, and Edison, Aylesworth and a few others could enjoy these sitting on chairs, but Fessenden stretched his long length on the asphalt floor with a Watt's Dictionary for a pillow and the soothing sizzle of an arc lamp overhead.

Batchelor, always concerned for Edison's welfare, worried over these protracted bouts of work and installed a canvas cot in an unused room which came to be known as Edison's bedroom; this Fessenden compared to a famous chapter headed "snakes in Ireland" and consisting of the words "There are none," for Edison would have none of it. Once however, having worked an unbroken stretch from Monday to Thursday before getting the desired results, he succumbed but even then apparently with an uneasy conscience for he called to Fessenden passing by, "Fezzy come on in here, there's a table in here." But a table offers scant attraction to a six footer so he pleaded an unfinished job in the laboratory and left Edison to his unwonted luxury.

There was a responsiveness in Fessenden to the Edison methods of investigation that won quick approval. In an interview which appeared about that time in a New York paper Edison was quoted as saying, "I can take a Yankee boy and a china mug and he will get more results than all the German chemists put together."

This no doubt referred to Fessenden for a few days later

he said "Fessenden you will take charge of the chemical laboratory in the future." "Oh," said Fessenden, "is W—— leaving? He is a much better chemist than I am." "Yes," replied Edison, "he is a fine chemist but he does not get results and he has another place which will suit him better."

Thus proudly came the news to me in Bermuda, "I am now Head Chemist of the Edison Laboratory."

Other lines of work were added, mostly connected with ore milling and refining the Sudbury copper-nickel deposits; there was also a good deal of analytical work. His chief assistant was Mr. John Dorr who had come direct from school; he later became an eminent mining engineer and the inventor of many mining processes.

In this hive of industry, with brilliant men giving their ardent best to very varied problems, there was naturally a contagion of interest each in the work of others. Fessenden recalled several of these developments, two of which are doubly interesting as showing the effects of monopoly—whether of labor or of capital.

Electric lighting by incandescent lamp was in increasing demand. Lamps at that time sold for a dollar and cost more to make. Glass blowers, believing they had a monopoly, refused to take on any apprentices, refused to work during the summer months and demanded and had to be given twice their old wage.

A cherished tradition was current in the glass blowing trade to the effect that an alcoholic breath helped to prevent glass from cracking; many did their best to ensure improvement along these lines. Fessenden recorded an amusing instance. The Edison 'Tasimeter', a device for measuring very minute quantities of radiant heat such as of the corona during an eclipse, was being tested one day. The device consisted of a bent strip of paper covered on one side with lampblack and shellac pressed against a carbon button; when radiant energy heated the shellac and softened it, the pressure on the carbon button was reduced, the resistance increased and the spot of light from a galvanometer in series with the button moved over a scale. An old-time glass blower came into the room and the spot of light danced off the scale. It was found that his breath took only 5 or 6 seconds to diffuse across the room and soften the shellac enough to give a big indication. But this is incidental. An imperative need was to find some cheaper method of manufacture and Edison finally evolved a machine which made the lamps for 15 cents so that they could be sold at a profit for 25 cents. Without this machine, electric lighting would have been retarded many years as under the old method it was costing $1.50 to make each lamp.

The man in charge of the development of this glass blowing machine was himself a skilled glass blower and taught Fessenden how to make many quite complicated pieces of apparatus in glass; this facility later came in very useful.

A second example of the effect of monopoly had to do with one phase of the phonograph development. It was found that minute traces of silica in phonograph wax quickly dulled the steel knives so sapphires were used instead; they were off-colored stones and the cost per knife was not great. But the dealers, as soon as they found there was a demand, increased the price about ten times. Edison gave instructions that every kind of very hard stone should be tested out in this connection and, while this was going on, decided to make sapphires artificially. The proper constituents were fused but even at the highest temperature and at the most fluid state of the mixture, tiny bubbles persisted which could not be removed and which spoiled the edges of the knives. Then, on the principle of the modern centrifugal milk separator, a circular trough was built on top of a big lathe, with the opening facing toward the center; this was filled with the mixture and a big arc heated it as it revolved—the idea being that the bubbles would be separated from the fused material. It gave promising results but in the meantime the first line of tests on different types of hard stone had shown that knives of oriental jade would do as well or better, so further work was discontinued.

Moving pictures was another art born at this time and as Fessenden said, it was pioneering from the ground up, for

Edison had to invent to satisfy every requirement that presented itself and he produced in the end a 'movie' that was also a 'talkie', without flicker and absolutely synchronized.

Fessenden and Kennelly proved very congenial; they were both of the scholarly type and though in charge of different lines of work under Edison, they drew together for extra scientific work and read mathematics together. Fessenden had J. J. Thompson's "Dynamics applied to Physics and Chemistry" so Kennelly got a copy too and they studied during the lunch hour. Edison once came looking for his Chief Electrician and his Head Chemist and found only the book open at a page filled with a lot of quadruple integrals; by way of a visiting card he wrote at the top of the page, "This inscription was found written over the top of the door of an ancient Aztec lunatic asylum."

Though Edison sometimes made fun of their mathematics, he was himself a natural born mathematician, like Faraday, and when, a little before, the mathematician he had employed had failed to find a rational solution of the problem of the size of the neutral in a three-wire system, he solved it himself and the solution stands today.

In 1890 Edison went to Europe to the Paris Exposition. Before he left, Fessenden asked him if he could take up work on the lines of Hertz's experiments which had recently been published. He said yes, but to wait till he came back. But hardly had he returned, when, owing to financial difficulties and the reorganization of the Edison Companies, substantially the whole laboratory was shut down.

CHAPTER VI

FESSENDEN FINDS HIMSELF

MANY YEARS LATER, Fessenden wrote a critical opinion of the great genius of Menlo Park—a tribute of the disciple to the Master. Here is what he wrote:

"The question has often been put to me 'Is Edison really a good inventor? Are not his inventions really due to his assistants?' Having worked with him for a number of years and having made a rather special study of the science of invention and of inventors, my own conclusion is that all of the inventions which go by his name were made by him personally, and that there is only one figure in history which stands in the same rank with him as an inventor, i.e. Archimedes.

The following partial list of Edison's principal inventions will support my position:

The phonograph
The moving and talking pictures
Incandescent lighting—both carbon and metallic filament
The system of electric distribution, including central station and underground conductors
The carbon microphone transmitter, without which the telephone receiver (which was invented by Gray) would never have developed into the present telephone system
Introduction of all modern methods of making cement, which have made its use practical for modern construction work
The Edison Valve (hot cathode tube, which is used as a receiver in wireless sets and is the basis of De Forest's great invention, the Audion)
The Edison storage battery
The mimeograph
The Edison duplex and multiplex telegraph systems, etc., etc.

From what has been previously said it will be evident that Edison allows to those of his assistants who have been 'indoctrinated' in his methods a very considerable opportunity of developing their individuality in the working out of problems. But the inventions are always his own; the particular assistant who does the work is not material. If an assistant leaves or is transferred to another job, the work goes on just the same.

There is an old story of a famous organist who came down from London to a country village and played for the evening service. At its close the vicar's daughter said to the sexton who had worked the bellows "That was a beautiful anthem." Said the sexton with entirely justifiable but disproportionate pride, "Yes, if I says it myself, I never pumped better." And of Edison himself the story is told that an assistant met once in Germany a glass-blower who had formerly been in Edison's employ, and was posing as the real inventor of the electric lamp. On remonstrating with him he received, as justification, the reply, "Why John, you know yourself that Edison never could blow glass."

It is, of course, true that without the organ blower there would be no music, and without the glass-blower no electric lamp. But as I have shown elsewhere, the responsibility for the music is measured by the ratio of the number of men who could play the anthem so well (perhaps four or five) to the number of men who could blow the organ (hundreds of thousands), and therefore the musician is substantially entirely responsible for the result. And so with Edison's work; while much credit should be given his assistants, the results are his. His knowledge is such that he does not need to follow out any one method of attack; he has many by which he can advance.

On two or three occasions I noted his method, for he frequently had me accompany him on his morning rounds to save time when difficult problems needed survey, of dealing with new assistants who were evidencing more than a reasonable appreciation of the value of their contributions. He would listen quietly, not say much, but next morning he would, apparently casually, shift the development to an entirely new and generally better line. This would be effective.

In these morning rounds of inspection he was, as always, most considerate and never found fault with the work, merely, when things were going wrong, explaining what should be done to make it go right. The nearest I ever heard him come to criticism was once when an assistant who had taken over a job on which a relative had worked for some time without result, was himself making no apparent progress, Edison turned to me and said, "I think, Fezzy, I shall have to make this job hereditary."

It will be evident then that the inventions previously described in the development of which I took part, were Edison's and not mine, and would have been made, though perhaps in slightly different form, if he had employed other of his assistants for the work."

There was a good deal of a XIXth century echo of King Arthur's Knights of the Round Table in those years at the Edison Laboratory. The following is a typical day: Work started at 9. The last half of the noon hour was spent by Fessenden on mathematics at which later Kennelly joined him. At 5 the two men walked at top speed to the Y.M.C.A. gymnasium, put in fifteen minutes on the bars and trapezes and with the medicine ball, then a shower and, more leisurely, to their boarding house for supper. At 8 P.M. back to the Laboratory—Kennelly to his electrical building, Fessenden to his chemical building with John Dorr keeping faithful tryst. The two worked till midnight, stopping short at the hour for strong hot coffee and biscuits; Dorr then called it a day and started for home while Fessenden put in another hour's work on theoretical physics or chemistry.

The only interruption to this schedule were the periods of day and night work already alluded to, and occasionally when Kennelly and Fessenden undertook the solution of some electrical problem.

Perhaps the most important piece of work they jointly accomplished was the determination of the resistance temperature coefficient of copper. There were a considerable number of formulas for this, some curves concave upward, some concave down. The discrepancies were due apparently to uncertainty and non-uniformity of the temperature of the copper wire and inaccuracy of the thermometers used. Kennelly had the beautiful idea of putting the wire coil inside the bulb of an air thermometer and heating it electrically, thus at the same time insuring uniformity of temperature and certainty as to its value. Fessenden had the theory based on some chemical investigations, that the curve was neither concave nor convex and was equal to the reciprocal of the volume expansion of the gas. Kennelly's method worked perfectly though they had a good deal of trouble getting the apparatus blown; after repeated attempts, the laboratory glass-blower gave it up in despair as impossible and Fessenden then took over the job and pridefully demonstrated that it could be done. The results came out absolutely consistently and gave a straight line curve. These findings were published in the proceedings of the International Electrical Congress which met at Chicago in 1893 and were shortly afterward adopted officially by the British Post Office authorities.

Both Kennelly and Fessenden recall long hours spent one sweltering summer night chasing an elusive variation of from 5 to 20 milligrams in the weight of the mercury content of the air thermometer bulb, traced at last by an irritated buzz, to a mosquito who had been trying to roost on the arm of the sensitive balance, and had at last lost patience at being disturbed so many times. Also another hot Sunday afternoon when they had lugged a heavy Kew Magnetometer far out into the country so as to be away from all iron, in order to get an accurate standardization of their galvanometer—but instead, got such remarkable readings that they searched around through the long grass of the field to find that they had set up the apparatus within ten feet of the only magnetic object probably within miles. This was an iron cannon ball, fired, as they found later, during the war of 1776.

But it was at this time also that Fessenden was exploring independently and without reference to laboratory assignment, certain unsolved problems.

Dr. Alexis Carrel in his 'Man the Unknown' (Harper & Bros.) has this to say: "Obviously, science follows no plan. It develops at random. Its progress depends on fortuitous conditions, such as the birth of men of genius, the form of their mind, the direction taken by their *curiosity.*"

It will be recalled that one of the requirements of Fessenden's first experimental job under Edison, i.e. an insulation compound, was 'as flexible as Indiarubber'. All the other requirements were satisfied, this one only partially so, and Fessenden realized that he didn't know enough about the theory of elasticity. The insulation compound met the requirements and passed to the production stage but an itch of curiosity was left in Fessenden's mind in regard to elasticity. By the time he had satisfied this curiosity, the trail had led him to what he described as the most important and revolutionary of the discoveries it was his good fortune to make and one which led, as will later be seen, to many inventions.

This was the *Electrostatic Doublet Theory* and the *Nature of Cohesion and Elasticity.*

First of all he made an intensive study of what had been done by others on the subject and deduced from that, that the mathematical work was not sufficiently advanced to give a solution and, more important still, that it appeared to be on the wrong trail, even as treated by such authorities as Kelvin and Sutherland. Both of them and all other physicists at that time, held that cohesion could not possibly be an electrical phenomenon, because conductors such as copper and silver had cohesion, and electrical charges could not exist inside of conductors. Both of them were agreed that cohesion was a gravitational phenomenon; Sutherland had published a paper demonstrating that the elasticity of rubber and similar substances was due to the gravitational attraction between very long and attenuated forms of atoms.

To the casual reader the step-by-step details of this prolonged investigation might be tedious; to the student however it is of incomparable importance and for that reason Fessenden's own account of this work is appended.

When concluded, a fundamentally new law of the nature of the electric charge of atoms had been given to the world; the true nature of the composition of rubber had been solved and an unknown metal—beryllium or glucinum, had been forecast.

Meantime Fessenden had made an invention in connection with the fascinating gyrostat. It puzzled him why it had not been used as a compass but, on reading up its history, he decided that the complicated method of driving it—with belts, steam etc.—had been the obstacle. He believed it could be made to work by using an alternating current drive and that furthermore there was an immediate commercial field for it as a sight for guns on shipboard.

He wrote an article for the Electrical Engineer, New York, published May 1889, describing the many uses to which this device could be applied by making electricity the driving power. It was his first scientific article and was well received by the editors. But inhibition prevented ship owners from supplementing the magnetic compass and it was not till Lake had developed the submarine into a serious means of warfare that the impossibility of the magnetic compass functioning within the steel shell of the submarine, forced the adoption of the gyro-compass. By that time Fessenden had carried the work further and had found that a frequency many times that of standard motors was necessary, 500 cycles being the best, and a patent obtained for this drive.

It has since been immensely improved and the principle ingeniously applied by Sperry to a great variety of uses, on aircraft as well as on shipboard.

A temptation overcome or an opportunity lost—call it which you will—came to Fessenden in 1889.

Mr. Pratt of Pratt & Lambert Company came to consult Edison on trouble he was having with blackening of varnish gums. Edison, busy, sent him to Fessenden. Fessenden in his work on elasticity had distilled great numbers of flexible and elastic substances, including fossil gums, in vacuum and under pressure, and thus had formulated certain conclusions as to their behavior, decomposition, etc. He was therefore able at once to show Mr. Pratt how to remove the blackening of the gums and also how to use the cheaper Zanzibar fossil gums in place of the more expensive copals, and at the same time get clearer, tougher and harder varnishes.

About a month later Mr. Pratt again appeared at the laboratory, this time, after consultation with his partner, to offer Fessenden one-third interest in his company, guaranteed at not less than $10,000 per annum—and this was 1889—not 1929. Perhaps it was as well that Fessenden was still a bachelor, free to make unhampered choice, for, being Fessenden, that choice was inevitably toward the chance to explore new fields of thought rather than toward greater material prosperity. He said, "I suppose any sensible man would have accepted it. But I wanted to continue my work with Edison and have never regretted turning this offer down and similar invitations received later from the Carnegie Company, the Baldwin Locomotive Works and others. At times it has seemed to me that it might have been more fair to my wife if some of them had been accepted, but on the whole, I think not. The richness and fullness of life depends on the amount and character of its experiences. My dear mother used to say that the only difference between a rut and a grave was that the rut was longer, and I am quite sure that the years of good, clean hardship, of wide experience and varied interests together, effect a welding between husband and wife which is the best personal thing that life can give; and that early marriages and simple living are best."

But 'the chance to work with Edison' was already passing. The Edison Machine Works at Schenectady and the Edison Light Companies were in financial difficulties and unable to continue to pay for the solution of their commercial problems by the Edison Laboratory. As a result many of the laboratory staff were laid off and had to seek work elsewhere. There may have been a twinge of regret then for the declined Pratt & Lambert Company's offer, for our wedding had been set for the coming September. But a job with a living wage and the opportunity to get practical experience in the design of dynamos and other electrical machinery as well as a chance to round out his mathematics amply offset, in Fessenden's opinion, the more lucrative offer. This job was assistant to J. D. Kelley, electrician for the United States Company, the eastern branch of the Westinghouse Company at Newark, which handled all D.C. work for that company.

CHAPTER VII

NEWARK, PITTSFIELD AND PURDUE

CERTAINLY THE YEARS between 1886 and 1890 were for Reg years of high pressure work, but the atmosphere of the Edison laboratory was congenial, every problem was a stimulus to wider research and the years were crowded with fruitful accomplishment.

One short Bermuda visit in 1887 or 1888 and a single Christmas trip to the Rectory at Chippewa were the sum of his holidays for those four years.

On the Bermuda trip he brought with him a laboratory model of the Phonograph—just launched commercially. Naturally the very great marvel of the reproduced sounds was a rare experience for us Islanders. We made our own records and put them through all the tricks of speeding up, slowing down and going off key. One of my sisters was critically ill at the time, just at the crisis, and odd as it may seem, we have always felt that it was her interest in those sounds drifting into her room, familiar voices yet capable of such funny distortions, that helped pull her back to safety.

For me, the years between 1886 and 1890 were filled with teaching—during the last three years, running a private school for girls which acceptably met a community need. They were full and happy years but four years of being engaged seemed a long time to both Reg and me, so in September 1890 I came to New York and we were quietly married at the Church of the Heavenly Rest by the Rev. Dr. Morgan to whom Reg's father had sent letters of introduction.

From Tiffany's had come my heavy, 22 carat wedding ring and guard and from Tiffany's too, a brooch with a small but very beautiful diamond. When these gifts had been selected to Reg's satisfaction and he had paid for them, there was little, in fact there was nothing left for incidental expenses. His plans for a holiday and our wedding trip were dissolving in thin air.

Fortunately a streak of thrift in my own character had trained me to be prepared for emergencies and the proverbial rainy day. This was indeed a rainy day, so with part of my savings we took our trip and spent a couple of weeks at the Rectory in Chippewa.

There I heard myself being called "Mrs. Reggie" by the parishioners—but somehow it sounded weak and characterless so we were pleased when family and friends fell in line and shortened the name to a clear-cut "Reg."

Together we tramped the paths by Clarke Hill Islands and Niagara River, visiting a hundred nooks Reg had loved in his childhood. The long hours out of doors brought health and color to the pale-faced, overworked young man who had awaited me at the dock of the Bermuda boat on the 21st of September.

Early in October we were in Newark, installed temporarily in a boarding house and Reg back at work with the United States Company. Boarding soon palled and we decided to go to housekeeping, making an appreciable hole in our small reserve to buy furniture. A tiny, two-story brick house in a row, in one of the suburbs of Newark was the best that came within our means and we were soon comfortably settled and I began my struggles with coal as a fuel. The kitchen range and I were not on good terms for quite a while and it was then that I missed recording a possible formula for linoleum that Reg always regretted, as he said it might have made our fortune—my first pumpkin pies— the filling spread out thin for economy and an oven that dried things but didn't bake—no linoleum ever had or could have had their durability.

The Newark Library reading rooms were a favorite resort but evenings were spent for the most part at home, in study and writing. The glow of two student lamps, the occasional 'glug' of oil siphoning through the tubes, the turning of a page, the scratch of a pen, do not make an exciting evening's setting, but it was the background for most of ours and a very satisfying and restful one.

Reg, hot on the trail of some solution, or deep in a new mathematical or physics book, was conscious of an expanding universe, while I, unable to soar on such pinions took the simpler flight of a metrical translation of Von Scheffel's "Trumpeter of Säkkingen." We were both keen on what we were doing and each knew what the other was about. We performed miracles of economy in housekeeping and it was well we could furnish our own amusement, for Reg's salary didn't permit of any extravagance.

Once for a whole night financial tragedy threatened us. Our small nest egg, some five or six hundred dollars, was in a Newark bank and we learned that a run on that bank had started. Needless to say we were in line at an early hour next morning and when the withdrawals began and the file moved slowly forward toward the cashier's window, and when we saw gold being paid out instead of 'greenbacks,' the suspense as to whether the money would hold out till our turn came was pretty tense. The account was in my name and when the thirty golden double eagles were pushed out to me we faded thankfully out of the milling crowd, rushed home and hid our treasure at the bottom of a trunk where my exploring fingers sought assurance of its safety many a time. Not so much to be wondered at. We all know what Kipling calls the 'black thought' and this was our sole and only bulwark against emergency.

A few acquaintances, a little neighborliness, but nothing of particular import marked our private life at this time, but at the Laboratory of the United States Company Reg at once began to do outstanding work. Both the business contacts of the period and the lines of development were striking and important.

Zimmerman, general manager, and Nassoy, shop superintendent, were both very able men. Kelley, the Laboratory chief, was a brilliant man and well up in his subject but disinclined to take trouble and with an absorbing interest in sociology; in consequence he seldom came to the laboratory and Fessenden, his assistant, was left to carry out the experimental work.

Always quick to appreciate the outstanding work of others Fessenden found that high traditions belonged to this laboratory of which he was placed in charge. Sawyer and Mann, Maxim and Weston had worked there; Sawyer and Mann had been among the first to use carbonized paper for incandescent lighting—a very important step though they failed to make a practical lamp. Maxim was said to have been responsible for the use of nitrocellulose for lamp filaments; later he was the inventor of the first practical rapid-fire gun and of cordite and of nitrocellulose rifle powder and also did some important work in flying. But Weston was the greatest of them all; his work stirred Fessenden's profound admiration. The field in which he made himself pre-eminent was the invention and perfection of electrical measuring instruments. In this he was supreme as was Edison in the field of electric lighting.

The crudeness of such apparatus prior to Weston's work is almost unbelievable, with errors amounting easily to $7\frac{1}{2}$ per cent. By brilliant invention, by the refinement and ageing of his metals, by perfection of construction, by a new type of jeweled bearings Weston gave to electrical engineers D.C. voltmeters correct to 1/10 of 1 per cent, and later, A.C. instruments. He also discovered an entirely new alloy with the unheard of property that its resistance diminished with temperature instead of increasing. This he called "Manganin" but Fessenden always insisted it should have been called "Weston."

The laboratory had run down shockingly and the first thing was to put it in shape so that quantitative measurements, which are the main secret of successful inventing, could be accurately made.

Next, a problem of insulation was put up to Fessenden, this time in connection with dynamos, the chief output of the United States Company. Shellac, nitro-cellulose varnish and japan were being used but the stuff always cracked and became hydroscopic so that the dynamos would not stand up. Linseed oil would have been suitable if it could have been dried more quickly but the raw oil took weeks to dry and when chemical driers were combined it would not insulate.

Fessenden found that the chemical driers, such as lead oxide, which had been used, combined with the oil to form water-soluble metallic soaps, thus rendering the insulation hydroscopic. But the search was extended and the fact established that borate of manganese in particular and some other similar substances did not do this; that instead borate of manganese was a powerful catalyst for oxygen and that a dynamo soaked in borated oil and placed in a drying oven would dry out in a few hours and with perfect insulation. In fact the results were almost too good for Nassoy came in one day complaining that the repair department no longer showed a profit.

In conjunction with this method of insulation, a very fine flexible insulating cloth was obtained by the addition of suitable gums in proper proportion. After the lapse of a quarter of a century samples of this material show no deterioration and are very similar to what is now known as Empire Cloth.

The work on the *Electrostatic Doublet Theory* and on the *Nature of Cohesion and Elasticity* had prepared Fessenden to attack this and allied problems with assurance and to arrive speedily at the correct solution.

Of all the dynamos insulated this new way, only two came back for repairs and one of these had been struck by lightning. So, although the repair department was idle a reputation was established that brought orders in so fast that there was difficulty in filling them.

The making of aluminum by electrolysis had just been developed and required an unusual type of dynamo, low voltage but about 200 h.p., a large dynamo for that time. The overload on these was at times excessive, amounting to a short circuit, and no organic insulation could stand the strain.

For this Fessenden applied radical remedies. He had noticed that pure asbestos cord soaked in silicate of soda turned, when dried and heated, to a sort of opaque glass with a certain degree of flexibility and fair insulating quality. He therefore gave instructions that the large copper straps, three or four inches deep and a half inch wide should be insulated in this way and simply laid in the grooves of the armature sheets. The testing department was horrified especially when it was noted that a whole bank of several hundred lamps lighted up between adjacent windings. But said Fessenden. "An inventor must never be intimidated by what appear to be facts when he knows they are not." So the dynamos were shipped that way and the report on them was that they worked well but that the brushes used to get red hot.

The new types of dynamos and motors which were being put out frequently brought about problems at the various plants which the regular field man could not solve so Fessenden began to do considerable outside work with street railways, lighting plants, paper mills, manufacturing plants etc., and in addition to straightening out technical difficulties he was often able to analyse and improve the financial condition of the plant. In his own Company's office he introduced a new system of accounting called the "Job Order" system which enabled jobs to be kept track of better than under the old classical method.

Contact with the Baldwin Locomotive Works and its capable and courageous Works Manager, Vauclain, was especially stimulating. It was in connection with some 100 ton cranes and the compound dynamos to drive them that Fessenden first visited the plant. When they were in working order, Vauclain, who had evidently sized-up the young engineer in spite of the fact that he nicknamed him 'The Parson,' turned to Fessenden for much more far-reaching advice on possible economies in running the plant. He was using too much coal. The steam-drive system in use, with a great number of engines scattered over the plant, involved excessive emissivity of the connecting steam pipes and consequent loss of efficiency. Fessenden knew what should be done—that is, scrap the entire steam-drive system and install motor driven groups of machine tools drawing their current from large dynamos and engines located next to the boilers.

He was himself aghast at the carefully estimated cost and hardly believed that Vauclain would venture on the change. But Vauclain was a man of nerve and far-vision; he decided to have it done and offered Fessenden the job of superintendent of motive power with a salary four times the amount he was then getting. I think it must have been the fear of falling into a rut, of limiting the range of his investigations that, time and again, made Fessenden decline this and similar opportunities. Though he was not to see this project through, it was successfully carried out a few years later and Vauclain stated in a paper on this big electrical drive that it saved him over 60 per cent of the power formerly used—just a little better than Fessenden's original estimate. Even as late as '95, Vauclain was still regretting this capable young electrician, for Kennelly writing to Fessenden in May of that year said "I was glad to hear a kind word spoken for you by Mr. Vauclain, Supt. of Baldwin Locomotive Works. He was speaking to a Westinghouse man about motors and he said that when you were called in you set the matter straighter than it had ever been either before your advent or since.—Vauclain doesn't dream how near he came to being publicly hugged.—"

Meanwhile whenever possible Fessenden studied and carried on independent experimenting. Alternating Current was coming into use and he worked on a commutator type of motor run by A.C. current which was a complete failure as it got altogether too hot. This was traced to high hysteresis and eddy current losses. Hysteresis means loss of energy; the required thing therefore was a kind of iron with low hysteresis and high ohmic resistance.

It appeared from Ewing's work on Magnetism that the molecules of iron aligned themselves differently when magnetized. The effect known as Hysteresis was probably also a matter of alignment of the molecules. Back to the Electrostatic Doublet Theory and the Nature of Cohesion and Elasticity for help.

Since the iron lost energy it must mean that some of its elements were such that they hindered the molecules from aligning freely. An element smaller in size, having sharp corners and a higher melting point could produce this effect and it was found that the carbon atom in high carbon steel did exactly this and resulted in high hysteresis. Therefore the thing to look for was some element whose atoms were larger than the carbon atoms, also with a lower melting point, cheap and easily alloyed with iron. Silicon seemed to be the element required and through the kindness of Mr. Perrine (former electrician of the United States Company and at this time engineer for the Roebling's Works) samples of low carbon iron alloyed with different amounts of silicon were obtained and when tested gave the anticipated low hysteresis and eddy current losses. Arrangements were made for obtaining this product in quantity and in sheet form for armature discs.

Until now platinum had been used for the wires sealed into glass vacuum bulbs and leading the current to the electrodes; but even then platinum was expensive and it occurred to Fessenden that his new silicon iron alloy, in wire form, with its low coefficient of expansion and its silicon relation with glass, might prove a valuable substitute. This was successfully tested out and he applied for his first two patents, with the permission of Mr. Westinghouse. These were U.S. 452 494, Feb. 18, 1891, covering alloys of silicon with iron, nickel, cobalt etc. and U.S. 453 742 Feb. 18, 1891, covering the method of keeping the joint clean by sealing in vacuum, driving off occluded gases by passing current through the wires, so that iron or nickel alloys could be used without addition of silicon, the oxide formed being forced to combine with and dissolve in the glass. No immediate use was made of these patents but they saved Westinghouse the contract for lighting the Columbia Exposition at Chicago in 1893. It is still a recognized method.

The condensers used in the unsuccessful A.C. motor experiments were next investigated for the reason of their failure. Though made of the purest cellulose and paraffin they heated badly, and again the Electrostatic Doublet Theory showed that this was caused by short conducting paths in the material of perhaps only molecular dimensions. It had been found by other workers that a molecule of water could be split off from cellulose by prolonged heating at a certain temperature. Perhaps a water molecule was causing this high hysteresis. So the paper was heated in high melting point for so many hours until the water molecule had come off and then boiled in vacuum, with the result that the hysteresis was reduced to the point when it could no longer be measured.

There was a remarkably fine library at Newark much ahead of its time. Fessenden made exhaustive use of its technical resources and kept abreast of Alternating Current Theory also of all work done by Hertz. He gave a paper on the Electrostatic Doublet Theory of Cohesion before the Newark Electrical Society and sent a copy of the paper to the Philosophical Magazine hoping for publication; but it was too new. Of all the scientists at that time, Fitzgerald, the mathematical genius and an extremely kind man, was the most encouraging. He wrote that if true it would account for Michelson's and Morley's results on light and ether drag.

Part of the plant of the United States Company had been unoccupied and this was rented to Mr. Stanley for an arc light machine he was developing. He also owned part of the electric lighting station at Pittsfield, Massachusetts.

An inventor and a good business man himself, he had with him Mr. C. C. Chesney a highly trained electrical engineer who was also a fine designer.

Out of the contacts and developments in various lines going on at the plant, a new combination arose which seemed to be a nucleus with fine possibilities. Stanley, Chesney, Kelley and Fessenden. Chesney had worked out new types of transformers which were better than anything on the market and he had also found that the idle current of transformers could be neutralized commercially and the all-day losses greatly reduced by a new type of condenser. Kelley had a brilliant idea of neutralizing the inductance of A.C. motors by winding a compensating winding in grooves in the pole pieces. It was thought that the Fessenden silicon iron would be of use in the transformers and A.C. motors. So, as the Stanley Company, it was proposed that this group should start work at Pittsfield, Massachusetts. Zimmerman tried to hold Fessenden with the offer of the position of chief electrician and a higher salary but this time there seemed to be wider opportunities in the new opening.

It was the late fall of 1891 that the offer of the Stanley Company was accepted and we left Newark for the Berkshires and our first experience of New England conservatism.

The law, 'what has been, is, and is to be' was still strong in Pittsfield. Two streets were the correct residential ones—East and South. A hen coop on either was more to be desired than fine gold of modern plumbing elsewhere. So it happened that on arrival we found a little group of newcomers housed on sacrosanct South Street in an antiquated place run as a boarding house by an elderly bachelor and his old-maid sister. Mr. and Mrs. Chesney, Dr. Withington, a Kindergarten teacher and ourselves were the intruders.

My recollection of the management is a series of dissolving pictures as in the movies. An apocryphal "Miss Lucy" who had already gone south because she could not stand New England winters, and whom I never saw—followed by "Mr. Theodore," tall, spare, gangling and that queer, occasional New England product, a man who does the housekeeping. He too disappeared south, dissolving into a woman housekeeper whose only capacity seemed to be for inertia. She endured for the winter and then to my intense dismay, she dissolved into *me*. By this time it was nearly June and the New England winter was beginning to be over; the Chesneys had rented a house for themselves and only

Dr. Withington, the Kindergarten teacher and the Fessendens were left. No other arrangements could be made so I was logically 'it.' Meantime charming hospitality had been extended to all of us by the old residential group, and interests and friendships then begun are still cherished.

The income of the new little company was to be derived from three sources—the lighting-plant and street railway, the manufacture of transformers, and from possible new inventions developed in the Laboratory. Mr. Whittlesey (father of indomitable 'Go to Hell' Whittlesey of war fame) was the treasurer and Mr. Hines was the business manager.

Once more, insulation was Fessenden's first job for the company—of transformers this time. By getting rid of hydroscopic effects by the use of the Fessenden catalyzed linseed oil and by a varnish made of the combination of this linseed oil and Zanzibar copal, excellent results were obtained. Later a peculiarly hard asphalt called Uintahite found only in Utah and with a very high melting point (above 400 degrees Fahrenheit) was combined with the catalyzed linseed oil and gave even better results. His silicon iron also proved to be a valuable contribution to the transformer development.

While at Newark, Fessenden had been invited by Dr. Dudley of the Pennsylvania R.R. to give a lecture on the design of telegraphic apparatus, before the Pennsylvania railroad engineers at Altoona. As delivered, it covered a wider field and was published in June 1900 in the Journal of the Franklin Institute under the title "Electro-Magnetic Mechanism" with special reference to "High Speed Telegraphy."

A discussion arose after the lecture of the difficulties with railroad telegraphic lines owing to the large number of stations in series. Fessenden suggested that by working the line multiplex, with different frequencies and tuned circuits, the difficulties might be overcome. Dr. Dudley approved further work along this line but when it was suggested to Mr. Stanley, he decided that there would be no money in such a development. For that period, it was no doubt the right decision and was further supported by an expert in the transatlantic cable business to whom Fessenden submitted the scheme.

"Mr. Fessenden, I think your system would work. But we do not want it. Every one of our cables has cost us $3,000,000 and we have to earn dividends on them and the greater part of the day they are hardly worked at all. But if you can invent something which will prevent all cables from sending more than four words a minute, we will give you a million for it."

This wasn't quite serious of course but at least served to emphasize the fact that high speeds of working were not wanted. Even as late as 1914 when Fessenden again proposed this method in another connection, the time was not ripe.

Welsbach had invented a mixture of thorium and cerium for incandescent gas mantles. Stanley was obsessed with the belief that this same mixture could be used as a coating for filaments in electric lamps to intensify the light, and Fessenden could not persuade him that it would not work. His own reasons for this certainty were that the effect was a catalytic one as shown by the small percentage of cerium, but Stanley wanted every line of investigation pursued which might make the idea succeed and Fessenden faithfully carried out the experiments until it was demonstrated beyond question that the Welsbach coating would not work.

Then Stanley sent Fessenden to England—his first visit—to see what was being done in high potential work especially by that engineering genius, Ferranti, at his Deptford station. He had seen that the right way to light cities was from a large central station outside the city and had designed and built great dynamos and was sending the current into London on concentric 10,000 volt mains. Admirable as was the development, Fessenden was forced to conclude that it did not seem to be adapted to conditions in the States at that time and he so reported to Stanley, adding that he was going to investigate the new steam prime mover, the steam turbine, which Parsons was operating at Newcastle. On looking it over he was convinced that it would take the place of the steam engine for central station work.

A side trip to Cambridge was most interesting. He visited the Cavendish Laboratory as a shrine where Maxwell had worked and where J. J. (now Sir Joseph) Thomson was making new traditions. Thomson showed Fessenden some of Maxwell's apparatus and some of his own experiments on vacuum tubes. To and fro went the rapid fire of ideas, experiments, theories still perhaps on the verge of confirmation, and inevitably Fessenden's precious jewel, his Electrostatic Doublet Theory of Cohesion came up for discussion. Thomson said he could not accept it. Fessenden pointed out that some of the formulas for conduction given in his book "Dynamics applied to Chemistry" were not at variance with the cohesion theory but Thomson still held that all conduction in gases, liquids and solids was electrolytic and that charges could not exist inside conductors except when conducting a current.

Fessenden met Ewing at the same time and witnessed an extremely pretty experiment of his, determining the hysteresis of a wound iron ring, the windings of which were connected to a galvanometer whose mirror threw a spot of light on a screen. He turned the handle of a zinc arrangement which produced slow alternating currents and the spot of light traced out the hysteresis curve of iron.

1892 was a 'panic' year and things were not going well with the Stanley Company; work was curtailed and the staff reduced. The promise of a share in the company made to Fessenden when he joined it had not been fulfilled nor was he reimbursed for many of the expenses of his English trip. Altogether the outlook was serious for us, but shortly after his return the offer of the chair of electrical engineering at Purdue University was made to him and gladly accepted.

The months of our stay at Pittsfield had indeed been somewhat kaleidoscopic—two moves, an unstable outlook and at a time of general as well as individual apprehension. It was therefore a piece of good fortune to receive the Purdue offer. It satisfied several problems, a stated and assured income and opportunity for teaching and for research, both of which were dear to Fessenden's heart.

He left for Lafayette, Indiana in August so as to have ample time for arrangements.

Dr. Smart, the President of Purdue, was a fine administrator. He had secured Dr. Goss for the Mechanical Engineering Department and under him it had become one of the best in the world. Now it was the President's ambition to provide equally good facilities for Electrical Engineering. Having obtained a good appropriation he gave Fessenden a free hand in the equipment of the electrical laboratory and everything fundamentally necessary for good work was provided, with especial attention paid to apparatus for alternating current work and for precise measurements of all kinds. In the course, mathematical work was emphasized, students being supposed to enter the senior year with a fair knowledge of differential equations, which was considered revolutionary at the time. There was also a course on the work of Hertz, high frequency oscillations, resonance etc. The men were a fine lot and many of them have since become eminent in their profession.

I did not arrive in Lafayette until October for the incubus of the house in Pittsfield was hard to unload, but Dr. Withington had established her office there and did not wish to make a change so finally decided to take it over and I 'dissolved' into her.

In Lafayette we rented comfortable quarters in the home of Judge and Mrs. Weaver. With their family married and gone they found the large house a somewhat lonely place and lavished kindness on us remembering their own children. Here in May our little son was born.

Research work was undertaken, sometimes independently, sometimes by suggestion and supervision of thesis work where a student had no preference of his own. Multiplex resonant telegraphy was resumed, carried to a successful conclusion and published in the Electrical World, September 1894. The more important findings were that pure sine waves should be used and the signaling done, not by interrupting the current at random points of the wave, by a key, but by operating inductively and so as always to start the signals at a definite point, generally the zero point.

Perhaps Fessenden's most important development at this time was his filament galvanometer in which he broke away from the use of a coil with a large number of turns to provide the moving element, to the use of a single fine wire. Optical calculations had showed that the motion of the single fine wire could be observed just as accurately as that of the coil by the mirror.

The importance of this can perhaps be appreciated by the fact that in later work Fessenden used this type of galvanometer with gold wire 1/10 000 inch in diameter for recording frequencies up to 50,000 per second and more, and for recording each individual wave of wireless messages. In a still more advanced state of the radio art it was, according to Fessenden in 1926, the one type of shutter of the Fessenden 'pallograph' or wireless moving picture transmitter and receiver, since it is the only method which will modulate a light beam in one-millionth of a second. A rapid shutter of this kind is necessary for the operation of the pallograph or 'radio Telescope.'

Reg was very happy in college life at Purdue. Everywhere there was an eager enthusiasm so typical of those parts of the country which have not quite lost touch with pioneer days. The University had a famous football team at that time which had defeated Chicago, Michigan and all the other Western teams. In faculty meetings the fateful balance of poor class work with its consequent conditions and the chance of keeping a man so conditioned on the team was often a matter of deepest concern. It was Fessenden's affair to bring every resource to bear in the way of special coaching, extra examinations, etc. to meet Dr. Smart's inexorable dictum that no man who failed in his class work could stay on the team. But he was very just and would not insist on 'the letter of the law if the work was done, somehow, and in time.

Lafayette was a pleasant friendly place where we would gladly have made our home; but already events were taking shape which seemed to hold greater opportunities for Reg.

Westinghouse had obtained the contract for lighting the Columbia Exposition at Chicago, but could not use platinum wire for the seals of his incandescent lamps, on account of patents.

The two Fessenden patents already referred to, using silicon iron wire and iron nickel alloys for sealing wires, were available as these patents were taken out under Westinghouse management. Some one else had proposed to make the incandescent lamps with stoppers, so that the filaments could be renewed when they burned out, without wasting the bulb.

These two ideas were combined and the arrangement worked sufficiently well to save the contract. Later the stoppers were abandoned.

After the Exposition opened Fessenden received a letter from Dr. Holland, Chancellor of the University of Pittsburgh (then called Western University) saying that Mr. Westinghouse had informed him that he had a particular regard for Professor Fessenden and wished, if possible, that he should be offered the newly created chair of Electrical Engineering at the University.

This was soon followed by a letter from Mr. Westinghouse enclosing a check for $1000 and stating that he wished to take up the gas secondary incandescent lamp if Fessenden should be offered the chair at Pittsburgh.

The decision was a hard one. It was difficult to leave Purdue especially after the electrical students had sent a committee to the trustees to ask them to ensure his remaining and the trustees had offered to do anything they could if he would stay; but the advantages as regards experimental work of being near and connected with the Westinghouse works were so great that Dr. Holland's offer was accepted.

As soon as College closed, the business of moving from

Lafayette to Allegheny City was undertaken—not very efficiently—for with a three-months old baby, reorganization was the 'mot d'ordre,' all along the line.

Household furnishings were packed and shipped and we followed. A Chicago stop-over was planned to coincide with the World's Fair Electrical Congress, a widely attended convention at which Fessenden had the pleasure of meeting the aged Helmholtz, also Preece, Mascart, Rowland and others, and of being appointed with Kennelly, Siemens and Preece on the committee on standards of Electrical resistance. Also Kennelly and Fessenden presented a joint paper—"Some Measurements of the Temperature Variation in the Electrical Resistance of a Sample of Copper," this based on work done during the Edison Laboratory period.

CHAPTER VIII

PITTSBURGH DAYS

ARRIVING AT ALLEGHENY CITY and not realizing the overshadowing importance of Pittsburgh as compared with its twin city in the matter of hotels, our instructions to a cabman to take us to a good hotel resulted in finding ourselves in a drab looking building of the small-town, railroad-hotel order. This wouldn't have mattered for the baby and I were too tired to be critical. But the first half-hour of rest revealed very positive reasons why it did matter. I promptly devised a crib out of two chairs, a censored pillow and a trunk strap so that at least the baby should be safe.

Bugs on the threshold of life in the "Smoky City." Was it prophetic of the disturbing events which were to be our last contacts with it?"

However there were happy years between.

The discomforts of the hotel intensified Reg's efforts to find a suitable house and this he did very quickly. A brick house on Charles Street gave us a fortunate combination of a considerate landlord, pleasant, kindly neighbors and a home as comfortable as our means permitted.

Western University occupied a hilltop overlooking Allegheny City and Pittsburgh. On one side of it was the Allegheny Observatory under the direction of Dr. Keeler. The Observatory was small and comparatively humble as to equipment but possessed nevertheless rich traditions. Thanks to the financial support of Mr. William Thaw, Langley had there made his famous measurements on radiation and his still more famous experiments which demonstrated for the first time, and contrary to the accepted scientific doctrine, that it was possible for man to fly.

The location of the Observatory was itself a handicap as

the atmosphere was very smoky and the telescope only 13 inches in diameter and of yellowish glass. These disadvantages had turned Langley to other lines. Mr. Very, his skilled assistant, who had helped him in the construction of his bolometer and in the measurements, was still there.

The flying tests were made by mounting small, thin, flat or curved pieces of wood of various shapes on long arms rotating on top of a post and measuring by very ingenious devices their lift and drag at different speeds. Langley found that the lift was much greater than had previously been calculated, owing to the fact that the inertia of the air had not been taken into account, and he became convinced that flying was possible.

Dr. Keeler, who had studied in Germany and was a great friend of Dr. Willy Wien, had succeeded Langley and was occupied mainly in spectroscopic work. He had laid out a plan for mapping the surface of the sun by means of the calcium and other spectroscopic lines but, without sufficient facilities, had turned it over to Hale and was working on the determination, spectroscopically, of the rotation velocity of the different portions of Saturn's rings. If they were solid they should give one kind of rotational shift of the lines; if made up of small planets they should give a different kind. He proved the latter was the fact and also measured the rotation of Venus.

He was a splendid technical man and fortunately, as Fessenden felt, did not care much for mathematics, so that the pleasure of supplementing his work in this direction often fell to Fessenden.

A warm friendship quickly developed between the Keelers and ourselves. They were a devoted and delightful couple with a small son and a 'baby sister.' Later he was made Director of Lick Observatory and there made another great discovery, i.e. that substantially all nebulae are rotating, which had never been suspected, except by a few, until his discovery.

On the other side of the University were the Brashear Optical Works and the Brashear home. The Brashears were both in middle life at this time and both already widely known and greatly beloved because of the romance of their natures that had compelled them in very truth to 'hitch their wagon to a star.' While still a mill foreman, the transcendent nightly panorama of the heavenly bodies had lured Brashear to a closer knowledge and the story of that first lens which he and Phoebe Brashear fashioned with their own hands, the fatal flaw, the undaunted fresh start is an epic dear to the heart of Pittsburgh. To those who knew them in life the words that now mark their resting place are a fitting tribute:

"We have loved the stars too fondly
to be fearful of the night."

Mr. Thaw had encouraged the young mill foreman and arranged for him to work in conjunction with the Observatory. He made the flats and concaves for Rowland of Johns Hopkins, on which Rowland ruled his famous gratings and later made the great photographic doublets for Wolff with which much good work was done. Though not himself a scientific man, he had a large acquaintance all over the world and a charming manner and told a good story. Joe Jefferson, the actor, always stopped with him when in Pittsburgh and it was a delight to hear the two of them after the theatre, their wits sharpened by Mrs. Brashear's good coffee and by Keeler's silent appreciation.

McDowell was Brashear's chief assistant, a fine optician and mechanic and a great chess player. He taught Fessenden how to make optical flats and his first 8-inch flat, correct to one-twentieth wave length, went on a galvanometer used for some specially accurate work on hysteresis.

University life was rich enough with engrossing lectures, laboratory work, keen students, private research and public service. Electrical Engineering had just been added to the curriculum of the University so that Fessenden had been able to select his own laboratory equipment and plan his own courses. In fact he was given a comparatively free hand in college work and sufficient leisure for private research.

The phrase 'happy is the country without a history' may perhaps apply to this period. They were years that seemed as if they might go on for ever, constructively, quietly, comfortably, with the University as a solid background; in fact life settled down to pleasant routine.

For the first time our house afforded a study—small it is true—but room for bookshelves, roll-top desk, typewriter and revolving chair and floor space enough for its tall occupant to stretch out at full length with a volume of Watts Chemical Dictionary under his head, reminiscent of Edison Laboratory days.

A glance at the appended list of Fessenden's published papers will show the lines of investigation at this time. Photography was an absorbing hobby and our bath room bore a Jeykell and Hyde existence of gradual but uncontrolled merging into a permanent dark room. One practical result of this hobby was described in the Electrical World, August 22, 1896—"Use of Photography in Data Collection." For this purpose a jointed wooden arm supporting a small camera using plates an inch square, was fastened to the top of the desk and there used for photographing charts, curves, references etc. which were to be preserved.

This little device constantly before his eyes stimulated Fessenden to its further development and was the genesis of the group of patents which in later years disclose his "Micro-photographic Book and methods of reading it." His objective was microscopic photographic records between transparent, fused discs of glass or quartz and with automatic devices for projecting the records in proper sequence, on a screen.

One wonders how long it will be before inertia and inhibition are overcome to permit this method of producing books in imperishable form. A letter which appeared in the New York Evening Post October 13, 1930, gives a clear concept of what Fessenden had in mind in his Micro photographic Book patents—(Nos. 1, 616, 848 and 1, 732, 302).

"To the Editor of the Evening Post:

Sir—In your editorial "Beautiful Books" of October 9 you discuss "the device invented by Rear Admiral Bradley Fiske which reproduces the printed page in a microscopic scale and reverses the process to permit its reading with comfort and convenience." I am not familiar with the details of Admiral Fiske's device but I should like to point out that, prior to 1919, Professor Reginald A. Fessenden had invented means for accomplishing precisely this result. Among other applications of his method Professor Fessenden's invention included means for recording the microscopic reproductions photographically.

From the standpoint of practical use, visualize the possibilities of the following: All the records of the largest corporation for a considerable period could be permanently preserved within the space of a single film reel; a complete file of the Evening Post since 1801 could be carried in one hand; vast collections, such as that of the Congressional Library, could be preserved for all posterity within a few sealed film tins; such priceless and relatively inaccessible collections of source material as that of the Vatican, the British Museum, etc. could be made forever available to scholars in every part of the world.

All such uses as the foregoing illustrate, and others too numerous to mention here, were foreseen by Professor Fessenden, and means for carrying out various adaptations of this general idea were worked out by him more than a decade ago."

(Signed) C. O. Gibbon.

New York, Oct. 9, 1930.

Social intercourse in the University group was simple and sincere. A frequent family dissipation was a picnic in the woods, always with the ceremony of a small fire to boil the coffee, followed by a quiet smoke in the hush of sunset. Golf was not yet a national obsession so Sunday forenoons were reserved by the men for congenial group gatherings and when Mr. Wilson became Musical Director in Pittsburgh, he and his talented family organized delightful Sunday forenoon musicals at their Sewickley house at which

Victor Herbert was a frequent guest and which Fessenden keenly enjoyed.

His closest friendship was with Professor Keeler and when in 1898 he was made Director of Lick Observatory, a sense of deep personal loss drummed its persistent beat to the higher note of rejoicing at his friend's well deserved promotion.

During the seven years of the Pittsburgh period, two summer vacations were spent in Bermuda and two in Canada, one of the Canadian holidays coinciding with a meeting of the British Association at Toronto, which Fessenden attended.

The Pittsburgh Academy of Science and Art was an active association of representative Pittsburghers and quite elastic in its undertakings and one of them must here be mentioned.

Lenard in 1893 and Roentgen in 1895 revealed X Rays and some of their possibilities. Thereupon in 1896 Mr. W. L. Scaife recommended that the Academy should construct and own an X Ray apparatus of the highest efficiency which should be available for use by physicians and surgeons and competent persons desirous of making investigations.

The construction of the apparatus was entrusted to a committee of three, the President (Dr. Keeler), Professor Fessenden and Dr. John A. Brashear and in January 1897 the completed apparatus was exhibited at a regular meeting of the Academy. The circular describing it stated that many novel features were designed by Professor Fessenden especially the 'Contact Breaker' which had a combined oil and magnetic 'blow-out' invented by Fessenden to increase the suddenness of the break on which the length of the spark largely depended.

In the Chicago Inter-Ocean, March 14, 1897 considerable emphasis was laid on the fact that it was the most powerful Roentgen Ray apparatus in existence, that it contained every modern device and that the advanced ideas of Fessenden, Keeler and Brashear had gone into its production.

A dramatic surgical operation had been performed. A chip of steel had struck a machinist in the right eye and blinded that eye but it was not known that the chip had embedded itself until the left eye began to give trouble. The X Ray revealed a chip a quarter of an inch long, an eighth of an inch wide which had worked to the rear of the eye. It was skilfully withdrawn by the operating oculist by means of a powerful magnet.

Keeler's and Fessenden's successful tests to detect blow holes in armor plate by X Ray photography also attracted wide attention. It was important and Mr. W. L. Scaife, himself a steel manufacturer, welcomed the discovery. The Carnegie Company had just lost a million dollars through defective armor plate and feared further trouble as it was claimed that plates filled with blow holes had escaped detection by Government Inspectors and were already incorporated in some of the new U. S. Cruisers.

A certain amount of newspaper fame ensued. In consequence Fessenden was approached by two men, Seely by name, who were manufacturers of an arc lamp under a German patent which they had not succeeded in making commercially operative. They proposed to switch to the manufacture of X Ray apparatus under Fessenden patents and an agreement was reached by which Reg was to have a yearly retaining fee for his X Ray patents and as consulting expert. But it was soon found that the X Ray company had been saddled with the losses of the prior lamp business as the Seely contribution; no retaining fees were paid and there was nothing to be done but liquidate the business and sever connections. This was agreed to, though several years later a preposterous claim was put forth by one of the Seely brothers for a share in all Fessenden patents. This of course was a silly and futile gesture and never reached a court hearing.

A second attempt at a business connection was with one, Grant McCargo, to manufacture a modified 'Nernst' Lamp covered by Fessenden patents, but this too was an unsuccessful venture.

The third and last business project of the Pittsburgh period was on a different basis. Fessenden opened an Electrical Consulting Office, taking into partnership Mr. Charles Ridinger. This gave good promise of success and was a going concern when we left Pittsburgh.

Two experiences which I recall had shown Fessenden the need for such a business. The Macbeth Lamp Chimney Company put a problem in his hands for solution. Loss from breakage in cutting chimneys to length was far too great—could he suggest a remedy? He devised a simple inclined plane with exposed, non-insulated electric wires at proper intervals, down which the glass tube rolled; this effected a perfect break at the required points and he was handed a check for the agreed amount, $400.00, the very day he submitted his bit of mechanism.

I well remember the feeling of affluence this check produced on us; it was almost as if we had picked $400.00 off the bushes. Both agreed we must celebrate and laughed at ourselves at the end of the evening when we found that we had walked blithely down to the Allegheny Library, spent a couple of hours there and, still uplifted, had climbed the hills again as our expression of wild and riotous celebration.

At about this time too, W. E. Corey, superintendent of the Carnegie Company came to Reg for help in correcting a serious trouble in annealing. The making of properly Harveyized plate was a delicate process, 'almost like making a peachblow vase' wrote an imaginative reporter; over-annealing resulted in cracks. It was a matter of guessing as closely as possible and too much or too little heat meant failure. The solution was a simple little appliance—a single wire, one end of which was placed in the furnace, the other leading to the cool air outside; in the center a heat measuring device, by which it was possible to tell to the smallest fraction of a degree, the temperature of the molten mass. This saved small fortunes annually.

Fessenden was offered a partnership in the Carnegie Company in recognition of this work, and again a second time in connection with some work done in the manufacture of steel tubing, but each time he declined.

It seems men go their destined and appointed ways.

In 1898 a change took Keeler to Lick Observatory where the high altitude attacked an unsuspected heart weakness which proved fatal in a few years.

In 1900 Fessenden made a change which demanded almost superhuman effort of him to the end of his days and made him the target of those who sought to reap where he had sown.

CHAPTER IX

A MOMENTOUS DECISION

1900 SAW THE BEGINNING of a new phase for Reg. Academic work came to an end, the class room and the laboratory knew him no more. Invention became his profession.

In the light of later years would we still have made that choice?

It was a 'via dolorosa.'

Picture for a moment what it means to be an inventor, a *real* inventor, not one of the pirate crews maintained by every large organization from Government Departments down, men whose duty it is to scout for new developments and to imitate them and to protect those imitations by Applications to the Patent Office which, all too often, issue as bona fide patents.

No. I do not mean that kind of inventor.

I mean the man who, by some Alchemy of Nature, some mysterious Mendelian transmission, some super distillate of mentality which, by unremitting investigation and study has been brought to a high perceptive state, sees beyond the known, discovers the laws of the unknown and expands our processes to accept them.

Such minds are rare, incalculable, not to be explained and of extreme importance to the world's progress.

But what happens?

The inventor discloses some of these laws, some of these remarkable facts brought back from the unknown land; they gleam like precious jewels; the glint of their possibilities catches the public mind. As the prospector who has returned to the rim of civilization with word of located goid, becomes on the instant a marked man with the rabble at his heels, waiting to track him down and jump his claim, so the inventor, as his daring concepts are affirmed, becomes aware of more subtle forces with fixed intent to reap a benefit from his invention.

I do not believe that there is an inventor who has not experienced this claim jumping, or who has not at some time led the utterly unworthy to wealth and public honors.

But at first he is unaware of this——. He is an optimist. In his brain whirl such far-reaching thoughts, such glimpses of things to be, such an urge to be at them, such splendid visions of benefits to all, he cannot conceive of anything but honest, willing cooperation. Nothing is really important except getting started on the project—once completed, he believes everything will adjust and right itself.

It was Sophocles who said in criticism of a contemporary —"He paints men as they are: I paint them as they ought to be." I am sure that my husband's abiding characteristic was to believe that a man was "as he ought to be."

And thinking thus we went gladly forth into a new life. Before it drew to a close we were to make acquaintance with treachery in many forms, but also with heartening loyalty.

The famous diarist, Greville, who held aside the curtains and revealed the stage settings and machinery of English Court life in the first half of the nineteenth century, writes on March 17, 1838—"Met Dr. Buckland and talked to him for an hour and he introduced me to Mr. Wheatstone, the inventor of the electric telegraph, of the progress of which he gave us an account. *There is a cheerfulness, an activity, an appearance of satisfaction in the conversation and demeanour of scientific men that conveys a lively notion of the pleasure they derive from their pursuits.*" One senses a twinge of envy in the noble earl that his contacts with this remote class were not more frequent. We can feel sorry for him, knowing what he missed. There *is* pleasure, and there *is* satisfaction, the atmosphere is wholesome and stimulating and the men who follow the call are a brotherhood in the cause of unveiling the secrets of the universe.

Looking back on the succession of young men who were

identified with my husband's work from 1900 on, the memory is of an amazing consecration to the job. Whether college graduate or day laborer, each gave a loyalty and zeal that took no note of times or seasons. A fine lot of men whom I am proud to have known.

That these men felt and responded to the influence of a mind beyond the ordinary is equally true. There was magic compulsion in it. Under Fessenden, work became an adventure; goals were set, preposterous and beyond the borderland of possibility. The men were in that constant state of mental gymnastics advised in *Alice Through the Looking Glass*—"practise believing so many impossible things before breakfast." The tasks set might seem like trying to grasp beautiful bubbles, but marvelously, the bubbles held, were brought down to earth and one by one linked to perform their appointed miracles.

Thank God for men who love work for work's sake.

It will be recalled that in 1889 while still in the Edison Laboratory, Reg suggested working on wireless telegraphy, the phenomenon recently disclosed by Hertz. Edison agreed but postponed it for a while and the opportunity was lost.

At Purdue in 1892-93 and later at the Western University of Pennsylvania he lectured and experimented on the production and detection of Hertzian waves, and in 1896-97 two of his students, Messrs Bennett and Bradshaw, investigated imperfect-contact receivers most thoroughly over a period of many months, incorporating their results in a thesis. These findings convinced Fessenden and themselves that such methods of reception could not be relied upon.

In 1898 Reg suggested to one of the editors of the New York Herald that the international yacht race should be reported by this new method of communication and in December of that year he was asked to undertake the work but declined, suggesting instead Signor Marconi, already widely known as a worker in this field.

This new and striking means of communication excited public imagination and the pressure to see it carried to further development grew steadily everywhere. In a paper read before the American Institute of Electrical Engineers, November 1899, speaking of this pressure, Fessenden said—"Having been forced some years ago into X Ray work with much loss of time and very little results to show for it, I considered myself proof against the seductions of liquid air and wireless telegraphy." But there was inward compulsion on him as well as outside pressure, for he was convinced that *a wrong turn had been taken* by other workers, as regards both generation and reception, and he must put to the test his theory that there was no essential distinction between the Henry high frequency oscillations and Hertzian waves. In which case, sustained oscillations and non-microphonic receivers was the answer, instead of the damped oscillation—coherer doctrine that Lodge, Marconi and all other workers were imposing on the scientific world.

Fessenden began to be recognized as an independent American worker in this new science. This recognition resulted in a proposal from the Weather Bureau that he undertake the development of a system to be used in the transmission of the Bureau's Weather Forecasts.

Professor Cleveland Abbe,—the "father of the Weather Bureau,"—came from Washington to discuss with Reg the necessary plans for such a service. For the consideration of Willis L. Moore, Chief of the Weather Bureau, Fessenden was required to put into writing his ideas and plans. This was done, and from the Chief the following letter was received:

          U. S. Department of Agriculture
              Weather Bureau
              Washington D. C.
              Jan. 4th 1900.

"Professor Reginald A. Fessenden
Western University of Pennsylvania,
Allegheny, Pa.
Dear Sir:—

 I am in receipt of your letter of the 29th ultimo.
 In general your proposition is acceptable to us, but some

modification must of necessity be made, because of the legal restraints covering the expenditure of public moneys.

I am authorized by the Honorable Secretary of Agriculture to make you the following offer:

You will be employed for one year in the Weather Bureau at a salary of $3000 per annum. The Bureau will pay your actual expenses while on the road to an amount not exceeding $4.00 per day. You will be allowed to remain in Allegheny and continue your local connections for not longer than 3 months. Two active young men of the Weather Bureau will be assigned to duty as your assistants, and if you are especially desirous of retaining the one you at present employ, he will also be employed in the Weather Bureau for one year, at a salary of $1200. Such apparatus as described in your letter of the 29th ultimo will be purchased at the expense of the Government, one of our own men making the purchases and auditing the accounts: the property to belong to the Government. At the end of the year, if your work is successful, your services may be continued at a salary not less than that paid the first year.

The Government cannot legally pay for the patents issued to you, but by the proposition herein made, *you* are allowed a salary that will enable you to easily bear such expense and *thus own the patents, the Bureau reserving the right to make use of such patents or of such devices as you may invent for its use in receiving meteorological reports and transmitting Weather Bureau information.*

I am of the opinion that you would have a better opportunity here not only to test your present devices, but also while enjoying a remunerative salary and having your travelling expenses paid be able to devise new apparatus that would inure both to the profit of the Government and to your own individual benefit.

Congress recently gave us $25000 which we expended in making additions to our buildings in Washington. We therefore have plenty room and can easily fit up such laboratory as you may need. You will also find instrument makers, blacksmiths, metal workers and artisans of many classes, the services of whom will be freely placed at your disposal.

If this general proposition meets with your approval, I

would thank you to sign the enclosed agreement and return same to this office.

Very truly yours,
(signed) Willis L. Moore,
Chief U. S. Weather Bureau."

Reg decided to accept this offer and March of 1900 found us pulling up roots that had begun to feel themselves almost in native soil. Household goods were stored, Lucifer, the kitten, was adopted by neighbours, farewells to friends of seven years standing were spoken and Professor Kintner succeeded Professor Fessenden in the chair of Electrical Engineering at Western University.

Professor Very of the Allegheny Observatory and formerly under Langley had been working with Reg on wireless and he was continued as assistant in the new work. The 'active young man' of the Weather Bureau appointed to assist as well as to thread the mazes of governmental red tape was Mr. Alfred Thiessen a Cornell graduate of distinct ability and a man of such equable and friendly disposition that we always counted ourselves fortunate in having him for a wilderness companion.

We—my husband, Ken, our little boy of seven and I, reached Washington early in April. After a short period of conference with the Bureau to crystallize plans, we started for an island where a series of quantitative experiments were to be made. This was Cobb Island, Maryland, sixty miles down the Potomac from Washington.

Only sixty miles, but sixty long slow miles on a river steamer that zigzagged from one small settlement to another. Alexandria was the first stop and the last link with adequate stores and, as there was always freight enough to discharge and load there to ensure a long wait, it was there we did our marketing and made arrangements for ordering supplies by mail.

Rock Point was our steamboat landing and from there to the island the colored caretaker was our Charon. All sorts of queer contraptions were ferried over by him; I recall one day a top-heavy boat load that looked like a small wireless hut but which turned out to be a packing case ice box with a lid that had to be hoisted by rope and pulley and into which, standing on a chair, I had to make headlong dives to reach the inner box and my perishable supplies.

Cobb Island was the summer home of a Philadelphia newspaper man. There were two houses on the place, a cottage occupied by the Very family and the main house by ourselves and Mr. Thiessen. No water was laid on and plumbing was a minus quantity, still the place was comfortable enough, even after the Philadelphia family arrived in force for the long vacation and the main house had to be divided into two housekeeping entities never dreamed of by the builder.

The sole water supply was a constant spring with perhaps a half-inch flow, about twenty-five yards from the house. Here we waited for our buckets to fill, for there was no arrangement for storage other than a large tub at which several head of cattle were supposed to slake their thirst and which, coming as they did all at once, was never adequate to their wants.

All through the day and night the little trickle wasted which might have been stored, and it was a relief when a long trough took the place of the tub so the poor beasts could drink in comfort.

The combination of a southern climate and cattle meant, of course, the presence of that southern pest, the tick; it was our first introduction but we soon learned *not* to sit on the grass and *not* to allow our clothes to touch shrubbery in passing. Swimming in the Potomac was pleasant and rowing was useful for we established a few mainland connections for food supplies, eggs and garden truck, and my son and I made little excursions to replenish the larder.

A few visitors hunted us up, some official, some friends of longer standing and all were welcomed with such hospitality as the place afforded. Our high water mark of entertainment was a picnic excursion to the Wakefield Estate famed as the birthplace of George Washington. He lived there only four years and the house now standing is not that in which he was born as that house was burned down in 1780. Nevertheless, it served as a pious and pleasant pilgrimage.

For construction work, early contact was made with a local man, Captain Chiseltine, the owner of a good schooner, a capable and reliable man. Incidentally he became an occasional purveyor to us of oysters of a size and succulence as will never come our way again.

Two fifty foot, wooden masts were erected exactly one mile apart and with hot wire barreters and ring receivers those exact quantitative measurements were continued that made Fessenden's work so sound. He describes this in "How Ether Waves move." Popular Radio, November 1923.

> "The exact method of transmission of the waves was experimentally determined by means of ladders placed at varying distances from the antennas. The course of the waves in the air was fully mapped out up to distances of several hundred yards from and to the antennas, and by burying the receivers at different depths in the ground and immersing them in different depths in sea water, the rate of decay below the surface and the strength of the currents flowing in the surface were accurately determined."

The basic features of the Fessenden System had been fully determined before leaving Pittsburgh. The quantitative measurements therefore that were continued during the Cobb Island period were for the purpose of building on an absolutely sure foundation and of perfecting each component part of the system so that maximum output and sensitivity of parts should be attained.

Distance in wireless telegraphy was neither desired nor stressed at this time, though in the fall of 1900 in order to demonstrate to the Chief of the Weather Bureau and to Professor Marvin, head of the instrument division, some marked improvements that had been made in the *sending* apparatus, a test of moderate distance and difficulty took place. This was between Cobb Island and Arlington, Va., a fifty mile stretch which included wooded country, open water and the City of Alexandria and was made with a single No. 16 B & S gauge wire, 65 feet long and no transformer—and, like the Irishman who included the irrelevant clause to make his riddle difficult—in this test the "energy wasting, inaccurate and slow coherer" was used at the receiving end instead of the Fessenden type of receiver which required only 1/500 of the power needed by the coherer. It was evident therefore that greater distance awaited only the erection of stations.

One milestone of Radio History marks the close of this Cobb Island period.

In 1899 before leaving Allegheny, Fessenden and Kintner had also done some work on Wireless Telephony and had found the need for a different type of apparatus, an interrupter to give at least 10,000 breaks per second. Mr. Brashear the celebrated optician kindly consented to make this up and it was ready in January or February of 1900 but not until December of that year were the Cobb Island stations ready for this apparatus to be tested. *There, between two masts 50 feet high and one mile apart, intelligible speech by electromagnetic waves was for the first time transmitted.* Poor in quality, since it was accompanied by an extremely loud and disagreeable noise due to the irregularity of the spark, but *distinct and entirely intelligible.*

At the close of the year all necessary data had been obtained—the Weather Bureau was so enthusiastic about results that work on a larger scale was decided upon and a chain of three stations planned, one at Hatteras, one at Roanoke Island and the third at Cape Henry.

This change involved considerable upheaval; dismantling of the Cobb Island stations, transfer of masts and equipment to the new sites, re-erection and a general lining up and adaptation of locality to requirements. Reg and Thiessen were to be on the wing for several weeks so Ken and I were bundled off to Bermuda for a Christmas Holiday.

Construction and experimentation was only a part of this

undertaking, one might almost say a small part, for patent work began to add a compelling pressure which grew always heavier and more demanding. It involved endless traveling, patent conferences, office actions and a mind tensely on the alert for the perfect phrasing of claims that would adequately and precisely protect these fundamentally new inventions. In Pittsburgh Mr. Darwin S. Wolcott of the law firm of Christy and Christy had been Reg's patent attorney in some Incandescent and X-Ray applications and he continued in that capacity for wireless work.

The Fessenden System has been referred to more than once. It is proper at this point to give some description of this System, not from a technical point of view so much as a comparative one. *What did it do for the art?*

Fessenden lacked the publicity sense commensurate to his contributions; he was always too busy doing things to take time to tell the world what he had done and what he was going to do. No glare of limelight, no fanfare of trumpet stressed the magnitude and importance of his work or his vital influence on the Art. These irrefutable facts are for the most part buried in patent files and in volume after volume of law dockets in which the validity of his inventions were established against tremendous odds.

By excerpts from sworn testimony and by Court decisions something of what Fessenden did for Radio may emerge. *Alone, he lifted it from a track down which it was moving to frustration and placed it on sound scientific principles.*

From Federal Trade Commission. Docket #1115
Typewritten record Library of Congress.

WITNESS

S. M. KINTNER (formerly receiver of National Electric Signaling Co., later Vice President Westinghouse Company) testifies—
"Fessenden is looked upon as one of the pioneers in the art . . . . one of the outstanding figures in the development of radio. . . He had invented wireless telephony." pp 492-3

"Fessenden was the first to disclose a particular type of receiving mechanism which was continuously receptive . . . and Marconi and all the other systems went to that particular type of receiving means." p 498
Same witness testified that Fessenden conducted the first two-way transatlantic radio communication. pp 501-2

Marconi Wireless Telegraph Company
of America, Complainant,
vs.   in Equity DE-23
National Electric Signaling Company

WITNESS

R. A. FESSENDEN—"I have not, nor has the National Electric Signaling Company, ever used in practice any Marconi system of wireless telegraphy, nor any coherer, nor any capacity areas such as described in the Lodge patent in suit. In fact, my entire work in this art, now including something like two hundred patents and applications for patents, was begun and carried on for the express purpose of developing a new system on a different principle from that of Lodge, (and later of Marconi), and at the very inception of the work my primary idea was that the Lodge system (and later, Marconi's modification of it) was based on the wrong principle and that a successful apparatus must be built which radically differed from it in the three essential points of generating prolonged wave trains, including continuous reception, of tuning circuits together in true resonance, and of employing a current operated constantly receptive and directly and proportionally acting receiver. All the receivers I or the defendants have used have been of this form, acting on a principle directly opposite that of Marconi and Lodge's coherers. In short, the Fessenden system was conceived and developed to take the place of the Lodge system (and later the Marconi system), and in actual practice it has displaced the Marconi and Lodge system so that at the present time there are few if any plants in commercial use which employ the highly damped wave, or the trigger acting receivers."

ALSO

JUDGE HALE U. S. C. Ct. Maine   sustaining Fessenden
patent 706, 736.

"I think it must be held to be a pioneer invention.—Fessenden found the loose imperfect contact coherer, he substituted for it the current operated wave responsive receiver, effecting an unobstructed path, a summing up of all the waves, however small, a constantly receptive avenue, an unbroken circuit. He made a new instrumentality in the art, different in conception from the instrumentality which Marconi employed. The whole progress in wireless telegraphy up to this time had been the coherer. Every imitator had assumed that by it alone he could obtain results in that mysterious art. Fessenden gave a new direction to the progress of the art. In making his invention he is entitled to be held a pioneer within his field." pp 16,17.

"I believe that the patent in suit is the first disclosure in the art of an announcement that the art was on the wrong track." p 25.

Of the tuning he says, "The patent in suit is the first disclosure in the art of wireless telegraphy of a wireless telegraph system in which the sending and receiving system is adjusted to its mutual maximum effect, not merely with the adjustment of mast wire to mast wire, as in the prior art, but with the reinforcement due to the additional effect due to a tuned local circuit, including the spark gap at the sending station and including the receiver at the receiving station." p 19

"Complete tuning was only possible in such a system as that of Fessenden. I am of the opinion that the tuning of the prior art was essentially and typically different from the tuning involved in Fessenden's invention."

Decree entered, injunction, and order for accounting.

ALSO

JUDGE BUFFINGTON   U. S. C. Ct. App. 3rd Circuit. sustaining Fessenden patents 918, 306; 918, 307. "The free admission and absolute neutralization of hostile static influence in wireless system made in our judgment a new era in the art."

p 24. Quotes London Elect. article of June 1909. 'A great change has taken place in wireless during the past few years, namely considerable increase in range and certainty of working. Both these have arisen from work done in the United

States, and both are due to two simple technical facts. The first is the abolition of a coherer as a detector and its replacement by an integrating detector, the other is the increase in the impulses in the secondary spark in the sender.' "That the latter advance, conceded to have come from the U. S. was justly attributable to any person other than Fessenden the proofs do not show.—"

"The process was first disclosed by Fessenden."

Decree and accounting ordered.

CHAPTER X

WIRELESS AT ROANOKE ISLAND

RETURNING FROM BERMUDA in January I found headquarters established at Manteo, Roanoke Island and the Hatteras and Cape Henry Weather Bureau Stations both making ready for wireless work.

Captain Chiseltine had been commissioned to transport the 50 foot masts and all wireless equipment from Cobb Island to Roanoke Island on his staunch schooner.

An expurgated account of this Odyssey gradually seeped through to me. Reg and Thiessen would not be separated from their wireless *lares and penates* so made the trip with the Captain. Weather was unfavorable from the start and grew worse. Thiessen soon succumbed and was conscious of but one wish and that was that ether waves might have the penetration, persistence and general overwhelming power of the large Limburger cheese which was part of Reg's lavish stores for the trip. To improve matters the cheese was hung overboard but there it appears to have upset the sea, for the storm became really serious.

Finally in Albemarle Sound the schooner with its unwieldy tow of two 50 foot masts became so unmanageable that Captain Chiseltine believed there was danger of foundering and proposed to cast the tow adrift. This, Reg refused to permit and the matter hung in the balance till another squall struck the ship when the Captain started to cut the tow ropes, whereupon Reg either threatened to or did in fact knock him down. This was mutiny on the high seas, but he saved his precious equipment, the wind began to moderate, a local schooner rendered assistance and the incident was over—without rancor on either side.

Regular transportation to the island in those days was by

rail from Norfolk to Elizabeth City, by boat from there to a landing on the west side of Roanoke Island and a tedious drive from there along roads of deep, shifting sand to Manteo, a town of two hotels and several stores. In many ways it was an enterprising community. Hunters and drummers were the usual run of visitors.

The larger of the two hotels was a two-story wooden building with long street frontage and verandas on both floors and two wings stretching to the back. When we arrived an attempt was being made to provide table accommodation, the dining room being run by a man who had looked after hunting camps. Most of the work was done by his wife for the man's greatest activity seemed to be practicing the call for wild turkeys. It was poor white cooking to an accompaniment of innumerable flies. As the place was screened this was unnecessary but our complaints about them only provoked the long-suffering query—"Did you ever see a place whar there warn't no flies?" We admitted we had and soon decided to relinquish effete hotel life and 'roll our own.'

The owner of the building, a sterling business man, rented us an upstairs wing, a long straight corridor with rooms on either side, eight or ten in all, which we transformed according to our needs into office, bedrooms, dining room and kitchen and made out very nicely, having, however, to 'tote' water upstairs from a central courtyard.

Directly after breakfast the men would start off in a rickety conveyance for the Wireless Station which had been located on the west side of the island. They took sandwiches with them and brewed coffee at lunch time. Home again about six and after supper two or three hours of office work, correspondence, patent applications, official Weather Bureau returns and accounts.

Our windows looked east and out on a small warehouse and wharf at which, twice a week, it was a joy to watch the schooner 'Manie Carlos' under Captain Johnson, swing alongside with the beautiful precision of a mathematical curve. She carried freight between Elizabeth City and Manteo.

The wharf was the habitat of the cat, 'Yellow Maria' who up to the time of our arrival had fended ably for herself. But after Reg had paid her the graceful attention of buying a mess of oysters and having them opened for her, evening and office time was the signal for her presence upstairs. Seated on the bare edge of the table beside her patron as, deep in dictation he swung and balanced in his desk chair, a yellow paw would reach out from time to time to rest on his arm—not to play—not to distract—but merely to touch.

Mosquitoes, ticks and chigoes were the pests of the island and smell of decayed fish used as fertilizer was another unpleasant feature. Mosquitoes were the worst since they could invade us in our own territory whereas the other two were only met with when we invaded theirs. Against mosquitoes the men wore voluminous veils of white mosquito netting tied round their hats and coming well down over the chest and pulled tight with another drawstring. When the pests were very bad sheets of newspaper were wound cuff-like around ankles and wrists.

Sometimes in the afternoons after lessons and housework, Ken and I would walk the four miles to the station to drive home with the men. In spite of the ticks which brushed from the undergrowth on to our clothes and which had to be shaken off very carefully, these walks were beautiful; sandy, shifting soil and low underbrush, but overhead stately live oaks, long strawed pines, holly and mistletoe. Near the station a strip of marsh stretched between beach and interior and this had to be crossed. We negotiated it by taking off shoes and stockings and wading happily through the amber brown water. When we learned that moccasins were apt to lurk there, the edge was taken off our enjoyment.

Roanoke Island cherished its traditions and we absorbed them and on those quiet shady paths other presences seemed to linger—the early colony, Virginia Dare, the first white child born on American soil; the disappearance, sudden and complete, of the settlement with only the letters R O A blazed on a tree to indicate a possible answer to the riddle.

In later times another mystery—the beautiful and brilliant Theodosia Burr (Mrs. Allston), who with her young son set sail from Charleston to meet her father, permitted at last to return from Europe. A storm off the Hatteras coast, and again disappearance, complete and mystifying. Some say not a storm but pirates brought this about, but it is not to be believed that a woman such as Theodosia Burr would not have come triumphant out of any man-made hazard.

Not that piracy was an unnatural suspicion, for a strong strain of it weaves in and out of local history—witness the name 'Nag's Head,'—that part of the Hatteras sand-strip directly opposite Manteo. The story of earlier days is that when a storm raged, lighted lanterns were fastened to horses' necks and these roaming beacons lured to destruction the richly laden merchantmen of the coast-wise trade. Later this place enjoyed some vogue as a fashionable seaside resort and practiced perhaps another form of piracy, for a ramshackle building proclaimed itself in circular, 'Here the beautiful Nag's Head Hotel pleasantly resides.'

Now, after the flight of thirty years and when the slow transportation methods of bygone years have yielded to a quicker tempo and automobile traffic has opened the way to the island, a large sign on the road leading from the ferry connecting with the mainland, reads as follows:—

MAINLAND FERRY FORT HUGER AND THE OLD WIRELESS STATION one mile	This road leads to the Ferry to Mann's Harbor and route 90. Near by is the Civil War Fort Huger and the old Station site where Fessenden's famous Wireless Experiments were made in 1902

So we have become part of the tradition of Dare County.

While Reg and his men were making Wireless history on Roanoke Island, history in a vastly different form was being made at Kitty Hawk by the Wright brothers. It was a companionable thought that in this element, the air, two men not so many miles away from us were achieving mastery in one form while we at Manteo were achieving mastery in another.

There was much passing to and fro between our three stations in 1901 in order to complete installation and to get each one properly tuned up. Quite early in the spring Fessenden had to visit the Cape Henry station and Ken and I accompanied him on the trip. There was work to be inspected and some mast or rigging trouble to be righted. When the spar was ready to be hoisted, Reg took the rope over his shoulder and ploughed through the deep sand, while others blocked and stanchioned the pole as it lifted. A piercing wind was blowing. That night Reg wakened me saying, 'I can't move.'

We were alone in a summer cottage but luckily supplied with plenty of wood and an air-tight stove. Also one other homely remedy—a mixture of lard and kerosene given me by a kindly soul the night before in case of croup on Ken's part. I soon had the stove red hot and the chill, damp air changed to genial warmth. It was a pretty bad bout of lumbago but he would not allow it to delay him and we managed to get back to Manteo the following day. It was while at Cape Henry, climbing the great sandhills where now and again topmost branches of pine trees show the constant, engulfing progress of the sand, that we were warned of the danger of breaking through a crust of sand into tubes that once were the straight columns of mighty pines.

One other outing of this same spring was to Norfolk, to witness an eclipse. Cameras and certain pieces of apparatus were taken along, among other things a coherer, to see if any interesting data might be obtained.

We sought an open field on the outskirts of the city as far removed from street cars and interference of that sort as possible. Everything was made ready as slowly daylight faded in mid forenoon. Birds were silent and we ourselves reacted to the weird, somewhat awesome spectacle.

Suddenly the coherer began to chatter, rather hysterically,

babbling all the gossip of the spheres—which we couldn't translate. Very effective as mise-en-scene, but revealing its own weakness.

As work progressed the staff increased. Mr. Eben T. Turner of Ithaca was chosen as an experimenter to fill the place of Professor Very, who had left at the close of 1900. Mr. Turner and his wife were a most welcome addition to our little community. Then Mr. Thiessen married and he and his wife established themselves in a couple of rooms off the long corridor. A machinist and some operators from the Weather Bureau arrived, so that the three stations could be kept in communication.

That Communication was satisfactory is shown by the following telegram—

"Washington D. C. Oct. 4, 1901
Professor Fessenden
Manteo, N. C.

Your report highly satisfactory. Please do not negotiate or communicate with anyone relative to your work or experiment until after you see me. We do not wish to become involved with promoters for the present. Professor Marvin and myself will leave Elizabeth City 6 P. M. Saturday boat. Meet me with team.
(signed) Moore."

There was possibly a portent in this telegram, for to revert to the opening theme of this wireless period—*a jewel of great worth had been disclosed—*

But if storm clouds were on our horizon the shadow was not yet very ominous and did not disturb the Christmas dinner at which the whole wireless staff gathered. Captain Johnson was commissioned to choose the turkey in Elizabeth City and brought down a noble bird. I knew there would be no waste when at sight of it came the timid request from an old char-woman—"Please ma'am, ef ye ain't got no use for de haid and de foots dey'll make fine brof for my young uns."

Local resources were drawn on for our feast, but in nothing so effectively as for the decorations; the dining room became a tent of small-meshed seine net stuck thick with hundreds of sprigs of holly with its gleaming red berries, mistletoe and brooms of long-strawed pine. It was really beautiful.

On Christmas Eve a cruising motor boat tied up at our wharf and word went round that it was 'the Edison boys.' Reg went down to call and found a party of four in their little cabin, ankle deep in feathers; with all the zeal of amateurs they were tackling the job of plucking a goose. The party consisted of Tom Edison, Billy Edison and his wife, a dainty little Virginia beauty, and her sister. They were Florida bound, cruising leisurely along inland waters, but finding at Manteo a colony that promised congenial companionship, they gradually abandoned thoughts of Florida and when we left for good in August 1902 they were still there.

In 1902 storm clouds began to gather everywhere, general as well as personal, and wireless work speeded up to an almost frenzied tempo.

With the business perspicacity that always marked Marconi's efforts, his company had closed a deal with Lloyds for 14 years. The British Government, at that time backing British systems, was alarmed at the menace of a Marconi monopoly, for the mutual advantages of cooperation which were exploited under the Lloyd George and Rufus Isaacs aegis were still in the future.

Propaganda was started by the British Government urging International Regulation. England was in fact asking other countries to join in legislation favoring a system owned by itself which at the same time barred the door to systems invented in other countries.

With that follow the leader spirit so characteristic of politicians, Congressmen on this side also rushed into legislation. Reg believed that any legislation at this time must of necessity be bad, for even if equitable arrangements could be arrived at, an infant art might have its growth entirely arrested by legislative bonds. Strenuous efforts to stem this uninformed legislation were made by him, in letters to the press, letters to and calls on men who were a power in Congress—John Dalzell, Quay, Hepborn, Chairman of House Committee on Interstate and Foreign Commerce, etc. Likewise he urged as a back-fire proposition to the English plan the establishment of an International Shipping League which should provide for the United States, France and Germany the same service that Lloyds did for British shipping.

So much for public endeavor. In addition to this, some difficult experimental problems presented themselves to Fessenden in the early months of 1902. The following letters to his patent attorney, Wolcott, reveal what they were and how magnificently they were overcome.

Manteo, Roanoke Island, N. C.
March 28, 1902.

"Dear Wolcott,

I have been having a frightful time this last month, but it is now ended with the very best of luck and I can give you a letter now which will make you open your eyes, and which will be a hundred times better than any letter that I could have written before, and which should enable you to get your men interested at once.

What do you say to a receiver which gives telegrams at the rate of a thousand words per minute and is so sensitive that it gives that rate when the coherer will not even give a click and when the coherer cannot be read when the power is increased over ten times, i.e., which measurement shows works at this rate with less than ten per cent of the power necessary to work the coherer at all. Also that it is perfectly positive and gives these results in its very crudest form and on the very first trial.

Well, this is what I have now and what I have been working over the Hatteras-Roanoke line, as fast as the man could handle the key. So it is no theory but an accomplished fact.

To begin with, I was almost worried sick last month. The coils were bad, and did not work, having been made different from my specifications. I could get no signals between Hatteras and Roanoke. I tried a number of things and finally found that the trouble was that the water had over

30 times the resistance of sea water, as measured by actual comparison of samples by Wheatstone Bridge, allowing for polarization of course, in making the measurements. This, in conjunction with the bad coils, and the fact that for some reason the coherers were working badly, prevented all good results, also the sending was bad. It was principally owing to the insulating water, which made the course equivalent to about 300 miles, and with bad coils it was no wonder that we did not get this.

I then tried my new receiver. I say new, but I used it some at Rock Point (Cobb Island) and have been working at it since, but had not considered it as ready for trial, as the material was bad, and for better results it should be in vacuo, and have a better mechanism, and a resonator and prolonged oscillations, and longer waves, and higher frequency break. So I did not think it would work. But it worked at the first trial, and I could hear every click of the key at Hatteras, and got every dot and dash as plainly as could be and as fast as they could send.

To do a little figuring. The resonator should increase the effect 10 times. The prolonged oscillations about 5 times. The vacuum about 20 times. Longer waves about 5 times. Salt water instead of insulating water about 5 times. Good coils about 4 times, i.e., the sensitiveness can be increased about 1,000,000 times over this crude apparatus. This would give about 1,000 times the distance or 50,000 miles.

As it is perfectly selective, perfectly positive, i.e., can give no false dots and cannot omit dots or dashes, I think we are at the end of all our troubles.

I enclose you a letter for your people. I suppose you thought you would make me mad when you wrote about not trusting you in the matter, and thought that I would have replied at once. So I probably would, but I knew that if I waited a few days longer I could give you a letter that would be worth writing, and so it has turned out.

About the patents, I have gone over most of them, and will send them on in a few days. I should have done so before, but have been nearly down with nervous prostration I have been working so hard and I found that I could do no intelligent work on them when in that condition. I am all right now, however, having slept for two days.—Hoping that the good news will to some extent mitigate what I acknowledge to be your most righteous wrath, and with very best wishes, I am,

Most sincerely yours
(signed) Reginald A. Fessenden."

Manteo, Roanoke Island, N. C.
April 3, 1902.

"Dear Wolcott,

I have more good news for you. You remember I telephoned about a mile in 1900—but thought it would take too much power to telephone across the Atlantic. Well I can now telephone as far as I can telegraph, which is across the Pacific Ocean if desired. I have sent varying musical notes from Hatteras and received them here with but 3 watts of energy, and they were very loud and plain, i.e., as loud as in an ordinary telephone.—I enclose telegram which was received with less than 1/500 of the energy which it took to work the coherer. The new receiver is a *wonder* ! ! ! "

The Public was by this time so wireless-conscious that demands for installations became urgent, by both Government Departments and foreign agents. General Greeley visited the Manteo Station and witnessed tests which were so convincing that, combined with a lower bid than from any other company, they secured for the Fessenden System an Alaskan contract.

The Navy wanted some sets, the Postal Telegraph asked for a chain of three stations on Chesapeake Bay—Cape Charles, Old Point Comfort and Norfolk; Mexico's agent placed orders, the Secretary of Agriculture wanted a Farralones installation.

So the formation of a company for the Fessenden System grew more and more imperative. But country-wide swindling in wireless stocks was in progress. Time and again fine endeavor and splendid inventive genius were thwarted and wrecked by the greed of promoters and sycophants. At this period Dr. De Forest was the most outstanding example of this sort of exploitation and one could only regret that for a time his brilliant, productive mind, under misdirection, suffered eclipse till a fresh start led up to sounder success.

Fessenden, knowing this, sought by all means to keep his System absolutely clear and free from stock jobbing. His broad terms were a company capitalized at $5,000,000; actual cash to be subscribed $500,000, of this Fessenden to be paid $300,000 in cash for the patents in the United States and abroad; the remaining $200,000 to be used as working capital.

He further proposed to take in addition the sum of $3,000,000 in bonds which he estimated to be the equivalent in value to $1,000,000 of stock—in such form that if the company did not pay profits above a certain amount he would get nothing, whilst if it did the company would have the option of exchanging the bonds for stock or cash. This to provide against possible loss of patents if the company were mismanaged. But as a further safeguard he stressed always connection with solid, conservative business men, a closed company and no public stock selling.

He was in communication with Mr. Henry Phipps and his nephew Mr. Lawrence Phipps; also with Mr. M.G. Parker of the New England Telephone Company; with Mr. Mellon; with Messrs. Coffin and Rice of the General Electric Company and with Sir Hiram Maxim.

Queen & Company, Instrument Makers, of Philadelphia, had supplied considerable apparatus for the work and built to specification a number of devices, in particular the coils, and the president, Mr. Grey and his technical men were so impressed with the effectiveness of the Fessenden system and its business possibilities that Mr. Grey proposed terms for a company, $200,000 cash and 50 per cent of the stock. A similar offer was received from one other party.

Reg had given his patent attorney, Wolcott, an interest in the expected proceeds but no voice in the disposal of the patents. Wolcott however was convinced that the original amount of $300,000 cash could be obtained from some Pittsburgh men and asked that acceptance of Queen & Company's offer be delayed until he had a chance to interest these men. To this Reg agreed.

Pending the formation of a company, Queen & Company were glad to be licensed to take contracts for supplying the Fessenden System on terms outlined in the following letters.

Manteo, Roanoke Island, N. C.
May 16, 1902.

"Dear Mr. Grey,

. . . About the company, that is of course a matter for discussion. You may be right or I may be right. It must not be forgotten that recent developments, since we had our talk at Norfolk, have immensely increased the field. Then I had succeeded in talking with Hatteras with a 1/4 inch spark. Since then I have got good results with a 1/32 inch spark. That means that there is absolutely no difficulty in getting across the Pacific. Now you will note that the Pacific Cable Co. is capitalizing for $50,000,000 and as it is in the hands of Mackey and other good men they doubtless expect to pay dividends on this, and their cable costs $10,000,000. Now if they can pay dividends on $60,000,000 with one cable, sending 15 words per minute, I do not see why we cannot pay dividends on $5,000,000 with what is the equivalent of 100 cables in different parts of the world, each plant costing only about $10,000 in addition to our other business. . . ."

Manteo, Roanoke Island, N. C.
June 12, 1902.

"Messrs Queen & Company,
Philadelphia, Pa.

Dear Mr. Grey,

The letter enclosing contract is received. I am glad to hear about the success of the microphonic contact etc. We have had similar good success here and are now reading messages on a Weston voltmeter which are almost inaudible in the first telephone. I enclose sketch showing connections. The question of calling up, you will please tell Mr. Hodge is entirely settled, and we can now receive on Morse recorder, sounder or telephone, and can call up any way desired, this removes the last objection to the system, and we can go out with an absolutely perfect system in all respects.

About the contract, I note that you have made a mistake. I made a memorandum of our conversation, so that I should not forget it, within a few moments of its occurrence as my memory is rather poor sometimes. 'Mem. of agreement with Mr. Grey. 50 mile transmission to sell for $5,000 or $100 per mile. Allowing $500 for the cost of apparatus, and allowing Queen and Co. an additional $1000 for manufacturers profit and office expenses, leaves $3,500 for division. Mr. Grey asked what portion of this I thought should be my share. Told him $2,000, leaving him $1,500 in addition to other $1000. Said he thought this satisfactory.'

I see that the contract was drawn up hurriedly, so possibly the amount allotted to me, i.e. $1250, is a mistake, as I do not think that you will say that a profit of $2500 on apparatus which can be bought in the open market for $500 is too small. According to the agreement sent, your profit would be $3250 and mine $1250.

I have assumed that there has been a slip, and have had another contract drawn up, in agreement with my memorandum of the agreement made in our conversation and forward it for your signature, if agreeable. I think that if you get, as you will according to this agreement, $3000 for each 50 mile transmission on outside work and $3600 on each pair for the navy, your company will make a good thing. 30 pairs at this rate would make over $100,000 and there is little doubt but that you will get at least this.

My object was to give you such liberal terms that it would be an object for you to push matters, and that you should be enabled to make a good round sum before any company was formed. Even in case the company was formed it was my intention to see that Queen and Co. retained a profitable connection, if my influence could manage it, and in case the company were formed sooner than anticipated, it is my intention to see that the contract is continued, if I can possibly arrange this, (and my influence would naturally be strong to this end) until you have made an amount of profit which should be entirely satisfactory to you.

Of course, on general principles, I do not care to make

definite promises which I may be unable to fulfill, but I can promise that my efforts will be towards this end, i.e. that you secure an amount of profit which will entirely satisfy you and which will cause you to feel satisfied with having taken up the work at this time.

It is very unlikely that any company could be organized and running before at least three months, and in this time you should sell a large number of sets.

In special cases, where it might be to your advantage to do it, I will make modifications of the contract, provided it is not plainly against my own interests, which however is unlikely as our interests in the matter are practically identical.

I am
Yours very truly,
(signed) Reginald A. Fessenden."

Meanwhile conditions had changed at our wireless stations.

For reasons which the following letters disclose, relations with the Weather Bureau became strained and intolerable. Fessenden severed his connection with the Bureau and left Manteo in August 1902.

Manteo, Roanoke Island, N. C.
Jan. 16, 1902.

"Dear Mr. Wolcott,

I enclose a letter received some time ago from the Chief. I send it to you and have referred him to you. I do not know if it would do any harm to give him the list of the application numbers, however I leave that in your hands.—I enclose the letter sent by Moore because it may be very important. I am afraid that he is not trustworthy. I have an idea that he will try to extend the meaning of our agreement, as he told me once that the Weather Bureau was authorized under Congress to do a telegraph business between ships and the Weather Bureau offices. In such a case, the lines I have underscored will be very important, indicating the scope of our agreement, i.e. that the rights are limited to sending meteorological information only. Incidentally he has broken the agreement on every point, and though I do not intend taking advantage of it, I shall use it if he attempts to play any more tricks.—

Yours truly
(signed) Reginald A. Fessenden."

Manteo, Roanoke Island, N. C.
June 16, 1902.

"His Excellency,
The President of the United States of America,
Washington, D. C.

Sir:

Whilst professor of Electrical Engineering at the Western University of Pennsylvania, I developed a system of wireless telegraphy which gave promise of better results than other systems. Inducements were offered me by the Agricultural Department to resign my position and my business as consulting engineer in Pittsburgh and to develop it under the auspices of the Weather Bureau.

The inducements offered were never made good, and consequently the work took nearly a year longer than it should, I lost considerable money and the value of my patents was depreciated.

When I had succeeded in developing it to such a point that its final practical and financial success was certain, I was approached by Professor Moore, Chief of the Weather Bureau, who stated that he considered that he should have a half share in the patents, and suggested that I permit him to go to the Patent Office and swear out some of the patents in his name. I stood him off for some months by pointing out that the oath required by the office was to the effect that the applicant had actually been concerned in making the invention, which had not been, to the slightest extent, the fact in his case. He finally stated that he had come to the conclusion that this was not meant strictly, and that I must let him take out some of the patents in his name, otherwise he had the power to have the Marconi system adopted.

On my refusing, he began to hinder and oppose the work in every way. He took away my assistants without consulting me, made gross misrepresentations to the Secretary of Agriculture, reflecting on my honesty and capability, issued arbitrary orders preventing me from carrying out the experimental work, and published interviews discrediting the capabilities of the system and the results which had been obtained in official tests.

I have steadfastly refused to allow myself to be blackmailed. But the situation has become really unendurable. Two courses are possible. The first is publicly bring suit against him,—the second to lay the matter before you.

The first would cause a public scandal, and in such cases the results are always unpleasant to all concerned.

The second has seemed to me more proper, if practicable. I am aware of the great pressure of public duties, of much greater importance than this, but it has occurred to me that you might be willing to designate some one of your officials, a man of business experience or a lawyer, who might consider the evidence in the case and report to you a fair and equitable action in the case.

I trust that you may see fit to give my petition favourable consideration, as the present situation is very prejudicial to the conduct of the work.

I would explain that in making this petition I am not concerned with what is past and done with, and should not have ventured to lay the matter before you if it related merely to injuries and losses which have already occurred. But I have reason to believe that Professor Moore does not intend to stop here, but is taking steps to make my system appear to be a public failure, and it is for this reason that I hope you may see fit to have investigation made as to the facts of the case.

I am,
Very respectfully yours,
(Signed) Reginald A. Fessenden."

Manteo, Roanoke Island, N. C.
July 1902.

"Dear Wolcott,

—About the Sec. of Agriculture I got on all right. He advised me to drop all matters with Moore and to go ahead and finish the work up. I think he is right. He said he would have to fire Moore if what I said was true, and showed plainly that he did not want to go into the question.

I intend following his advice if practicable, i.e. if Moore will let me alone.—

(Signed) Reginald A. Fessenden."

Manteo, Roanoke Island, N. C.
July 3, 1902.

"The Hon. Sec'y of Agriculture,
Washington, D. C.
Sir:

During my last visit to Washington I called upon you, and you advised me to put all matters of dispute between me and the Weather Bureau to one side and confine myself entirely to developing my system. I was and am grateful to you for your advice for I believe it was prompted by consideration for my best interests, and I had hoped to find it practicable to follow it.

But on my return I found a communication from Professor Moore which takes away my last chance of doing this. He has taken away all my assistants and left me only a machinist and a telegrapher.

I would respectfully ask you to consider the nature of the work I am doing. I am making experiments on wireless telegraphy, a subject which has been characterized by Prof. Slaby as the most abstruse in modern physics. I put it as an obvious fact that I can absolutely make no experiments with this force. To take an example, suppose I sent a telegrapher to Hatteras. In the first place he could not adjust the coil, as this takes practice which he has not had, and which it would take him at least three months to learn. Secondly, suppose I telegraphed to him for example to change the inductance in the tuned circuit to get better resonance, or gave him any other simple direction like that. He could not do it for he knows nothing about electricity and does not even know what inductance is.

How then can I follow your advice and develop my system under these conditions.—

(Signed) Reginald A. Fessenden."

Manteo, Roanoke Island, N. C.
July 19, 1902.

"Professor Willis L. Moore,
Chief U. S. Weather Bureau,
Washington, D. C.

Sir:

—I note that you state that the progress of the work has been very unsatisfactory since May 1st. I repeatedly pointed out to you as far back as April that the limitations and obstacles you had put in the way of the work had practically stopped it even then and since then, so far from removing the obstacles, you have continually added further ones.

The work which I have been attempting to do, under conditions which I believe no scientific work was ever attempted before, is the tuning of the wireless circuits. This involves the variation of the inductance and capacity of four circuits, in each case, and delicate measurements simultaneously on these quantities and the effects obtained.

In order to do this work I have at the present moment two men neither of whom knows an ohm from a volt or has ever done any experimental work in his life.

With reference to your statement that there has been little practice by the operators, recently, I would remind you that Mr. Dorman, the only operator under my direction, left here June 23 by your direction, and has just returned, having been meantime engaged in work at your Washington office, as you are well aware. You are also aware that previous to that he was laid up with an abscess in his leg. The only other operator here, Mr. Pickels, is under Mr. Thiessen's charge, and has not yet been able to learn how to manage the coil arrangement. Kindly indicate, since there must be two to practice, i.e., one to send and one to receive, how it was possible to practise.

I should be glad to have reference to any letter of mine stating that the work of installing stations and instructing operators was unpleasant to me, or stating anything beyond the fact that it retarded the experimental work; or making that statement more than once.

As regards your statement that you learned from interviews with me that I was to resign Sept, 1st, I believe that the Secretary of Agriculture will be able to recall to your mind that you were present and took part in the discussion when this arrangement was made.

Very respectfully,
(signed) Reginald A. Fessenden."

As arranged, Reg left the Bureau in August 1902. The work between Manteo and Hatteras was continued by the Bureau in a desultory fashion for a few months, then the stations were closed and the equipment ordered sold at auction.

CHAPTER XI

NATIONAL ELECTRIC SIGNALING COMPANY

THINGS WITH US were chaotic. The terms proposed by Queen and Company for a company had not been accepted and the Pittsburgh men with whom Wolcott was negotiating were still holding off.

Meanwhile patent expenses were mounting with staggering rapidity, for patent interferences with their heavy legal costs were beginning and foreign patent fees were swelling the total. From the start we had drawn on our own small personal resources for patent expenses and in June 1902, with these exhausted, Fessenden sought financial help in Bermuda knowing that his patents, which were protected in the Colony, were ample security.

Therefore it was with considerable relief that he was able to write to me from Pittsburgh on September 17th that Given and Walker, Wolcott's men, had made an acceptable financial proposition.

The arrangement made in September was formally ratified November 1902, signed by Fessenden, Wolcott, Given and Walker. By it the National Electric Signaling Company came into existence. All present and pending Fessenden Wireless patents were to be transferred to the Company by Fessenden and Wolcott, and in return the entire capital stock of the Company was to be issued to them but turned over by them to a Trustee to be held. Fessenden to be paid a salary and travel expenses.

Given and Walker agreed to advance $30,000.00 to erect, equip and operate commercial stations at stated points, the proposed sites being Cape Charles, Old Point Comfort and Bermuda, to demonstrate the commercial use and success of the Fessenden inventions. If the tests proved satisfactory, Given and Walker were to have a 9 months' option to purchase 55% of the stock for $300,000.00. If they did not exercise their option Fessenden and Wolcott agreed to return to Given and Walker the $30,000.00 advanced for the tests.

Reg was, as he said, up to his neck in work. The main station was at Old Point Comfort on the beach just outside the massive, granite-walled emplacements that bordered the moat at Fortress Monroe. The contrast between life at a fashionable army post and our islands of the past two years was great and we were quite ready to appreciate and enjoy the change. The parade ground with its fringe of fine homes and magnificent live oaks was an effective setting for the daily pageant of drill and sunset flag.

The Club House across the moat was a delectable and joyous rendez-vous for the men and sometimes for the women and the welcome extended to us generally by officers and their families has left pleasant memories. With Colonel Erasmus Weaver who was then at the Post we had a ready-made friendship for it was in the home of his dear father and mother that our year in Lafayette, Indiana was spent and where our son was born.

In the spring of 1903 we rented a summer cottage near one of our testing stations, at Ocean View, across the bay from Fortress Monroe. Here we lived until October, moving then to Washington where we rented a house on Riggs Place.

At Old Point Comfort huts were built, masts erected and machinery installed. Our two first operators were Messrs Pannill and Roberts who for a number of very active years were closely indentified with the installation and telegraphic work of the N.E.S. Co. In the late fall Mr. Frederick Vreeland applied for a position with the N.E.S. Co. His training and credentials were such that Reg considered him a very promising applicant and engaged him. As always, and following the methods of the Edison Laboratory days, the first thing was to 'indoctrinate' the newcomer and he was set to work on tuning devices and by repeating the various stages of their development to familiarize himself with the

Fessenden method of work and with the Fessenden System.

But to our great surprise this young man in a very short time was demanding an interest in the company, an interest which according to a letter from Fessenden to Wolcott would have amounted to $30,000.00 a year. The demand was refused and Vreeland left immediately.

Six months later he wrote to Messrs Given and Walker claiming the Liquid Barreter as his own invention.

The Liquid Barreter had a stormy career. It was one of our 'Jewels of Great Worth' and at this time and for many years was the master key to the wireless situation. Here was a receiver Fessenden had been working towards in 1899, based on the necessities of his conception of wireless—a conception which he alone in all the world at that time believed to be the correct one. In 1900 he had experimented with it in one form and in the spring of 1902 had used it in the transmission of signals between Hatteras and Manteo, making at that time exact measurements of its effectiveness. Recalling his letters to Wolcott at that time, one feels his exultant thrill as its reliability and sensitiveness were proved again and again.

But because of its exquisite perfection and simplicity, it was a target for all. As it became known, companies used it and inventors claimed it with such desperate persistence and ingenuity that Reg and the N.E.S. Co. fought and won no less than four hard-fought suits over it.

For Vreeland's behavior there is a possible tolerant explanation of an introvert type of mind which could believe that in the few weeks of work under Fessenden he had evolved an improvement or invention of which Fessenden was unaware.

At the Fortress Monroe station, wireless adopted its first mascot—a half-drowned black and white kitten that crawled out of the moat and took refuge under the wireless hut. Its cries attracted attention and Reg soon had it in the warmth of the station, rubbed dry and full of milk, but as a final touch and to encourage that 'chez-soi' feeling that a good spell of washing induces in a cat, Reg rubbed him liberally with butter, figuring that by the time it was licked off he would feel at home.

But the kitten decided that he would leave impossibilities to other people so promptly made himself comfortable in the coal scuttle and went to sleep. A laundry squad was organized while he slept and on wakening, cleaning and christening was done in one operation and Michael Faraday, 'Mike' or 'Mikums' came into his kingdom.

The routine of establishing stations went quickly forward. Operators were constantly busied with sending and receiving and with minute attention to their apparatus to obtain maximum output and sensitivity. Projected lines of research were extended by the experimenters, Reg everywhere supervising, directing and experimenting when not engaged on patent work. This, as the number of his applications in the Patent Office increased, made ever heavier demands on him. Distinguished visitors both American and foreign must frequently be received and informed of the possibilities of the System.

It was found impossible to obtain a Bermuda license owing to restrictions imposed by the British Government and a far-reaching cable monopoly. Therefore three stations, Washington D.C., Collingswood N.J., (sometimes called the Philadelphia station) and Jersey City (sometimes called the New York station) were substituted by agreement to fulfill the clause of the November 1902 agreement to equip and operate commercial stations where 'actual commercial or ordinary telegraph messages' were sent and received.

These were the first wireless stations to operate regularly over land.

The following letter refers to tests between the above stations.

"Mr. Hay Walker Jr.,
Farmers Deposit Bank
Pittsburgh, Pa.
Dear Mr. Walker,
I wish to call your attention to the manner in which the stations between Jersey City and Philadelphia are now working.

During the past month the average number of messages which had to be retransmitted was less than 2%.
Several thousands of messages were sent, hence the results are superior to most wire lines.
During the last ten days not a single message had to be retransmitted.
I enclose a letter from Jersey City from Mr. Pannill. He encloses thirty messages, fifteen of which he sent to Roberts and fifteen others which Roberts sent to him, without a single mistake and all done within one hour, i.e. $7.50 per hour or $100 per day of 16 hours.
This means you will understand an average of a message every two minutes. This would be extremely good working for best wire lines, and as regards wireless it is so immensely superior to anything that has heretofore been done that no comparison can be made. Please return Mr. Pannill's report.

Yours very truly,
(signed) Reginald A. Fessenden."

Now, rumblings of a volcano beneath us began to be heard. A few extracts from letters between Wolcott and Fessenden in the months of September and October 1903 show how apprehensive they were about their prospects in this new business enterprise.

Pittsburgh, Pa.
Sept. 24, 1903.

"Dear Prof.

I enclose copy of agreement which Walker states is in accordance with the understanding you and he reached Saturday night. It seems to me to put us entirely in their power. The option is done away with and if nothing is earned between now and July 1st 1904, they need not advance any more money but will have their 55% of the stock which can be sold by them in three years without consulting us. As soon as the stock is distributed in accordance with the enclosed agreement they will have control and we cannot do anything and may never receive all of our cash consideration.

It is my opinion that we should never agree to the distribution of the stock until the cash consideration has been paid.

And further the three hundred thousand should not wait the dividends of the Co.

I am willing that any money earned by the sale of instruments as contemplated in our present plan should be credited on the cash consideration, but under the present plan we would be paying part of the consideration ourselves.

It would be better for us not to take any more money from Given and Walker but to make the test Saturday and Sunday between N.Y. and Philadelphia, give notice that the option begins to run from that date and then lay back and await developments.

We could probably get money from some other source to build the apparatus for which we might get orders during the interim. Of course they have to pay your salary during the option. It would be unfortunate not to push things for the nine months but it would be more unfortunate to lose everything. I wont sign the agreement in its present form.

Very sincerely yours,
(signed) Darwin S. Wolcott."

September 25, 1903.

"Dear Prof.

. . . Be very careful in discussing terms for the new agreement. I told Walker a little while ago that I could not sign the one I sent you for the reasons I gave you. He has just called me to come down. I suppose to discuss the agreement. I think I shall tell him to go over the matter with you and therefore suggest that you watch out for the points mentioned in my letter. I do not care particularly about the payment of the $300,000 from the first earnings but will not agree to turning the stock over before the consideration has been paid. I consider this vital.

I have just told Walker that while I did not consider the manner of paying the consideration consistent with the original agreement I would (not) kick if you were satisfied. They agree that stock is to be held as in the first agreement until cash consideration has been paid. This practically extends option, you should see that provision is made to pay your salary until option terminates.

Very sincerely
(signed) Darwin S. Wolcott."

September 28, 1903.

"Dear Wolcott

——With reference to the agreement sent, I am entirely of your opinion, i.e. that it is not in accordance with our understanding. In order to prevent any possibility of mistake I have written today to Mr. Given pointing out this fact. I am in hopes however, that everything can be amicably arranged at our Philadelphia meeting. It seems to me that there is money enough for us all and since we are willing to do all we can to help G. & W. with their part of the work that it ought to be a matter of give and take. If we all work harmoniously everything will come out all right, for all we have to fear is a split amongst ourselves. It would be a great pity if anything should happen which would separate us from two good business men like G. & W. and I do not believe it would be to their interest to have any agreement drawn up or agreed to which should put us in such a position that we would feel that we were not being treated right. It is absolutely essential that all four of us should be satisfied, and I am in hopes that everything will turn out all right.—

Yours very sincerely,
(signed) Reginald A. Fessenden."

October 5, 1903.

"Dear Prof.

. . . I have just had an interview with G. & W. at their request. They commenced by stating that you were anxious to pay Christy's bill, (firm of patent attorneys of which Wolcott was a member) and said they had inquired of you the nature of your agreement with me and then went on to state that they thought my services to you did not justify my having such an interest. I told them you had voluntarily given me that interest and that it was a matter which did not concern them and that you were the only party to complain. They then stated that they thought that I should assume Christy's bill and when I stated I did not have the money they agreed to pay it if I would give them enough of my stock to make their holdings 60%. This I positively refused to do but said that I would assign them $6000 out of the first money due me, if they would pay the bill. This they refused and there the matter stands. I suppose they will try a squeeze in some other way.

I notice that in the new agreement of which I was shown a rough draft, that provision is made for paying the cash consideration from sale of stock. I cannot agree to this as all money received from stock should be used as capital for running the company and if part is used to pay the cash consideration then more stock will have to be sold for capital and you and I must contribute our proportion.—

Are you dissatisfied with the agreement you made with me and is it your opinion that I should return some to you? And further is it your opinion that I should assume the Christy debt?

Very sincerely
(signed) Darwin S. Wolcott."

October 6, 1903.

"Dear Professor,

. . . I have nothing further to report in regard to the matter I wrote you yesterday. I suppose nothing more will be done or said until the new agreement is prepared, when we may look for some new surprises probably. I wish very much that it were possible for us to have a few minutes consultation to agree on proceedings.—I am willing to do anything in reason to clear up Christy's acct. and will accept any suggestion *you* make. But the suggestion of G. & W. amounted to giving them stock worth $500,000 for a cash payment to Christy of $6000 on the basis of a $10,000,000 company. I came very near telling them that I would not sign any more agreements but would proceed on the last agreement. What terms have you agreed to in regard to the next money they agreed to advance. They said your tests were decidedly satisfactory.

Very sincerely yours,
(signed) Darwin S. Wolcott."

October 15, 1903.

"Dear Wolcott,

The letters you sent were duly received, but I have delayed answering hoping to hear from you more fully with reference to the agreement. Not knowing exact details of contents of the agreement I cannot discuss the matter with advantage at present.—With reference to G. & W.'s proposition I have already told you my opinion over the telephone. As regards my part in the matter it simply amounted to this. That when they suggested that you should assist me in paying some of the legal expenses I told them that my agreement with you did not call for this, and that I should not propose the matter to you.

They asked me if, in view of the fact that you were getting half as much out of the invention as I was, whether you should help me to bear some of the expense of the legal end.

I told them that I did consider it fair but told them that I should not propose any such thing to you. This is the status of the matter as far as I am concerned.—The second point that I wanted to speak about is the fact that you seem to think that I am getting money from the company for my living expenses. This is a mistake. You are overlooking the fact that I have been shouldering by myself during the past year all patent expenses, foreign fees, besides other expenses in connection with the work, of which you are not aware, so that while normally I have received $3,600 from the company, the actual facts are that I have paid out $3,800 to keep things going. When I started work last October I had about $2,400 in the bank and out of that I have had to pay my living expenses and about $200 additional for patent work. I trust that this statement will make plain what the facts of the case are i.e. that I have been shouldering all these expenses myself which were not covered by our contract.

Finally in altering these agreements I hope you will bear in mind the understanding upon which I made over to you half as much as I am getting myself. As you will remember I had received an offer of $250,000 for a half interest and you asked to be allowed to make a better bargain. I agreed to give you the opportunity to make a better bargain and I signed over to you the share you have in the business for this reason and on this account. Therefore I hope that you will not forget the consideration in connection with these agreements. I do not of course expect to hold you strictly to our original written understanding, because things have turned out not so well as had been expected but I trust you will keep it in mind in acting for me.—G. & W. told you I suppose how the tests went off. They worked perfectly all morning and lost only one word which was repeated and got correctly a few minutes later.

Yours very sincerely,
(signed) Reginald A. Fessenden."

The outcome of all this juggling was that when, upon the successful completion of the tests, Given and Walker were asked to exercise their option, they declined to do so, giving as their reason that the stations were not capable of handling the *ENTIRE* business between New York and Philadelphia.

They demanded immediate repayment of the $30,000 or the alternative of selling the company out to recover.

IMMEDIATE. Not the leisurely nine months provided for their own option but *WITHIN THE WEEK.* They even refused an offer of 10% of the company's stock in lieu of the amount.

Neither Reg nor Wolcott could raise the money.

As a result a second agreement was signed, the main difference of which was that the cash consideration was *to be paid out of the first earnings of the company.*

Optimistic as they justifiably were over the ultimate prospects of the company, this concession did not appear too serious to Reg and Wolcott as the foregoing Wolcott-Fessenden letters show; the arrangement was not satisfactory yet neither was it apparently dangerous.

But looking back, the implications are clear and the outcome almost inevitable.

In establishing relations with a foreign people, with a new race or tribe, it is the man who can most fully understand their way of thinking and the *Why* of that way, who best succeeds with them. Fessenden had lived in Pittsburgh for seven years—his University and social contacts were congenial, he numbered among his friends representative minds in science, music and art—year by year the plastic material of Youth of the district came under his quickening influence. We both felt at home in Pittsburgh and thought we knew the spirit of the place.

But there was an aspect still unfamiliar and one which forever would be foreign to Fessenden's nature.

Out of the seething volcano which vomited coal, iron and steel on to a wide-spread area and upon an unprepared people, and out of the frenzy of adaptation, came a ruthless habit of mind. To be proficient in this, to acquire it by whatsoever Spartan suppressions of natural, kindly instincts, was the hall mark of success.

Mr. Given had attained the Presidency of the Farmers' Deposit National Bank and the power of a multi-millionaire.

Mr. Walker was a manufacturer of soaps, perfumes, and food stuffs.

Throughout the period of their connection with wireless Given and Walker were held up to the public, and conceivably thought of themselves, as courageous pioneers backing their faith with unstinted funds.

Mr. S.M. Kintner who after 1910 became Manager and later Receiver for the N.E.S. Co. and subsequently vice-president of the Westinghouse Company, lauded these financiers in glowing terms, in a paper "Pittsburgh's Contributions to Radio" read before the IRE Conv. Pittsburgh, April 7, 1932.

". . . This experimental and development work of Fessenden's was made possible by two other courageous Pittsburghers. These two men, Messrs. T. H. Given and Hay Walker Jr., in wholesome contrast to the methods followed by most of the Radio Companies of the period prior to the war, dug down into their own pockets for the necessary funds to carry on. Mr. Given remarked to me several times, "If this radio business turns out as I expect it will, I'll be satisfied with my returns on what I've put into it—If it does not, I, at least, will not have on my conscience the thought that I've wasted the savings of poor scrub-women, widows with dependent children or others who fell such easy prey to the high-powered salesman."

"The courage of these two men who put more than $2,000,000 of their own money into this radio company, is one of the most striking recollections I hold of genuine confidence in the future of radio. Unfortunately, neither reaped the benefits of their sacrifices—as Mr. Given who bought Mr. Walker's interest during the war, died about one year before broadcasting raised radio to its full stature and it has always been a great regret to me that he could not have lived to see his dream come true." "The company organized by Given, Walker and Fessenden was operated solely for the purpose of developing the latter's inventions. It was called the National Electric Signaling Company and not one dollar's worth of stock was offered for sale to the public. Particular emphasis is laid upon this fact because these were the days when selling stock in a new wireless company was the racket of the time."

But half-truths are never the truth.

It is true that Given and Walker caused large sums of money to be spent in developing the Fessenden System. The amount was nearly $1,000,000 at the time Fessenden's connection with the N.E.S. Co. ceased. But Kintner failed to state that out of that considerable sum not a single dollar was ever paid to Fessenden for his patents which constituted the company's sole assets.

Such was the treatment accorded the man from whose brain gushed the living spring of invention which justified the investment.

It is not intended to depict Fessenden as a mild and pliable nature, or one easily put upon. On the contrary he was extremely strong willed.

He was a man ahead of his time. Without conceit he knew his mind for the high-powered, high-pressured engine that it was. He knew how wide the range of knowledge it absorbed. What his co-workers saw and understood he had seen, understood and passed beyond, and, standing on a height, realized other factors still unperceived by the slower plodders.

Because of this broad scope and vision be believed his judgment to be wiser than most and having made a decision, with every ounce of his energy he strove to make that decision stick.

His 'time constant' under stress was almost intolerably quick, giving to those working with him an impression of extreme impatience and he could be a whirlwind for action when the need arose—though at times his patience in explaining and making things clear was amazing.

In describing the physical Fessenden of this period, a thought expressed by the poet Spenser in his "Hymne in Honour of Beautie" may well find application:—

> "For of the soule the bodie forme doth take;
> For soule is forme, and doth the bodie make."

It was as if, with the magnitude of his work and the certainty that he had the true vision and was ahead in the field, a Viking spirit not earlier apparent possessed him and expanded his body to its expression. Shoulders broadened, he took on weight and a ruddy tan replaced the paler coloring; habitually his head was uplifted as if to scan a far horizon. There was distinction about him that commanded respect.

There was no hint of meanness in his nature. He was generous to a fault and had a natural spirit of lavishness that was hard to curb. He performed his share of a contract in complete measure and was always willing that those associated with him should share liberally in the profits. His associates may at times have felt themselves urged by him against their own convictions, in the same way as he on occasion disapproved of an adopted policy. That is a part of partnership.

Especially in later years it appeared sometimes as if difficulties arose because of imperfect meeting of minds. His personality was very striking and, in conference, this unusualness was apt to distract. Further, he courteously assumed in his listener a mental capacity on a par with his own and was apt to touch only on the high lights of a subject without going into the details that linked them. The listener heard with mind agape, promising himself to digest the matter later, but there was not complete understanding.

A silent witness to many such meetings, I have often said afterwards. "I dont believe he understood you." "What part didn't he understand?" would be the quick reply, but the only answer to that was that there hadn't been the same 'ting' of the bull's eye as when equal minds meet.

Not that habitually he estimated the general run of minds as of high order—he did not—and an impatient phrase often on his lips was "Don't *try* to think"—being convinced beyond doubt that he knew and that his own thinking was sufficient.

But with his mind prolifically filled with great matters, it is certain that he gave scant heed to safeguarding his legal rights. It was his nature to believe that "everything would be all right."

When fate dealt him a blow, whether the loss of a friend or a business misfortune, he found refuge in sleep, exhausted by his reactions to the event. In sleep his sub-conscious mind restored life to an order and calm from which he could carry on. So now, in 1903, with the new agreement signed, what was done—was done—no use crying over spilt milk—he would not waste himself in regrets.

The urgent need was to 'carry on.'

CHAPTER XII

WIRELESS AS A BUSINESS ENTERPRISE AND TRANS-ATLANTIC STATIONS

THE WASHINGTON STATION was intended to be permanent headquarters, so required a more complete equipment than any previous station. A larger staff must be recruited and trained since technical men and operators must be available to erect and install other stations on order, abroad as well as at home.

Mr. Le Conte Davis, Mr. Edward Bennett, Mr. Adam Stein were all technical men of the Washington period. Mr. Glaubitz a mechanical engineer of Western University was construction engineer. Among others, Mr. Lee, Mr. Wescoe, Mr. Isbell and Mr. Beakes joined the ranks of the operators.

In the patent field, interferences swarmed like seven-year locusts—Marconi, Shoemaker, De Forest, Vreeland et al. Everything that legal minds could devise mutually to harass and delay was being done. Writing to Wolcott in October 1903 to change the date set for a hearing, Reg reminds him that a rival firm had tried to serve an injunction on him in the New Jersey district and since such service would be valid up to November 2nd it was inadvisable for him to be in that jurisdiction until after that date, particularly as he was obliged to be in Germany by the first of December on patent matters.

This was an extremely hurried trip planned to allow just time for his testimony to be taken. Writing from the "Deutschland" while lying off Cuxhaven he said "I did not get a chance to try the receiver coming across, the arrangements were too poor and there was no room. I may try coming back."

On his return shortly before Christmas he found us settled at 1677 Riggs Place, a very nice house in a dignified locality which we considered essential for the standing of the company, though with it went the penalty of a basement kitchen which was a nightmare to mistress and maid.

For the first time our boy was able to attend public school and find companionship and competition with children of his own age. Also he was alive to the cosmopolitan thrills that Washington affords. I recall his return from some back-yard expedition round-eyed with excitement at having seen lots of Chinese pigtails hanging on a line to dry.

Next door to us was the Persian Minister, Morteza Khan, who sent his secretary to express the hope that we would be friendly neighbors. His establishment was small and without ladies and I think the Minister and his secretary were lonely in their isolation. We exchanged occasional visits and their reception rooms contained rug treasures that even my untutored eyes recognized. French was our medium of conversation and sometimes was put to a severe strain, as on the occasion when we had taken them to supper at Chevy Chase and were returning on a crowded street car. Some of our party were among the strap-hangers and our vocabularies were taxed considerably when Reg attempted to convey to the Minister his opinion that evolution from monkeys would have been a far more successful affair had we been permitted to retain their prehensile tails.

The N.E.S. Co. was now ready for business, prepared for orders from all and sundry. Negotiations with various U.S. Government Departments, as well as with foreign Governments, were started and no opportunity lost of demonstrating the superiority of the Fessenden System. Among the many exhibition tests was one for the head of the Australian Postal Department. The Russian Legation asked for a demonstration. For them a special train was chartered for the run between Washington and Philadelphia, lunch served on the train, followed by a splendid test between the New Jersey and Collingswood stations.

The U.S. Navy having no system of its own, adopted a

coldly critical attitude, demanded certainty before commitment and inaugurated a series of tests between a naval station at Sandy Hook and the U.S.S. Topeka. All systems, foreign as well as domestic were given the opportunity of test. Not only systems as a whole but more particularly selected pieces of apparatus, such as receivers, tuners, interference preventers etc.

It is correct to say that in these tests the Fessenden System showed marked superiority. A swashbuckling yarn about one of these tests is told from two different angles by Mr. Pannill now of the Radiomarine Corporation and by Mr. J.W. Scanlin of the U.S. Navy.

Mr. Pannill writes:

> "While tests were being conducted for the Navy between the U.S.S. Topeka and the Sandy Hook station, there had been installed a station by the De Forest Wireless Company within a few feet of the Navy Station and the operator in charge of the DeForest Station had received instructions to interfere with the Fessenden Tests.
>
> In an endeavor to head off this interference the DeForest operator was kept under the influence of strong liquids during the tests, but in an unguarded moment he slipped away from his guards, got back into the radio station and started up a powerful transmitter, placing a brick on the key. In a few moments there was a knock at the door of the Navy Wireless station and there appeared Mr. Dan Collins, the DeForest operator, who demanded that food and drink be supplied forthwith or he would refuse to take the brick off the key.
>
> Of course the Fessenden tests were halted because of the powerful spark transmitter operating next door and it was not till Mr. Collins was finally induced, thru the supply of food and drink to withdraw the brick, that the Navy tests proceeded, much to the amusement of the Navy officials observing the tests."

Mr. Scanlin tells us:

> "In 1904 Professor Fessenden was developing his so-called interference preventer which, among other apparatus, was

submitted to the Navy for test and his engineers, Pannill and Isbell, came to the U. S. Naval Radio Station at Highlands. Navesink N. J. to conduct the test. The preventer was supposed to be quite secret and was contained in a box about 30 x 15 x 15 and held together by at least 50 screws. The engineers carried this box, which was quite heavy, each evening to their hotel and brought it back each morning, as they claimed it was so secret they had orders from the Professor to trust no one.

About 500 yards from our station was the DeForest Station (WS) and the operator apparently had orders to interfere on the Fessenden test, for when the test started WS would hold down his key and a half inch spark would jump the Fessenden electrolytic detector, compelling them to throw out the antenna to save the detector.

The Professor was on the Navy Yard end and could not understand the messages his engineers sent him. He had so much faith in his preventer that he could not believe anything could interfere, so after several hot messages to them, he came down by train and when he got up the steep hill to the station he was red as a lobster and out of breath, but enough left in him to cuss out both engineers, telling them they had the preventer hooked up wrong. When he attempted to hook it up and saw the sparks across the detector, he called for a screw driver and not only opened the box up before us but when he found the circuit was correct and realized it would not prevent the particular kind of interference we had, he called the Board of Officers and explained the workings of the circuit. I never saw a more disgusted couple than Pannill and Isbell, after lugging the heavy box up and down the steep hill to their hotel, to have the boss open it up and explain the thing fully was too much for them, and they certainly expressed themselves to me."

In a series of articles to the Electrical Review in 1906, "Interference in Wireless Telegraphy and the International Telegraph Conference," Fessenden discusses this test among others and quotes from the report of the Bureau of Equipment showing that with the *normal* interference anticipated and arranged for the test, satisfactory results were obtained but that it was not possible to cut out malicious interference from a high-powered and very near-by station.

This of course was the interference preventer in its earlier form.

These interference yarns have an important bearing, because interference was one of the arguments by which the U.S. Government sought to gain control of wireless, justifying its proposal to make wireless telegraphy a Government Monopoly (though it had contributed nothing to its creation) on the ground that it was not possible for stations to work without interfering with each other, and proposing to transmit all messages free.

It is easy to see that talk of Free Government Wireless Service was a monkey wrench big enough to jam any works, and chance of business with the merchant marine vanished like the morning mists. Legislation to effect this monopoly fortunately failed since tests demonstrated positively that interference could be cut out. But the attempt to make it a monopoly had the effect of discouraging sales. No national backing was given to American systems,—Fessenden's, De-Forest's or other's, and there was no real commitment on the part of the Government, nothing indeed beyond 'sample shopping.'

More and more there was revealed the tendency which later grew to alarming proportions, for the Government Bureaus to enter the inventing (sic) and developing business themselves. The U.S. Navy installed more than 100 liquid barreters without paying the owners a single cent though the N.E.S. Co. had successfully maintained its ownership of the patents in not less than four hard-fought Court Proceedings.

In much the same way the Brazilian Government frustrated wireless working. The N.E.S. Co. received an order for a 100 mile installation on the Amazon between Manaos and Para. On the arrival of the company's engineers and operators with the apparatus, the distance was found to be nearer 150 than 100 miles and changes had to be made to adapt the apparatus to the longer distance. When this was finally accomplished and the two stations had worked perfectly for two weeks, day and night, without interruption, a decision of the Brazilian Courts put a stop to the work.

It will be seen therefore that the financial prospects for a commercial, land-operating company were not very bright. Reg, alive to the situation, was most anxious to develop the business of manufacturing and selling wireless sets. The policy of Given and Walker, however, as will be seen repeatedly, was *not* to manufacture and sell, but to concentrate on selling as a whole the entire group of Fessenden patents that constituted the system to some firm already in "Communications." So, the "first earnings" of the contract agreement became more and more remote. Evidently Fessenden didn't willingly relinquish then or later the selling-of-sets plan for in July 1905 Walker wrote as follows, on receipt of a copy of a bid by the N.E.S. Co. on apparatus for the U.S. Navy.

"Dear Professor,
——We had thought this matter of the Navy or any one else being offered or furnished anything of ours had been settled in the negative—and we do not wish to complicate any deal we may be able to make for the whole of all we have.
(signed) Hay Walker Jr."

And again in August of the same year he wrote:

"Dear Sir,
. . . We note what you say about the Bureau of Equipment and the West Indies stations.—When you receive a written request from these refer them to this office; as we must soon face the situation of a comprehensive deal for the whole system we think we ought to act with—extreme caution.
(signed) Hay Walker Jr."

In order to sell the system as a whole something dramatic had to be done, and already in 1904 this something had been decided upon, i.e. *Trans-Atlantic Working.* It cannot be said that Fessenden really approved of this decision.

Difficult and discouraging as the sales situation was, it was still his conviction that the proper and sensible thing for the company to do was to engage in business and obtain its share of orders for wireless apparatus instead of loading the company up with debt for all kinds of development work.

Hitherto our stations had been planned for limited transmissions—120 miles being the greatest distance planned for. Now, at a single jump, 3000 miles was to be attempted! A glorious objective beyond question. But was it sensible?

Fessenden believed that it was not. The practical and business side of his brain told him that the interests of the company and of the public would best be served by progressive, stage by stage development. No art is ever complete and perfect beyond change and improvement. But the public does not want to wait for ultimate perfection, it wants the best that the present state of the art affords, and that is what the Fessenden System admittedly could supply.

But Given and Walker wanted the grandstand play of Trans-Atlantic working. They were putting up the money and in the ensuing burst of glory they expected to sell out to the highest bidder.

I have said that the practical and business side of Fessenden's brain disapproved of the proposed step. That is correct, but on the other hand, the side that leaped ahead to far-flung goals, that gloried in the buoyancy of supreme confidence in his own ability to overcome difficulties—that side could not be other than thrilled at the task to which he was pledged. Once embarked upon the undertaking, he was single minded in his devotion to its accomplishment.

Thenceforth the Washington station and our own house at Riggs Place fairly seethed with plans and preparations. Large scale maps littered the floors like autumn leaves— eastern and western Atlantic seaboards were scanned and measured for sites—gnomic projections were consulted— and, since in view of Government obstructions it was by no means a matter of what we would like but rather of what we could get, our Mr. Boyle in England, with the assistance of our London patent attorneys, was instructed to see where in Great Britain the British Government would permit the erection of an experimental wireless station.

There were difficulties, but finally the choice of one of two sites was submitted. Of the two, Machrihanish on the far side of the Mull of Kintyre opposite Campbeltown seemed the more desirable. With this as a fixed point, the line of the great circle led out from the coast of Scotland across the Atlantic to Newfoundland, down a valley of its contour, across the Isthmus of Chignecto and the Bay of Fundy and out across another waste of waters to our own shores of the Massachusetts coast, specifically Brant Rock. Land was leased at both places and construction operations begun.

But this was only the *where*.

The *how* was infinitely more important.

Trans-Atlantic working at that time and for fully two decades afterwards, required very high masts or towers. Reg believed in using where possible, construction methods that had stood the test of time and that were already standardized, and in his opinion the smoke stack was a well tested type of tower.

So he designed and patented an antenna which was to consist of a cylindrical steel tube, 400 feet high, with the N.E.S. Co.'s patent "Umbrella Capacity" at the top. Each tower, i.e. the one at Brant Rock and the one at Machrihanish, was to rest by ball and socket on an insulated base and to be supported by sectionally-insulated wire-rope guys of the company's standard type. There were four sets of guy ropes of four each at 100 foot intervals.

The contract for the steel work and erection of the two towers was given to the Brown Hoisting Machinery Company of Cleveland, Ohio, and for the insulators to the Locke Insulator Company of Victor, N.Y.

The specifications called for the tower to stand a wind pressure of 50 lbs. per square foot of flat surface, and for the tower to be capable of being extended to a height of 500 feet if desired—and to be capable of standing a pressure of 50 lbs per square foot of flat surface even if one set of guys broke.

On these specifications the Brown Hoisting Company gave the following calculated stresses:—

	Lbs.
Top Guy	18,400
Second Guy	14,750
Third Guy	13,200
Fourth Guy	12,800

At the Massachusetts Institute of Technology, Professor Miller made tests to determine the breaking strength of the insulators. The tests showed that the insulators were stronger than the forgings to which they were attached—the holes in the steel forgings elongating $\frac{1}{4}$ inch at 46,000 lbs. With a different method of attachment the porcelain insulators cracked at from 51 to 56,000 lbs.

The tower was insulated to stand approximately 500,000 volts and safety gaps were provided for discharges if the potential rose above 500,000, to prevent injury to the insulators. The design was carried out in a very creditable manner by the Brown Hoisting Machinery Company but with unexpected delays, so that the towers were not completed until *December 28, 1905*.

The Brant Rock station was begun first and during the early months of 1905 this work was actively pushed by the Brown Hoisting Company and by our own construction engineer, Mr. Glaubitz. By midsummer when the work had advanced far enough for the bare essentials of equipment to be in place, we left Washington for Brant Rock and soon after our arrival Mr. Glaubitz proceeded to Machrihanish.

Since the Fortress Monroe days Mike the cat, had retired to private life but now, with a railway permit for "one small cat" from Washington to Boston, he resumed his official position as Mascot of Western Tower.

Two summer cottages were on the tract of land leased

for the station, one of them became the office and our living quarters, the other was used for precision testing and as living quarters for the stenographer's family.

Mr. Hadfield our engineer at Brant Rock recalls the day in late summer when the insulators successfully withstood their test. He writes.—

> "This was the occasion for an invitation to all hands and the cook to come to the office. 'The Old Man' as we always called him when he was not looking, broke out a case of Pabst Export and we all drank to the success of the venture. But the Professor raised his glass and said *"Here's to the Trans-Atlantic Telephone."*
>
> After we returned to our respective stations one of the fellows said—'Now isn't that just like the Old Man, dreaming about telephoning across the Atlantic before he knows whether or not we will be able to telegraph as far as Plymouth. A thousand miles ahead of himself, that's the way he has always been. But the toast was prophetic, the dream came true, and it is a fact that although he was a thousand jumps ahead of himself he was always able to catch up with himself and make a wild-looking dream an accomplished fact in a very short time."

But of course, it wasn't a dream really; Reg had already done enough to *know* that it was possible.

Sometimes instead of "The Old Man" Reg was designated by the sine "Z." Mr. H. C. Gawler one of our operators of the Brant Rock days and now Sales Manager of the Federal Telegraph Company writes of this—

> "All of us operators had sines, i.e. Pannill's was "CN", Wescoe's "W5", Lee's "MW", mine "W", and so on. It is natural that we referred to Glaubitz as "G", Stein as "S" etc. I believe that Pannill was the first to use the letter "Z" to designate Prof. Fessenden and soon all of us used Z even in our conversations. As evidence that the practice was not objected to by Prof. Fessenden you will find numerous memos, I feel confident, still in existence signed with Z.
>
> The professor's signature resembled a train of erratic but rapidly decaying oscillations, as you must admit, so

that may account for the acceptance of Z for some of the more informal acknowledgements on memos. There were few in Naval service having to do with Fessenden equipment who did not know that Z was Fessenden, and this applied generally within his zone of activity."

Sea air off Massachusetts Bay was invigorating after sultry Washington and the summer and fall months were delightful but with cold weather we became aware that "rock bound coasts and bleak New England Shores" were more than mere poetic license.

Water supply was cut off at the first sign of frost, since piping was too near the surface to permit winter service. A water cart brought periodical supplies for the entire plant and new zinc ash barrels constituted our household tanks. It often seemed to me that an appropriate title for our work was "Wireless and Waterless Telegraphy and Telephony."

The winds blew gale force and for days on end. The foundations of the cottages had been sodded up to afford some protection but even so, the linoleum on the office floor undulated to a height of six and eight inches and elsewhere the breezes frolicked freely through cracks of the flooring. A coal stove of the railroad waiting-room type heated the office and Mike was made supremely happy with a box lined with one of his master's coats and placed back of the stove; its perfections never staled and each return to it was marked by a paean of purrs. For Ken and myself, the kitchen stove was a refuge, especially during the inactive hours of lessons, when we were apt to sit with our feet at the open oven door for warmth.

The men at the plant met all discomforts—and they were many—with utmost good cheer and only after a week or more of high winds did nerves grow a bit edgy. Not to be outdone by the office, they too adopted a cat giving her the aristocratic title of Ermyntrude; this quickly simplified itself to "Minty."

Mr. Lee, one of our tried and true operators tells a story of a cricket that took up residence in the receiving room. One winter night Reg blew in and heard the cricket doing a little rival Morse sending. "You'd better see what he's talking about, Lee." "Yes sir," said Lee, "I have and all I can make out is something about Icicles."

An interesting relic was unearthed during the foundation digging at Western Tower. Arrow heads were a frequent find but the real treasure was an Indian pipe, a most delightful and whimsical bit of artistry. The small black bowl and about three inches of stem were perfect. Up the side of the bowl clambered a bear cub, using obviously every ounce of strength to hold on; along the stem making straight for the smoker's mouth was the second bear cub, absolutely fearless. Were those the two qualities the Indian carver of long ago sought to depict?—endurance and fearlessness?

The workman who ran across it was glad to sell it for a few dollars to Mr. Campbell, one of our technical men and through him this treasure has been admirably preserved to the public. When it was learned that Mr. Cyrus Dallin was commissioned to make a statue of Chief Massasoit, to be carried out in bronze and erected on Cole's Hill, Plymouth, as a feature of the Ter-centenary celebrations, Mr. Campbell offered Mr. Dallin his pipe as a model for Massasoit's Peace Pipe. The offer was accepted and a copy of the pipe is now a noteworthy detail of a notable work of art.

CHAPTER XIII

TRANS-ATLANTIC WORKING

WESTERN TOWER WAS a veritable beehive and to and fro the workers went gathering their precious stores of measurements and facts. As activity increased at Brant Rock men were transferred from the Washington Station till only the skeleton of a machine shop force was left behind.

It would be vain to attempt to describe these activities. Fessenden's technical papers of the period, as listed, will satisfy the technical reader on this point, and in touching on these matters I am much in sympathy with Mr. Bryan's explanatory remark to the Secretary of the Navy on a certain occasion when he demanded a battleship and was pacified with a gunboat. "Roosevelt, after this when I talk about a battleship don't think I mean anything technical."

Neither do I mean anything technical but it is essential to convey something of the tremendous surge of development that went on.

What should be brought out above all is Fessenden's inflexible requirement that every component part of sending and receiving apparatus *must* be brought up to maximum efficiency. The strength of the whole is measured by its weakest link and there must be no weak links. He often attributed superiority of his results to this rule. *Know by quantitative measurements what a thing is capable of and see that it does it.* Be satisfied with nothing less than the best.

For sending, every type of spark gap was investigated, a compressed gas spark gap invented, a rotary spark gap giving 20,000 sparks per second was built, different electrodes were tried,—in short nothing was neglected that might make any one of these types the most perfect thing of its kind. Yet all the while Reg was nursing to adequate practical form the *High-frequency Alternator* that would generate the wave directly without any spark gap and which he *knew* was to supersede them all.

Equally, the liquid Barreter—the wonder of 1902 was still a wonder and still being groomed for more perfect performance—some rarer metal, tantalum for example, in place of the platinum point, and yet Reg *knew* that it would soon yield place to his still more wonderful *Heterodyne* receiver, of which he said in 1907, "This is undoubtedly the most efficient form of receiver in existence, and it is doubtful if the method will be improved upon so far as most classes of work are concerned."

Ten years later, in 1917, this great invention after having run the gauntlet of every possible legal investigation was passed on by Judge Mayer, Southern District of New York, (Federal Reporter, Vol. 241, p. 956) as follows:

> "These patents . . . are concerned with the systems of radio signaling known as the beats system, or more expertly the 'heterodyne'—a name created by Fessenden which has survived in the art. . . . The beat system in acoustics was old and well-known but Fessenden was concededly the first to apply this principle to signaling in the radio art. . . . . When, therefore, Fessenden, by his patent No. 706,740, applied for Sept. 28, 1901, and granted August 13, 1902, announced 'Broadly my invention consists in the production of electric beats analogous to sound beats and their utilization in receiving conductors . . .' he made, in the best sense, a new contribution to the knowledge of the time; for nowhere and by no one had there been even a suggestion of the applicability of the 'beats' system to radio. . . . On the question of invention therefore. . . . there can be no doubt but what Fessenden accomplished world invention of a high order. . . . ."

On the heels of this decision came the following generous and sporting letter from Dr. DeForest to Fessenden which it is a pleasure to quote:—

April 16, 1917.

"My dear Prof. Fessenden,

I have just been reading Judge Mayer's recent decision in the Heterodyne suit and wish to congratulate you on the result of the suit and on the very high opinion of the heterodyne invention which the court has expressed.

I fully agree with the Judge that the heterodyne was an invention of the highest order. It stands in the very small class of pioneer inventions from which great and revolutionary commercial developments result.

The court's decision will undoubtedly seriously embarrass some of our proposed work unless it is possible to arrange licenses with Nesco; but notwithstanding this, I am glad, as a follow inventor, that the patent has been so sweepingly upheld.

Believe me,

Sincerely yours,
(signed) Lee DeForest."

So, every device came up in turn for intensive consideration.

It might be compressed air condensers. Then, by long distance 'phone, telegram and letter, aluminium rolling mills would be besieged for sheet production that would be absolutely free from buckle. It might be head 'phones; the best commercial types would be tested and better demanded or made. And so with amplifiers, tuners, relays, interference preventers, what-not. The draughting room under Mr. Mansbendel designed and designed again and yet again, then the machine shop and lastly the experimental department relentlessly analyzed the quantitative output.

Mr. Edward Bennett head of the experimental department and Mr. James C. Armor, his assistant, came on from Washington to take part in 'tuning up' the tower for trans-Atlantic work. Since Mr. Armor worked first at Western Tower and then at Machrihanish, his account of the two stations will be quoted.

"The equipment of the two stations was identical. The sending apparatus consisted of a 40 horse-power steam engine driving a 35 K.V.A. 125 cycle alternator which, in turn, supplied current to transformers in which the voltage was raised to the value required to operate the spark gap. This was a rotating spark gap driven from the generator and arranged to give one spark each alternation at a predetermined point on the voltage wave. These rotating gaps produced clear, almost musical signals, very distinctive and easily distinguished from any other signals of that time. They were very superior to other signals commonly used which, by comparison, were very rough and ragged.

At first we used oil insulated condensers but these were superseded by Prof. Fessenden's compressed air condensers which were greatly superior to the oil insulated ones.

The receiving apparatus was housed in a small building located perhaps 100 feet from the building containing the sending apparatus so that the operator would not be disturbed by the noise of the revolving machinery. The receiving apparatus was of a type developed by Prof. Fessenden and was very efficient and very selective. While the equipment of the two stations was identical the terrain was quite different. At Brant Rock the country was flat with sandy beach, while at Machrihanish the shore was generally rocky with hills back of the station rising to a height of about 600 feet.

At Brant Rock during the months of November and December 1905 we made many measurements of all kinds, calculated to throw light on the performance of the equipment and of the station as a whole. As a result of this study of the characteristics of the station three wave-lengths were adopted as standard. These were designated A, B and C tunes.

Sometime in the latter part of November or early December, 1905, we started to send regularly to Machrihanish, which station at that time was equipped to receive although it could not send signals. The schedule adopted was as follows:—

At 8 P.M. U. S. Eastern Standard Time, Brant Rock would call Machrihanish using the "A" wave-length. They would then send the letter D repeated three times every ten seconds for a certain length of time after which any desired message would be transmitted and Brant Rock would sign off. The total time of sending on "A" wave-length between 8 and 9 P.M. occupied thirty minutes, leaving thirty minutes scheduled for Machrihanish to reply on the same wave-length. The rate of sending the letters D was accurately timed so that the three D's took up exactly $7\frac{1}{2}$ seconds with a silence of $2\frac{1}{2}$ seconds before the 3 D's would be repeated.

Beginning exactly at 9 o'clock Brant Rock would send in the same way except that "B" wave-length was used and the same program was repeated at 10 o'clock using "C" wave-length.

From the time the regular schedule of sending was started until the night I arrived at Machrihanish no signals from Brant Rock had been heard there."

Mr. Armor sailed for Machrihanish the Saturday before Christmas. He was thoroughly trained in the handling of the apparatus and was to be in charge of the experimental work at the Scottish station. On the Sunday following Christmas Day, Fessenden put in a very hard day and night of mathematical work checking the figures on which the different "Tunes" were based. He found that an error had crept in through a faulty conception of the tower's electrical characteristics. The corrections necessitated a new set of figures for the "tunes" and these I coded on New Year's Day but the cable was not sent off until the morning of the 2nd.

So at last we come to the momentous opening days of 1906, *when for the first time in the history of the world two-way trans-Atlantic wireless telegraph messages were sent and received.*

We knew that Mr. Armor was due to reach Machrihanish just about this time, also the 'Umbrella Capacity' of the tower was now in place, so we earnestly prayed for success.

On the afternoon of the 3rd a long cable in code began to come in over the telephone. Happening to be in the office at the time I said in an undertone to Reg—"It sounds as if they've been getting us, doesn't it?" "Oh, probably something about the tune" he replied, but took the code book and began to decode the first few words. In a few minutes he came into the dining room saying "They're getting us all right."

Strict secrecy in case of success had been enjoined by Given and Walker, so the message was brought into our dining room to be decoded but long before it was fully deciphered we were certain of the good news, and so exalted and excited with the joy of it that it was difficult to settle down to final particulars. When it came to "Get you 150 ohm shunt" Reg said to Miss Bent, his secretary and to me —"That's all I want to know. I told them they should get us 140 ohm shunt. You can finish the cable by yourselves now—that's all I want to know."

It was a tremendous relief, this realization of hopes that had been built up on theory and calculation. Newfoundland had lost its terrors, it didn't deflect our waves in some unexpected manner. The Bay of Fundy was no longer a nightmare for what it might possibly do.

However carefully this System had been built up fact by fact, nevertheless no one knew better than Fessenden that wireless still had its riddles and that we might have struck a particularly hard one in this trans-Atlantic work. But, so far, luck was with us, and we were like to burst from having to bottle up our glorious exaltation.

For the Machrihanish side of the picture we must see through Mr. Armor's eyes. After a very rough voyage he reached Campbeltown about 5 P.M. on January 2nd and drove on to Machrihanish in an open cart and through a driving hail-storm.

"As soon as possible after reaching Machrihanish Mr. W. E. Beakes (who was the operator on duty that night) and I went to the station and that night we, for the first time in Machrihanish heard signals from Brant Rock, picking up all three wave-lengths, that is tunes A, B, & C.

The operator that night felt, of course, that if anything could be heard from Brant Rock he did not want me to hear it first, so he listened through almost the entire first period without getting anything. When I did listen Brant Rock was signing off but I picked them up almost immediately. I turned the phones back to the operator, Brant Rock, however, had by that time signed off and had stopped sending. I therefore was the first person to hear Brant Rock signals received in Machrihanish.

I had watched the operator and saw that he passed too quickly over the instrument settings on which I expected to hear Brant Rock. I told the operator on what instrument settings I thought he could hear the next period and as I had had a very hard trip from Glasgow and was very tired I lay down on the work bench in the operating room and went to sleep. The next period the operator picked up Brant Rock almost immediately and woke me up and we heard the whole period, also picking up the third period without difficulty.

The next morning Mr. Glaubitz cabled Prof. Fessenden using the phrase "credit due Armor".

Work continued, each night Brant Rock sending signals and messages and Machrihanish cabling us the results. Each day the signals seemed to improve until on one occasion they got us on 14 ohm shunt and the sound could be heard with the telephone held $2\frac{1}{2}$ inches away.

On January 10th, Brant Rock asked Machrihanish if it could manage to send the next night after our sending period was over. The cable came in reply "Every effort will be made to send." But we knew there were heavy odds against getting them on their first attempt at sending. They did not know about the snappy type of signal that the operators at Brant Rock found to work best—atmospheric might be extra heavy, anything at all might happen to disappoint. But hopefully after 11 P.M. when our own sending period ended, I went down to the receiving room to get news and report to Reg who was ill in bed.

I found Mr. Bennett, Mr. Pannill and Mr. Wescoe there, Mr. Pannill listening in. They greeted me with "We haven't got them yet." We all sat quiet as mice, Pannill listening as hard as he could, Mr. Bennett sometimes listening and Mr. Wescoe turning the inductance roller, I think. Suddenly about twenty minutes to twelve Mr. Pannill said "There he is—just as pretty as possible—way down," and he removed the telephone he had been using to adjust the more sensitive Lambert Schmidt one to his ears. "That's it all right. You couldn't mistake that spark," and Mr. Bennett was given the telephone to listen.

"Oh, that's it, you couldn't mistake that musical note."

After listening a minute or so he handed the phone to me. The boys had said that there was little atmospheric though lots of interference, and true enough I found it; four or five different sets of signals that I could distinguish, and very near ones apparently, but presently—way, way off sounded zzz-zz-zzz and I knew I was listening to Machrihanish. Then the point was adjusted and I heard the spark several times again and then handed the telephone to Mr. Wescoe who had been whispering "Hurrah!"

The boys at first said that we were getting Machrihanish at about 400 ohm shunt and this on tune "A," which was the poorest one. The best one was to be used from 12 to 1. I did not wait for that period but went back to the cottage to tell Reg the results so far.

Next morning Mr. Bennett said that we got Machrihanish on 150 ohm shunt but that interference continued and atmospheric increased considerably so that only one message came through well. We got "Condensers working very satisfactorily." That was about as good as could be expected for the first time, seeing too that Machrihanish did not have the best selector installed.

To another generation and more than thirty years later, all this may seem very tame, but then it was *HISTORY*—new from the mould of Time. Once again in "Communications" it could be said "What hath God wrought" and in all humility the medium of the miracle was the Fessenden System.

Given and Walker had said that if we succeeded in getting across that they would feel like riding down Pennsylvania Avenue, Washington D. C. with their legs hanging out of the cab windows. So still in the spirit of secrecy, **Fessenden** wired them on January 3rd that they had better get ready for that drive. But perfect moments don't last forever.

To return to Mr. Armor's account:—

"About the second week in January 1906 we were able to start our scheduled sending to Brant Rock and messages were exchanged nightly for some time, allowing us to transact our regular business between the two stations in that way. However, at times the weather conditions were such that we could not get across. As summer approached with correspondingly short nights the interchange of messages became very difficult and the company decided to greatly increase the capacity of the sending apparatus. In the meantime the regular schedule was suspended for the summer."

Atmospheric absorption was the factor on which calculation had gone astray. Tests made on shipboard at distances of 1500 miles had shown that 90% of the radiation was lost in atmospheric absorption—that is, that 10% got through. Since messages could be received if *only one-fifth of one per cent* got through it was believed that the margin of safety for this 3000 mile transmission partly over land, was sufficient.

But after the first few months of working in 1906 it was found that with the same sending power, the range of received signals on different nights was all the way from 400 times stronger than audibility to signals so weak that they could not be read.

During the period of good working successful demonstrations were given to representatives of the General Electric Company and others at Brant Rock and to Mr. Shields, the technical expert of our English Patent Attorneys at Machrihanish, but it was evident that the stations were not yet sufficiently powerful for regular commercial work.

CHAPTER XIV

DASHED HOPES

IN THE EARLY DAYS Brant Rock Tower possessed all the attractions of a new toy. To climb it was one of our small stunts—not for the men of course for in the line of duty they were up and down it all day long—but for the 'laity.'

One squeezed through a manhole at the base and started a perpendicular climb via a steel ladder built at one side of the tube. Darkness all the way except for the light that came through the manholes at each 100 ft. interval; then at the top one crawled precariously out on to a small platform that surrounded the tube and enjoyed the panorama of land and sea below, and in a small way gloried in one's own sense of achievement. Crawling back into the tube was the most ticklish part of the performance—a 400 ft. drop wasn't a comforting thought, especially as in our case, my young son would not be denied the adventure and climbed with me.

Mr. Pannill contributes a story in this connection.

> "It was not intended that people of large 'rotunda' should proceed to the top of the tower by this means and therefore the hole was not of very large proportions. This made no difference to Professor Fessenden who one day when something went wrong decided to go to the top of the tower. He squeezed in all right, but the difficulty was coming out, as he had evidently 'swelled' somewhat since he entered the tower.
>
> To make a long story short, it was necessary to grease the hole thoroughly with axle grease and for him to get most of his clothes off, before we were able to push him thru the hole.
>
> It goes without saying that within a few days after this incident, the riggers suddenly appeared to install an out-

door swinging elevator to the top of the tower, which the Professor used thereafter."

Another stunt, this exclusively for the men, was to be in the tower when sending was going on and it was functioning as an antenna. I recall seeing Mr. Bennett standing inside the tower holding in his hand a lamp bulb. On extending his arm through the manhole the lamp filament glowed brilliantly.

Brant Rock was popular as a summer resort and in consequence we were pestered by the idle and curious, who disregarded notices and signs against trespassing with the traditional aplomb of the tourist. This was not only disturbing and time-wasting but might be fraught with danger, and more than once Fessenden staged a realistic tempest in a tea-pot to teach the public proper respect for our regulations.

Another important reason for keeping the public out was that spying by other companies was by no means uncommon. A watchman was always on duty and hourly rounds of inspection was one of his chief functions, the exact performance of which was certified by the registers of the time clocks at ten different points on his route.

Fire, too, was one of our hazards and once in the middle of a winter night Western Tower underwent its baptism. The watchman sounded the alarm whistle and quickly all the men within its radius of sound responded. Fire drill was so well organized that no time was lost and only a small amount of damage done. It was exciting while it lasted and there was no more dejected man on the plant for days afterwards than Mr. Hadfield, our engineer, who lived furthest from the station, had not heard the whistle and had missed the excitement.

There were, of course, many official visitors and these grew more numerous as the work progressed.

Patent work increased daily and with it, legal expenses. In order to reduce these costs somewhat Given and Walker decided to make a change in the company's patent attorney, switching from the expensive firm of Christy & Christy of which Mr. Wolcott was a member, to a young attorney, Mr. F. W. H. Clay who with his way to make, was willing to work at lower rates. Mr. Clay was a hard worker and a keen and skillful lawyer but until he had mastered the technical details of the 150 odd Fessenden applications in his charge an extra burden developed on Reg to see that no mistakes were made, no oversights, no office action overlooked.

Also at this time Reg, as will be seen from the appended list of his papers, kept the scientific world informed as to his work by numerous contributions to foreign and domestic technical journals.

One incident in this connection may be of interest. A certain statement was received by an English technical publication, typewritten on National Electric Signaling Company stationery and with Fessenden's stamped signature. It appeared to be genuine, but to the Editor the statement in this communication did not ring quite true. It seemed to clash with previous printed statements by Fessenden; he sensed something queer about it and before printing the communication, wrote to Fessenden to make inquiries.

On investigation it was evident that the original communication on the sheet of paper had been washed off and a different communication substituted, neatly fitted to the available space.

It was not very important since it had been caught in time, but it intrigued us to try to trace the thing. We anticipated that the original letter might have been the reply to some applicant for a job. All files were ordered sent on from the Washington office and though no one had much time for sleuthing I undertook to hunt the needle in the haystack. This was tedious but not difficult. The first thing was to narrow the choice down to carbons of N.E.S. Co. letters that came within the dimensions—about twelve double spaced lines. Then such idiosyncracies of the machine and typist of the original letter as could be discerned were carefully charted. Under the microscope a period caused a minute puncture, a comma or certain letters were struck more forcibly and not completely obliterated by the wash. With this skeleton chart on onion skin paper some hundreds of selected letters were compared, and beyond shadow of doubt the search brought us at last to the Patent Office. The letter used was an unimportant one as it was concerned with routine matters only, and would hardly be missed from Patent Office files.

Trans-Atlantic working was not resumed until October 1906.

Great difficulty had been experienced in getting suitable aluminium discs for the compressed air condensers, so that even in October only half of the required number of condensers were in place. This gave the station a margin of safety of 2000. With the full number installed it would have been 4000 and Fessenden further intended to use a new form of receiving apparatus which he estimated would have brought the margin of safety up to 400,000.

But even with the 2000 margin of safety the stations, barring shut-downs for a couple of nights for mechanical reasons, operated continuously until December 5, 1906.

During these two months, demonstrations were numerous and to widely diversified interests. U.S. Army and Navy officials, Associated Press, Foreign Attaches, technical experts of American Telephone and Telegraph Company and of the General Electric Company, and scientific experts, Dr. A. E. Kennelly, Dr. G. W. Pickard, Mr. Hammond V. Hayes, Dr. Louis Bell, Professor Webster, Professor Pierce among others. It can readily be imagined that these were strenuous days for all. Everyone was keyed up and on his toes to get best results.

Winter isolation and limited accommodation at Brant Rock were not the least of our problems, for visitors must not be allowed to experience discomforts. They were met and entrained with minimum effort to themselves; offices and testing rooms were specially heated if the weather proved uncommonly New Englandish; meals were planned with care for anticipated events and when unexpected guests arrived and the proverbial bare cupboard yawned at me, housekeeping magic was in order as well as wireless miracles. Nothing must detract from the effect of the tests.

Reg was always at his best as host, whether at a meal at his own table or at a feast of scientific achievements, though in regard to the latter he often in my opinion erred in laying too little emphasis, touching too lightly and casually on the wonders he revealed, almost as if they were a matter of course.

Indeed this habit of disclosure of his most advanced findings to other workers in the wireless field in the belief that such disclosure established his priority of invention, led to many serious consequences. In 1904 one of his patent attorneys referring to two occasions of that period when such disclosures had been abused, wrote to Fessenden—"we remarked that you would never learn to keep your great discoveries to yourself."

One evening in November when no tests were on, permission was given me to send a personal message by wireless to friends in London. The message itself went in code and was decoded at our Machrihanish Station but the name and address, both entirely unknown to anyone at our Scottish station went straight, of course. Two nights later a reply via Machrihanish came from my London friends, who I think, may not be aware that they were the first to receive a personal message by trans-atlantic wireless telegraphy.

Mr. Pannill too has a recollection of this period.

"One morning about 3:30 I was on watch in the receiving station listening for signals from Scotland. It had been snowing all day with a heavy gale and very cold. I was startled by the opening of the door of the receiving room, when there appeared Professor Fessenden in bath robe and slippers and smoking a Pittsburgh stogey. He explained that he would like when I heard the signal from Scotland, to listen intently for an echo $1/5$ of a second later and he explained that the echo would be the signal coming round the world.

My first thought was that he had been giving too much attention to his work and was a little goofey, but what he had to say was not only true but has been demonstrated in many ways since that time, in other phases of wireless telegraphy. You could not help but have the greatest admiration, regardless of how startling some of his ideas seemed to be at the time, for his wonderful insight into the future of wireless."

On December 5, 1906 came another cable with vital tidings but this time of far different import. *The Machrihanish Tower had crashed in a storm.*

It was as if Death were in our midst—a staying hand on all that moved and glowed with such promise but a minute ago.

How? Why? Brant Rock had stood storms as bad or worse with no sign of weakness anywhere.

For the answer to these questions we waited till letters and complete sets of photographs could reach us. These revealed that the primary cause of the disaster was *faulty joining of the guy ropes!*

When construction details were being settled the Brown Hoisting Company had pointed out that the method used by Roebling in Brooklyn Bridge had proved very satisfactory, so this method was decided on.

The cable of galvanized wire is first introduced into the small end of a cone-shaped socket, open at both ends. The cable is drawn through a certain distance and bound with a piece of binding wire; then the end of the cable is unlaid so that no two wires remain twisted together but are bunched like a brush: this is then pushed back into the socket and where the cable emerges from the socket a second piece of binding wire is wrapped around it. Then into the socket where all the untwisted wires are bunched, melted zinc is poured to fill every smallest crevice.

Tests at the Massachusetts Institute of Technology showed that forgings had gone at 46,000 lbs., the insulators at 56,000 lbs., but the cable hadn't pulled out of its socket.

So, properly made as at Brant Rock, these joints left nothing to be desired.

But at Machrihanish the Brown Hoisting Company had adopted a somewhat different method, in which the outer circle of unlaid wires were turned back on themselves, a wedge driven into the balance of the wires to spread them and melted zinc poured into the socket.

That this is an inferior type of joint is proved by the fact that after the fall of the tower it was found that five or six of the joints had pulled out of their sockets, though sockets and insulators remained intact. But even this type, faithfully carried out, would probably have stood the strain.

The cross section of the joint that first failed showed that a wedge had split in the original work and an indifferent workman or superintendent had allowed the defective wedge to remain, merely pounding the top of it flatter, thus shutting off more space from the free flow of the melted zinc. Then, as a final touch, the zinc had been poured almost *cold,* and instead of becoming a solid binder, it was merely a *crumbly* filler of space. The only wonder is that the tower did not fall before!

Fessenden said "The accident came at a very unfortunate time, as work had just been begun on a new method for eliminating atmospheric absorption, which had given very promising results, the absorption having already been reduced to one-tenth of what it was formerly. Moreover, the new receiving apparatus had only been partly installed and no opportunity had been afforded of trying it between the trans-atlantic stations.

It was a body blow, but Given and Walker no less than Fessenden took it with fine courage. The word was "Carry on."

CHAPTER XV

WIRELESS TELEPHONY AND THE HIGH-FREQUENCY ALTERNATOR

WESTERN TOWER STOOD staunch against blast and sleet and ragings of nature. With it as an operating base, work went forward with scarcely a halt in its stride and the Wireless Telephone moved to the center of the stage. Fessenden was often asked how the wireless telephone came to be invented.

His explanation was that in November 1899 he was experimenting with a Wehnelt interrupter for operating the induction coil used in sending. In the receiver, the ring of a short-period, Elihu Thompson, oscillating-current galvanometer rested on three supports, i.e. two pivots and a carbon block. A storage battery was used in the receiving circuit. It was noticed that when the sending key was kept down at the sending station for a long dash, the peculiar wailing sound of the Wehnelt interrupter was reproduced with absolute fidelity in the receiving telephone.

It at once suggested itself that, by using a source with a frequency above audibility, wireless telephony could be accomplished. But it is one thing to conceive the idea and to know the sort of apparatus required and another thing to get it constructed. Reg gave an order in 1900 for a high-frequency dynamo, but instructions were not followed by the manufacturer and when it was delivered in 1903 it was found capable of giving only 10,000 cycles.

Meantime a 10,000 frequency spark gap had been built to his specifications in Mr. Brashear's machine shop and it was with this piece of apparatus, as already noted, that wireless telephoning was for the first time accomplished, over a distance of one mile, between 50 ft. masts, at Cobb Island in the fall of 1900. Speech was perfectly intelligible but accompanied by an extremely loud and disagreeable noise due to the irregularity of the spark.

Between 1901 and 1903 half a dozen or more types of sources of continuous waves were invented and developed. The oscillatory arc, the regenerative mercury tube types, both static and magnetic, compressed nitrogen and compressed neon oscillators, the quenched gap and fly-wheel types, etc.

Some of these gave very good results. Bureau of Standards tests on the compressed nitrogen gap showed one-half kilowatt of pure sine waves at frequencies measuring as high as 2,000,000.

By 1904 a 20,000 frequency spark gap and compressed nitrogen gap gave such good results that a demonstration was given before scientists who testified that transmission was commercially good over twenty-five miles, and thereupon telephone sets were advertised for sale.

But all this was in line with Fessenden's method of getting the best out of every different type so as to pit that best against the still better type that he was preparing.

Mr. Kintner vividly describes the development of this final method.

"——how to make the continuous waves was not so apparent. Fessenden boldly said, "Take a high-frequency alternator of 100,000 cycles per second, connect one terminal to the antenna and the other to the ground, then tune to resonance. ." That looks simple now, but it wasn't then I assure you.

I remember very distinctly the impression I formed when Fessenden told me of his plan. First I asked him how he could get sufficient voltage and he said, "Several hundred volts will be ample, as by resonance I can raise the voltage in the antenna one hundred times, which will be all that I require." Even then I was sceptical because I didn't know of any 100,000 cycle machines—neither did he, but he was already working on it and after about five years of strenuous effort and considerable expense, his first machine was delivered to him at Brant Rock, Massachusetts, in September

WIRELESS TELEPHONY

1906. From this machine he was able to get 750 watts at 80,000 cycles." (Pittsburgh's Contributions to Radio)

But it wasn't so simple as that; there were difficulties and intermediate stages of which Mr. Kintner did not know. It was a far cry between the high-frequency alternator as received from the manufacturers and the transformation it had to undergo before it was capable of giving the 80,000 cycles required for telephonic transmission. The high-frequency alternator that was delivered in 1906 by the General Electric Company which had been doing the work on it, came with the statement that in the Company's opinion it was not possible to operate it above 10,000 cycles.

Thereupon Reg scrapped everything but the pole pieces—designed a new armature and had it built at his Washington shop. After this rebuilding by Fessenden machinists under Fessenden supervision the alternator gave from 70, to 80,000 cycles and about one-half kilowatt of electric wave radiation.

A second dynamo built to a different type in the Washington shop with an 8 inch armature gave the same power but 100,000 cycles and operated as reliably as any other dynamo until 1911.

To his own engineers,—Mr. Stein, Captain Hill and Mr. Mansbendel, Reg always felt profoundly grateful for splendid cooperation in this difficult work. To the General Electric Company engineers Messrs. Steinmetz, Alexanderson, Dempster and others, he also felt a debt of thanks for their very earnest efforts to fulfill his admittedly unusual specifications. They did their best but that best could give only 10,000 cycles as against the 80 to 100,000 cycles that he demanded.

When Fessenden had showed the way with his two home-built, high-frequency alternators, the General Electric Co. began to see light and went seriously to work. As the world knows, under Dr. Alexanderson the high-frequency alternator was carried to great perfection and Fessenden was generous with enthusiastic praise for what he accomplished. But as far as the world is *permitted* to know Alexanderson is given sole credit for the invention. It is a good instance of what big organizations can do in the way of manipulating History, by blotting out here and building up there till the desired impression is indelibly etched on the public mind.

Many years later Reg in a letter to Mr. Albert G. Davis at that time Vice-President and head of the Patent Department of the General Electric Company, wrote.

> ". . . Of course for business reasons your company has never given me credit for this (High Frequency Alternator), but if you will look at the back correspondence you will see that I built the first one after the G. E. engineers had said that nothing above 10,000 was possible: and that Alexanderson, who is a splendid engineer) did not come in until after three months running at 100,000."

In his reply of November 15, 1924 Mr. Davis said:—

> ". . . As far as concerns the high frequency alternator, I thought that we had always given you credit for the work which you did in this connection. Alexanderson never claimed to have invented the high frequency alternator, as such, but merely to have invented certain structural features which worked very well in practice. His patents were limited to what he invented." (in testimony, Federal Trade Commission, Docket 1115, p. 4433. Library of Congress.)

Surely a disingenuous statement. For even though Alexanderson himself may not have claimed the invention, the General Electric Company has sedulously permitted and encouraged the attribution of it to him, so that even in publications such as "The Radio Octopus" (American Mercury, August 1931) written to reveal the iniquities of the Radio Trust, the writer, Dane Yorke, accepts implicitly the Alexanderson Myth, in regard to conception and reduction to practice of this invention.

> ". . . During the war, it seems, the General Electric Company put into use a very valuable wireless device known as the Alexanderson alternator. After the war, impressed by the

device, the British Marconi Company offered General Electric a $5,000,000 contract provided it were given exclusive rights. The deal was nearly closed when President Wilson, then in Paris at the Peace Conference, sent two high officers of the Navy to protest against the granting of exclusive rights to the British Marconi Company. So fundamentally important was the Alexanderson device to wireless transmission that without its use the United States would be effectively barred from the radio field. The cable systems of the world, argued President Wilson's representatives, were already under complete foreign control; to surrender air communication also would be a tragic mistake.
But Owen D. Young and his associates of the General Electric Company pointed out that much money had been spent in developing the Alexanderson apparatus. Save for the Marconi Company there was no real market for it, and thus no seeming hope of any return on General Electric's investment. Here the official story grows vague. . . ."

Another group of investigators out to tell the truth as they see it "Empire of the Air"—Ventura Free Press, Ventura, California, while attributing the invention to Fessenden and referring to the early abortive efforts of the General Electric Company to build a high-frequency alternator for him, appear nevertheless not to know of the two perfectly operative, high-frequency dynamos built by Fessenden with which he accomplished regular wireless telephonic transmission up to several hundred miles (exclusive of freak transmission) between 1906 and the close of 1910.

In the fall of 1906 wireless telephone work went on between Brant Rock and Plymouth a distance of eleven miles, also between Brant Rock and a small fishing schooner. A well known technical journal November 10, 1906 alluded rather incredulously to this latter feat. It is headed "A New Fish Story"—and reads as follows:

"It is stated from Massachusetts that the wireless telephone has successfully entered the deep sea fishing industry. For the last week experiments have been conducted by the wireless telegraph station at Brant Rock which is equipped with a wireless telephone, with a small vessel stationed in the fleet of the South Shore Fishermen, twelve miles out of Massachusetts Bay. Recently it is asserted, the fishermen wished to learn the prices ruling in the Boston market. The operator on the wireless fitted boat called up Brant Rock and telephoned the fishermen's request. The land operator asked Boston by Wire and the answer was forwarded back to the fishermen. This is a rather fishy fish story."

It was realized that the use of the wireless telephone would be seriously curtailed unless it could operate in conjunction with wire lines, so relays were invented both for the transmitting and receiving ends. Transmission itself was more perfect than over wire lines. Since development was so far advanced, it was decided on the heels of the Machrihanish disaster to issue formal invitations to a demonstration of the wireless telephone. The invitation to the American Telephone Journal of New York City follows:

Brant Rock,
Dec. 11, 1906.

"Dear Sirs:—

A limited number of invitations have been issued to witness the operation of the National Electric Signaling Co.'s wireless telephone system between Brant Rock and Plymouth, Mass. over a distance of between ten and eleven miles.

The tests will be as follows:

1. Transmission of ordinary speech, and also transmission of phonographic talking and music by wireless telephone between Brant Rock and Plymouth.

2. Transmission of speech over ordinary wire line to wireless station at Brant Rock relaying the speech there automatically by telephone relay and automatically transmitting the speech by wireless to Plymouth, transmitting same at Plymouth automatically directly or by telephone relay over regular wire lines. Invitations have been issued to the following gentlemen,—" (here follows a list of the guests, including Dr. A.E.Kennelly, Professor Elihu Thompson etc. and a request to the Telephone Journal to send a representative.)

Yours very truly

(signed) National Electric Signaling Co."

A report of these tests appeared in the American Telephone Journal of January 26, and February 2, 1907, the Editor having attended the tests in person.

This article unequivocally confirms the success of this demonstration of the wireless telephone and is in the nature of a landmark and an historical record; so much so that on the occasion of a formal meeting of the Radio Institute in New York City, at which Fessenden gave a talk on "Inventing the Wireless Telephone and the Future," (Jan. 19, 1926) he presented a Photostat and Certified copy of the article to the Library of the Radio Institute.

On Christmas Eve and New Year's Eve of 1906 *the first Broadcasting* occurred. Three days in advance Reg had his operators notify the ships of the U.S. Navy and of the United Fruit Co. that were equipped with the Fessenden apparatus that it was the intention of the Brant Rock Station to broadcast speech, music and singing on those two evenings.

Describing this, Fessenden wrote:—

"The program on Christmas Eve was as follows: first a short speech by me saying what we were going to do, then some phonograph music.—The music on the phonograph being Handel's 'Largo'. Then came a violin solo by me, being a composition of Gounod called 'O, Holy Night', and ending up with the words 'Adore and be still' of which I sang one verse, in addition to playing on the violin, though the singing of course was not very good. Then came the Bible text, 'Glory to God in the highest and on earth peace to men of good will', and finally we wound up by wishing them a Merry Christmas and then saying that we proposed to broadcast again New Year's Eve.

The broadcast on New Year's Eve was the same as before, except that the music was changed and I got someone else to sing. I had not picked myself to do the singing, but on Christmas Eve I could not get any of the others to either talk, sing or play and consequently had to do it myself.

On New Year's Eve one man, I think it was Stein, agreed to sing and did sing, but none of the others either sang or talked.

We got word of reception of the Christmas Eve program as far down as Norfolk, Va., and on the New Year's Eve program we got word from some places down in the West Indies."

It is not surprising that it was widely heard even beyond the group of Fessenden equipped boats—for as he further states—

"As a matter of fact, at the time of the broadcast, practically everyone was infringing the liquid barreter. When the broadcast was made, practically every ship along the coast was equipped to receive it."

One other happening of this period of the wireless telephone was a private communication about November 1906 from one of the Machrihanish operators to Fessenden. He wrote that he had been listening at the Scottish station and had heard a voice which he recognized as Mr. Stein's voice, quoted what he had said and gave the time at which he heard him, but so astounding did it seem to him that he refrained from discussing it with anyone until Professor Fessenden should advise him in regard to it.

The matter was at once investigated and without giving any hint as to the reason for finding out, it was established that on the specified date and hour the words quoted were spoken by Mr. Stein in the Brant Rock-Plymouth transmission.

The operator's theory to explain the occurrence was that Mr. Stein must have been standing near the rotary gap and that the arc had been the medium of transmission of speech, which was, as Reg said, an ingenius explanation and could under certain conditions produce such results.

What the operator did not know was that the high-frequency dynamo had just been received at Brant Rock from the Washington shop and was being tested on the Brant Rock-Plymouth transmission. A second time he wrote that he had heard talking from Brant Rock and Reg was just preparing a schedule of telephonic tests between Brant

Rock and Machrihanish when the disaster to the tower cut the work short.

In July 1907 the range of our commercial wireless telephone was considerably extended; speech was successfully transmitted between Brant Rock and Jamaica, Long Island, a distance of nearly 200 miles, in daylight and mostly over land; the mast at Jamaica being approximately 180 feet high.

The evenings when Reg was free from exhibition tests and able to be quiet, it was his habit to play game after game of a difficult Patience—one that required the planning of many moves ahead. This seemed to supply a surface activity beneath which his sub-conscious mind could sort and arrange data and material in orderly fashion, so that when next a problem came up for consideration, its factors assumed more complete significance. Another soothing accompaniment to the pad-pad of the cards as he laid them down was the purr-purr of 'Mikums' in the center of the table beneath the one beauty spot our cottage afforded—a ground glass, rose painted lamp shade, one of the earliest and loveliest of its kind. Not that the beauty appealed to Mike but the light and the warmth did, and so did the chain pull. When he managed to switch off the light we always applauded his cleverness.

It was a time when such peaceful diversions were needed, for discouragement lay heavy on the men who owned the N.E.S. Co. Magnificent as was the technical superiority of the Company's System, its business policy was still not getting it anywhere.

When it was seen to what lengths Government Departments were going in ignoring patent rights, Given and Walker had refused to attempt to sell any apparatus. Now that Trans-Atlantic working had been achieved and the success of the wireless telephone was admitted, it was essential to find a market, to quote Mr. Walker "for the whole of all we have." So in 1907 serious and protracted negotiations were started with the American Telegraph and Telephone Company, the Postal Telegraph Company, the Western Union Telegraph Company and with Mr. John I. Waterbury.

This involved minute investigation by technical and legal experts of the various companies and under Mr. Frederick P. Fish, the American Telegraph and Telephone Company had reached the decision to buy, but at the very moment an upheaval occurred in the management of the A. T. & T. Co., Mr. Vail succeeded Mr. Fish and the incoming president was pledged to a different policy.

CHAPTER XVI

DIFFICULTIES—LEGISLATIVE AND COMPANY

PROFOUND UNCERTAINTY MENACED the future of this new art and all wireless companies were seriously concerned. An International Radio Convention met in Europe in 1907 and delegates from the various countries attended. But rarely are Conventions representative of what they represent.

No doubt most of the delegates were able, conscientious and willing to be impartial but in very many respects they were uninformed, for, speaking for the United States, no opportunity was given the various wireless companies to present their views to these delegates prior to the Convention.

On the other hand the large group of Government representatives were far from being impartial. Each national group very properly sought to protect the interests of its own country but above and beyond that and with the immemorial habit of bureaucracy, each department, and in particular the Navy, manoeuvred to secure control for its own Bureau.

When the findings of the Conference were made public Fessenden wrote:—

> "The fact that the proposed Regulations are unsuitable does not reflect in any way on the ability or conscientiousness of the delegates.—The main difficulty however, is that no one, no matter what his knowledge of the present state of the art can foresee future developments. The question of wave length and daylight absorption is an illustration of this, as is also the question of syntonized circuits. The time has not yet come for any such hard and fixed regulations as proposed."

The restrictions proposed were in fact so crippling that both the Marconi Company and the National Electric Signaling Company asked for a hearing before the U.S. Senate Committee of Foreign Relations, before ratification.

They were heard on January 15 and January 22, 1908.

Both companies argued that the proposed regulations amounted to confiscation of property and service of the wireless companies, with no provision for adequate compensation.

That the regulations were impracticable and throttling.

That they expressly excluded the use of a number of the most important developments in the art.

That they were of such a character as would prevent future development.

Happily there is a limbo for troubles eventually overcome, but it is well sometimes to refresh the public mind about them. Take for instance Regulations II and III.

Ships were required to use two tunes only, so that stations were placed, so to speak, on two-party lines, thereby producing the maximum of interference.

Regulations required each ship before sending its message to call the coast station, have a number assigned to it, inform the coast station of its distance, its true bearing in degrees, its true course in degrees, its speed in nautical miles, the number of words it had to transmit; must then be informed how long it would have to wait, whether the transmission was to be in alternate order or in series, interrupt the sending after 20 words, send an interrogation mark, wait for the repetition of the last word, etc.

Ordinary commercial messages were barred, such as money order telegrams, repeat telegrams, or prepaid reply telegrams.

The restrictions laid on the mechanics of the Systems were even then antiquated.

The accusing finger points to the machinations of Governments, not for the exercise of their legitimate duty to regulate, but for the underlying and sinister attempt to control.

This impersonal appropriation by Governments of things

they have not created, have not paid for and have not understood must in the end so rifle the rich stores of honey which science and industry have created that the hive weakens and dies.

The Senate Committee after these hearings decided to do nothing for the present but shortly thereafter another set of regulations was forwarded by the Administration to the Senate endorsing the recommendations of the Secretary of the Navy that a law should be passed making it an offence punishable by imprisonment for one year, or a fine of $2000, or both, for a private station to continue sending when called upon to discontinue by a Navy Operator, or to produce interference with a Navy Station when the latter was transmitting an official message. This recommendation was not accompanied by any recommendation to the effect that the Navy Station should use any means for keeping out interference.

A hearing was sought on this but without success.

The following memorandum of an interview between Secretary Straus of the Dept. of Commerce and Labor and a representative of the N.E.S. Co. is illuminating:—

"*Representative.* Will you not, Mr. Secretary, be willing to assist us in obtaining a treaty which, while giving the government all it desires in the way of intercommunication between different systems, reservation of wave-lengths for government purposes etc. will at the same time avoid driving the wireless companies into bankruptcy?"

"*Secretary Straus.* The treaty was reported by experts of the government departments, and we propose to carry it out, as it is the policy of the administration."

"*Representative.* But, Mr. Secretary, these regulations virtually prevent the wireless companies from doing any commercial business. With every body on one party line, even without the numerous other restrictions, it will not be possible to handle a sufficient number of messages to pay operating expenses, and the companies will necessarily be driven into bankruptcy."

"*Secretary Straus.* That has nothing to do with this department. If you are injured you should go to Congress and ask them to reimburse you."

"*Representative.* Mr. Secretary, you know that it would be practically impossible to get a bill to reimburse a private company through Congress. Why should the government crush out a new and important method of communication which will save the country millions of dollars yearly, when the government will gain nothing by the action. We feel that your department ought to assist us in the matter."

"*Secretary Straus.* It has been decided by the administration that the treaty should be approved as it stands."

Fessenden fought this government tendency throughout his whole life. Not solely, not even chiefly on his own account, but because he saw that *National Decadence* must follow the frustration of *Individual Initiative*.

An inventor had no legal remedy against the confiscation of his patents by the United States Government, and impregnable, the Departments of the Government availed themselves of their power.

It was thought that if this situation was placed clearly before the administration and Congress that legislative remedy would be forthcoming.

President Theodore Roosevelt was asked if the administration would introduce such a bill. He replied that the administration had too many bills of its own to look after, but later he stated that if such a bill were introduced the administration would not oppose it.

Thereupon a suitable bill was drawn which passed the House of Representatives by a large majority, both Republican and Democratic parties speaking in favor of it. It passed the Senate unanimously but did not become law as President Roosevelt refused to sign it despite strong recommendations by Secretary Taft and by Senator Knox and others. The reason for this refusal is not exactly known but it is thought to have been because the ratification of the Wireless Treaty was opposed by one who favored the passage of this present Bill, No. 184.

So we came to the summer of 1908 with nerves under extreme tension. In such discouraging legislative atmosphere Given and Walker could make no headway in their negotiations for a deal with some Communications company. Fessenden was increasingly conscious of the unsatisfactory status of that long-deferred payment by Given and Walker for their share in the patents.

Our family exchequer was beginning to be very inadequate in spite of utmost economy; $300 a month is not inexhaustible and our son was now at Phillips Andover and Prep school fees had to be budgeted for. To ease this situation I persuaded Reg to consent to give up the Washington house. Because he had felt that it might reflect on the solvency of the Company, the rental of this place had been going on since the summer of 1905 when we moved to Brant Rock.

A horrible fortnight alone in Washington during the dog days to pack and place in storage our belongings, brought at least to me, a sense of relief at getting rid of that much financial burden.

There were, it is true, gleams of hope ahead. Reg had been approached by Colonel Firth who for some years had been interested in wireless and had acted as agent for other wireless companies in negotiating extensive sales of sets and parts. He, with Mr. Musgrave, then in charge of Communications for the United Fruit Company, were deeply impressed with the superiority of the Fessenden System and deplored the N.E.S. Co.'s policy of the closed door in the matter of selling apparatus.

Colonel Firth was convinced that he could make 'the leopard change his spots' and turn the U.S. Navy into a good customer. Mr. Musgrave was considering full wireless equipment for the fleet of the United Fruit Line and the erection of several high-powered land stations at strategic points. Fessenden knew that he could deliver the goods if permitted to do so and once more he urged on Given and Walker the wisdom, the necessity of selling apparatus, at least until the System could be sold as a whole.

Finally, to keep him pacified, they yielded—but with restrictions. Permission was strictly limited to contracts with the U.S. Government and with the United Fruit Company.

Given and Walker had not then, nor ever, the intention of going into the electrical manufacturing business. Each had his own highly profitable business. Fessenden's output as an inventor was for them a 'flier,' an opportunity to control a scientific jewel brought to perfection by the most skilful lapidary of the art. When in due course its last revealing facet should be burnished, the final touch given, then in their hands it would be taken to the market place and there sold to the A.T. & T., or the Western Union, or the Postal, or the Westinghouse.

In the summer of 1908 Colonel Firth succeeded in placing orders to the amount of $152,000 with the U.S. Navy and the United Fruit.

But far from regarding this prospective payment in the light of FIRST EARNINGS,—that will o' the wisp which had kept our courage up since 1904,—Given and Walker now began to urge that Fessenden give them MORE of his share of the stock of the Company.

He was between two mill-stones. His own family needed increased income. Given and Walker, with a controlling interest in the Company for which they had not paid him a single cent now asked for even more of his stock.

Fessenden stood at bay. He must make a stand or be lost!

At a meeting in Pittsburgh in September 1908 he brought the matter to a head. He was well aware of the large sums of money that had been expended on the company by Given and Walker, largely in pursuance of a policy of which he did not approve. On his part he had contributed, on a bare living wage, six years of brilliant and successful experimental work and had added another 150 patents to the 32 of the original contract.

The money that Given and Walker had advanced was all on demand notes bearing interest at 6 per cent. Fessenden's $330,000 due him from Given and Walker for their controlling interest in the company was contingent on FIRST

EARNINGS, and bearing NO interest. Reg notified Walker that the only terms on which he would stay with the company were that the deferred payment of $330,000 be placed on the same basis as the debts of the company to Given and Walker—i.e. demand notes bearing interest at 6 per cent, and that his salary be doubled.

At the first interview Walker flatly refused these terms. His answer was—"If you don't behave, don't do what we say you won't get anything. Mr. Given and I have the company tied up so that if you make any fuss you won't get a cent. Mr. Given will take it all over himself."

Given was ill at the time, unable to be at his office, Fessenden offered to wait till he could be out again, but Walker said "No, we'll settle it here and now."

Following this interview Reg wrote that night to Walker restating his terms.

Sept. 11, 1908.

"Mr. Hay Walker Jr. Pres. National Electric Signaling Co., Farmers National Bank Building, Pittsburgh, Pa.

Dear Sir,

In 1902, before I met you and Mr. Given, my system had been under development for six years; and had been in operation for a distance of fifty miles; and had been favorably reported on by the Army and Navy officials, and I had been offered $200,000 cash for a half interest in it by Mr. Grey, President of Queen and Co.

By the agreement which Mr. Wolcott persuaded and advised me to make with you and Mr. Given, I was to get $300,000 and 45% of stock (Mr. Wolcott to get one third of this).

When I had succeeded in transmitting hundreds of messages daily between New York and Philadelphia, you and Mr. Given refused to pay the purchase price and threatened to withdraw, leaving me so tied up that I could do nothing, unless I made a new agreement by which I got nothing except 30% of the stock and you and Mr. Given got the rest of the stock and my patents without paying anything for it.

The business of the company was conducted in direct

opposition to my urgent advice, with the result that a heavy debt was piled up against the company.

Since that time I have put in six years additional work and contributed more than 150 patents in addition to the 32 of our original contract, with the sole result that a short time ago you approached me with the proposition that I give up some more of the small amount of stock which was left me.

Present Situation.

During the Six years referred to, I had continued to work, maintaining myself and family on the sum of $2000 per year, my wife doing her own scrubbing and washing.

When you agreed to sell apparatus I secured for you the services of Colonel Firth, probably the best man in the United States, and during the last couple of months he has succeeded in placing orders for $152,000 as follows:

Navy		
100 K.W. and 10 K.W.		$97,500
2 telephones		6,500
United Fruit		
2 Large		$32,000
5 telephones		16,000
		$152,000

There is strong probability that we will succeed in placing the following order, most of which has in fact been promised:

Navy		
6 Large		$450,000
7 10 K.W.		77,000
10 Arcs.		40,000
West Indies		200,000
Condensers		50,000
United Fruit Co:		
100 Vessels		300,000
		$1,117,000

The designs and working drawings for these stations have been practically completed by me. I leave behind me a corps of capable assistants.

I have worked out the system, demonstrated the apparatus could be sold, got you a man to sell same, sales have been made and the apparatus has been designed.

There is nothing, therefore, which you can possibly complain of in my actions. I am not bound to you further in any way, either by contract or morally, in fact the reverse is the case.

I would ask you to please accept this as a notification of the fact that I shall leave the company on the 15th of this month.

During our conversation last night I offered to remain until the 1st of October to superintend the completion of the apparatus, but you informed me that you did not wish this.

Proposition No. 1

I have till the 1st of October to arrange my affairs. As stated yesterday, I do not feel, in view of your statement last night in regard to the matter of interest, and to the effect that Mr. Given and you had so arranged matters that he could shut the company down at any time, and in view of your statement that if the company was wound up I would have nothing to say in regard to the matter, that I would be acting wisely in doing any further work for the company without having my interests protected.

The sole and only condition under which I would feel justified in continuing work, and a condition which I feel is only fair, in view of the fact that the sole assets of the company consist of my inventions, for which the company has never paid a cent, and the orders obtained by the company which were secured by the men whose services I obtained for the company, and based on my inventions and work, which also the company has paid nothing, is this:

That the $330,000 which the company is to pay me for my patents be secured me as a first lien, bearing 6% interest, upon the patents themselves.

This sum represents 2% of the total investment, and as I have placed the company in a good position and am not bound to it in any way whatsoever, by contract or otherwise, it is purely a business proposition for you to accept or reject.

I would be unable to consider any modification of this

proposition except that during the first year I would be willing to refund one-half ($\frac{1}{2}$) of the interest to the company, and I would not ask any salary.

As above mentioned it will be necessary for me to have the matter decided one way or the other, and all papers signed, provided any arrangements are made, by Oct. 1st, 1908.

Proposition No. 2

Should you not care to accept this proposition, I shall be glad to buy either you or Mr. Given, or both, out, as I have offered before. I should much prefer that you should remain with the company, because the amount of business coming in under the new business policy, and the business in immediate prospect, although only a few openings have been touched, indicates that the operations of the company will be exceedingly profitable.

Proposition No. 3

Failing acceptance of either of these two propositions I propose that we amicably arrange to have the company placed in a receiver's hands.

I believe that a receiver could manage the business in a satisfactory manner considering the good condition I have left things in.

Any attempt, such as proposed last night, to wind up the company without consulting me, would be met immediately by me placing my interests in the hands of a syndicate, and applying for a receiver. In view of the number of circumstances, including the fact that the company has never paid me a cent for my patents and the discrimination which has been placed upon the various indebtednesses to the company, I am informed there would not be the least doubt but that my motion would be granted.

Yours very truly
(signed) R. A. Fessenden."

Colonel Firth arrived in Pittsburgh from New York and acted as mediator between Walker and Fessenden; as a result Walker, President of the Company, agreed to the Fessenden terms.

The contract signed by Walker and Fessenden took the form of a letter to Colonel Firth.

Sept. 12, 1908.

"Col. John Firth,
Fort Pitt Hotel,
Pittsburgh, Pa.
Dear Sir;—

After considering the demands of Professor Fessenden in regard to the National Electric Signaling Co., which I understand in a general way to be:

FIRST:—That the $330,000 that under our contract is a deferred payment without interest, to be paid out of the first profits, be put upon an equal basis to the money advanced on promissory notes by Mr. Given and myself—I will agree to this proposition to date from the time the Fruit Co. contract was signed, and think the best way to do this is by the issuance of 6% per annum preferred stock as of that date.

Whenever the company accumulates a surplus of $100,000 of cash in bank, then immediately they are to appropriate all such balance over a working balance of $50,000 to the purchase of preferred stock in pro rata proportion among the holders thereof.

SECOND:—Hereafter, or say from September 1st, Prof. Fessenden to receive a salary of $600 per month.

THIRD:—Messrs. Given and Walker to advance from time to time if it should be needed, a further sum of money up to $50,000 to construct stations under contract and provide funds for the running expenses of the company, they to receive notes for said advances bearing interest at 6%, said notes to be paid out of first receipts of money received on account of various contracts.

FOURTH:—It is further agreed that all questions of policy in the company, or all questions as to the erection of new stations, or all questions of licensing subsidiary companies or all questions of patent suits shall be voted upon by the stockholders according to their holdings, and should any difference arise between the majority and a minority amounting to 25% of the stock then the question shall be referred to an arbitrator, and it is hereby agreed that the present arbitrator shall be Col. John Firth, but, either side can ask for a new arbitrator at any time to be appointed by both sides in the usual way.

It is also understood that any or all questions that may arise in the company shall be covered by this arbitration clause.

Sept. 12, 1908.   (signed) Hay Walker Jr.
           accepted (signed) Reginald A. Fessenden"
Witness to both Signatures
           (signed) John Firth."

"It is understood that the clause above providing for the issue of preferred stock for the debts, and other obligations of the company is to include all money payable by the company under its contracts with accrued interest on such obligations as call for interest.

           Hay Walker Jr.
           R. A. Fessenden."

It had been a sharp fight but Fessenden knew that he must stand his ground. Thereafter he shook from his mind all irritating financial disputes. The Company's debt to him was on the same footing as its debt to Given and Walker. They were shrewd financiers enough to make sure of getting 'their own back,' therefore his, (Fessenden's) share was safe too, and untroubled, he could now take up once more work that really mattered.

He returned to Brant Rock relieved and relaxed. Knowing the effort it had cost him, he gave me his copy of the contract with the caution "Put it somewhere where it will be safe."

CHAPTER XVII

SERVICE ABROAD

VARIOUS MATTERS HAD delayed decision as to the re-building of Machrihanish Tower. For one thing Brant Rock was constantly busy expanding the range of its wireless telephone, first to Plymouth, then to Jamaica, L. I., then to Washington, D. C. Another reason was that Fessenden was on the trail of a new type of antenna *which he called the Horizontal Antenna,* which he believed would obviate the costly and more vulnerable tower type. More important still, a crisis loomed ahead in the matter of obtaining commercial licenses or concessions.

At a meeting of Colonial Premiers in London in 1909 a resolution was passed to the effect that the British Government should establish trans-Atlantic and trans-Pacific government wireless stations; a similar resolution was passed by the Imperial Institute of Journalists. The British Postmaster General thereupon announced in Parliament that the Government would make trans-oceanic wireless telegraphy a government monopoly and a similar statement was made by another cabinet minister.

Reg had long realized the disabilities under which an American Company would labor if the British Government imposed such restrictions and in anticipation of this possibility, the Fessenden Wireless Company of Canada had been formed with a distinguished and influential directorate—Sir Frederick Borden, Colonel F. Minden Cole, Mr. Gear, President of the Montreal Board of Trade and Chairman of the Shipping Federation of Canada, and Mr. G. W. Stephen, President of the Montreal Harbor Commission. Through them Lord Strathcona interested himself in London on behalf of the Canadian Company and Mr. McNab of the Montreal 'Star' enlisted the interest of Lord Northcliffe. The gentlemen of the Directorate were prepared to bring pressure to bear where and when needed.

When the policy of Government Monopoly was announced in London, Walker and Given instructed their British agent to apply for a license, but it was then too late and the license was refused. At the same time the matter of sending Colonel Cole and Mr. McNab to Newfoundland to try for a concession was considered. As the seriousness of the situation became apparent, Walker and Given decided that Fessenden himself must go to London to see what could be done.

But Fessenden by this time was in a precarious physical condition. The years of intense concentration and strain were taking their toll and his doctor had warned him that he must have a prolonged rest. Arterial pressure was nearly double what it should be and twice he had been refused as a risk by insurance companies.

Incredulous of this, Mr. Walker insisted on going with him to an insurance company and when this condition was confirmed he suggested that Fessenden should go to Muldoon's whose training methods had become famous and who numbered among his grateful patients, many high pressured workers. Reg agreed, and after some days of intensive patent work, bringing all applications up to date, and outlining schedules of work for the various department heads, he left for White Plains.

In one respect Muldoon certainly could guarantee 100 per cent results and that was in obliterating past problems and perplexities. He saw to it that diversified exercise pushed to the limit of endurance, drained a man of every concern except the one grim resolve to stick it. As Reg wrote, "Muldoon keeps close watch on the men and runs them up to the limit, the very limit, but not beyond" and the intervals between exercise were passed in a sort of torpor to make ready for the next effort.

Reg never did anything half-heartedly and after the first few days of training he was coming in with the first batch from the seven and ten mile walks and runs. Three weeks of this training from February 3 to 24, benefited him vastly. On leaving he plunged at once into final preparations for the English trip.

There were conferences with Given and Walker, two separate trips to Washington, and between times at Brant Rock, planning for an absence of several months. I was to accompany him and Reg had imposed the condition that the expenses of my trip as well as his own should be paid by the Company.

At Brant Rock all department heads were made responsible for their own departments. Miss Bent, the secretary, was in charge of the office and to her kind and efficient care we likewise entrusted 'Mikums,' not such an easy task as he had already been in hospital for some obscure ailment and the days of his prime were passing.

This trip involved more than obtaining a license. Both Given and Walker were now convinced of the necessity of forming an English Company and Fessenden's mission was an onerous one.

At last, on March 12, we sailed on the S. S. Adriatic for Southampton—our cabin filled with roses and fruit from the staff at Brant Rock and from other friends and a sheaf of last minute messages, farewells and good wishes.

Three pleasant and helpful contacts of the voyage were with the Hon. Mr. E. C. Grenfell, English representative of J. P. Morgan & Son, Mr. Christopher Turner and Mr. Sutherland Macklem of Niagara Falls, an old friend of the Fessenden family.

On reaching London a suite was engaged at Claridge's, Brook Street, that hostelry of Royalty, and here Reg remained for the entire seven months of his English visit. This was in line with his standard way of attacking any problem,—to be satisfied with nothing less than the best. He expected to meet and to match his ability with the highest in British Officialdom. The vantage ground from which he launched his campaign must therefore be above criticism. His letters of introduction from the State Department at Washington, from Ottawa and from Montreal could not be improved on.

Recalling the succession of events with which he inaugurated his undertaking, it is seen that within three weeks of his arrival he had accomplished the followings:—As host at lunch he met his patent solicitors in conference to discuss his line of action. He had met U.S. Ambassador Reid, First Secretary Mr. Phillips and Naval Attache Commander Simpson. He had called at the Colonial Office and presented a letter of introduction to Mr. Cunningham, the Secretary of Lord Crewe. He had met Mr. Johnson in charge of Colonial Permits and with him planned the proper procedure for presenting a Plea or Memorandum before the Royal Commission. There had been two interviews at Whitehall, meeting first Mr. Beddersley, Chief Secretary of the First Lord of the Admiralty, then the chief officer in charge of wireless work. He had had a long and satisfactory interview with Mr. Sidney Buxton who made an appointment for him with the Post Master General.

He drafted and redrafted the Memorandum and presented the final draft at the Colonial Office. He attended two banquets, one in honor of Sir John Murray and the Michael Sars expedition given by the Atlantic Union, the other that of the Chartered Institute of Patent Agents. And all this with Oxford and Cambridge boat race day, Good Friday, Saturday and Easter Sunday and Monday Bank Holiday, intervening.

Then came King Edward's sudden illness with its fatal termination and the complete halt to negotiations of every kind. During this interlude, Reg went to Cambridge for a few days to confer with the Cambridge Instrument Company on some preliminary work being done by that firm on his Pherescope. While there, he was entertained by Sir J. J. Thomson, Mr. Darwin and Mr. Wood, dined at Trinity and Caius and returned to London, May 19, the day before the King's Funeral.

With an unprecedented concentration of Royalty in London, Claridge's became a minor Court. Its rubber-paved porte cochere presented endless comings and goings, and to and fro in lobbies and corridors passed dignitaries of every race and nation, their uniforms and robes of state of unparalleled splendor.

The pageantry of London is always arresting, but the gorgeously somber spectacle of that Lying in State is unforgettable. By comparison the Funeral Procession itself was almost gala with every Emperor, King and Princeling present in person or by proxy and each bursting with his own importance.

The Lying in State was the tribute of the people and I wanted to become a part of London for it. Alone, I joined that moving U-shaped stream whose constantly augmented flow started near the Abbey, extended mile after mile to Vauxhall Bridge, turned there on itself to flow back slowly, silently, till St. Margaret's Chapel was reached. Muted and tense the living stream entered the upper level of the great chapel and for a moment looked down on the mortal remains of The King, then passed on.

At each corner of the Bier stood King's Orderlies, bronzed, bowed, motionless figures, picked Ghurka Officers. Two of them we had met a short time before at the home of a friend where they had called to pay their respects to the family of their Colonel's lady who had died in their far-off land.

Very appreciatively they had eyed Reg's stalwart figure and through the interpreter conveyed to him a genial invitation to be on their side if he ever felt inclined to do any fighting. Linked with my recollection of these native Indian Officers is a wisp of talk of a mutual Masonic grip, but that is vague.

With funeral ceremonies over it was possible to resume work on the dual task of overcoming Government opposition and sizing up desirable and available men or concerns for the English Company. In the latter connection Reg was already in touch with the Dunlop Tire Company, with the engineers of the Maxim Company and, through friends, had met a former Government Official eminently fitted to pilot a young concern through official shoals—Sir Montague Ommanney who for many years had been Permanent Secretary for the Colonies. He was approached and was very favorably inclined.

Through Sir Montague, another bit of pageantry fell my lucky way—attendance at the annual meeting in St. Paul's Cathedral of the Knights of St. Michael and St. George. In this Order, Sir Montague Ommanney was 'King at Arms' and next in official rank to King George. He came up from the country for the event and was guest at my friend's home. We, (my friend and I) had the feminine thrill of tying the shoulder ribbons that held the massive gold chain of his order. Since Sir Montague had only one guest card of admission, my friend unselfishly insisted that I should be the one to use it, so for an hour I rubbed shoulders with the Great of England, great by inheritance but also and very largely great by accomplishment in service of Empire. It may be incorrect to term it a memorial service though my recollection is that part of the ceremony was the placing of Banners of those of their Order dead within the year, on the walls of the private chapel of their Order in St. Paul's, but in any case it was Pageantry to the Nth degree.

Another glint of what might be termed Pageantry lingers in my mind in connection with London banks. Beside the elbow of each paying teller was a pile of golden sovereigns and a gleaming brass shovel. As a check was presented for payment the clerk nonchalantly scooped up an abundant measure of coins and shook out the required amount like sugar at the grocery store. In these lean, gaunt years of depression and financial restrictions this memory strikes a note of lavishness but at the same time of finality for its dirge has sounded and we intone 'sic transit.'

Reg had called once or twice on Lord Strathcona and on the occasion of his Lordship's reception to ex-President Theodore Roosevelt, we received invitations. The typical Roosevelt greeting was in evidence, beaming teeth and vigorous handclasp, but we recalled the while that he had turned down House Bill No. 184 for a petty grudge. Contrasted with all this vigor was the silent, aloof little old lady who was his hostess—Lady Strathcona—the American Indian who became the wife of young Donald Smith during his ten years as factor in the Hudson Bay Territory. With keen black eyes that were aware of her guests and with attentive grandchildren to bridge the intangible gap, she was in but not of this crowded gathering and except with intimates was as remote as the Sphinx.

At a dinner in honor of Sir George Reid at which Lord Strathcona presided, Reg was asked to speak and to propose a toast to the Atlantic Union, coupled with the name of the Bishop of Norwich. In this speech his theme was "Natural Resources" and of this he chose to say—"The true and only natural resources of a nation are its men." This was his fundamental article of faith.

We were also invited to a Dominion Day dinner given by Lord and Lady Strathcona. There, Reg met Lord Crewe, Lord Balfour and Sir George Reid. Lord Balfour told Reg at that time that the Commission would be unanimous in recommending that his permit for a wireless license should be granted.

It was now however mid-June and Reg was alone. His mission owing to the King's death had dragged on longer than anticipated and I was uncomfortably aware of being an added expense to the company. Ken was graduating from Andover with highest honors for Yale entrance examination and after that had nowhere to go, so it had seemed best for me to return alone to the States and to have him join me in a summer vacation in Bermuda.

Reg's letters must tell the rest of the story. He established very cordial relations with the editorial and engineering departments of the London Times, also with the Editor of the Morning Post.

"June 17. I saw Johnson (Colonial Permits) yesterday and he said that the Colonial Office intends making me a proposition. I am going to find out what it is, later, when the Commission put in their report, so as to let them know whether we can accept it before they formally make it. This will be better than letting them make it and then turning it down."

"June 22. Fielding is over and I have got the correspondence up for Balfour and seen Cowell several times, also Strathcona. Think I shall pull it through."

"July 18. I do not like the idea of Ken going sailing. It is very funny—whenever I come across anything that is really dangerous I never feel satisfied till I am doing it and getting all the thrill out of it that there is in it. Often and often I have gone ahead when I felt absolutely certain that I was going to be killed. But I hate like anything to see or think of other people running any risks. If he does go out make sure that there are enough life preservers on the boat and GOOD ONES, not like the old hay-stuffed one that I had to save from sinking to the bottom when it should have been holding me up."

"The Lorentz Company of Germany sent a representative over to see me (in regard to taking up the Fessenden System in Germany). I have been preparing a full statement of our patent situation also of the wireless situation generally, for them."

"July 28. Am going up to Cambridge for a few days to see the Cambridge Instrument Company, and also Prof. J. J. Thompson. The new instruments I designed should be coming along and I want to see them, also I want to see J. J. about some mathematical things. I may go to Machrihanish for a few days."

"Aug. 28. This week, Lemieux, the Canadian Postmaster General, is coming over on his way to South Africa. He will see the English Postmaster General about the cable companies and I want to see him first. It is pretty important that I should, as although I have the Commission on my side, a good deal will depend on what he says. I have been hard at work getting my arguments for the Colonial Office in final form. The Commission's report is finished but will not be published for another week.—The legal expert whom I saw (of the Commission) asked me if I did not intend making an exception in favor of any of the cable companies. I knew what he meant for Lord Balfour is Chairman of one of the cable companies in Panama etc. and I had taken the bull by the horns and told Lord Balfour that I was sorry our interests were opposed. So he said at once that that made no difference and that as far as he was concerned he had no objection to our competing.

Ordinarily, of course, I would look on such a statement as a bluff, but I can tell about men pretty well, and I think he was entirely open and honest. So when we come to settle up things I am going to fix up his company on the ground floor, but, of course, I have not told anyone this, especially not Lord Balfour. So when the expert asked me that, I told him 'No', then went on and said I supposed he referred to Lord Balfour's company which he did not deny, and then told him of my conversation with Lord Balfour. Incidentally, I got out of him the chief arguments of the cable companies. But this goes to show how things are run here. If in the States a Committee was formed and one of the Committee was interested financially in the matter under consideration, wouldn't there be a howl in the newspapers and wouldn't the man be fired from the Senate!"

In the doldrums of August he went down to Canterbury for a week, to browse around old St. Martin's church and find out what he could of the place where his family had its beginnings. He needed to be away from London and the burden of his task, for in one letter he had written "if I could ever get mentally rested"—and in another "I am getting very weary, more so since you left."

Sept. 7. I have just got back from Sheffield where I went for the British Association. I wanted to see Thompson, also to present a paper on "Storage of Power". The Times had been after me for a long time for an article on it, as you know, so in order not to break my rule of never giving out a discovery to the newspapers until it had been presented to some scientific body, I took advantage of the B. A. meeting. I sent you some clippings.

It was well enough received by the meeting but it was a fizzle in one respect. I had gone into details and given exact figures for everything, prices of machines, cost of power etc. I had hoped for a good discussion to bring out all the points. But not a single soul seemed to know anything about large scale power work. This to some extent explains why all the big power plants in South Africa and India are built by U. S. or Canadian engineers.

But I was disappointed at the total ignorance displayed. Not a single definite criticism was made. Sir William White, the big battleship designer, was the only man who referred to the figures at all and all he said was that caution should be taken in accepting the figures, as they might be too low. When I asked him to say which ones he referred to, he said he could not say any particular figures but was merely making a general statement as to the necessity of caution. He then said that there were some figures given before a parliamentary inquiry which he thought would show a higher cost for Niagara Falls power then I had taken. But I found out that these were merely my own old figures from the Power Commission. I did not wish to hurt his feelings by calling the attention of the Section to this, though I felt like it.

Altogether I was disappointed at the lack of knowledge in regard to large power plants and the absence of any useful discussion. However the paper went off O.K. and will do good in a number of ways."

". . . The reason for the delay in the work is that everybody connected with the Government goes out of town July 1 and does not come back till September 15, so nothing can be done in the meantime.

"For example, the report of the Royal Commission has not been printed yet though it was made eight weeks ago. I would have gone out of town myself but for the fact that I wanted to see Fielding and Lemieux. I had seen Fielding in July and in August, and when Lemieux came last week I saw him and he promised to work for us. I have also had my brief for the Colonial Office printed and have fixed up everything that possibly can be fixed up until the report of the Royal Commission is printed and in the hands of the Colonial Office.

It cannot be long now before I hear from the Colonial Office and have things fixed up. It is the only way to save the Company from being cut off for good and all from all opportunity of doing any cable work, so we must make some sacrifices for it."

Oct, 1. I have at last succeeded in getting a Trans-Atlantic permit, that is the Post Office has written me that they have decided to give me one and on terms that they think will be satisfactory to me. As I told them that I would not accept a short term license or one which did not make provision for a fair return if the Government decided to buy at the end of the long-term license, I am in hopes that this matter is now closed up. They state that the formal offer will be mailed me in a few days.

I got this by gradually working up and getting everything going simultaneously. I have been keeping in touch with Major O'Meara and wrote the Post Office about distributing news from a wireless station in London. This is where the P. O. loses a lot of money. They wrote back that there were other reasons (afraid they would have to discharge some employees I believe).

Then the Commission's Report came out and I asked for an interview and told them I was writing an article on it (which I had previously arranged with the Times). So I got a good discussion (two hours) of the entire situation with Sir Matthew Nathan and he finally explained that the real reason was the fear of monopoly owing to the stations interfering with each other. I offered to demonstrate that this was not the case, and got him to say that if so, I would get a license.

Then to prevent their asking for a lot of tests which would take six months time, I wrote a formal letter to the Admiralty asking them to advise the Post Office if I was right. The Admiralty was solid with me on account of my offer of two sets to the Canadian Navy and I had also seen Lemieux the Canadian Post Master General and Major O'Meara and Sir George Reid on account of Australia, so they all got together, also Sidney Buxton, and the next morning I got my notification that a license would be granted me on terms which it was thought would be considered satisfactory by me.

Such a lot of wires to pull. But everything worked like clockwork. It was a tough thing to do, to convince three Governments that their policy was wrong and should be reversed, but it is done and even if the proposed terms are not exactly what I want they can be changed easily now that the principle is settled.

You would be amused at the mixture of bluff and persuasion and apparent indifference to results which I had to put on at the interview.

The Post Office is thinking of reconsidering its decision in the matter of distributing news and may order a number of sets.

The next thing is the West Indian license. That will be easier now that the P.O. has agreed to give us our Trans-Atlantic license. The report of the Royal Commission has been issued and recommends wireless but suggests Government ownership and the Colonies buying the cables out. This recommendation was forced on the Commission by later instructions from the Colonial Office.

I will send you later my article in the Times on this subject. I think there is no doubt but that we shall get the West Indies license and that very soon."

"Oct. 20. I meant to sail on the 26th, but Mr. Samuels, the Post-master General, was away this week speechifying so I had to wait till November 2nd before sailing. Everything is coming O.K. The Post Office has agreed to everything I wanted with the single exception that they want me to take a 15 years' license and I want 20. Sir Matthew Nathan seems very reasonable however and he is going to see the P.M.G. again and will let me know in a few days.

The West India Matter is not decided yet for the Colonies have to be consulted but I think it will come out O.K. in the end as I have the Colonial Office on the jump. In fact the article I am writing for the Times may practically do away with the Colonial Office and result in the West Indies and other Colonies running their own affairs through a West Indian Commission as Canada does.

One curious result of my work is that if I wished I could become a member of parliament here for one of the Kentish districts—Conservative of course—If it were not for the fact that my inventing work is so much more important I would almost feel like doing it. On the whole, my trip has been a big success. I have saved the N.E.S. Co. for if I had not come over exactly when I did, Government would have gone too far to have gone back in the matter of making Trans-Atlantic Wireless a Government Monopoly.

I think that my visit will be a good thing in a number of

ways. For instance, when I came over all the Government officials were very strong for Government Monopolies for everything. I know I have shaken their views and there is now a reaction setting in and five years from now I think you will see that the Municipalities will begin to sell out to private companies."

As a postscript to this it may be added that a letter from Sir Matthew Nathan followed Fessenden to the States confirming the 20 year license.

CHAPTER XVIII

DESTRUCTION AT HOME

Reg arrived in New York on November 10. I met him at the dock as did Mr. Walker. We were all at the Astor Hotel, dined together and went to the theater afterwards, a very pleasant social evening with business touched on only occasionally and lightly.

It had been increasingly apparent in letters from Brant Rock during the past six months that work was not running smoothly there. Rivalries and petty jealousies had cropped up with all the lowered morale that comes when personal importance rather than the importance of the work is at stake. But Reg knew that as soon as he was on the job again, all this would disappear.

At long range he attributed this state of affairs to Mr. John Kelman, an electrical engineer whom he had met in the Pittsfield days in the Stanley Company. He had appeared to be a suitable man for General Superintendent during Fessenden's enforced absence in London and had been engaged for that purpose. Fessenden said to Walker on the evening of his return that he thought they would have to let Kelman go, but Mr. Walker said he did not agree with him.

At the Brant Rock station in addition to the lines of work laid out for the engineering staff for the summer of 1910, Dr. Cohen had been engaged on special mathematical work and Dr. Louis Austin of the Bureau of Standards had also spent the summer there, on special work. On previous occasions Dr. Austin had been afforded the facilities of the station for investigations of his own and found it particularly suited for research.

There had been outside jobs in connection with the Navy

and United Fruit Company orders. In April, two scout cruisers, the Salem and the Birmingham equipped with the Fessenden System made important tests, the chief objective of which was ship to ship, day and night communication over a distance of 1000 miles, and when possible, between ship and Brant Rock over a 3000 mile stretch.

At New Orleans the United Fruit Company had a highpowered station in course of erection which was to attempt, as a test of efficiency, transmission between New Orleans and Brant Rock.

Some difficulties had arisen at the New Orleans station so, almost before Reg had chance to analyze conditions at Brant Rock after his eight months' absence, he was obliged to leave for New Orleans.

He quickly found out the trouble, corrected it and in two or three weeks established successful wireless transmission between Brant Rock, Massachusetts and New Orleans, Louisiana, a distance, *over land,* of 1600 miles, this being a feat heretofore believed to be impossible. He returned to Brant Rock only a short time before Christmas.

On December 24 a long distance 'phone call came from Mr. Walker asking Fessenden to come to Pittsburgh for a conference. Reg answered that he would come as soon after Christmas as possible.

On December 26 came the following telegram: "On account of other engagements must know what day you will be here. Wire answer. (Signed) Hay Walker Jr." Fessenden replied "Arrive Thursday morning, telegraph if satisfactory. Had intended arriving Wednesday but delayed account important patent and other business."

Accordingly he left for Pittsburgh on the afternoon of the 28th. Everything went on as usual at the station until just before the noon hour on the 29th, when Mr. Kelman came to the office and showed the head stenographer a written order addressed to Kelman.

The authorization which he showed was signed by Hay Walker Jr., President. The instructions were to the effect that it had been decided to discontinue the Brant Rock Office. That all papers, records, etc. in the office should be packed and shipped to A. E. Braun, Treasurer as legal custodian of same. That particular care must be taken to obtain all papers in the safe and, if it could not be unlocked, to ship the safe itself.

This extraordinary notice was brought at once to my attention.

I talked with Mr. Kelman and told him that while it might be perfectly sound Company policy for the records and papers to be transferred to Pittsburgh, this order, coming as it did with such surprising suddenness, could not be carried out until we had consulted Professor Fessenden by telephone in Pittsburgh.

Mr. Kelman agreed to wait till this could be done.

We immediately put in a long distance call for Fessenden at the Farmers' National Bank, Pittsburgh. Promptly the answer came back that Professor Fessenden was not at the Farmers' Bank Building and it was not known where he was.

At half-hour intervals we renewed the call, always with the same reply.

Then we put in a call for Mr. Clay, the Pittsburgh patent attorney. He answered the 'phone himself and I told him that it was extremely urgent for us to get in touch with Professor Fessenden—that he was reported not to be at the Farmers' Bank and would he personally institute a search for him and tell him to call Brant Rock. This he promised he would do.

About 2.30 Kelman came again to the office from the wireless station, this time accompanied by two strangers. These men, we afterwards learned, were detectives hired for the job, who had been introduced at the plant as construction men. He said he would now proceed to carry out his orders.

There were two stenographers and myself in the office and we knew that we could not hold three husky men at bay; nevertheless I told Mr. Kelman he would have to use force. With my back against the largest set of file shelves,

I stood with arms stretched out across them. There was some vague notion in my mind that if they used physical force some legal advantage would accrue to the victim.

Both stenographers were more than willing to help but I did not wish for any employee to run counter to a company order without permission from Professor Fessenden. So I clutched the shelves until my grip was forcibly loosened; then Kelman and his gang started to carry out the box files.

At any moment a call might come from Reg, so delay was essential, if not by force then by strategy, and I demanded that each box file should be sealed and initialled by the stenographers as a safeguard against the contents being tampered with. This gained half an hour or so and all the while our call kept going through to Pittsburgh and always with the same response.

When perhaps a third of the files had been removed the men apparently thought that we would offer no further resistance for all three of them were out of the office at the same moment. We saw our chance, slammed and locked the door in their faces and carried the balance of the files to my bedroom.

By this time the men at the station were buzzing like a hive of angry bees. They had given but scant allegiance to Kelman at best, and now still less. But what could they do? They knew of the President's order—but they took orders from Professor Fessenden—only he couldn't be reached to give orders in this emergency. What to do?

Five o'clock; work shut down; the men went home to their suppers.

About six the 'phone rang. I answered and it was Reg. He began as usual—"Hello dear, is that you? Have you pencil and paper?" meaning to give instructions about sending one of the men to New Orleans. He got no further with his instructions for I burst in with my story of what had happened and told him we had been trying to reach him all afternoon by 'phone.

"Why" he said "I've been in the room next to the telephone exchange all day." All day he had been at the Bank in conference, friendly conference as he supposed, with Given and Walker, and all telephone calls had been kept from him.

He just *happened* to call up Brant Rock.

When he learned of the removal of the files through Walker's order to Kelman he said—"Hold the 'phone a moment," and went back into the room to hurl at Given and Walker the charge—"Well, you've done it now." Then turning his back upon them he came again to the telephone and told me "Don't let a paper get away—get a lawyer and find out what to do to hold things till I get there."

THOSE WERE ORDERS.

The men rallied round and had themselves sworn in as special police by our landlord, Mr. Blackman, who had authority for this.

All evening they patrolled the plant with rifles and shot guns, for most of them went hunting now and then. Kelman meanwhile was packing the loot and planning for its transportation. Two local trucking firms were called; one refused point blank to touch the shipment, the other came but turned tail when I warned him that he would be a party to the theft if he transported the boxes.

At the office we were keeping the telephone wires hot in our efforts to get the necessary legal advice. A Boston lawyer who had done some minor work for the company was reached and he said we must get the county sheriff to put an attachment on the boxes of files. But easier said than done to locate a society sheriff, twelve miles away, in mid-evening of holiday week.

By dint of every urgency we could think of he was found at last and we tore an unwilling officer of the law from a dinner party. By 11 P.M. the boxes were under attachment, under guard and the first skirmish won.

This may seem like melodrama at which in the 'movies' we would turn up our noses, but for us it was a desperate and crucial struggle to hold fast to the results of twelve years of supreme effort of a man who was one of the master minds of his age.

Meantime, in Pittsburgh, Fessenden was finding that this was more than a one-act play. Hardly had he returned to his hotel to fetch bags and catch the night train for Boston than he was served with notice of an injunction brought by the Company against him to enjoin him from further participation in the affairs of the Company. The papers in this action were drawn up in complete readiness in NOVEMBER 1910 in the jurisdiction of Pittsburgh and were calculated to hold him in Pittsburgh till the Brant Rock 'coup' was accomplished.

But Reg, in a whirlwind series of moves, found a lawyer, dictated a comprehensive argument to outline his case and satisfy the court and caught the night train for Boston.

I met him there the next morning having carried out our plan of the previous night to transfer our personal account from the bank where the Company also had an account. We feared that in some way our small savings might be attached and thus leave us even more defenseless.

On January 8, 1911 Fessenden received telegraphic notice of his dismissal from the Company.

He could beyond doubt count on his men, for with fine loyalty they had resigned in a body in protest. But he could not possibly run the Brant Rock station on his own funds and the only thing to do was to leave and bring suit for breach of the contract of September 12, 1908.

A judicial minded public is not interested in the details of personal fights but this much has been written to disclose the essential facts and to convince, if truth can convince.

Our feet were set on that grim road which many an inventor had already trodden.

Would it lead us at last to the heights or to the depths?

CHAPTER XIX

DUST AND ASHES

On January 22, 1911 we bade farewell to Western Tower and to the Brant Rock station and found temporary quarters in Boston. Ken had gone back to Yale, we hoped it might be possible to keep him there, at least to wait until impossibility confronted us.

Those who have watched their life's work crash down to negation will know how utterly our world had gone to pieces. Even poor little Mikums caught by impending doom had died early in January and we had buried him beside the concrete base of one of the guy anchors of the Tower.

We did not delude ourselves about the hazards of the legal fight we proposed to make. However just our cause there were terrible odds against us—odds of great wealth and of political power—and the outcome lay 'in the lap of the gods.' But, come what might, we must fight and we made this pact with ourselves—to exhaust to the utmost limit our own resources but neither to seek nor to accept financial aid from anyone.

From January 1911 to May 1912 an endless succession of futile and expensive legal proceedings hampered us. Attachments and sheriff's fees—bills from lawyers for advising us that we *hadn't* a case—from other lawyers who found, mirabile dictu, that we *had* a case—preliminary hearings—postponements—affidavits—preparation of and printing of briefs—injunctions—appointment of a Master—examinations and cross-examinations—all the weary round of actions with which the law crucifies those who have to seek its help.

To prepare for these hearings required prodigious effort

on our part. All our files were in storage, in packing cases, and though the contents of each case were listed for reference, the mere physical task of consulting files was exhausting—it was always the packing case at the bottom of the heap that needed to be opened up. Every fresh list of wanted papers acquired all the horrors of a nightmare; more often than not, it was an emergency call that demanded an all night session of work till the data was assembled and the argument written.

Throughout this period the marked prudence of scientific friends and acquaintances impressed me deeply. A crude acrostic welled up in my heart to express the equation.

F R I E N D—Take away my first and my last and you have in French my equivalent.

Sharp and clear-cut as was the break with the N.E.S. Co., echoes of the Company's activities reached us from time to time. A number of the employees resumed their jobs, some, driven by necessity, some by a keen sense of expediency. A stalwart few kept the faith and sought new connections.

Mr. Stein was offered the job of General Manager to replace Fessenden, but declined.

Mr. Kintner on the other hand, ex-Fessenden student, ex-Fessenden assistant, successor to Fessenden in the chair of Electrical Engineering at Western University, vacation job hunter at Fessenden Laboratories, with an alacrity singularly free from restraining memories, resigned his position with the Westinghouse Company to accept the vacant post.

Patent complications were of course numerous and in the matter of new applications emanating from the N.E.S. Co. amusing situations arose. The new brooms must justify themselves in office and, from afar, we noted the delving into the scrap bag of abandoned Fessenden applications for claims on which to base new applications—the searchers often unaware of the fact that such claims existed already in other Fessenden patents.

There was a touch of Gilbertian humor in the way these were shared around to make a good showing:—

> "with one for him and one for he,
> and one for you and one for ye
> but never oh never a one for me."

Our immediate goal was trial by jury in the Massachusetts Courts.

Recourse to every possible postponement was taken by our opponents thereby frustrating our hopes of getting the case placed on the 1911 Fall docket.

Ebb tide in our funds set in stronger and stronger.

Ken had left college and found a job.

For the first time in our lives since childhood Christmas passed without a gift or a card from us to anyone.

Reg, whose nature was always lavish and constructive and which led him to spend in order to produce rather than to save by stinting and penny-paring, even he in those days put the pressure of economy upon himself to keep expenditures to the minimum.

Our last source of income was tapped—i.e. loans on our life insurance policies, the premiums on which for a period of fifteen years had been paid with unfailing regularity and promptness.

But here, because of a clause which made our son a joint beneficiary, he being still a minor, we met with such grudging and obstructive tactics and rulings on the part of the company in which we were insured, that for several months we despaired of overcoming the difficulties placed in our way. Innumerable interviews with the agent, legal help, conferences with the State Commissioner, and a considerable expenditure of money, all were required before the loan was obtained.

But May of 1912 brought the desired climax. Colonel Firth's testimony and cross examination on the September 12, 1908 letter had been taken earlier in New York and was in strong support of our claim that said Letter was intended as and constituted a Contract.

The case before the jury began on Friday, May 3, 1912 and the four men whose word was opposed to Fessenden's confronted us—Given, Walker, Braun and Wolcott. We did not know whether Wolcott was an involuntary witness by subpeona or whether he was convinced that Fessenden could not possibly win against Given and Walker and that his only hope lay in throwing in his lot with the stronger party.

The case lasted till Monday, May 13—contested every inch of the way—and at 8 P.M. of that day the jury returned a unanimous verdict in our favor and for the entire amount $406,175.00.

The relief was enormous. Those iron bands around the heart of the Faithful Henry of Fairy Tale pressed no harder on him than the clutching anxiety of the past seventeen months on us. It seemed almost too good to be true—and it was.

Judgment was entered in August for the amount above stated with costs, whereupon the N.E.S. Co. sued out a writ of error asking an injunction against execution of judgment.

Further tedious delays until January 24, 1913 when the attorney for the N.E.S. Co. made his argument before the Bench, Judges Brown, Hale and Aldrich sitting. On January 30 our attorney made his argument. Some advantage may have lain with our opponents at this time because the N.E.S. Co. had brought a new attorney into the case who could take a fresh grip on the subject whereas our own very fine lawyer had of necessity given his splendid best at the jury trial.

Then followed silence until the oracles of the law should speak. This was not until August 23, a lapse of seven months, and then the disheartening news was that a dissenting opinion had been handed down—Judges Brown and Hale against us—Judge Aldrich for us.

Meantime to safeguard itself the N.E.S. Co. in July 1912 had petitioned for a receivership and their own General Manager, Kintner, was appointed receiver and one, Barrett, appointed with him.

A rehearing was possible, a new trial by jury was possible but in reality the situation was one of stalemate. A chronological abstract of court actions and negotiations in this litigation shows hardly a month in the period 1911-1916 that is free from some phase of the conflict which was wearing us down and getting us nowhere.

In October 1914 the Marconi Company faced the necessity of working under Fessenden patents and therefore sought to negotiate an agreement with the N.E.S. Co. whereby all Fessenden's wireless patents could be licensed to the Marconi Company. Fessenden had assigned the U.S. patents to the N.E.S. Co. but a large number of his foreign patents were still unassigned and these, equally with the U.S. patents, covered the basic and fundamental radio inventions.

The N.E.S. Co.'s receivers in their deal with the Marconi Company had deposited $20,000 with the Marconi Company as guarantee of having good and valid title to the Fessenden patents. In order to avoid forfeiture of this deposit and to continue to receive large royalties from the Marconi Company it was necessary for the N.E.S. Co. to secure proper assignment of the foreign patents from Fessenden.

By this time, Fessenden was actively engaged in another field of work. He wanted to be free to bring the full force of his ability and achievements to this new yet allied art. So in response to the demand of the N.E.S. Co. for assignment of foreign patents, Fessenden proposed sweeping and inclusive concessions on his part—withdrawal of all litigation, assignment of all foreign patents, surrender of stock and of money claims and a complete cessation of hostilities. In return he required a *License* to use his own patents.

Endless bickering and arguing. But the nub of the consideration for this comprehensive withdrawal on Fessenden's part was fully understood by everyone concerned—*License to use his own Patents.*

It was claimed that such a license could not be granted as long as the company was in the hands of receivers but as it was only a matter of a few months before reorganization would be completed the license would then be granted.

Matters dragged on till October 19, 1916. At that time photostat copies of some Fessenden note books were required by the N.E.S. Co. and Fessenden took this opportunity to stipulate in writing that the license to use his own patents previously discussed should be confirmed. After considerable discussion this stipulation was informally O-Ked and signed by Kintner as Receiver on October 19, 1916—a final agreement made by the N.E.S. Co. destined, as all the others had been, to be broken—for this license was never granted.

Thus the echoes of this conflict fade for the time being into the background.

CHAPTER XX

POWER AND POWER–STORAGE

THE ARID AND FUTILE legal preoccupations of this period had to be endured and prosecuted with all the energy and ability that Reg possessed, but this alone could not satisfy him. He might be blocked and frustrated in one line of effort and until the debris of that wreck cleared away he must turn to something else, for never would he yield to disaster. Always a remedy could be found, a difficulty overcome and still his old philosophy of the days when he tramped the streets of New York guided him. "The more things you try and the quicker you try them, the sooner you find the solution."

Whatever this solution might be it must be work that would bring benefit to mankind and this he conceived to be Power—Horsepower energy, that should labor for the world, that should be available everywhere, to everyone, in the simplest form and at the lowest cost.

This was a job that had inspiration and purpose in it and it was also an old love coming to his help in his hour of need. For back in 1898, the American Electrician published a short article of his "A Sun Storage Battery" which shows that he, like many another before him was attracted by the problem of putting to work the intermittent forces of nature, sun, wind and tides.

This problem had stayed with him, turning and taking shape in his mind. A strong impetus had been given it in 1904 when he was asked to be the technical member of the Commission then forming to consider municipal development of power at Niagara Falls, later known as the Ontario Power Commission.

This invitation coming from the land of his birth and

early training pleased him very much. Also the project it involved of cheap power to an extended community was a matter of deep interest, so he accepted gladly though greatly overburdened with work.

The first conference took place at Toronto on January 30, 1905. The five Commissioners—E. W. B. Snider, Chairman, P. W. Ellis, W. F. Cockshutt, A. Beck, R. A. Fessenden and the consulting engineers Messrs. Ross and Holgate at this meeting considered the entire problem and each assumed his share of the undertaking.

Considerable investigation, correspondence and a further general conference in the summer of 1905 followed: Then sub-reports were drawn up and embodied in the final Commissioners' Report of March 1906.

Reg always took much pride in being connected with this great and successful enterprise. His special report to the Commission reviewed the following considerations:—

Cheap Power
Niagara Falls
The aesthetic value of Niagara Falls
The incidental advantages of the use of Electrical Power
Engineering Undertakings considered in relation to State and Municipal Control
Is the Generation at, and the Transmission of Power from Niagara Falls by the Municipalities advisable from an Engineering Standpoint?
Loss of Capital through New Developments
Is the Operation by the Municipalities of Lighting Plants advisable from an Engineering Standpoint?
The Engineering Features of the Proposed Undertaking
The Estimates of the Proposed Undertaking, Power Plant, Transmission Lines and Distribution
Estimate of Cost of Power
Electric Lighting Estimates
Load Curves
Electricity as a Heating Agent

Fessenden's views on State and Municipal control of public Utilities were very positive. He believed it to be absolutely sound that the State or Municipality should control these utilities *through its powers as a Landlord,* but for the State actually to engage in such undertakings was another matter and, from an engineering standpoint, only desirable for such undertakings in which there is no immediate prospect of or need for improved methods.

Power development and transmission as proposed for Niagara Falls came, he believed, under this heading and was therefore a proper Municipal activity.

Lighting on the other hand did not, in his opinion, fall within this class because it was an art still in a state of Flux and Change and therefore liable to heavy losses on superseded methods. Where such an undertaking by State or Municipality was a necessity he urged that large financial provision for possible future developments be made.

Enormous benefits accrued to the districts that could be supplied with Power from this source, but not many parts of the world have a Niagara to draw from nor yet the simpler requirement of suitable high hills where suitable reservoirs could be created to simulate smaller Niagaras.

One cubic yard of water at a gravitational potential of 1000 feet gives one Horse Power Hour. Hydraulic head was the obvious answer for Power. But the real problem was Storage. Cheapness of Storage is more important than efficiency of generation. Fessenden felt that universal cheap power must be achieved somehow but for a time the thing 'hung fire' till the answer came to him and in 1907 he applied for a patent on a System of Storing Power.

A part of the specification of this application reads as follows:—

> "Applicant has now discovered a new instrument for storage of power which is applicable irrespective of locality and by which intermittent power may be stored at an annual cost of less than one-tenth of the cost of generation from coal.—This instrument, never before suggested or published is extremely simple in its nature and corresponds, in the simplicity of the method to the historical change of the eye of the needle from its end to its point. It consists in

making every point on the earth's surface the top of a hill by placing the upper reservoir, not on a tower or on the top of a hill, but at or near the earth's surface and placing the lower reservoir, not on the surface of the earth, but subterraneously, so as to have a high negative gravitational potential with reference to the earth's surface. This apparatus enables, for the first time, power to be stored for general power purposes."

This application met with many vicissitudes in the patent office and required a brief on appeal before the Commissioner, but after ten years it was finally granted November 20, 1917. No. 1,246,520.

Another patent forming part of this Power Storage Group is No. 1,217,165 which has particular application to generation of power from the sun's rays.

In September 1910 as already shown by extracts from Fessenden's letters from England, this method was fully discussed in a paper read before the Sheffield meeting of the British Association. His disappointment at the lack of discussion or constructive criticism, apparently because of unfamiliarity with the subject, will be recalled. It received however considerable press notice. The London Times, Sep. 8, 1910 published the paper in full with a further review in the Times Engineering Supplement, Sep. 14, 1910. The Illustrated London News in its September issue gave a full-page diagram with descriptive text. So to some extent the public had become acquainted with this project and Fessenden's mind had reached very definite conclusions in regard to it.

From Chambers Journal, Nov. 1910 the following is quoted:—

"The address of Professor Fessenden to the Engineering Section of the British Association has aroused widespread interest owing to the magnitude and novelty of his proposals for utilizing the heat of the sun and the force of the wind for generating power.

Obviously power must be stored in either case, as both of these sources are intermittent and uncertain in character.

Electrical storage is rejected in favour of a novel system of water-storage, consisting of a reservoir at the ground-level in conjunction with a shaft sunk to a great depth and provided with another reservoir at the bottom. In order to store power by these means, the water in the lower reservoir is pumped to the surface, to be run back through a water-turbine whenever the power is needed. The professor advocates this system in connection with a combined installation of wind and sun-power, an example being worked out for the production of about three thousand horse-power continually.

The apparatus for utilizing the heat of the sun consists of a tank containing a thin layer of water at the bottom, and covered by wired glass so as to be steam tight. The sun's rays are stated to be powerful enough to boil water under these conditions; hence steam is generated, and can be used in low-pressure turbines. Power from the wind is developed by a number of large windmills mounted round a circular frame which can be made to turn so as to face the wind. Each windmill drives the usual vertical shaft from which the power is transmitted by wire ropes to a central power shaft.

Powerful pumps are installed for pumping the water from the underground tank to the surface reservoir, these pumps being driven by either the sun-power steam turbine or the wind-power central shaft. (Or when necessary by an auxiliary engine.)

At the lower end of the storage system—one thousand feet below the ground level, water-turbines are driven by the water flowing back from the surface reservoir. Powerful dynamos are coupled to these turbines, the electric current being brought to the surface for transmission to factories in the vicinity or at a distance."

This Power Storage scheme included secondary arrangements for receiving power from one point and delivering to another simultaneously, the net, if surplus, going into storage; if deficit, being drawn from storage.

Reg visioned beyond this of course—seeing everywhere small and large centers,—Power Banks he called them,—with a wide transmission network and every farm and home connected. The farmer with a windmill need only hitch on to it a synchronous generator with a sealed reversible meter and, letting his windmill run all night, get credit for the power pumped by him back into the storage network, and debited with what at other times he drew out.

He saw Fuel Alcohol coming into its own, made from almost any kind of waste, each plot of ground its own small dynamo in embryo, growing vegetation to supply its own power needs; the West Indies turning their waste banana and fruit surplus into fuel alcohol and with it as a source of power, restoring past prosperity.

For the present, he knew this to be a Tantalus vision; not that it was not practicable—it was, completely so, and simple enough to be readily within the scope of all. But embattled Oil Magnates with incredible and world-wide power and ceaseless vigilance would see to it that nothing so simple and readily available should be allowed to undermine their monopoly of cheap liquid fuel.

Experience was teaching Fessenden that the world can only be pushed a little way at a time along the road of progress. He never really learned the lesson completely, one can be thankful that he never did. It would have been like condemning a high powered plane to perpetual trundling on the flying field.

Allied with his general scheme of Power Storage Fessenden had a project that was demonstrably sound and money saving and with no unknown equation.

Figures for a one-thousand or two-thousand foot shaft with excavation for subterranean reservoirs were obtained from mining engineers in different parts of the country and each set checked against the other. All necessary equipment could be of known and standard type.

It was proposed to operate with a 500 mile radius. The service it pledged itself to perform was to supply power to contracting plants for all peak loads, for all needs above average, and to receive, purchase and store power during the periods when demand fell below average—in other words, A Power Clearing House.

To this project Fessenden added a further feature which opened the way to still greater economy. Coal Dust which is practically waste fuel at the mine mouth and but little more expensive when blown by air blast or floated in water through pipes to a settling basin, was the fuel he intended to use. The engine to utilize this type of fuel was the first problem he attacked as shown by his patent "Method for using Pulverulent Matter as Fuel," No. 1,191,072 and his fluid piston engine for power generation No. 1,214,531. These details were worked out by the end of January 1911.

He then went to Schenectady to discuss this matter with the General Electric Company. In a letter from there he wrote—

> "Am on here to talk my storage scheme over with the G.E. I do not know whether they will take it up or not, but think they will if they are wise. My scheme for power storage substations for street railways and electric work generally should appeal to them when I explain it."

Again on November 9, 1911 at Lynn, there was a conference with nine G.E. Co. engineers—Messrs. Elihu Thompson, R. Rice, Stone, Hobart and Kreussi among others, at which it was decided to recommend setting aside $25,000 for the experiments. The matter would have to come before a Board, however, with the chance of being sidetracked.

Undoubtedly they were interested, unquestionably alive to the importance of the project—but co-operation with the inventor was a different matter, and for success the scheme required co-operation and long-time contracts with the large power producers and users of any given district.

There was the rub, the Achilles tendon of the project. Thus too when the Boston Edison Electric Company was approached on the same subject, not so much by Fessenden himself as by a business man who had studied the Power Storage scheme and was fired with enthusiasm over it. He wrote to Fessenden:—

> "Every step I take shows this thing bigger and more necessary and I have yet to find an objection."

But after a year or more of besieging the citadels of Power, he too lost hope of prevailing not against, but with them. Writing once more to Fessenden he said:—

> "I had M. and W. of the Edison at lunch yesterday and we went over the revision of the Power Bank report—costs and efficiencies, afterwards. I believe their interest is increased and really confirmed. *I doubt greatly however, the likelihood of the company taking the project up until it is forced on them by outside activities.*"

In line with this, at the close of 1930 we find the *American Committee World Power Conference* releasing for publication as though something very new had dawned upon the world, a leaflet headed "Pumped Water for Power" and beginning—

> "Ever since the war German Engineers have made an intensive study of water storage as a means of supplying the peak load demands of their light and power stations."

The solution found by these German Engineers was storage reservoirs *above* the level of the water to be pumped; in one case 985 feet, in another 400 feet above.

In 1907 Fessenden's investigations had shown that of the two possible locations, i.e. above or below the normal level of the water, the excavation of the reservoir *below* the level was by far the more economical method of construction.

To one unversed in Committee procedure it would seem that such isolated reports as the one above referred to, made public without reference to the state of the art in other and especially one's own country, are calculated to produce false impressions and perhaps to stifle initiative.

Edison's laconic phrase of forty odd years ago:—"I can take a Yankee boy and a china mug and he will get more results than all the German chemists put together" might well find a place somewhere on the walls of our Committee rooms as a warning to look first in our own country for creative talents. But foreign competition is here of small moment.

Fessenden's problem in 1911 and subsequently was to obtain co-operation from the big business organizations for projects which he knew to be sound. In this attempt he failed and failed so consistently that, presently, out of the unreason emerged a *law* and the forces that evoked it. This law he later promulgated:—

"NO ORGANIZATION ENGAGED IN ANY SPECIFIC FIELD OF WORK EVER INVENTS ANY IMPORTANT DEVELOPMENT IN THAT FIELD, OR ADOPTS ANY IMPORTANT DEVELOPMENT IN THAT FIELD UNTIL FORCED TO DO SO BY OUTSIDE COMPETITION." (Radio News, January 1925)

Government Departments and major Industrial Organizations stand at the gates of Progress. They admit or they bar, as the case may be. To these gates, which are the logical market for new ideas, comes the individual inventor to submit his conception.

He encounters very effective policies for delaying the introduction of such inventions. There are many ways of suppressing them—Nominal down-payments to the inventor, promise of royalties and a pigeon-holed and inactive patent; Or blocked openings by reason of secret trade pacts; Or most frequently of all, a 'Chinese Copy' of the invention that has been divulged.

An invention is available to the public *only* when the control of it has passed into the hands of business organizations and not before. The Report of President Hoover's Commission to investigate social trends has this to say in regard to "Delays in Invention."

> "The industrial research laboratories may solve it in some cases, for in these laboratories the delay between conception date and success date is said to be less in general than with the individual inventor."

But Fessenden did not find in Research Laboratories the natural habitat of Invention. They contribute magnificent detail and development work which carry inventions to supreme perfection, but *not* Conception, and because of this he found that too often they are required to operate as Fagin schools for pickpockets. So brazenly is this the case in Government Departments as well as major Industrial Organizations that Fessenden risked being counted a 'knocker' and a Jeremiah in order to make an uninformed public aware of this cancerous growth in our national development.

CHAPTER XXI

TURBO-ELECTRIC DRIVE
THE FESSENDEN COMBUSTION ENGINE

ANOTHER NOTABLE INSTANCE of delayed invention, of the laborious quickening and kindling of the engineering mind to another step forward, is the Turbo-electric Drive for marine propulsion.

Fessenden made a chronological abstract of these hesitating, grudging steps, each stage substantiated by letters of the U.S. Navy Department, General Electric Company and himself.

"1. In 1891 Fessenden, as Consulting Engineer to George Westinghouse, recommended to him the purchase of the American rights to the Parsons steam turbine for electric generating plants.

2. When the steam turbine came into use for marine propulsion, Fessenden was struck by the great loss in efficiency due to the fact that the speeds of maximum efficiency for the propeller working under water and the blades of the steam turbine working in steam were so different.

3. Fessenden took up the problem of obtaining increased efficiency.

4. Through the kindness of Admiral Taylor data as to the efficiency of screw propellers at different speeds was obtained, and from the Westinghouse Company data on the efficiency of steam turbines at different blade velocities.

5. Applying this data Fessenden discovered in 1900 that a marked increase of efficiency could be obtained by driving the propellers by electric motors, which in turn were driven by steam turbine generators.

6. He went to Washington and laid the matter before the U.S. Navy who stated that they were not prepared to take up the problem but would consider a proposition from one of the Electric Companies.

7. Westinghouse Company was not interested so Fessenden went to Schenectady to the General Electric Company who promised to look over Fessenden's figures on the subject.
8. Six months later, i.e. the fall of 1900 Fessenden was advised that the G.E. Co. had gone into the matter but were of the opinion that while the Turbo-electric Drive might be suitable as an auxiliary it would never be of use as a main drive.
9. Fessenden called the matter to the attention of the British Naval Attache in Washington.
10. During the period 1901-1907 the method was recommended from time to time by Fessenden to the U.S. Navy but without success until 1908 when, as a result of a conference with the Assistant Secretary of the Navy, Fessenden asked permission to obtain plans of Battleships 30 and 31 then being designed, in order that he might present actual designs and actual figures demonstrating the advantages of the Turbo-electric Drive for Battleships.
11. This request was granted and Fessenden designed a Turbo-electric Drive of 28,000 horse power suitable for these battleships and in July 1908 forwarded these designs to the U.S. Navy accompanied by two Memoranda demonstrating the advantages of the method.
12. In January Fessenden was notified that the matter had been considered by a Board and adversely reported.
13. March 20, 1909 a copy of the adverse report was received by Fessenden, whereupon he asked leave to take the matter up with the Chairman of the Naval Committee and the G.E. Co.
14. At a personal interview with the Assistant Secretary of the Navy in August 1909 permission was granted and the further promise made that in the event that Fessenden was able to secure proposals from any of the large Electric Companies, payment to be based on successful trials, that the Navy would place at their disposal one of the new Scout Cruisers, Salem type.
15. Again Fessenden took the matter up with the G.E. Co. and on August 26, 1909 received from Mr. Emmet of the G.E. Co. a letter stating that the use of the Turbo-electric Drive was not considered feasible and explained the method proposed by him of using the Turbo-electric Drive as an aux-

iliary to a main direct steam turbine drive, further stating—
"I cannot explain my reasons for preferring a main direct steam-turbine drive in a letter of this kind."

16. On September 21, 1909 Fessenden wrote to Emmet giving his own figures for weights and asking for Emmet's figures. Mr. Emmet replied September 23, 1909 giving a summarized statement of his figures which had been derived from the Fore River Company.

17. On examination of these figures Fessenden found that they could not possibly be correct. He therefore wrote September 27, 1909 to Mr. Emmet stating that they appeared to be incorrect and asking for the figures in detail. These were most courteously supplied by Mr. Emmet in his letter of September 28, 1909.

18. Examination of these detailed figures disclosed to Fessenden where the Fore River Company had made its mistake in the computations and these were pointed out to Mr. Emmet in a letter of September 29, 1909.

19. Mr. Emmet perceived that the G.E. Co. had been misled by the figures given them by the Fore River Company and at once arranged that Fessenden be asked to come to Schenectady to discuss the whole question of Turbo-electric Drive.

20. Two conferences followed—one with the engineers of the G.E. Co. at which it was unanimously agreed that the Turbo-electric Drive was a practical engineering proposition and embodied the advantages claimed for it; the second, with the Vice-President of the Company, Mr. E. W. Rice and other high officials who after a thorough investigation decided that it was a sound commercial proposition and should be taken up by the Company.

Thereafter work on the Turbo-electric Drive went on under the G.E. Co.'s engineers with bold and efficient skill to a brilliant conclusion.

But with the Turbo-electric Drive an accomplished success and accepted as standard equipment, the man who had visioned this, who had studied the problem and applied his skill to the solution of it, who urged it against opposition, indifference and misconception and who finally overbore inertia until his recommendations were acted on,—the work of this man disappeared, was lost sight of, as far as engineering and public recognition went.

Years later in correspondence with Mr. Albert G. Davis, then Vice-President of the G. E. Co., on this and other matters of engineering History, it is clearly to be seen that History is only permitted to begin when big business, convinced of commercial success, enters the field.

(Fessenden letter, November 6, 1924 to A. G. Davis)

"*Turbo-electric Drive.* You know all about this, and the long fight I had with the Navy and to convince Emmet, and Emmet's letter telling me how mistaken I was and that "Electricity could never be used for anything but auxiliaries on shipboard." By the by, the G.E. was to have this for nothing so far as U.S. Navy vessels were concerned, but I was to get something if it was used for mercantile and passenger ships. I wish you would remind Rice about this; I think he has forgotten it. I saw the other day that it was being used for commercial work."—

(A.G. Davis' reply to above—November 15, 1924)

"—I know nothing about your connection with the turbo-electric drive matter. I will remind Mr. Rice, as you request, but I was not aware that you had ever done any work on it. Of course the broad idea is very old.—"

It was Fessenden's intention to push recognition of the fact that he was the originator of direct Turbo-electric Drive for marine work. Sherman L. Whipple, that brilliant and beloved Boston lawyer had already gone into the facts of the case and had forecast a sweeping victory and was preparing to enter suit when his untimely death brought the matter to a standstill.

Lest anything of engineering value be lost, which to Fessenden was always more important than a question of recognition or non-recognition, attention may be called to a part of his original specification which was subsequently omitted in practical construction but which he believed offered improvement both in operation and economy. This was a two phase drive using acyclic generators, which boost each other's speed in pairs.

Two other lines of work may properly be included in the period following the drastic halt in his wireless work. These were a System for "Storage and Care of Wheeled Vehicles," Patent No. 1,114,975 and an "Internal Combustion Engine," Patent No. 1,132,465.

In view of phenominal increase in automobiles, parking and storage was already a problem. By means of certain novel car conveyers and improved methods of handling cars in garages patented by Fessenden, the way was opened for the storage of a greatly increased number of cars per given area, as well as greater speed in handling.

Fessenden hoped in 1911 and 1912 to start this in a small way by showing Garage owners and prospective Garage builders that an increased rental per given area was possible. A company was incorporated and circulars printed but that was as far as it went. A decade or more later other engineers were struck by the same idea only to find the Fessenden patents blocking the way. This brought him again into the project for by this time the congestion in automobile service that he had anticipated was at flood with no prospect of an ebb.

But Garages were no longer an approved banking investment as extensive failures had occurred in that field; also the looming business paralysis was making itself felt so again the project was given its quietus.

Fessenden's Internal Combustion Engine *was* and *is* more important. Its genesis is of interest, being an output of the years 1911 and 1912 when his mind was intensely active and when he felt himself obliged to produce under forced-draft both as an antidote to disappointment and because of the urgent need to make a fresh start.

POWER as we have seen was the main theme of his labors and engines large and small were adjuncts to the scheme. Past experience with two types of automobile engines, each with its special inherent weaknesses and defects had no doubt made him critical of existing types of combustion engines and therefore he sought something that would be simple, foolproof and adapted to use cheap fuel and suitable for airplanes and cars.

I well recall the particular time when these problems were revolving in his mind. One afternoon he was asleep on his lounge and frankly snoring; all at once he raised his head energetically and said, "That's what we'll do—put the piston outside."

"Why Reg" I said "You've been sound asleep, what started you off on the engine like that?" "Oh" he answered "even when I'm asleep my subconscious mind is busy. It's just as if there were a lot of little slaveys always tugging out one fact after another in my brain and holding it up for inspection—Is that it? Is that it? an endless number of times, till suddenly the right fact is hauled out and—click—the whole problem fits together complete."

This outside piston, or more correctly, piston sleeve, was the basically new feature of the engine, doing away with piston rings and being self tightening. He started designing at once and I find such diary entries as the following:

"Feb. 13, 1912. R.A.F. working on drawings for Mr. Rivett. Spoke yesterday of having a new mechanical movement, being able to drive a rotary thing direct.
Feb. 18, 1912. R.A.F. doing calculations for his motor over again, as he finds the Hiscox tables not reliable.
Feb. 19, 1912. R.A.F. in all day. Still at his calculations.
Feb. 23, 1912. R.A.F. very active in his motor work—up most of last night developing it and also today.
Feb. 24, 1912. R.A.F. made a blue print of his last drawing before going to town. Up most of the night working on it."

When the whole thing was worked out on paper he took it to his old friend Mr. Edward Rivett of the Rivett Precision Lathe Works, knowing that if he would consent to have the machining done in his shop, the work would be as nearly mechanically perfect as precision tools and skilled human labor could make it.

Mr. Rivett agreed to what must have involved considerable disruption to the regular routine. By the middle of May the model engine was made, assembled and brought home. As soon as it was completed it was shown to representatives of the General Electric Company, the General Motors Company, Stone and Webster, to Mr. Stanley of the Stanley Steam Car and by letter and blue print was called to the attention of the Wright Brothers. It was taken to Lynn to show to Professor Elihu Thompson and to Mr. Rice. Mr. Coffin of the G. E. Co. was consulted and he said that if Professor Thompson thought it ought to be tried, it ought to be tried, but Professor Thompson felt that the Patent Department would have to pass on the situation first.

All was done that the inventor could possibly do. He had made the invention—he had, through the kindness of Mr. Edward Rivett, built a 40 H.P. working model. He had disclosed it by detailed blue prints and by working model to such concerns as might be expected to be interested. With that, the 'dead center' was reached—without outside co-operation he could go no further.

The 40 H.P. working model of the engine as produced was something infinitely superior to anything which had been devised or marketed to date. In the first place it was light, lighter even than the aeroplane motors of those days —less than one pound per horsepower and that without any special light-weight alloys. It was compact—three engines could be put inside an ordinary suitcase. The pistons were opposed and it operated on the Diesel principle on low grade oils without electrical ignition system, vibration or noise from exhaust. In short, the best engines turned out today —a quarter of a century later—are just beginning to approach the efficiency of that machine.

In a Memorandum to the British War Office, Fessenden described it as an "Aeroplane engine, entirely silent, balanced at all speeds, lighter and more simple than present engines."

It was certain that this engine was the machine par excellence for aeroplanes and as Reg believed, for automobiles as well. With this new power plant, he felt that the design of the motor car could at last break away from the hybrid tradition of the horse drawn vehicle. His studies in naval architecture and the resistance of fluids had impressed him with the tremendous waste of power in overcoming resistance. He made tentative plans for a new type of vehicle, stream-lined, tapering to a point in the rear, with the driver and passengers in front and the power plant behind.

This of course was too radical for that day and age. It is only as the result of twenty years of cautious inch by inch development, that modern automobile manufacturers have arrived at the stream-lined body and according to the most informed minds in the automotive worlds it is expected that the shifting of the motive power to the rear of the vehicle will take place within the next few years.

However, co-operation was forthcoming in the case of this Internal Combustion Engine. For a few months it stuck on the "dead center" and by that time Reg, by magnificent results in another line of work, had' won the confidence and enthusiastic support of his associates of the Submarine Signal Company of Boston. Also the perfect operation of the 40 H.P. model which was on exhibition at the testing rooms of the Submarine Signal Company was its own best salesman and a group of men undertook to finance the further development of the engine.

Reg would have preferred to commercialize the 40 H.P. type but his associates more closely affiliated with marine matters decided on a 500 H.P. type for Submarines. Designing started at once and when these were finished the Fore River Ship Yard agreed to do the work on it. This was in March 1916. On completion at that plant it was sent in August to the New London Ship and Engine Company for tests. It was not until November 22, 1916 that fuel was turned on for the first time and it worked on its own power, starting up at once without any trouble though the lubricating feed needed some changes.

Throughout the tests the engineer in charge was most enthusiastic as to its future but as tests proceeded it was seen that the large engine had been designed too efficiently. It was a question of fuel intake and exhaust. The smaller model had operated perfectly because of certain friction and turbulence inevitable in small intake and exhaust ports. But, when the larger engine was built, it was found that the larger surfaces involved, created a new set of conditions.

This larger engine was *too* efficient. The intake of the explosive mixture and the scavenging of burnt gases were so complete and instantaneous that it was difficult to create the proper conditions in the explosion chamber at the proper point in the cycle. In short, to make it a working proposition it was necessary to create a certain turbulence in the fuel.

But the miracle would have been if it *had* operated without a hitch at the start. Compared with most new types of engines the performance of this one was full of promise. Von Tirpitz in his Memoirs discussing submarine motors of the combatant nations said that when in 1910 France sought to develop a large-size Diesel Engine so as to extend the cruise radius of her submarines, so many difficulties were encountered that the Diesel type was abandoned for the steam engine type in spite of all its known disadvantages; and when in 1915 the Diesel type was again decided on, Creusot, the most important of the motor firms, *failed forty times running* in the development of one of these bigger motors.

In 1915 Fessenden offered his 500 H.P. engine to the Navy if the Navy would standardize it in six months. It was an offer well worth considering, remembering especially the rivers of gold that flowed to waste later when Boards and Committees attempted to develop an aeroplane engine. But the Navy did not accept the offer. The money put up by the Boston group to develop it was exhausted before complete success was attained so work on the engine stopped. Fessenden never doubted however that its destiny was still in the future and that in days to come its great possibilities would be appreciated. Indeed on April 10, 1921 we find him writing as follows to one of his associates of this development;—

"About the Engine, the Germans have already taken it up and made a big success of it, as you will see from the enclosed, (which please return to me at your convenience; I would like Harry to see it as he will recognize how little difference there is between it and ours.) You will note that they have found all the claims for efficiency, safety, reliability, etc. just as I claimed, and the weight even lighter, as I claimed 2 lbs. per H.P. while they give it as 1½ H.P. Our compressor for scavenging is really somewhat better than theirs, but that is about the only difference, except that they use 210 lbs. where we used about 250. One amusing thing is that they evidently had just the same trouble as we did, but they went ahead and used spark plugs and gasoline, having no one to object as Mr. ——— did, and being unhampered, made a big success of it. And you will note that they have not got over the difficulty yet but are using spark plugs and gasoline in the commercial engines; while I have located the trouble and have a patent in the office for the remedy.

There is no doubt in the world but that this will be the standard type of engine in the future and will supplant all other types, on account of its efficiency, simplicity, etc."

But in 1916 War trends were such that ways of *destroying* Submarines became a far more vital matter than motorizing them. Fessenden's entire scientific training made him the man above all others best fitted for this task.

CHAPTER XXII

SUBMARINE SIGNALING AND THE FESSENDEN OSCILLATOR

FESSENDEN'S CONNECTION with the Submarine Signal Company of Boston came about to a certain extent by accident. In the Company Magazine 'Soundings,' Mr. Harold Fay, an executive of the Company says:—

> "Our first meeting with Professor Fessenden was in the Bell Laboratories in 1905 when, in connection with his radio-telephony developments at Brant Rock, he was looking for a better telephone transmitter to use in his work."
>
> "Our second—was a number of years later in 1912, when I met him quite by accident one evening at the South Station, Boston. I asked the Professor to come down to the Submarine Signal Company plant to see what we were doing. With characteristic promptness when interested, he came down to see us the next morning. We all enjoyed his visit and instinctively felt his interest and enjoyment in delving into the new line of work presented by our submarine problem."

This was in August 1912. It must be recalled that on April 15, 1912 the stark tragedy of the 'Titanic' iceberg collision shocked the world and since then Fessenden's mind had grappled with the problem of divesting sea travel of this horror.

A possible connection with the Submarine Signal Company was therefore undoubtedly very attractive to him, offering as it did a chance to extend his work in the field of "communications" and in an element where, though wireless was beginning to pierce the curtains of its isolation, there still remained those soundless perils of rock and shoal, of iceberg and fog, dumb agencies of Nature to menace and destroy.

The problem first put up to him by the Submarine Signal Company was the elimination of water noises. Finding that the state of the art as then practiced by the Company was limited to the use of microphones for listening to a bell over *short* distances, he saw that the real need was the development of an apparatus for transmitting telegraphic signals under water for *long* distances.

His proposal to experiment along this line did not meet with approval, it being assumed that the Company's engineers having had more experience, would be better able to develop such an apparatus if it were desired.

Reg thereupon suggested building a new form of *receiving apparatus*. This being approved, he proceeded to invent and develop the Oscillator and within three months had completed a working model of this submarine telegraph apparatus which not only proved an efficient receiving device but which, when power was put on, was capable of telegraphing *fifty* miles under water.

The Oscillator in Mr. Fay's words:

—"revolutionized the art of Submarine Signaling, doubling and trebling the range at which it was possible to send sound signals through water. The ease and speed at which sound signals in the form of dots and dashes could be sent through the water with the Oscillator marked a tremendous advance over the older slow method of submarine signaling by means of dots with a bell."

The rapidity with which this invention was accomplished was a typical Fessenden achievement. He did not approach the problem as it was presented to him by the Company's engineers. A small improvement of an already existing method could not satisfy him, he must devise something that would place the art on a new plane. Nor must it be inferred that the invention involved merely the application of work he had already done in Sound, for, as he said, "Signaling and detecting submarine sounds is a much more complicated matter than signaling and listening in air."

In the Oscillator Fessenden had an apparatus of remarkable power and efficiency by which were brought into existence electric forces very much more intense than those that occur in the ordinary dynamo or motor.

Describing one particular type of Oscillator he said:

> "This copper tube weighing only a few pounds is driven to and fro with a force of more than two tons, approximately one thousand times per second.—In the Oscillator we possess a source of great intensity and one capable of acting almost instantaneously, the time-constant of the Oscillator being less than one ten-thousandth of a second."

But as Mr. Fay justly remarked:—

> "When Professor Fessenden thought out a problem and had arrived at a mathematical solution of this problem, to him, putting the device in final form and the ultimate development which might take months and years, was to his mind but an aggravated detail with much unforgiveable delay."

In the case of the Oscillator however, everyone was so stimulated by the possibilities it opened up, that delay was slight. Mr. Perkins, Vice-President, coined the happy phrase "a Wall of Sound" with which the Oscillator could encircle the coast of every country.

With such a tool perfected it is easy to see that Fessenden's mind ranged wide and free in regard to the uses to which it could be applied. Its primary purpose of signaling through water to a suitable receiving apparatus, whether oscillator, microphone or other device, was but half the story.

Its *Echo* possibilities opened up a field of extraordinary promise. With the unsuspected iceberg of the "Titanic's" doom uppermost in his calculations, Fessenden anticipated that such a submerged base would echo back such oscillations.

The answer to that thought had to await the conjunction of ships, men, apparatus and icebergs—not to be assembled by a magician's wand. But terra firma was available and he experimented with it to find out how oscillations would penetrate and echo in the earth. My diary records that on May 10, 1913 Reg was at South Framingham making tests of this nature.

With satisfactory business connections established in Boston, Fessenden again and for the first time since University days in Pittsburgh and a few months at Old Point Comfort, had opportunity for the social relaxation of clublife. Whether at the St. Botolph Club of Boston or on the golf links he thoroughly enjoyed the varied contacts of men at play. There was always 'bonhomie' in those contacts and there was also the tendency to regard him as an unknown equation—someone from whom the unusual, the unexpected, the illuminating was always to be looked for. Not as an 'enfant terrible' but rather as a friendly giant.

Early in 1914 Professor Kennelly of Harvard, then president of the Lawrence Scientific Association suggested to Reg that he give a lecture on the Oscillator before the Association and a second society, the American Academy of Arts and Sciences under its president Dr. John Trowbridge, joined in the request.

Reg consented and the lecture was given on February 25 at the testing rooms of the Submarine Signal Company where the apparatus could be demonstrated. It created a real sensation among the technical members of the audience.

With the lecture out of the way, Reg went off to Washington to try and arrange for the iceberg test that had been stirring in his mind ever since the "Titanic" went down. Through the kind offices of the Revenue Cutter Service this was made possible. Its ships on patrol on the Grand Banks could afford the desired opportunity.

Although by this time the engineering staff of the Submarine Signal Company was well skilled in making tests with the oscillator, Reg was not content to leave this work to anyone else. Answering my apprehensions about this somewhat perilous trip he said—"It will be a delicate experiment at best and they may get results and yet not know it, if the work is carried out by inexperienced operators."

So on April 7, 1914 a jolly group of Submarine Signal

men gathered at the North Station, Boston, to see Fessenden, Mr. Blake, Mr. Price and Mr. Gunn off for Halifax where they were to join their ship the U.S.R.C. "Miami," under Captain Quinan.

The following survey and analysis of the problem had been made by Fessenden prior to his departure for these tests: —

"Determining the presence of icebergs by submarine echo has one obvious advantage in that more than 80 percent of the iceberg is submerged. But the method did not at first sight seem promising because—

a. The index of refraction of ice for sound is almost identical with that of water.

b. The shape of the iceberg being irregular, echoes could not be expected unless the iceberg happened to present a flat side towards the ship from which the signal issued. As the result of investigation it was found however, that closely adjoining the melting icebergs there was a thin layer of somewhat denser water from which sound reflections could be obtained. Also as the result of some mathematical work along a line which had never previously received mathematical treatment it was found that although specular reflection could not be obtained nevertheless if a prolonged oscillator signal were sent out, interference fringes of sound could be obtained no matter how irregular the surface. (Several years later this mathematical work was called to the attention of Lord Rayleigh and the results obtained were confirmed by him and applied to some optical problems)."

Fessenden's letters and Captain Quinan's report give the results of this expedition.

Letters from Fessenden

The Queen Hotel
Halifax.
April 11, 1914.

"—Well, we have got everything here O.K., tested out the dynamo, oscillator, sound-standards and commutator, so that the delay in harbor has been a very good thing, as otherwise we would have had a tough time when the time came to make the tests, whereas now they are all drilled in getting the oscillator overboard etc. Price leaves for Boston Sunday night or Monday morning and will get back about the same time as this letter will reach you.

We go aboard tomorrow, Sunday, at 10.50 A.M. and sail Sunday afternoon. I am afraid we shall not be very comfortable as the boat is quite small and they have only one spare stateroom which I have turned over to Blake and I shall sleep in the Captain's diningroom.

She is a very tubby little boat about the same size as a fishing schooner but her Captain is very proud of his command and believes her to be just a shade smaller than the Olympic, and as I said to Blake, walks around as if he were not even in soundings (being a short man) while I have to duck every beam.

Halifax is a very dull place. I was disappointed, for the Geography we studied at school (1878) said it was a very gay place, in fact was celebrated for its gaiety.

I suspect it was Early Victorian gaiety. By the bye, we have a lot of Early Victorian pictures, steel engravings, "Return of the Life Boat" etc. in the Hotel here.

The trip up was a slow one. We did not get in till 1 A.M. Government-owned railways of course.

Your letter came this morning and I was mighty glad to get it. I certainly needed it for the weather has been abominable, till today, and stormy today.

I got some pictures of our little boat which I will bring back, D.V. We go out to the S.E. corner of the Grank Banks direct and cruise up and down around there—We will not be back till about May 1st or possibly 7th though I hope for the former.—"

U.S.S. Miami
Off Banks.
April 14, 1914

"—We expect to meet the Senaca tomorrow and may get a chance to send this letter by her. We had a very tedious trip to Halifax as I wrote you in my last letter, but when we sailed Sunday the weather was fine. But when we got out of the harbor the fog came down and that night it blew a fresh gale and only now has slacked off. This ship is a great roller, (very small and about the size of a schooner) and even now I am writing you with one arm coiled round a stanchion so as to keep from being thrown out of my chair, though now it is *comparatively* quiet. I was not sea sick but had an awful time the first night. The rolling was so bad that my mattress got thrown out of my berth four or five times with me on it. Then I got tired putting it back and left it on the floor and tried sleeping on the leather cushions under the mattress. But it got rolling worse till even these were thrown out several times. So I gave it up and tried the floor, but could not stick to the mattress even on the floor and in addition six or seven chairs etc. took charge of the room, broke the ropes they were tied with and started charging up and down the room. So then I tried sleeping on the bare planks of my berth, but soon the chairs started jumping upon that and one of them gave me a bad crack on the ankle. So after that and much profanity, as it was then 4 A.M. and dawn breaking I got up and dressed.

It was very fatiguing all day as I could not lie down anywhere and even sitting up had to hold on all the time. When night came I had boards fixed on the bunk and after about ten minutes they broke so I took the mattress and put it in a narrow alleyway where I could not roll far and the chairs could not get at me and got a good sleep.

Tonight it is not so bad and as I have got extra strong fastenings, expect to last out O.K. There was a good deal of breakage. One air cowl went and a lot of glass and the Captain's cherries encarnadined the floor.

I was afraid for the oscillator and went out to look for it several times the first night in the intervals of dodging chairs, but it stood O.K.

Blake had an easier time as I gave him the cabin with the good walled-in bunk, and Gunn was in sick-bay. He was pretty sick but is getting over it.

It is quite a trick to eat meals as you can imagine and we do not run to liquids at present.

The Captain O.K. and very pleasant and all the officers and crew. I tried the polarizing prism in fog and in sun glare today and it works fine, also before sailing I tried the oscillator and got the same reading as in the tank at the shop and at 10 ft. depth as at 4 ft. (within 5%) which is very satisfactory showing that we do not need deep forepeak tanks on the ships.

Tomorrow we are going to put the oscillator overboard and have the Senaca pick us up by it. If this works out it will be a good thing for now they sometimes cruise around for several days before finding each other, if there is fog, and once or twice have failed entirely. There are two cats on board and they don't seem to enjoy it. I got some photos which I will have developed when I come back. The Senaca reports by wireless that there is quite some ice in 44.30 latitude, where we are going about 20 miles East of the Banks, which is lucky as we might have had to chase round for it. Several big fields and one big berg and seven small ones, so we will hope to be able to get to work at once.

I find I have everything I needed except that I should have taken six boxes of stogies instead of three as I give away a good many and they aren't going to last me out so the last week I shall have to smoke a pipe.

The dressing gown comes in very handy and I am glad you put it in. I miss not hearing from you. Your last letter was just at the right time and caught me just before sailing on Saturday night.

I enclose a photo of the Miami, the ink line shows how the waves come in right over the top of the flag pole in the stern. X is the cowl which was washed off (not the smoke stack of course but the little cowl at its foot.)

I am very anxious to get to work at the tests on the icebergs and the soundings and hope to in a few days.—"

REPORT OF CAPTAIN J. H. QUINAN OF THE U.S.R.C. "MIAMI" ON THE ECHO FRINGE METHOD OF DETECTING ICEBERGS AND TAKING CONTINUOUS SOUNDINGS.

"From the Hydrographic Office Bulletin of May 13, 1914.

"We stopped near the largest berg and by range finder and sextant computed it to be 450 feet long and 130 feet high. Although we had gotten within 150 yards of the perpendicular face of the berg and obtained no echo from the steam whistle, Professor Fessenden and Mr. Blake, representatives of the Submarine Signal Company, obtained satisfactory results with the submarine electric oscillator placed 10 feet below surface, getting distinct echoes from the berg at various distances, from one-half mile to two and one-half miles.

These echoes were not only heard through the receivers of the oscillators in the wireless room, but were plainly heard by the officers in the wardroom and engine room storeroom below the water line.

Sound is said to travel at the rate of 4,400 feet per second under water. The distance of the ship, as shown by the echoes with stop watch, corresponded with the distance of the ship as determined by range finder. On account of the great velocity of sound through water, it was our intention to try the oscillator at a greater distance for even better results, but a thick snowstorm drove us into shelter on the Banks again.

On the morning of April 27, anchored in 31 fathoms of water with 75 fathoms of chain in order to make current observations. . . . . Professor Fessenden also took advantage of the smooth sea to further experiment with his oscillator in determining by echo the depth of the water; the result giving 36 fathoms, which seemed to me very close."

Fessenden gave further details:—

"When the signal sent was very short no echoes were received from the iceberg, or only very occasionally, though the echo from the bottom, depth about one and a half miles, was always very clear and loud. When, however, a prolonged train of waves was sent out, an echo was invariably received and always in the form of sound fringes; i.e. whereas when a long signal was sent out a prolonged and loud echo was received from the bottom after the lapse of three or four seconds, the echo from the iceberg, arrived in the form of a number of short disconnected dots loud enough to be heard in the ward room and engine room, and after a lapse of from one to ten seconds depending on the distance from the iceberg.

The "Miami" steamed around the iceberg but no measurable variation in the intensity of the echo could be observed with variation of aspect."

THE FESSENDEN OSCILLATOR

The men returned from this trip on May 5 and found things moving briskly at the shop and office. June was a month of tests. On June 3 a series of demonstrations were made for the Press at which all Boston papers were represented. In the morning, in Boston Harbor, the Submarine Telephone was operated up to half a mile and the Submarine Telegraph up to ten miles. The evening test was to get in touch with the collier "Devereux" fitted with an oscillator, as she rounded the Cape on her way from Norfolk.

On June 9 tests were made for some Japanese and Argentinians, and on June 11 another test with the "Devereux" off the Cape.

In addition to obtaining data on signaling between surface craft, Fessenden carried his investigations to the next stage, that is signaling between surface craft and submarines or between submarines.

A diary entry of July 23, 1914 reads—

"R.A.F. returned late last night. Since July 14 he has been in Newport taking part in submarine tests. He has been down in a submarine a good part of the time. Says tests were very satisfactory. At a Directors' meeting today Major Higginson told him his life was too valuable to risk in that way and that he must not take such chances again."

CHAPTER XXIII

THE WORLD WAR

WITH THE DAWNING of August 1914 a considerable section of the world entered the confines of a mad house. Through its portals the United States gazed on chaos but as yet were not obliged to enter the inferno.

As far as the Submarine Signal Company was concerned it was obvious that not only great commercial opportunity but also opportunity for service lay in these recently developed Fessenden devices. As soon as their existence and scope were realized by the public, it was inevitable that they would be of incalculable service.

It was decided by the Board of Directors that a mission to England should be undertaken to tender the Company's devices to the Admiralty. Preliminary steps to this were:—

    a. A conference with Special British Agent, Captain (Admiral) Gaunt, formerly of the "Thunderer". Fessenden and Mr. T. R. Madden of the Submarine Signal Company went to New York on August 18 for the purpose. Captain Gaunt's reaction to the proposal was that if the Oscillator could do what was claimed for it that the Admiralty would jump at it.

    b. August 21 Captain Gaunt came to Boston for a demonstration of the Oscillator, on a trial run out of the Harbor; the tests were very successful.

    c. August 25 Fessenden and Mr. Madden went to Ottawa. Fessenden had already tendered his services to the Canadian contingent in any capacity the Minister of Militia might approve and at an interview August 28, Sir Sam Hughes, on being told of Captain Gaunt's urgency that the submarine signalling devices be submitted to the Admiralty, agreed that in no way could Fessenden render more valuable service. He therefore wrote a warm endorsement to the British War Office and to the Admiralty—

"I recommend him (Professor Fessenden) most cheerfully to the British War Office and Admiralty. He should be invaluable to the authorities there now.

(Signed) Sam Hughes."

A Canadian agency for the Submarine Signal Company was arranged and it was expected that large orders would result. Thus prepared and with blue prints, patents and all necessary data, we sailed on September 2, a party of four, Mr. and Mrs. Madden, Professor Fessenden and myself, on the "Olympic," Captain Haddock commanding.

War time sailings were still a novelty and as the "Olympic" slipped out of her dock the "Adriatic" at the next pier gave her a fine send-off, band playing, crew assembled at the stern, cheering, waving Allied flags and singing the songs of the hour. Then in sweltering heat a southerly course was set and held till we neared the other side.

There was a small passenger list, not more than fifty or sixty first class, and we were assigned luxurious quarters, ours as I recall being the Louis Seize suite. William Corey the steel magnate was a passenger, very concerned for his Chateau near Paris. Late in the afternoon of the 9th we landed in Liverpool, the port having been closed all day for the despatch of troops.

Inspection of passengers was rigid and to our surprise Fessenden was one of those listed for investigation. Passport, letters of introduction, blue prints, papers, patents and printed copy of Fessenden's lecture on the Oscillator were all required for inspection without any reason being given for such particularity. Finally we disclosed the letter of Special British Agent, Captain Gaunt and then the officials fell over themselves in cordiality and courtesy.

We spent the night in Liverpool, going on the next day to London and from there to Bushey Hall, a country Hotel or Hygeia, run much on the lines of a country club and within commuting distance of London. It was a magnificent estate developed half a century earlier by a member of the firm of Burdett & Coutts and had changed hands owing to financial reverses.

On September 11 the Admiralty was approached. At that time fortunately Winston Churchill's first Secretary was the Honorable Rear Admiral Hood, former Naval Attache at Washington. Reg had met him there many times on business and at Chevy Chase as well and in 1908 he had arranged a wireless telegraph and telephone demonstration for him at our Brant Rock Station. Mr. Perkins, the vice-president of the Submarine Signal Company, was likewise a personal friend, so there were no barriers to overcome and Admiral Hood at once promised the fullest and most expert consideration of our proposition.

A conference was arranged for the following Monday, September 14, and was attended by six or seven men, all Admiralty experts, heads of departments, called in some instances from outlying places. A full description and discussion of the Oscillator followed. At the close the Senior Officer said "I'm for a demonstration," qualifying his remark with the statement that he could only *recommend;* the power to *authorize* lay with the First Lord of the Admiralty.

Mr. Madden stated that the Oscillator had not yet been offered to any other government and if there was prospect of speedy action other negotiations would be deferred. He was assured that in those days miracles were happening and that "red tape" was being cut. After the meeting Reg was conducted to the office of Admiral Hood, who had asked especially to see him.

The demonstration was authorized on September 22, but on cabling the Boston office to that effect, both Fessenden and Madden were much upset to receive word that the oscillator would not be ready for shipment until about October 15. This seemed like unpardonable delay and called forth urgent cables from the London office, with the result that on October 11 Messrs. Price and Vaux reached London with the oscillator.

These men were two of Reg's very able assistants. Mr. Price in particular was indoctrinated with the Fessenden methods of development. He had come straight from college to the Brant Rock Staff and had proved a reliable lieutenant. At the time of the break-up at Brant Rock he was one of those who kept the faith and made his resignation permanent.

On arrival of these two men the Admiralty was notified and the test was set for October 29 at Portsmouth, the "Vernon" being placed at the Company's disposal for installation and demonstration. The results were most successful.

A submarine Detector of the type known as the Fessenden Long Wave Method had also been taken to Portsmouth along with the oscillator, but the "Vernon" officials stated that their instructions read to test submarine signaling apparatus and that they had no instructions to test submarine Detectors. Unfortunately for us Admiral Hood left the Admiralty shortly after to take command in the Channel, and our subsequent efforts to obtain a test of the submarine Detector were unsuccessful. The apparatus lay at Portsmouth until January 1917 when it was returned to the United States and employed in the successful tests at New London in April 1917 and also on the U.S.S. Aylwin.

Following the tests on the "Vernon," Fessenden visited the Thomson-Houston Company at Rugby on November 11 and there heard rumors of very large orders for Oscillators being under consideration. When however on November 16 an order came from the Admiralty it was to our consternation for *four* sets of Oscillators only.

The reason for this was later found to be the results of tests on the U.S.S. "Delaware" and U.S.S. "Utah" made by the Submarine Signal Company subsequent to Fessenden's departure for England.

The installation on these ships was carried out in a manner directly contrary to the method stipulated by Fessenden, a so-called skin type installation having been adopted instead of the tank type installation specified by him.

Such skin type installation gave good results *abeam* but did not work satisfactorily *ahead or astern*.

This was so reported by the Fleet Officer who further

made a confidential communication of his findings to the Admiralty. Since the first requirement for submarine signaling between vessels is for signals ahead and astern, this failure was a pertinent objection.

Prior to July 1, 1914, four tests of the tank type of installation had been made on the S.S. "Devereux" which had given dead ahead signals at thirty-two miles and more.

The Inventor, Fessenden, out of the completeness of his scientific knowledge of the complications of the problem, had specified that the installation *must* be of the *tank type,* it is therefore difficult to understand a Company policy which at so critical a time ran counter to that advice. It opened the way to competing developments which later caused the Company extended and tedious claims for infringement against the British Government and elsewhere.

An understanding may perhaps be reached by a knowledge of certain facts. At the time Fessenden became connected with the Submarine Signal Company it was a moribund concern. Almost as by a miracle a new lease of life was restored to it when the fresh vigor of the Oscillator coursed through its system.

But now with recovery assured, fresh factors cropped up —jealousy and wounded egotism, engineering rivalries, divided policies, cross currents and eddies.

Indeed as the war period progressed the most anyone could hope to do was to set down events in their sequence, without ascribing motives and intentions but noting only effects and results.

While negotiations with the Admiralty were pending Fessenden carried on with other war plans that he had in mind. His letter from General Hughes brought him in touch with Colonel (Sir Sefton) Brancker in charge of aviation at the War Office. Through his courtesy and interest the various Memoranda drawn up by Fessenden were brought to the attention of the different Departments concerned.

But before touching on these it is necessary to refer to an

incident of an earlier date related by Fessenden in his "Deluged Civilization" (By-products of History.)

"There is one thing which I should like to tell here, out of respect to the memory of the late King Edward VII, and that is that a good many citizens of London owe their safety during Zeppelin raids to him, though he was dead. If it is not told here it never will be, for it is buried in a report in the files of the War Office.
Early in 1910 Major E. C. Godfrey-Faussett called on me at my rooms and informed me that he was one of the king's aides, and that the king was interested in the problem of communicating between artillery batteries in action, and had asked him to call on me to ascertain if I could suggest a suitable system, and if not, if I would take up the matter. With the aid of Major Godfrey-Faussett's instructions and information I worked out a good system, using the loop direction-finding antenna shown in the first figure of my patent of January 14th, 1907. While testing it I noticed that the position of aeroplanes could be determined very accurately with two such loops. Owing to the king's death nothing more was done at the time.—But later the "King Edward Method" of locating aircraft fell into the hands of some enterprising officer of the War Department and they made good use of it during the Zeppelin raids. The Germans not knowing how to use the loop of Fig. 1 of the January 14, 1907 patent, used the star figure 2, which necessitated the Zeppelin commanders sending out signals so that the star stations could give them their positions, and the officers referred to were able to locate the Zeppelins and plot their course long before they reached England, and so give warning in ample time and let our own aircraft know where to look for them. If it had not been for King Edward's request the matter would never have been taken up and the apparatus never developed, and it seems as if this should be known."

After Reg's arrival in England in 1914 he drew up four Memoranda for the War Office.

No. 1 Location of Concealed Artillery
No. 2 Aeroplane Engines

No. 3 Aircraft in Mass and the Influence of Space Properties in Warfare
No. 4 Rifle and Machine Gun sights

The first he described as "Earth Tremor range finder" and summarized its characteristics as those of a long base range finder utilizing sound waves instead of light waves. The Aeroplane Engine has already been alluded to. It will be recalled that, as built and run, the small size operated perfectly. Fessenden's description of it to the War Office reads:—

"A fundamentally new type of engine in which the bearing between piston and cylinder is on the outside of the cylinder —is vibrationless at all speeds and has no unbalanced forces in it at any speed except the expansive force of the fuel and the torque of the shaft. The enclosed photograph shows an engine which is equivalent to an 8-cylinder 4-cycle engine, but which is capable of running at much higher speeds, much greater pressures and running continuously for several thousand hours without attention (there being no valves, springs, magnetoes etc.) The highest power so far obtained from it, its weight being 52 lbs. is 40 H.P., but it is believed to be capable of being operated up to 120 H.P."

No. 4 had to do with improved and simplified methods of sighting both with rifles and machine guns, also a method for night sighting.

The above Memoranda may be considered as a natural outcome of Fessenden's advanced work on Sound, Fuel Motors and Precision Firing.

But Memorandum No. 3 stands apart and distinct from these, as something instinct with vision, a remarkable and brilliant conception of means to overcome conditions that had as yet scarcely revealed themselves. It was written on November 5, 1914 at the London office of the Submarine Signal Company. I well recall Mr. Madden's return from the office that day thrilled with the newness, the greatness and withal the simplicity of this scheme of Fessenden's. The wonder of it fell on me too when a copy was given to me to read. It is difficult to recapture and almost impossible to convey the sense of a miracle that has since become a commonplace. But for us, that day, there was need to tip-toe softly because a shining bird of peace seemed to be circling above which might spread its wings over war-torn Europe. Briefly, Fessenden's idea was this:—

The manufacture of ten thousand airplanes, each capable of carrying four 100-pound, high-explosive bombs, to be built in Canada* by Mass production methods and to be delivered at the front by May 1, 1915. The most important feature of the plan was that these airplanes were to be used as airplanes had never been used before—IN MASS. This was an absolutely new concept in warfare; but it was practical. Because of their high speed of manoeuvre airplanes by the hundred or by the thousand could fly in column or in echelon; each distinct from its neighbor, yet passing a given point so rapidly as to maintain a continuous shower of bombs on that point. This meant that for the first time it was possible to end the war by some other means than the destruction of man-power. Using aircraft in mass, and striking again and again at the lines of communication and depots, the enemy in the front lines would be kept without food, ammunition or reinforcements until they were ready to give up.

Already it was perceived that decisive frontal attack in what Fessenden called one dimension was impossible. Therefore accept that fact and overcome it, but above all, overcome it FIRST and COMPLETELY before the enemy had time to reach the same conclusion and act on it.

Hence the need for prompt action; hence Fessenden's attempt to make the War Office realize that Mass production as practiced in the States and as readily applicable in Canada, was perfectly capable of producing airplanes at the rate of several hundred a day as it was of producing automobiles, and that six months of winter intervening was ample time.

In the training of men, Fessenden doubted whether it

* Note, it is interesting to see how literally the recommendations of this memorandum are being carried out in the present war.

would require more time to turn a chauffeur into an airman than a man with no motor training into a chauffeur, particularly if the plane included a stabilizer.

But it was asking too much for one creative spark to 'animate the whole.'

Colonel Brancker replied:

> War Office
> Whitehall,
> S.W.
> Nov. 9.

"Dear Professor Fessenden:

I have placed your remarkable memorandum on the subject of 10,000 aeroplanes before Lord Kitchener.

I am afraid that I lack your optimism after seeing the efforts of the British trade to make efficient aeroplanes during the last two years. You might start making aeroplanes in a year's time but not by Feb. 1st I fear.

> Yours sincerely
> (Signed) W.S. Brancker."

"Before Lord Kitchener:"—Further it could not be followed. Did it reach his mind, his pigeon holes or his waste basket? We never knew for sure, but in the Illustrated London News, May 30, 1931, in a review of "The War in the Air" by H.A. Jones, the following paragraph is found:—

> "Whatever opinion may be held of Lord Kitchener's action regarding munitions, it is evident that the Royal Air Force, at least, owes much to his judgment and foresight. In a section on recruitment and training for the Royal Flying Corps early in the war, we read; "The outstanding factors in the creation of new squadrons were the vision and backing of Lord Kitchener, Secretary of State for War. The day after the original squadrons left for overseas, he sent for Lieut. Colonel Brancker and told him he would require large numbers of new squadrons to co-operate with the new armies." An estimate was prepared as a forecast of requirements for some distance ahead. "But," the writer proceeds, "it did not look ahead far enough for Lord Kitchener. When

the papers reached him on December 21, 1914, he gave his approval in these words: 'A.D.M.A. ought to be prepared to double this.' These few words lifted the whole subject to a different plane. They came as a tonic and incentive to the directing staff of the Flying Corps, created an atmosphere in the War Office favourable to a generous consideration of the air service demands."

This makes it seem as if Fessenden's creative spark may have served in some measure to kindle Kitchener's imagination.

In June 1915 H.G. Wells in an article in the Daily Express came out with a plan to build and send a tremendous fleet of aeroplanes to the rear of the German lines to destroy ammunition factories. Said he "It is cheaper to launch 2000 aeroplanes against Essen than to risk one battleship."

The account of this period must not close without some mention of golf. Mr. and Mrs. Madden and Reg were all devotees and Bushey Hall provided ideal conditions for play. Links at the very doors of the Hall and stretching over beautiful country where often a pheasant rose with a whirr as we hunted balls and where, after eighteen or thirty-six holes as the case might be, all the luxuries of an up-to-date Hygeia could be enjoyed.

An exceptionally fine 'Pro' was in charge of the links and Reg worked under Batley (an ex-champion) with zeal and built up and unbuilt his game many times as a fresh conception of some factor of it came to him. I recall a set of three challenge foursomes in which Mrs. Madden and Batley consistently won over Mr. Madden and Reg. Two other matches gave him abiding satisfaction—one with Ray and Fessenden against Batley and a friend of ours; the second when three champions, Taylor, Ray and Batley with Fessenden made the foursome and though the outcome is forgotten I do remember that in spite of badly blistered feet he came back blissfully happy because he had played golf adequate to the occasion.

Meantime lack of co-operation on the part of the Boston office was becoming increasingly apparent. News of the changed method of installation had been withheld from Fessenden until the arrival of Mr. Price in London. The request of the Canadian agent for a demonstration of the Oscillator with almost certain orders to follow, had been disregarded. Then came a cable proposing changes in measurement of certain parts of the oscillator itself. This exhausted the last shreds of Fessenden's patience and on November 22 it was decided to return as soon as possible to the States.

Before sailing he made a hurried trip to Oxford to visit Sir William Osler, and for a meeting with Smith of Balliol and an introduction to Palmer of the Saturday Review who sought to bring Fessenden and G. Bernard Shaw together on the subject of "Phonetics."

Then a return to Bushey for last minute matters, dinner and theater in London with the Maddens and our life-long friends the Beaches, a jolly send-off from them all at Euston the next morning and so to Liverpool and a very stormy voyage on the "New York" sailing at midnight December 5.

On board were Lieutenant Hooper and Commander McCrary, both U.S. Navy and Arthur Ruhl, Colliers—War Correspondent. Reg saw a good deal of all three. It developed that Lieutenant Hooper had made the oscillator test on the U.S.S. "Utah" already referred to.

We landed December 14 and Ken who was taking law at Columbia met us at the dock and we had a happy day and evening together before leaving at midnight for Boston.

CHAPTER XXIV

SUBMARINE SIGNALING IN WAR TIME AND CIVILIAN WAR BOARDS

FOR A FEW WEEKS after our return to Boston in December 1914 it seemed probable that connections between Reg and the Submarine Signal Company would be severed. By official order all reports to Fessenden on Laboratory activities had ceased during his absence in England. Gathering up the threads on his return it was learned that a Mission had sailed for Germany, the representatives taking with them several oscillators and, more important still, description and copies of drawings of the submarine Detector, a model of which Fessenden had taken to England though no opportunity of demonstrating it had been afforded him there.

Impartial Company neutrality justified this it is true, but to Fessenden it was more than Company business. These advanced signaling and detecting devices were the product of his brain, designed to save rather than to destroy.

The successful demonstration in Germany of these devices, operation over 40 miles it was said, produced in Fessenden little pride of achievement, since he believed it was power fallen into wrong hands.

Germany was a compact unit. No far-flung bits of Empire sent troopship after troopship laden with loyal sons to Germany—her sons were within her borders—in her hands a Detector became a weapon against the laden troopships— in the hands of the Allies a weapon against the submarine. Just as Fessenden's 10,000 airplanes were meant to blast munitions and lines of communication, so his submarine Detectors were devised against those gadflies of the deep, to nullify the enemy's powerful weapon of offense and hasten the termination of the war.

By the Grace of God (if He concerned Himself with this man-made debacle) and owing to a faulty conception on the part of a rival German company of the correct frequency for the most effective use of the Detector, a wrong frequency was decided on as the standard specification, and it was not till very near the end of the war that this mistake was discovered, otherwise the resulting losses to the Allies might have been far worse.

In January 1915 certain changes in the Submarine Signal Company management took place; certain differences were composed and Fessenden found himself again in accord with the policies decided upon. A period of great activity for all ensued. By May the Oscillator as a magnificent aid to navigation was coming into its own, the Submarine Signal Company's shop was working overtime and work had spread to three other shops and 10 oscillators a week were being turned out.

The Admiralty was putting in repeat orders in quick succession and by early 1916 was making it standard equipment with the name of Fessenden on every part. In July 1915 the Company paid its first dividend. Rights to the Oscillator for submarine signaling were vested of course in the Submarine Signal Company but other uses were reserved to Fessenden by agreement. As the fame of this apparatus spread the General Electric Company began to evince interest in it. Its use as a dynamo was thoroughly appreciated, also I recall that one of the possible uses discussed was as a vibrator for the thorough shaking down of sand in molds of large and intricate castings. Likewise tentative consideration of it from a therapeutic view point started, these inquiries coming as I remember from Johns Hopkins Medical School; Reg urged extreme caution in such application.

Intermittent negotiations on the part of the General Electric Company continued until the spring of 1917 and on the occasion of a visit to Schenectady to obtain some material for his submarine Detector, Reg was told that in general conference the purchase of the Oscillator for rights other than submarine work had been recommended and certain terms discussed—a cash payment and royalties till a certain sum had been paid a total in excess of $100,000. This was still pending when in October 1917 the Submarine Signal Company, unwilling to let any part of so valuable an invention slip through its hands, made Fessenden an offer of 4000 shares of the Company's stock for these rights and in recognition of his services in pulling the Company up to Success.

This offer Reg accepted, as he believed in the future of the company. Even when feverish war activity should have subsided, the company under progressive management ought to be extremely prosperous—indeed with the opportunities open to it, it was inconceivable that it would not be.

Meanwhile to return to 1915, Reg as usual, went hither and yon—New York and Washington—mostly on patent matters. In New York in March of that year a last interview with his quondam wireless partners occurred—without lawyers and without results—the meeting seems to have been formal and colorless and to have etched in sharper lines the impassable gulf between them.

In Washington he was always sure of a good reception. My diary record of late February has this to say:—

"R. A. F. seems to have met a number of influential officials on various matters. Secretary of War, Chairman of the Army and Navy Committee, Senator Tillman, Senator John Sharp Williams, General Weaver of course, Mr. Ewing the Patent Commissioner, Zenneck the German wireless man, the Russian Ambassador, Admiral Gaunt and a number of others. He has offered his Engine to the Navy for Submarines if they will standardize it in six months."

In the summer of 1915 three parties had the Fessenden engine under consideration—the Lake Torpedo Boat Co., for Navy Submarines; the General Electric Company; the Submarine Signal Company. By October plans had crystallized so that Mr. Frederic Parker, President of the Submarine Signal Company, Mr. Gordon Dexter one of the Directors and another Mr. Parker, a brother of the President, associated themselves with Fessenden in undertaking the construction of a large size model, suitable for submarines.

In September 1915 Reg met Mr. Thomas,—later Lord Rhonda,—head of munitions, and Lloyd George's representative who was on a special Mission to Canada and the United States. Reg sought by personal interview to rivet attention to those war recommendations which he had submitted in writing to the British Government and had a two or three hour interview with a full discussion of the various devices and suggestions which he had to offer and Thomas expressed himself with much sarcasm at the failure of the War Office to adopt them.

In November 1915 Reg testified on behalf of Admiral Little at a Court Martial at the Boston Navy Yard to investigate defective batteries in submarines.

1916 was tense as the other war years were and filled with many undertakings. There were tests on ways of mounting oscillators, for in spite of Fessenden's recommendations, there was always pressure being brought to bear to mount them in different ways. There were patents and trips to Washington in connection with them. Draughting work on the big engine was going on and the lining up of materials for its construction. In July Reg took over the job of daily inspection of the engine construction work in progress at Fore River. By August the work neared completion and he planned a very elaborate series of tests to be made on the engine. But lest he be tempted to hurry matters and permit short cuts, and also because he was sorely in need of a holiday, a month at a hunting camp in New Brunswick, was decided on.

We left Boston August 21 with much talk of trout and salmon fishing, of duck and shore bird shooting, the enthusiasm being really for the wilds. The technique of sport interested him but not the objective. The delicate precision of fly casting as practiced by one member of the club in particular so intrigued Reg that in zeal of emulation the fate of the poor little trout was forgotten.

It was a great change for us and a very pleasant one.

Commodious club quarters, a few club guests all in relaxed and holiday mood, all enjoying long days out of doors on stream and beach and one very delightful, and for me novel experience, an overnight camping trip at the head waters of the Tabusintac River.

In late October more submarine telephony tests took place at which some General Electric men were present; at the test the report was that the weather was bad and part of the machinery broke down, but they got 'talking' for a distance of five miles.

In January Reg suffered a very acute and alarming attack of indigestion following a hard game of squash at the Union Boat Club. He received medical aid at the Club and later was brought home and a stomach specialist called on the advice of his physician. By midnight the pain had eased and he began to rest though the exhaustion lasted for many days. Indeed three different times in the first few weeks of 1917 he was in the doctor's hands for different ailments, conclusive sign that the pressure and anxiety of the times coupled with the stress of his own work were beginning to tell on him.

Early in the War the U-boat danger assumed menacing proportions and from the beginning and before the entry of the U.S. into the war, Reg had worked steadily on the problem of submarine detection, and what was equally important, on establishing friendly relations with the Naval Officers in charge of submarine work. He visited the Submarine base at New London and was personally acquainted with most of the officers connected with the work and at intervals kept the Navy Department informed of such antisubmarine devices as the Submarine Signal Company had developed or were in process of developing.

In April 1917 instructions were received from Admiral Grant to furnish submarine detector apparatus for test. These tests took place April 26 and 28 at New London in the presence of Naval Officers.

Two types of Detectors were tested—the Long Wave Method and the Echo Method.

In the measured terms of official report Fessenden states:—

"With the Long Wave Detector submarines were accurately and readily detected at the farthest distance tested, i.e. three miles. Also of interest as demonstrating that the indications were positive and not influenced by the knowledge that submarines were in the neighborhood, it will be noted that during one of the tests the presence of an unsuspected U. S. submarine not known to be in the vicinity was detected at a distance of three miles.

With the Echo Method as will be seen from the report, a submarine was detected at a distance of one mile. This was the only echo test made as the submarine was leaving for some other work.

On May 9th in Boston Harbor these tests were repeated, again in presence of Navy Officials and with equally successful results. From the report it will be noted that even when the submarine was running at the slowest speed, at which it could operate it was detected up to the furthest distance of its run—i.e. two and one-half miles. During the Boston tests the detecting apparatus was successfully operated by every member of the two details of radio officers and men who had been assigned by Admiral Grant to the test for purposes of instruction."

So much for formal report. My own diary has this to say:—

"The test at New London April 26 and 28 went off wonderfully. Submarines manoeuvred and could be detected invariably up to a distance of 5 miles and probably 10. (Note. The difference in distance as given is based of course on the intensity of signals—the loudness at the three-mile run assuring a five-mile transmission and probably more.) Reg sent me a telegram on Sunday 29th that tests were entirely successful. He returned the evening of the 30th; the Navy man turned in his report and R. A. F. his to the company and such tremendous enthusiasm started up in consequence that matters have simply been hitting the high spots since."

On May 15 Reg and Blake went to Washington for important interviews, the primary purpose of which was to acquaint the U.S. Navy in detail with the tactical method which had been devised by Fessenden for the best use of this detecting apparatus. Admiral Benson in the press of all other duties arranged for an interview. On the strength of the data furnished him by his own officers and the further plans submitted by Fessenden, he telephoned the British Embassy and arranged for a joint conference the following morning, to be attended by Admirals Benson and Griffin of the U.S. Navy, Admirals DeChair and Gaunt of the British Navy and Fessenden and Blake of the Submarine Signal Company.

The devices and tactics proposed were approved by all four admirals and arrangements were made to put same in practice. Later on the same day Reg called on Balfour who likewise approved the arrangements.

In view of the foregoing it may be stated without bias or exaggeration that the U.S. and British Navies looked to Fessenden as the man of the hour in this overwhelming danger of the U-boat which at this time constituted a major threat of defeat for the Allies.

In a spirit of full co-operation the U.S. Navy prepared to place at the disposal of the Submarine Signal Company every facility to further the work.

It was assumed and intended that all anti-submarine development work should be under the direction of the Submarine Signal Company's Laboratory.

Two yachts, the Margaret and another, were detailed to Boston for use in tests by the Laboratory. Two submarines were detailed to Boston Harbor for use in tests by the Laboratory. Arrangements were made to enable the Laboratory to secure without delay apparatus and appliances necessary for the work.

Such was the situation as America entered the War, at which time, by reason of the vastness and complexity of the burdens laid on Government Departments, authority and power had to be delegated.

In anticipation of war, Secretary Daniels had earlier proposed an advisory inventors' Board headed by Edison, and Fessenden's name was freely mentioned in a nation wide press as a likely appointee. But he was seldom a politician and never in his own behalf and he was not appointed to this Board.

Now, with a multitude of Special Problems coming up for investigation, a further solution was sought in *Civilian Boards and Committees*.

It should have been a good solution, if men were "as they ought to be." The pick of the land was available; but in many instances our civilian army let the nation down. There is a patriotism that rallies to a country's need and there is a patriotism that stands aside if there is a better man for the job. Our country was swamped with the first sort of patriotism but there was very little of the second.

With the appointment of Civilian Boards an entirely new set of conditions came into existence.

It is with the Navy Special Problems Committee and in particular with that on Submarine Detection by Sound also known as the Submarine Board which came into being on February 10, 1917 and was headed by Dr. W. R. Whitney of the General Electric Company that we are chiefly concerned.

In telling the story of how Fessenden's work in U-boat detection was obstructed and largely nullified, forces will be seen at work whereby the adoption of high scientific developments, of which the world stood in dire need, was prevented.

On February 17, at Dr. Whitney's suggestion, Mr. H. J. W. Fay of the Submarine Signal Company, the only company that had from its inception engaged exclusively in transmission and reception of under-water sounds, appeared before the Naval Consulting Board to discuss submarine signaling and the possibilities of detecting submarines.

On February 28 the Submarine Signal Company wrote a letter to the Government proposing that their company start an experimental station at Nahant, just north of Boston. At a meeting of the Naval Consulting Board on March 10 the Board passed a resolution endorsing the proposal and appreciating the patriotic suggestion. The Chief of the Bureau of Steam Engineering also approved the plan and recommended that the General Electric Co. and the Western Electric Co. be invited to co-operate with the Submarine Signal Co. in work at this station. By April the station was completed, the Submarine Signal Co. furnishing the buildings, the power plant and the oscillators. Work by the Submarine Signal Co. and the General Electric Co. started at once and in May they were joined by the Western Electric Co.

On April 26 and 28 at New London and again on May 9 in Boston Harbor trial tests in locating submarines, by means of Fessenden apparatus under Fessenden direction, took place, with the successful results already mentioned.

On May 11 a Civilian Advisory Committee was appointed. Brilliant as were many of the men on this Submarine Board, notable as the work they have done in their own lines, it cannot be denied that for the most part they came as apprentices to the art of submarine signaling and detection.

Since Dr. Whitney had accepted the Chairmanship of the Committee on Sound, it must be assumed that he knew something of the state of the art and who had contributed to it. But Fessenden, the man who had invented the Oscillator, had detected icebergs with it, had sounded the ocean's bottom with it, had telephoned under water with it, had detected submarines with it, this man was not asked to join this Committee.

That the omission was intentional could not be doubted.

The President of the Submarine Signal Co. was fully alive to the necessity for closest technical co-operation with Fessenden and made verbal arrangements, later confirmed in writing, that all technical matters should be referred to Fessenden as Director of the Submarine Signal Co.'s Laboratory.

But the able tacticians of Big Business soon reduced this understanding to the status of a 'dead letter.'

As showing how swiftly control was effected, already in May the following decisions were reached by the Submarine Board.

>   1. No information in regard to Submarine matters should be furnished to the Director of the Laboratory (Fessenden) or to any of the Laboratory engineers.
>   2. That the arrangements made by Admiral Grant (i.e. placing of two yachts, "Margaret" and another, and of two submarines for use in testing the Submarine Signal Co.'s detection devices) should be cancelled.
>   3. That no facilities for tests or developments should be furnished the Laboratory.

Thus the inventions and devices of the man most skilled in the art were halted while slowly the members of the Submarine Board groped their way in unfamiliar fields.

A particular instance is recalled which occurred early in August. Fessenden as already stated had been able to make only one test to locate submarines by the Echo Method. This was at New London in April, at which time the Long Wave Method had been more fully tested. A submarine had been located by the Echo Method at a distance of one mile and Fessenden was anxious to experiment further with this. He sent his assistant, Mr. Price, to Nahant to set up the necessary apparatus and to ask of the specialist in charge, the loan of the General Electric Co.'s Oscillograph.

Mr. Price was obliged to report to Professor Fessenden that the use of the Oscillograph would only be permitted under four conditions.

>   1. The work must be, in the specialist's opinion, of such a character as would justify the time spent.
>   2. He must know fully at all times what we are doing.
>   3. He must get copies of all data, curves, oscillograms, etc.
>   4. He will reserve the right to omit any part of the work or to stop it altogether if he considers that the time is not being well spent.

Was this co-operation as between distinguished scientists?

Was this patriotism as between men pledged to give their best services to their country?

When Fessenden fully realized the implacable determination of the majority of the Submarine Board to disregard his work, it dashed his hopes of any decisive results in curbing the U-boat menace—a menace which at this period was at its peak of destruction.

The average daily loss from U-boats was officially estimated at $5,000,000 (London Engineering, September 19, 1919) and the average daily loss of life was 40 (London Times, January 19, 1919.)

Hazarding a guess as to the ostensible ground on which Fessenden was excluded from participation in this work, it may be that the old propaganda of wireless days was revived, when it was broadcast that Fessenden was a difficult man to work with. Fessenden was never a difficult man to W O R K with but he was an intensely difficult man to play politics with. Nothing seemed to him so futile.

In one of his many attempts to get the Submarine Board to test his detecting apparatus he said to one of the staff of the Submarine Signal Company,—"Why is it they are not willing to try it? It wont cost them a cent." "Well you know Fessenden, ninety-five per cent of a man's time is taken up fighting things through against other men who are trying to block him." "I know nothing of the sort" said Fessenden, "not five per cent of my time is spent that way, if it were I should never get anything done. You men are in hell and dont know it."

To justify his exclusion on technical grounds, the Board, perhaps honestly through failure to understand it, proceeded to discredit Fessenden's work. In May it made a test of the Fessenden submarine detector without permitting Fessenden to be present and thereupon reported that it was of no use for detecting submarines.

What had happened, though it was not known to Fessenden for six months, was that the detecting apparatus had been attached to the *skin of the receiving submarine.* Since the Long Waves to be detected were given off by the vibrations of the skin of the submarine to be detected, these vibrations must necessarily set in similar vibration the skin of the receiving submarine and consequently no indication could be produced by the receiving apparatus so attached, because there would be no *relative* movement between the armature and field of the oscillator.

Then, still groping in the darkness of apprenticeship days, a mathematical monograph was received from England which was interpreted by a member of the Board as meaning that Long Waves could not be transmitted through water,—another fine weapon with which to discredit Fessenden's claims. Just before the Armistice this, too, was brought to the attention of Fessenden. He immediately pointed out that the interpretation of the mathematical formula was erroneous. The question was submitted by the Chairman of the Board to the Board's mathematician, Dr. Wilson, who confirmed Fessenden in every particular. Subsequent to the Armistice official information was received that the Fessenden Long Wave apparatus had at last been tested in England shortly before the Armistice with the result that *thirty times the intensity of submarine sound* had been received by it as compared with any method previously used.

One more instance to press home the fact that these self-appointed arbiters of a most critical phase of the war, were really at the apprenticeship stage of the art, is a terse marginal note by Fessenden in his copy of the Scott "Naval Consulting Board" report, p. 135 which attributes a certain discovery or improvement to a member of the Board—Fessenden's comment is "Used by Sub. Sig. Co. years before. Williams' patent."

Another angle from which the Board sought to damn the Fessenden apparatus was on the score of its weight p. 75 of the Official Report Naval Consulting Board, on the Fessenden Oscillator.

> "It was decided that the oscillator was not the thing to use, because it was heavy and couldn't be installed on very small

boats. It had a big motor generator as part of its equipment, and therefore work was immediately started to produce portable devices that could be put upon any boat."

This hardly checks up with Admiral Grant's statement as to whether weight was a detriment. He said:—

"Every extra ton the oscillator weighed saved the Department $70 because it took the place of that much lead ballast."

The Board inspired, and then entrenched itself behind some very useful Departmental rulings. It suggested, for instance, to the U.S. Government that all communications from foreign governments relative to anti-submarine devices should be referred to the Submarine Board, and obtained the following letter of approval:—

"The Department approves the recommendation of the Special Board that information relating to anti-submarine devices be given out by the Special Board only and instructions have been issued to that effect."

The ruling "Secrecy should be a governing factor" was made to work overtime by the Board when it served its purpose. For instance the United States Merchant Marine felt the need for protection against submarines and formed a "Submarine Defense Association." The Submarine Signal Company's Long Wave Detector was brought to the attention of this Association and the United Fruit Company in particular was much interested and proposed the installation of these Detectors on several of their boats until advised by the Defense Association as follows:—

"We were advised by Dr. Whitney, who is also upon the Naval Consulting Board, of the contents of a letter from one of the Naval Bureaus imposing complete secrecy upon the group and saying that if anything practicable and useful were developed the merchant ship interests would be apprised in due course. Thereupon we refrained from following up this lead awaiting word which, however, has not yet come."

In other words the Submarine Board had things completely 'sewed-up.'

Fessenden and the President of the Submarine Signal Company fought back as best they could. Secretary Daniels was appealed to and from his reply he was evidently completely unaware of the situation, he believed that there was "no stoppage of the work in Boston" and that "a boat was kept on experimental work"—which of course was true enough except that at no time was it at the disposal of the engineers of the Submarine Signal Co.'s Laboratory. And it is easy to see how little chance there was to untangle the red tape which so skilfully ensured certain fixed procedures.

Edison was appealed to, but he too had met with obstruction and negation, as his reply shows:—

("Meadowcroft—send this to Fessenden)
Fessenden—Yours received. You are not the only one who is being turned down. Up to date everything I have done has been turned down and I think this is true of all others.
(signed) Edison."

Thus, *little* Great Men sat in the seats of the mighty, with unlimited facilities at their disposal and expended millions of dollars with negligible production, and took the places of men who could have done the technical job better. As Fessenden wrote:—

"The total failure of these committees has been openly admitted and regretted by every naval officer and every eminent engineer and inventor of whose opinion the writer has information. Historians will probably regard as one of the most striking features of the World War the complete failure of each and every one of the committees appointed by the Government to accomplish any object for which they were constituted."

In one instance the Submarine Signal Company did succeed in going over the head of the Submarine Board and that was when the Company's able and loyal President made application to the Naval Department through Admiral Benson for permission to install at the Company's own expense, a set of its apparatus on a destroyer.

Admiral Benson arranged that permission should be

given to install the apparatus on the U.S.S. "Aylwin" while she was docked in Boston to install other experimental apparatus for the Submarine Board, and also that test should be made of the apparatus.

The installation was effected in accordance with Admiral Benson's permission but upon the "Aylwin" coming out of dock the Submarine Board ordered that no tests of the Submarine Signal Company's Laboratory apparatus should be made.

It can well be imagined that Naval men at this time were eating their hearts out for the chance to get something that would work and to be off with it to the fighting zone. Therefore the Naval Officer in charge of the work, on his own responsibility and actuated by a high sense of public duty, disregarded the instructions issued by the Submarine Board and arranged for a two day test of the Fessenden apparatus.

On November 14 and 15 1917 Fessenden and the Submarine Signal Company had their one and only chance since the Submarine Board took control, to demonstrate the efficiency of their apparatus.

Every possible precaution was taken to make the tests severe and conclusive.

On both days Fessenden and the Submarine Signal Company's operators were stationed in a small windowless booth on board the Aylwin. The door was kept closed, so that the sea was not visible, the compass could not be seen nor could the directions given the helmsman be heard.

The course of the submarine had been secretly prearranged by the Captain of the Aylwin and the Commander of the submarine, but was unknown to any of the Submarine Signal Company representatives. As later learned, the plan for the first day was for the submarine to proceed on a definite course, on the second day on an unknown and varying course and to seek in every way to elude the Aylwin.

At every minute of time after the submarine submerged and the chase started, the log shows the location of the submarine as reported by the Company's representatives. At one time during the first day, a strong tide carried the submarine to the left of her intended course and the Submarine Signal Company's operators reported being on top of her and in position for bombing. The officers of the Aylwin believed the submarine to be approximately a mile away and 45 degrees to port and therefore said that the report must be in error. However, the Captain was asked to come to the booth to listen and verify the facts. This he did and when, a few seconds later, the operator reported that the submarine had just sounded her bell five times, (her rising signal) there was a hurried jump for the bridge and orders given to clear the Aylwin. Hardly was the manoeuvre completed when from the starboard could be seen the air bubbles from the submarine's whistle—just clear of the ship. Then the periscope came into view followed by the gleaming length of the underseas craft herself.

There were two reports of these tests—that of the Naval Officers who conducted them and that of the Submarine Board which had forbidden them. But the Submarine Board had the last word:

Before allowing the Aylwin to proceed to European waters—without any word to Fessenden—they partly dismantled the Submarine Signal Co.'s detecting apparatus, removing the Long Wave commutator and absorption coils. They installed a sea tube (C tube) through a hole cut in the bottom of the Aylwin and gave strict instructions that the C tube was to be used on all occasions.

On arrival at Bournemouth an Admiralty test was arranged and the Captain of the Aylwin reported that even with the Aylwin at rest and without commutator or absorption coils, a submarine could be detected further with the oscillator than with the sea tube, and while the sea tube could of course not be used at all with the Aylwin in motion, the oscillators operated perfectly up to fifteen knots speed. A second test was just beginning when the sea tube broke off through being accidentally lowered while the Aylwin was slightly underway, flooding the compartment so that the destroyer was obliged to return to dry dock.

When it was learned that the Long Wave Commutator and absorption coils had been removed from the Aylwin, Admiral Benson was again petitioned to permit a complete installation of the Submarine Signal Company's detecting apparatus on some other destroyer,—again at the Company's own expense of course, for the Submarine Board were disbursing Government funds only on their own experiments.

The U.S.S. "Calhoun" was the first one available and was equipped.

Some time after the Armistice there took place a competitive test between this detecting device as installed on the Calhoun, developed before the war and with little or no opportunity for test,—and the very latest type developed by the Submarine Board with every facility for test at their disposal and at the expenditure of very large sums of money. The Fessenden pre-war type proved superior at all points.

In conclusion, one letter from Fessenden to the Submarine Board records and summarizes his attempts to overcome these discriminating and partisan tactics:—

February 15, 1918

"Special Board on Submarine Devices
Navy Department,
New London, Conn.

Sir: 2206-999RAF-L

Your letter of February 12th in reply to my letters of November 27, 28, December 4 and subsequent, notifying me that the Board is not willing to allow me an opportunity of meeting the Board and that "it has not been found desirable to have persons appear at a meeting of the Board" is received.

As my efforts to obtain an opportunity of meeting the Board have now extended over a period of seven months, I appreciate the fact that the Board intends this decision to be final and have taken up the matter of obtaining facilities from another source.

2. It is noted that your letter contains no reference to any vote of the Board rescinding the Board's notification of September 15th that—"any protest or objection on my part in connection with any of the tests would be met by the Board's cutting down or canceling the contracts of my clients," or of the Board's notification of November 12th that—"the Board would hold no further communication with me because I had written the Submarine Signal Company that the Aylwin ought to have a preliminary run before leaving Boston."

3. Summarizing my attempts to cooperate with and obtain facilities from the Board subsequent to the demonstration of the detector portion of my apparatus, New London, April 28, 1917.

May, 1917 a. Board notifies me we will not be allowed to use the Margaret which had been detailed to Boston for our tests, as they will need it for the General Electric and Western Electric companies.

b. Board does not acknowledge or reply to my letters of May 9, July 16, October 26, November 2, et al., pointing out that we have no boat to make tests with and requesting one.

c. Request is made, letter May 9, 1917 that a destroyer be sent to Boston to be installed with our complete equipment for running down and destroying submarines.

June 1917

d. Board, contrary to my recommendation and advice that they would not be able to get direction, sends over six destroyers to Europe with only half the proper number of oscillators and without sound screens or water noise cut-outs, etc.

September 1917

e. Board, having docked the Aylwin to install their keel oscillators, allow us to install fore and aft screens. A test, Sept. 15th demonstrates fore and aft screens enable operator to tell whether submarine is to port or starboard. Board declines however to permit complete equipment of screens and oscillators to be installed on the ground "it is not sufficiently promising."

November 1917

f. Board, while Aylwin is being docked to install their apparatus, permit us at our expense, to install athwartship screens. On Aylwin coming out of dock, Board refuses to permit Aylwin to be tested in Boston, Aylwin being ordered to leave November 12th.

Aylwin being held contracy to Board's instructions, completely successful tests are made November 13 and 14, submarines being picked up and run down at 15 knot speed and on second day Aylwin placed on top of submarine nine minutes after starting and four times during the hour. Board then takes Aylwin away, so no further tests possible to date.

December 1917

g. Board removes commutator and other apparatus from Aylwin without notification or consulting me.

January 1918

h. Captain and 1st Lieut. of Aylwin and Captain of Submarine, telegraph in reply to inquiry from Operations Bureau, stated Aylwin capable of running down and destroying German Submarines with certainty and efficiency, recommended that Aylwin proceed at once to European waters, and approved proposal that twelve destroyers be equipped at once with similar apparatus.

Board, in reply to similar inquiry (from Operation Bureau) sends in strong recommendation that Aylwin should not be sent abroad and that the equipment of the twelve destroyers should not be proceeded with.

November, December 1917–January, February 1918

I. Board declines, in response to letters of November 27, 28, December 4, January 2, 1918 to allow me an opportunity of meeting the Board and explaining the operation of my apparatus with a view to obtaining permission to install it completely on a destroyer.

4. No one, I am sure, regrets more than the Board the fact that their action in refusing facilities to men who have made practically a life study of submarine work has resulted in the terrible loss of life of our soldiers on the Tuscania and the unnecessary continuance since July 1st of the submarine warfare which is costing us more than five million dollars per day.

If I might be permitted, with all due deference to the Board, to make a suggestion it would be that the difficulty which the Board finds in permitting me to cooperate with them and meet them and the necessity of bringing before Congress the bill now in preparation to enable me to obtain facilities, might all be overcome if the Board would pass and transmit to the Navy Department the following resolutions:

A. "The Special Board on Submarine Devices recommends to the Navy Department that an oil burning destroyer be sent to Boston before March 1st, if possible, and there equipped with Professor Fessenden's complete four oscillator apparatus, similar to Aylwin but including commutator and water noise cut-out screens. Same to be available for experiments and tests in Boston Harbor for a period not to exceed two months. Work to cover ground recommended in Professor Fessenden's Sub. Sig. Report No. 87, May 9, 1917, i.e. best location of water noise cut-out screens, taking oscillograms of submarines, secret sending method, small oscillator and submarine telephone.

B. The Board also recommends that twelve oil burning destroyers be equipped with Professor Fessenden's four oscillator apparatus, similar to Aylwin but including commutator and water noise cut-out screens, and that same be sent to European waters for use under actual working conditions.

The Board understands that the sets can be furnished within fifteen days from receipt of instructions to equip."

Respectfully,
(signed) Reginald A. Fessenden."

Needless to say, the Board turned a deaf ear to this proposal.

The whole tale of industry in war was to us an unsavory interlude. Progress towards solution of the various scientific problems posed by the war was impeded by the lack of cooperation between scientists, as typified by Fessenden's experience with the Submarine Board.

It must also be realized that during the war there was disclosure and temporary pooling for the nation's benefit of patents and methods in almost every field of investigation. It is easy to see what a supreme opportunity this provided for big business to encroach upon hitherto private enterprise.

America was in the mad house along with the rest of the world.

CHAPTER XXV

OTHER EVENTS OF WAR-YEARS

THWARTED AS HE WAS in his work of U-boat detection, Fessenden nevertheless rendered service wherever possible. It was brought to his attention that some sort of recognition signal between Allied craft was greatly needed, as the substantial bonus paid for destruction of German submarines stimulated the zeal of crews on trawlers and anti-submarine craft to the point where they were disposed to sink first and investigate afterwards and quite frequently allied submarines were attacked by allied anti-submarine craft.

Something that would enable the submarine commander to notify near-by surface craft that his was not an enemy 'sub' was what was needed. Fessenden worked out two devices to cover this. In one, the recognition signal was produced by means of a code wheel controlling the field of the submarine motor. The dogs on the code wheel which produced the secret signal were re-arranged from day to day in accordance with a program sent out every week or fortnight by the Admiral in charge. This type was installed on a submarine and tested on a number of occasions by the Submarine Base at New London and operated most successfully, the signals being easily read up to the farthest distance at which the submarine could be detected and with the added advantage that the presence of the submarine was not disclosed until it would have been detected and then detection and recognition were simultaneous.

The second type was more in the nature of an emergency signal. A certain chemical was discovered which could be loaded into cartridges in such a way that the cartridges would not explode even if the submarine were completely filled with salt water, and which could be ejected from the submarine in such a way that they would float to the top of the water and then explode with a report capable of being heard for several miles, giving off at the same time a bright light of any desired color and producing a considerable quantity of smoke as well.

This method was given a practical trial in Boston Harbor in 1918. It was realized that a first trial of such a cartridge had a strong element of risk attached to it and when Fessenden went on board to make the test, volunteers were called for to assist him.

An officer and an enlisted man responded and the three took their places in the compartment with bulkheads securely fastened.

The cartridge was to be ejected through the torpedo tube. When all was ready Fessenden pulled the lever to release the compressed air but, with his abnormally quick time-constant he probably did not hold it long enough to release sufficient force to eject the cartridge. Each man was fully alive to the possibilities of the situation and Fessenden found himself saying in formal, social tones to his two motionless and silent companions:—"Why, it didn't go off, did it?"

Then a longer, stronger pull and up shot the cartridge and the tense moment was over. But always when telling of this experience he recalled the fine composure of his two companions, the perfect blend of personal courage and navy tradition. For himself he had the work of his own brain as guarantee but his companions were taking his work on faith.

The Submarine Signal Company's Laboratory was called upon on one occasion by the U.S. Secret Service to solve a problem in sound detection. It was known with reasonable certainty that the officials of a certain neutral European power in Boston were in reality strongly pro-German and were lending themselves and their offices to the gathering and distribution of German propaganda. But they had taken very thorough precautions against being overheard. Their offices were in a building with extra thick walls and doors; the walls and all door recesses except one were lined with bookcases filled with books; all electric wires had been removed to avoid risk of dictaphone attachment, in short such meticulous precautions safeguarded them that the Secret Service men had been unable to obtain the necessary proof for legal entry.

Fessenden realized that microphones and amplifiers could only be relied upon for a clear transmission of the words spoken in that office by connecting them up with absorption coils of such a type as entirely to cut out the effect of the natural vibrations of the walls and doors. As soon as these disturbing vibrations had been eliminated by suitable coils, conversation came through clearly and at once disclosed much valuable information—among other things the location of a book containing the name, residence and other particulars of every German reservist living in New England!

This book was subsequently secured.

In the later war years, Reg took up the study of singing, primarily for diversion and relaxation but also with utter seriousness, for *Sound,* its laws and manifestations, had absorbed too many years of his life for any phase of it to seem lacking in importance. He loved music and had a thorough appreciation of it, but beyond some early attempts with the violin had never had a medium to express it.

The St. Botolph Club was a gathering place for musicians of note and virtuosity where technique came in for exhaustive discussions and Reg was stimulated to try to overcome a voice handicap which,—though his analysis of sound was most acute,—seemed to prevent harmonizing with a given key.

Two men, Mr. Charles White whose science of voice production contributed materially to Helen Keller's later achievements, and Mr. Charles Bennett, a White pupil and one of the most successful and beloved voice teachers of the New England Conservatory of Music, were his inspiration. For a number of years, Mr. Bennett found in Reg a pupil such as he had never had before, for together—teacher and pupil—they tackled the how and why of voice production. Mr. Bennett placing his beautiful voice and masterly technique under a Laboratory microscope as it were, with Reg supplying from his store of scientific knowledge the reasons for thus and so and trying to follow where reason and example led.

It was a fruitful and happy experience for them both and Reg achieved quite respectable results. It led to the habit of music for an hour or so every evening at home for which I had to brush up my small skill as an accompanist. Characteristically, there was for Reg no such thing as a limited repertoire and we roamed far and wide—though with halting performance—among the choice songs of the world.

Very much a doubting Thomas at first, I gradually began to note improvement and to join more wholeheartedly in practice. But it remained an unsolved mystery to me by what method Reg arrived at a given note or which note in a given chord he needed to hear in order to arrive at a contrasting note and so there were sometimes stormy interludes. But it was certain that he was getting something out of it beyond my perception and a few years later when a young niece came to Boston to study voice under Mr. Bennett it was 'Uncle Reg' who was her sternest critic and most helpful adviser, pointing out unerringly her faults and how to remedy them. Now after years of study, she is able to say—"I know now what he was trying to get me to do, and he was right every time."

Through work and play ran the somber knowledge that shortly we, with other parents throughout the world must lend, perhaps must give, our only son to the holocaust that showed no sign of burning itself out.

To Youth, of course, it was Adventure, though by this time the starkness of it had been revealed; but Adventure plus Duty brooked no denial. The glamour of soldiering had dazzled our Ken's eyes ever since those early days at Fortress Monroe; in a hall bedroom in the Washington house he created for himself a parade ground which lacked no appointment that hoarded pocket money could buy or grown-ups provide. Grass-green denim stretched taut across the floor for greensward whereon all branches of the service paraded with all the precision and glitter that lead and paint and imagination could supply.

In due time he joined the National Guard and in New York for a time held a commission in a company pridefully known as the "dirty shirts"—one wonders whether that may have been an echo of 1750 of a line regiment under Governor Shirley of Massachusetts, known as Shirley's own, "the dirty half-hundred" whose uniforms with white linings and laces were impossible to keep clean.

At Harvard in 1917 for his last year of law, he joined of course, the R.O.T.C., going thence to Plattsburg and from there to Camp Devens as a first lieutenant in the 301st Infantry.

Quicker and quicker beat the tempo of life, and War. From Plattsburg, Ken came to take his Massachusetts Bar exam, from Devens to get his Masonic degrees and finally, when orders came that sent him overseas in advance of his regiment he and his fiancee decided on the gravely important step of marriage. He sailed early in March, 1918 and from then on letters became the high-lights of life.

In September, 1918, Reg's mother died—Clementina Fessenden, known throughout Canada as the Founder of Empire Day and in all parts of the British Empire by those who interest themselves in the origins of movements.

Devotion to England as the Mother Country stirred in her heart as well as in her husband's and his prolonged Missions in England strengthened it. It will be recalled how strong at the close of the century were the Americanizing influences pulling Canada towards the United States,—commerce, press and literature all contributed. But the Fessendens were among those who believed that Canada's stalwart identity should be preserved and not merged with that of her powerful neighbor. To the cause of knitting Canada more closely to the Motherland, Mrs. Fessenden bent her efforts during twenty or more years of widowhood, and through whatever channels she could find, worked towards that end. An ardent spirit passed when Mrs. Fessenden died and one who cherished her distinguished son's successes as only a mother could.

Slowly the War drew to a close. Hope had been deferred so often that the world waited for what might happen with grim endurance. Then in the darkness of a November night came the wild clanging of bells from far and near to tell the tidings of an Armistice. The news was premature and official confirmation came a few days later but the Peace that came in the stillness of the night to our thankful hearts was more real to us than the wild abandon of November 11.

At last it seemed safe to plan to live again and for us one expression of this was hunting for a home of our own. Coincident with Ken's return in the Spring of 1919 unwounded, but with a nerve strain that was to take him years to overcome, we found the place that pleased us all, and there, on Chestnut Hill, we assembled goods and chattels that had languished in storage since 1900.

The Submarine Signal Company had tasted prosperity during the war but it had been a period that made great demands on its able and admirable president, Mr. Frederick Parker, and with the close of hostilities he welcomed the opportunity of retiring from the presidency.

Thereafter the Company entered upon another phase— the adoption of a policy which in the unbalanced 'twenties' came to be widely recognized as the policy of bankers. With this, Reg was not in sympathy, believing that business must progress by means of new developments and thus be prepared always to keep ahead of a possible saturated market.

Under these conditions Reg withdrew somewhat to himself and, with a temporary relief from economic pressure, began to take stock of his experiences, his philosophy, his deductions, and finally to take up intensively those researches into the beginnings of civilization which enchanted him to the end.

CHAPTER XXVI

INVENTION

FESSENDEN GAVE A GREAT DEAL of attention to the subject of Invention from a historical viewpoint.

Believing as he did that "Conservation," "Natural Resources" etc. were shibboleths and bogeys whether raised by altruistic or predatory groups, he set himself to analyze and to preach the "Conservation" that he did believe in, namely "Man."

In a speech at an Atlantic Union dinner in London in 1910 he said:—

> "The only thing that really matters, materially as well as spiritually on this earth are its men. It is not the so-called "Natural Resources" which should be conserved but the Administrators, the Discoverers, the Organizers, the men who give these resources their value. Given the *Men* they will create all the Natural Resources necessary out of whatever may be at hand."

Again quoting from a proposed catechism on Economics in his "Deluged Civilization of the Caucasus Isthmus" we find:—

> "Q. If a nation does not produce indigo or sugar or nitrates or oil, must it not conquer some nation which produces nitrates or oil?
> A. This was formerly thought to be so, but nations which desired these products and were not strong enough to take the producing countries away from the nation which held them, found that it was not necessary to maintain armies and fleets to obtain indigo, but that refuse from the nearest gasworks dump could be turned, not only into better and cheaper indigo, but also into thousands of other valuable dyes, with new properties which have opened up great fields

in medicine and science and industry generally; that the nearest farm grew beets which could be developed till their juice carried more sugar than the sugar cane, and at less cost; that nitrates could be obtained by sticking two wires close together and passing oxygen-freed air over a catalyser. The total cost to date of these three developments is less than the cost of a single scout cruiser. There are literally hundreds of plant industry engineers who are capable of working out processes for producing fuel alcohol at a cost much less than gasoline is now selling for, and the total development cost would be less than required to maintain one battle ship in commission for three months."

In his unfinished autobiography, Radio News, 1925, elaborating the same theme he says:—

"This is an extremely interesting age, one which will be famous for many things. It is the age of great art. Our sculpture has been finely influenced by detailed and scientific knowledge of anatomy, for lack of which the older masterpieces are always slightly reminiscent of lard. Scientific knowledge of color has raised painting to a new level. There has never been any architecture to compare with the dreams of steel and concrete which we build. We shall be remembered for a hundred things, our literature, our surgery, our medicine, our chemistry, our wars. But most of all we shall be remembered for our inventions."

Fessenden's deductions on Invention seem to fall under the following heads:—

1. Its effects on Progress.
2. Where may Inventors be looked for?
3. What type of mind achieves invention?
4. What constitutes invention?
5. Its problems and pitfalls and the dangers that threaten it.

Of the first he says:—

"All our civilization is based on invention; before invention, men lived on roots and nuts and pine cones and slept in caves."

Macaulay once, in shining words, estimated the effects of invention:—

"It has lengthened life; it has mitigated pain; has extinguished diseases; has increased the fertility of the soil; given new security to the mariner; furnished new arms to the warrior, spanned great rivers and estuaries with bridges of form unknown to our fathers; it has guided the thunderbolt innocently from heaven to earth; it has lightened up the night with the splendour of the day; it has multiplied the power of the human muscles. It has accelerated motion; it has annihilated distance; it has facilitated intercourse, correspondence, all friendly offices, all despatch of business; it has enabled man to descend to the depths of the sea, to soar into the air; to penetrate securely into the noxious recesses of the earth; to traverse the land in carts which whirl along without horses; to cross the ocean in ships which run many knots against the wind—the goal of today is but the starting point of tomorrow."

This was written when the world still stood on the threshold of this "Great Age" which by now may have passed its zenith.

Fessenden continues:—

"And invention must still go on for it is necessary that we should completely control our circumstances. It is not sufficient that there should be organization capable of producing food and shelter for all and organization to effect its proper distribution. Nature has tried this again and again, as with the ants and the bees, and it was substantially effected by the Chinese at certain stages of their history. But the ant-hill civilization has always proved a failure and insufficient; we must work for still more complete control."

"Even if it were physically sufficient it would not be so mentally. One of the most interesting things in ancient history is the difficulty the Hyperboreans had with their messengers. They lived in a country which was considered ideal by those who lived elsewhere, for everything grew there without cultivation, there was little or no rain but a heavy dew each night and a cool breeze blew all day, and while it was never hot there was but little frost in winter. Yet when they sent envoys and messengers to other countries, as they did at first, from time to time, the messengers and envoys never returned to Hyberborea and they were finally reduced to sending their offerings to other temple shrines packed in wheat straw and handed on from tribe to tribe until they reached their destination."

Therefore something beyond the monotony of pleasant security is essential.

2. Since Invention is the very soul and spirit of Progress, where may Inventors be found? Fessenden, from a very comprehensive historical survey was of the opinion that the inventive faculty is a characteristic of certain races and not of others, of certain families of those certain races and not of others.

Therefore as a first deduction *Invention is a matter of Heredity.*

He found that the Greeks attributed most of their fundamental inventions to the Hyperboreans, a North Caucasus race, and to another North Caucasus race that settled Corinth and Syracuse. The Mongols also appear to have been inventors—the compass was used to guide the Mongol carts across the steppes many centuries before it was put to use on the sea.

The Semites, the Ethiopians and the Phoenicians on the other hand, appear not to have been inventors, though the latter race did invent or disseminate the alphabet; they were primarily great traders and had a college for teaching navigation and wrote great histories. The Mendelian Law that Heredity is a matter of mathematical probability can be and has been applied to controlled examples of plant and animal reproduction—as for example, new wheats of enormously greater value than older kinds.

But says Fessenden:—

"Applying these laws to people is obviously much more difficult and uncertain. In the first place we do not know whether a supposed characteristic, e.g. inventive ability, is a real characteristic or due to circumstances. Again, the pairs which form the second descendants do not come, so to speak, all out of the same pair of original boxes. One reason why the son of an inventor may not give evidence of inventive ability is that, contrary to general belief, the inventor has

as a rule, and as might be expected, exceptional business ability, provided he can be induced to exercise it. Stephenson, Edison, Ford, Weston, are examples. One of the most remarkable financial feats known is Edison's putting the phonograph back on a sound business basis after it had been run into the ground by professional business men. So if the inventor *does* decide to pay attention to business, the son may lack incentive or be swamped by administrative detail. And if he does not, the son may decide that it is a mighty poor profession to take up."
"Still, we have notable inventive families. The two Stephensons, the Stevensons, (Robert Louis' "strenous family":—

> "Say not of me that weakly I declined
> The labours of my sires, and fled the sea,
> The towers we founded and the lamps we lit,
> To play at home with paper like a child.
> But rather say—In the afternoon of time
> A strenuous family dusted from its hands
> The sands of granite, and beholding far
> Along the sounding coast its pyramids
> And tall memorials catch the dying sun,
> Smiled well content, and to this childish task
> Around the fire addressed its evening hours."),

the Maxims (Hiram, Hudson and Percy), the Parsons, etc. This last ran to three generations. Lord Rosse made many inventions relating to Telescopes and astronomical work. Sir Charles Parsons invented the steam-turbine and other important devices. His son, a young man of remarkable ability, had made a number of inventions and would have made many more without doubt, but that he was killed in the war. Parsons' son, Kipling's son, Osler's son—as I think over the long list I am not sure but that the greatest evil of the war is that to come; the loss to the time which should have been theirs of the work these brilliant young men should have done."

Dr. Charles B. Davenport of the Department of Genetics of the Carnegie Institute, Washington, D.C. says that:—

"The qualities which make a man a genius are determined principally by heredity. Eminence depends on three qualities. They are capacity for abundant output, technical ability and strategy in the planning of life work. The more the facts are analysed by objective quantitative methods, the clearer emerges the conclusion that the work of successful effective persons is largely if not chiefly determined by genetical factors."

Therefore, when recognized, such a strain should be safeguarded and preserved.

3. Fessenden gave the following definition of the inventive type of mind.

"An inventor is one who can see the applicability of means to supplying demand five years before it is obvious to those skilled in the art."

"What characterizes an inventor's mind?

Obviously, that he sees relationship between things to a greater extent than the average individual does. This may come about in two ways:

1. By extensive knowledge, gained by experience or by study. This explains the reasons for Edison's (scholarship) tests, which have been so much ridiculed but which are so sound fundamentally. Those tests showed whether the man was one who existed in a mental rut or was one who spread his thoughts.

2. By naturally thinking that way.

When I first began to invent I held the opinion that there was no natural aptitude for invention, and that anyone could be technically trained to be an inventor. This came from the fact that I have always been extremely fortunate in obtaining good men for my assistants of whom I have always been very proud, and who have placed me under obligations which I can never adequately acknowledge.

But in going over the history of all the inventions for which data could be obtained it became more and more clear that in addition to training and in addition to extensive knowledge, a natural quality of mind was also necessary.

For one thing, this was indicated by the fact that an inventor makes not one but many inventions, depending on the length of time he lives after he starts inventing, and his opportunities. Take for example Stevenson, Watt, Edison, Weston, DeForest, Parsons, Henry, the Wrights, Rowland,

Michelson, and you will see that they made not one but many inventions. How many men know that Watt invented the copying press, the parallel link motion, the condenser, the pantograph method of copying sculpture; that Stevenson invented the safety lamp; that Edison invented the mimeograph and the modern method of making cement."

In Fessenden's own case, not only was the inherited natural aptitude present, but extensive knowledge gained by study and experience, and, as already described in connection with his internal combustion engine, the process appeared to be a search in the vast storehouse of facts in his mind, carried on by certain wardens of his brain without the need for conscious supervision.

There must be distinction between Research, Dreaming and Invention.

Fessenden says:—

"These three groups are very generally confused with each other, but they could hardly be more distinct than they actually are.
The dreamer and the inventor are confused because they are both apt to omit discussion of details. But their reasons for doing this are exactly opposite. The dreamer does so because he is ignorant of them or does not appreciate their importance. He has merely the idea that he would *like* to do something, but does not know how.
The inventor does so because he is and has to be, or become, a complete master of detail to such an extent that when he has the fundamentals of the problem solved he does not care whether he can or cannot do what he wants in one particular way; if he cannot do it in that way, his knowledge of detail is such that he can merely turn around and do it some other way.
The research man and the inventor are confused because they both examine results of physical or chemical operations. But they are exact opposites, mirror images one of the other, positive and negative. The research man does something, and does not care what it is that happens, he measures it whatever it is. The inventor wants something to happen,

but he does not care how it happens or what it is that happens if it is not what he wants.

The research man will sometimes make an invention, but it will be really a discovery.

The inventor will sometimes conduct a research, but it will only be a step toward an invention."

4. What constitutes invention?

Fessenden says of this:—

"New and important improvements may originate in a number of ways.

1. *Discovery.* A man working in one field may observe a phenomenon which is immediately and obviously applicable, as an important development in another field. For example, Roentgen, working in a field which had been opened up by Lenard, but with different apparatus, noticed that when an object of non-uniform density, such as the hand, was interposed between the cathode and the screen or photographic plate, the image produced varied as the interposed density, and that he could observe and photograph the bones of his hand. This was a magnificent *Discovery* and has had far-reaching results. The *Discovery* of the light sensitiveness of selenium by Sale was also accidental. Such instances are extremely rare, I know of but four or five and would be obliged for information of others. But for some psychological reason the theory that all inventions are of this class has always appealed to the public and consequently there have been innumerable false stories of the origin of inventions. The Phoenicians are stated to have discovered glass through the accident of a wood fire on a sandy beach but glass has been dug up made more than four thousand years before the time of the Phoenicians. Myth-making of this kind is going on today; for example, in the radio supplement of a well-known New York newspaper there appeared a few weeks ago (1923) a very interesting and circumstantially detailed account of the accidental discovery, at the Brant Rock Station, in the presence of a very competent radio engineer, obviously speaking in good faith, of the *Heterodyne.* Though the records of the Patent Office show that the heterodyne patents were filed five or six years before the

Brant Rock Station was erected and three or four years before the apparatus described as being used was built, the story told fits better with the general idea of how inventions are made and will probably become the standard version. But it is important that the student of economics and of the science of invention should note that it is very rarely indeed that an important improvement arises in this way.

2. *Substitution.* Commercial conditions of engineering methods may change so as to make a well known but previously unused method preferable. Aluminum is known to be a conductor; if the copper mines became exhausted aluminum would be used. A method of signaling a few miles might be well known but not used; if a demand for apparatus capable of signaling a few miles arose, it might become important.

3. *Design.* A new and definite problem may be presented which can be solved by well known means in suitable combination. For example, at one time lamp-black was caused to deposit quickly on copper plates by electrostatically charging the plates and passing the smoke from burning oil between them. This method was found too expensive, but if occasion should ever arise for precipitating other finely divided material it would be a matter of design to ascertain the proper non-corrosive depositing sheets, the proper means of producing the electrostatic potential etc.

4. *Invention.* Here a definite problem is set, but the means is not well known, and invention is required.

It will be seen that Substitution, Design and Invention shade imperceptibly into one another. How then shall we determine which is which? I think it determines itself in this way: If the demand is new or the means for supplying it is new, then it is probably not an invention and most certainly not when the use of the means to supply the demand is suggested by several individuals. On the other hand if the demand has existed for a long time, then the suggestion of applying the means to the demand does involve invention. So I would suggest the following definition: *When a demand has existed for more than five years, and when it has been known for more than five years that there would be adequate financial reward from supplying the*

> *demand, and when all of the means for supplying the demand have been in known existence for more than five years, then the application of the means to the demand will be presumed to involve invention.*
>
> It may be asked, why set the term of five years? The answer is that this is merely a basis to work from. It may be held as quite definitely settled that when a strong pecuniary incentive has been in known existence for more than five years, and every element of the means to supply the demand has also been in known existence for more than five years, that invention has been necessary to see that the demand could be supplied by the means. But if either demand or means had been in existence for less than five years it does not imply that there has not been invention but merely that invention is not clearly established and that the claim for invention must be supported by other evidence."

The application of such a definition would, in Fessenden's opinion reduce the work of the Patent Office between 60 and 70 per cent. It would also do away with patent parasites, which always follow the trail of every important invention.

In his "By-products of History" (Deluged Civilization) Fessenden writes:—

> "It is sometimes said, by those who have not studied the history of inventions, that inventions are not made by the individual inventor but are the product of the time, and that if one man does not make them another will.
>
> Now the first Phonograph was made of two pieces of thin sheet metal, one wrapped round a cylinder, the other fixed and with a point fastened on it. Any one of Tutankamen's mechanics could have made it in a few hours. But what good did it do Tutankamen to know that if his mechanic did not invent it Edison would. I happen to know just how the phonograph was invented, for shortly after I came with Edison, I had the luck to work out some minor bothering details in a way which pleased him and saved his time for more important problems, and took the opportunity to ask him about it. In the course of some other work he had run a strip of embossed paper under a thin disc which had

a point fastened to it and had noticed that it made peculiar noises. I suppose thousands of Tutankamen's mechanics had run rough things across the diaphragm of drums and tom-toms and noticed that they made peculiar noises without thinking any more about it.

But to Edison it conveyed the suggestion that if he were to reverse the process, i.e. talk to the disc while a smooth piece of paper was being run under the point, he would have a reproducible record of what he said. He tried it and it worked. "Yes", said Batchelor, his old partner, who had come up and was standing by as we talked, "you can bet I was scared when I heard that thing say 'Mary had a little lamb' when he turned the crank." Batchelor had very distinct and painful recollections, for he had bet Edison twenty-five dollars that it would not talk.

If it be objected that Tutankamen's mechanics, though they built penny in the slot machines and made better carriage wheels than we do now and made speaking tubes for the oracles, had no scientific knowledge of sound, it is easy to prove that this was not the cause of their failure to invent. For, during more than a century before Edison, eminent physicists, engaged in the study of sound, Duhamel, Koenig, Helmholtz, to mention a few names, had been using the vibrograph, which was a diaphragm carrying a point, resting against a cylinder carrying a strip of smoked paper (i.e. the Edison phonograph exactly, except that the paper was smoked) to record the sound waves, *but it never occurred to one of them to run it backwards.* They must have discovered it through running it back accidentally if they had not been too much concerned with the injury to the lamp-black record to listen to the sounds it made.

Here then we have had, for more than a century, eminent physicists, studying the subject of sound vibrations, without it ever having occurred to one of them that by running the apparatus backwards they could reproduce the speech. On the other hand, Edison hears once the peculiar sound made by a rough strip of paper, and immediately builds the apparatus, and while it is building bets his partner that it will talk.

I have gone into this in detail, and have also called attention to the fact that inventors make not one but many inventions, because we cannot intelligently plan for development of our civilization until we realize that neither scientific knowledge nor the possession of facilities for inventing, nor the desire to invent, imply in any way the least ability to invent; any more than a knowledge of sound and the possession of a piano and the desire to compose is an index of musical ability; or a knowledge of metallurgy, possession of machine tools and the desire to make things implies that a man is a good mechanic.

Every man has his own ability and whether one is more important than another is a matter of no consequence; the point to grasp is that the abilities are distinct; the problem to solve is, how we can best obtain the development needed."

5. But though Invention is revealed as the motive power behind Progress, there is also Entrenched Business constituting a very ponderous and static bar to its onward movement. It was with something of the effect of a bombshell that Fessenden in his autobiography promulgated the following Law:—

> "*No organization engaged in any specific field of work ever invents any important development in that field, or adopts any important development in that field until forced to do so by outside competition.*"
>
> "e.g. 1. The telegraph companies did not invent the cable, and after the first cable had been laid continued their efforts to build lines in Alaska and Russia to communicate by that route.
>
> 2. Neither the telegraph nor the cable companies invented the telephone. It was offered to them for $300,000 and they declined it.
>
> 3. The telegraph, cable and telephone companies did not invent the wireless telegraph, and declined it when offered.
>
> 4. The telegraph, cable, telephone and wireless telegraph companies did not invent the wireless telephone, and turned it down when it was offered to them for $250,000.
>
> 5. The gas companies did not invent the electric light.
>
> 6. The horse-car street railways did not invent the electric railway.
>
> 7. The steam engine companies did not invent the steam

turbine. Nor did they invent the internal combustion engine.

8. Neither the steam engine companies, turbine companies, nor the electric companies, nor the shipbuilding companies, invented the turbo-electric or the Diesel-electric drive, and the chief engineer of one of the largest electric companies put on record his opinion that "electricity could never be used except as an auxiliary on ship-board."

10. The electric companies did not invent the high-frequency alternator and when persuaded to make one up at the inventor's expense, the electric company returned it with a letter stating that in the opinion of its engineers it "could never be made to operate above 10,000 cycles."

11. Neither the shipbuilding companies nor the ship instrument companies invented the gyroscopic compass, the inductor compass or the wireless compass.

13. The silk producers and manufacturers did not invent viscose or artificial silk.

14. The collar manufacturers did not invent the soft collar and turned it down when it was offered to them. Etc. Etc.

This is a law to which so far as is known, there are no exceptions. Is it not therefore worth while for an inventor of an important improvement in methods of making tea or of storing power to know that he should *not* take his invention to those engaged in selling tea or in generating power, because there is less prospect of their adopting it than substantially any other class or organization; that it would be merely wasting his time; that he should adopt other means?"

Fessenden long ago saw that business cannot be *conserved*—it must grow or die.

Invention must be its key-note—a steady progression from one new thing to another. As each in turn approaches a saturated market, something new must be *produced*.

Personality and salesmanship do not produce except in a competitive sense.

Standardization does not produce though admirable as an efficiency method.

Combination does not produce though mergers and combinations are still the accepted panacea. In Big Business there appears to be increasing aridity, bureaucracy, the stultifying sacrifice of initiative and above all fear.

An article in Atlantic Monthly for February 1933 "What can a young man do?" by William J. Nichols presents the theory that different callings or professions have been the *center of force* at different periods—soldiers, churchmen, explorers, statesman,—till in our own day Big Business has played the star role, intending to be the *super-center of force* for all time.

But already misgiving is in the air. It is not what the 'young men' thought. The spirit of freedom and of pioneering is lacking, the vital spark is gone.

Will the big body sink slowly to decay?

With buoyant optimism the 'young men' are advised to turn to other callings—medicine, teaching, engineering, scientific research etc.

But is it as simple as that?

Do not the methods of Big Business already permeate these callings?

Can the System, willingly or unwillingly undo its work and once again permit initiative and individuality to play its vitalizing part?

Fessenden hoped that this might be so but he perceived that sinister forces were at work which might prevail and all unwittingly bring about the downfall of our present civilization.

The following chapter from his autobiography gives this warning in his own words.

CHAPTER XXVII

GREAT AGES

(THE INVENTIONS OF REGINALD A. FESSENDEN
—RADIO NEWS, JULY 1925)

"THE GREAT AGES pass quickly; that they were passing has never been believed at the time; nor has the cause, which has always been over-organization brought about by well-meaning but too narrowly educated men, been appreciated.

The first thing every student of community affairs should study is real history; not the history of names and dates and battles, and not for the purpose of exterpolating curves based on empirical data, but for the analysis of the causes which have led to the results shown by the curves and of the modifications of the curves produced by variations of the causes. Such study makes it clear that the only vital growth of a civilization is that which comes from its own internal kinetic pressure, and that the application of statical and mechanical directional forces result only in wreckage.

The essential thing is freedom to expand in all directions, because there are fundamental reasons, which will be given later, why no body of men can ever determine the true direction for growth.

As an illustration, the "Great Age" of Plato, Aristotle, Demosthenes, Aeschines, Menander, Diogenes and Epicurus was succeeded in the very next generation by Ptolemy's great organization of literature. The production of great works was to be carried out by hundreds of writers, co-operating. Every effort was made to discourage the independent writer and to make literature a monopoly. The great Library of the Museum at Alexandria had finally more than half a million volumes. The export of papyrus was forbidden by law, and when the king of Pergamus, in an attempt to break the monopoly, gathered together a library of books written on a newly invented substitute for papyrus, i.e. parchment, his library was seized and carried to Alexandria.

Through generation after generation the foundation was the hobby of the kings of Egypt. It was richly endowed and the poets, scholars and scientists who lived in what Timon called "the coop" were free from all material worries. And the result?

In the five hundred years of its existence (B.C. 300 to A.D. 270) not one single original work of any importance was turned out by any member of the foundation, except the "Argonautica" of Appolonius of Rhodes, and that, on its reading before the members, was laughed out of the hall so that its author "flushing with mortification" as his Greek biographer records, severed his connection with the foundation and fled to Rhodes. This is of course not the first of the inventive ages. Invention has appeared so far only intermittently, as Kipling's torch, "rekindling thus and thus." There was a time extending over more than 5,000 years, during which science was in the hands of an international council, called the Cabiri, apparently exactly similar to our present Research Council, during which there was absolutely no development.

Will their antiquated and discredited policy, now revived by our own Research Council, of eliminating the individual inventor be successful?

These plans, which were formerly kept secret, (and for the most part are now) were recently divulged by a number of the members of the Research Council in the New York Times for March 1, 1925, p. 4. The article opens by saying that the day of Edison, Wright and Ford is past: that "Henry Ford worked on his automobile almost unaided in a little room at the back of his house. The Wright brothers designed the first airplane in a bicycle shop. Edison experimented in a baggage car."

"But the old-fashioned inventor has ceased to be the all-important factor in invention that once he was. The work of experimenting and inventing has been made the work of vast organizations, of immense and adequate equipment, and of virtually unlimited financial backing."

This is of course the old story. The "Do away with the individual author and give everyone access to a great library and a pension and we will have innumerable great literary works" of Ptolemy. The "Do away with the individual painter, and teach all children to paint, and we will have innumerable masterpieces" of another set of enthusiasts. The "Do away with the individual owner of property and we will all have all the property we can wish" of yet another set.

One must sympathize with these objectives.

We do want more inventions, because every invention, e.g. that of steam which manumitted the galley slave, lifts a burden and broadens comfort so that now the luxuries of Babylonian kings and Roman noblemen have become the necessities of our day laborers.

We do want more great works, in literature and art, and we do want every one to have all the property he can use efficiently.

But should there not be some demonstration, even on a small scale, that the objectives can be reached by the means proposed before throwing away the present system, which has given us what we have.

What the United States, and the world, owe to the individual inventor we all know. Take away the cotton gin, the steamboat, the telegraph, the electric light, the automobile, electric power, the typewriter, the sewing machine, all the other work of the individual inventor, and there is substantially nothing left.

On the other hand, it is admitted by all who have studied the subject that, to quote Russell, (Nature, November 1, 1924): "It is of course true, as others have pointed out, that epoch-making discoveries have not yet come direct from teamwork or organized research." Is it wise then to eliminate the individual inventor until teamwork has produced at least one such important invention?

Of course, the failure of the Research Council, after the expenditure of so many millions, has had to be covered up by propaganda. The following is a list of inventions which the Research Council has prominently published as its work:

> Inductor compass for airplanes.
> Ultra-violet light signalling.
> Under-water wireless.
> Audion oscillator.
> Sonic depth-finder
> Wireless compass.
> Liberty Motor.
> Submarine detector.
> Airplane wood-drier.
> Wireless transmission of pictures.
> Ultra-audible sound signalling.

but each of which was to my personal knowledge communicated to the Research Council officials by the inventors, e.g.

> Inductor compass by Pickard.
> Ultra-violet light signalling by Louis Bell.
> Audion Oscillator by DeForest.
> Under-water wireless by Rogers.
> Liberty motor by an engineer of the Packard Co. etc. etc.

in each case after practical and successful tests, many of which I witnessed myself, e.g. I operated Louis Bell's ultra-violet signaling apparatus perfectly over a distance of five miles. And in each case the Research Council, after witnessing the tests and privately constructing duplicates of the inventor's apparatus, arranged that the U.S. Departments should procure the apparatus from members of the Research Cabiri, without paying the inventor anything, and propagandized the U.S. at government expense, with statements that these inventions were due to the Council.

The list given in the New York Times of March 1, 1925, is of similar nature, e.g. the first invention claimed by the Research Council or Cabiri officials, the "invention that makes it possible to photograph sound on a motion picture film" is of course DeForest's.

The next, the microphotographic talking book, in regard to which the article states, the Research Council official was asked "Are you working on such a device now?" he smiled, "Not as a whole. I just happened to think of it," was really a matter of recollection, for it was shown to the official in the inventor's laboratory in 1920, and his company was asked if they could furnish the quartz discs referred to in the following account taken from a book published in 1923. (Deluged Civilization p. 134).

"The microphotograph-projection book—made from two quartz discs, one-sixteenth inch thick and an inch and a quarter in diameter.—When it is not desired to read visually the book may be read audibly, by a parallel phonograph record." A photograph of the apparatus used for making the phonographic records appeared in one of the radio journals the previous year.

The next "we have done away with the small diaphragm" was shown to the same official by the inventor in 1919 and written acknowledgment of receipt of a full description of the theory is in the inventor's possession.

The next, the single crystal wire, was developed in Germany before the war and applied to tungsten filaments.

The next, the nitrogen lamp is old, and will be found described in the back files of the American Institute of Electrical Engineers.

Will the effort to eliminate the Edisons, Wrights, and Fords be successful?

Personally I do not think so, because I have hopes that the seriousness of the situation will be realized before it is too late; it is one of the main objects of these articles to bring about that realization, and to suggest means for combating the schemes for the elimination of the individual inventor.

But it must be admitted that the Cabiri have had a certain amount of success so far. The writer, having other and many resources, has not been much affected; he has had to give up his researches on cancer, which were very promising and had effected a permanent cure, (no return after three years) in a case pronounced one for operation by the head of perhaps the most authoritative cancer hospital staff in the U.S.; and has had to obtain the fine grain protographic plates for some of his researches from abroad and secretly, to prevent the supply from being cut off. But many have felt the effects seriously. The suicides of McDowell and Webster are especially regrettable. McDowell's because his firm, the Brashear Optical Co. had always freely communicated all its optical secrets to interested members of the Research Council. Consequently he could not compete with the Mt. Whitney Observatory, which was heavily endowed from the Carnegie funds, and could make lenses at less than cost. (I see also, by last week's *Nature,* that the big English Optical Works of Sir Howard Grubb has also had to go out of business, and in another paper that the Mt. Whitney associates have obtained the contract for the great Switzerland telescope). Knowing Carnegie as I did and the affection he bore to Brashear and McDowell, and the fact that he intended his foundation for the use and assistance of just such men, I feel that Carnegie must have turned in his grave when McDowell died. Of Webster, whose great work is known all over the world, it is said that he had been in a nervous and unsettled state before his suicide. But he was very proud of Clarke University, and how many men would have preserved their full equanimity on receiving word that the Research Council had decided that the laboratory which had been hallowed by the work of Michelson and Wadsworth and his own work on sound was to be turned over into a school for geography, and that he must look, at his age, for a new position.

And minor cases are innumerable; as the pressure is being felt I receive requests for help almost every day.

Power at the command of the Research Council.
Let us first make a survey of the tremendous grasp which

the Research Cabiri has on the wealth of the United States and the despotism which it exercises.

1. The total funds at its disposal or in the shape of foundations from Carnegie, Rockefeller, Eastman and others, and from other sources, is in excess of $10,000,000,000.

2. This is, however, but a fraction of the total amount of Capital which it controls. In the first place it is international.

In the second place, all the industries in the United States (and in the principal foreign countries) are divided into groups. These the Research Cabiri rules with a rod of iron through secret international reports. As the description of this system should be made authoritatively, I will quote from the authorized statement, made by the head of one of the U.S. Government Bureaus and printed in the Boston Transcript of April 6, 1925. After describing the specific equipment, which has cost the taxpayer of the U.S. many millions of dollars, he says: "Our laboratory facilities are unusually complete. We have a research associate plan. Under this arrangement an industrial group can send to this department a representative to work on some particular problem of interest to that industry. His salary (alone) is paid by his employers, but in other respects his status is that of a member of the department's research staff. He has the use of the laboratories and the benefit of the experience of our people." (i.e. they assist him without pay). "The results of his work are published by the bureau *after approval by those interested.*"

The exact number of publications approved by the new form of trusts may be judged by the fact, disclosed in *Nature,* issue of February 7, 1925, that of 29 such reports of research work done almost entirely at government expense, and in a government bureau, not a single one has been published; every one is the secret information of the members of the trust. The total number of scientific publications for the past year available to the manufacturer outside of the trust, or to the inventor, or to the independent scientist, from the department referred to, with its millions of dollars of equipment, and its large annual appropriations, was just *nine* and those of minor importance. But the independent manufacturer and the independent inventor paid their share of the cost of these trust and Cabiri secrets.

It will readily be understood that the manufacturer who desires to be independent is virtually black-jacked into the trust, at government expense, and that the patent office is virtually eliminated.

3. If an invention is made in any industry, say in the piano manufacturers, and is submitted by the inventor to any one member of the industry, that manufacturer cannot adopt it. It has first to go before the branch of the Research Council which controls that industry. If the Research Council can see no way of eliminating the individual inventor in that particular case, the reply goes back, through the association to the particular manufacturer and thence to the inventor, that the manufacturer has decided not to adopt the invention. And if the inventor goes to any other piano manufacturer, no matter where, in the United States, he will find that they each and all know of the invention but are each and all decided not to adopt it.

If any manufacturer did adopt it he would be put out of business by the Research Council in short order.

If, however, the Research Council believes that the patent is loosely drawn and can be evaded, the council puts its own men to work to do so.

The immediate net result is of course elimination of the independent manufacturer and independent inventor; then stoppage of all improvement in the art, for as shown in a previous section corporations never invent or adopt any improvement of importance unless forced to by outside competition: then a hectic prosperity; then stagnation in the industry and high prices to the consumer, and finally hard times.

The Research Council thus controls absolutely every industry and every manufacturer in the United States, except a few, like Ford and Edison, who are able to hold out.

4. The present plans of the Research Council call, it is understood on good authority, for the placing of all stock of trusts as far as possible in the hands of small shareholders, and placing members of the Research Cabiri on the boards in influential positions.

5. On the Universities, the first hold of the Research Cabiri is through the Carnegie and other pension funds. No professor who opposes the Cabiri can hope for any support for his declining years. It will be remembered that his pension was arbitrarily denied President Wilson though he was strictly entitled to it.

The second hold is through endowment shares in industrial corporations controlled by the Research Cabiri. In a recent case this has gone even further, and one of the great universities, endowed with millions of dollars by independent donors, is now an actual partner in one of the trusts, and cannot sell the stock, but must depend on the trust being profitable.

A third is through control of positions for the university graduates. A student who enters one of the universities (with the exception of a very few who still hold out) has parted with his liberty for life. No matter how brilliant his class record, he cannot obtain a position unless he satisfies the Cabiri and the trust which controls his chosen field of work, and he cannot engage in business as an independent manufacturer, as shown above. Nor can he become a consulting engineer, for all that work is now turned over by the Research Council to its own universities, where the students are detailed to the work for little or nothing, and the professors must take charge of the work for nothing or lose their positions. To all intents and purposes the student is therefore a slave to the Research Corporation as much as any negro was to the plantation owner.

Defenses of the independent inventor against the Research Cabiri.

1. *The patent Office.* This institution, on which the wealth of the United States is founded is an obstacle in the way of the Research Council which has already, by the "con-

fidential research report" system outlined above, neutralized the chief function of the Patent Office which its founders intended it to fulfill. It has also (but much less than might have been expected, to the honor of the men, be it said) had a bad effect on the morale of the Patent Office employees, necessarily, for with the elimination of the individual inventor there is no longer any opening for a Patent Office official except with one of the trusts. And soon there will be none at all, for obviously when the combines are completed by the Research Council and the results of all researches are preserved in confidential reports, there will be no object in the trusts taking out any patents, and we will have returned to the medieval system of "trade secrets" which it was found, proved so detrimental to civilization, and from which the Patent Office was created to free us. Efforts will naturally be made by the Research Council to block the purposed functioning of the Patent Office; are, in fact, now being planned, it is understood. All legislation must be carefully watched.

2. *The Courts.* We still have the Courts. That they are a real defense is shown by the complete failure of the recent attempts of the Research Council to seize Rogers' under-water wireless and De Forest's regenerator. No doubt courts are occasionally fallible, as is every human institution, but they are a stronghold of civilization.

3. *Elimination of Secret Reports of Work, any part of which is at the expense of the Taxpayer.* The publication immediately on completion, of all work conducted in part or wholly at the government expense, should be called for by law. This would give the independent manufacturer and taxpayer a chance.

4. *Taxation of Endowments and Regulation of Endowment Official Salaries.* These endowments are not, in perhaps most cases, now being used for the purposes which the founders had in mind. They are a drain on the resources of the country. No foundation which does not continue to enlist the financial approval of the public should continue in existence for more than the generation which created it.

The taxes on foundations should be proportioned with this end in view, to lift the dead man's hand when rats shelter beneath it, or when the end he sought is no longer for the common good.

5. *Making our Universities Independent.* First by ruling as illegal bequests which make the university the servant of any trust or corporation. Next by making pensions dependent solely upon fixed rules, service and vote of the university itself.

With these defenses, provided and maintained, there is reason to hope for a long maintained age of invention. Without them we may confidently expect a long period of retrogression.

Preservation of Art of Inventing.

All that I have written above has been because I am firmly convinced that if the decision of the Research Council to eliminate our Edisons, our Wrights and our Fords and the Patent Office, and to return to the "trade secret" system is successful (and it may well be . . .), then, as has happened in past ages from exactly the same cause, the progress of civilization will be halted for many years, even for many centuries.

One reason why it is hard to recover "Great Ages" is the penetrating growth of vested interests into their foundations, which is hard to remove.

Another is that arts, and Invention is an art as well as a science, require what may, not irreverently, be called a form of apostolic succession; because so much more is to be learned by seeing and assisting in the actual doing of the thing than can be told in writing."

CHAPTER XXVIII

LOOKING FAR BACKWARDS
THE DELUGED CIVILIZATION OF THE CAUCASUS ISTHMUS

THE RESEARCH WHICH FESSENDEN took up intensively soon after the war and which continued to be his most vital interest to the end was on the beginnings of History—the pre-deluge Civilization.

It was a topic that had attracted him as a classical student but in the driving years that intervened it only cropped up occasionally as a matter for pleasant speculation. Now however the way opened for a thorough exploration of the subject and by *thorough* is meant thoroughness of the Fessenden order.

He started with an examination of the Geography of the Greek Myths—those delightful tales of Hercules, of Jason, of the Argonauts, which at school we accepted so gratefully for their rich glow of fiction in an otherwise drab field of facts.

He assumed first of all *Reasonableness* in connection with them—certain expeditions or journeys seriously undertaken and successfully concluded. What did the Geography of these Myths require in order to make them logical and reasonable?

Again the Fessenden touch—the premonition that *a wrong turn had been taken*—that somewhere in the long trail of History something had been misunderstood or misplaced. Tabulating all the Myths and the countries traversed by them it was seen that it was in the district bordering on the *Atlantic* (?) that discrepancies and impossibilities developed; therefore that there must be something wrong with the location of this district; that apparently it had nothing to do with our present Atlantic but instead with an *Ocean of Atlantis* (that former vast Mid-Asian sea now dwindled to mere remnants) and that *something* must have occurred to destroy or block a district that had once been accessible.

On such an assumption the Myths became normal and reasonable.

This *something* must have been a catastrophe of first magnitude.

The Deluge may have been such a catastrophe.

So every known, existing tradition of the Deluge was studied from literal translations and the results tabulated and compared.

There are five of them. The Greek, the Phrygian, the Egyptian-Phoenician, the Cimmerian and the Hebrew-Babylonian, so they were not derived from a common source.

Each tradition nevertheless relates to some region in the neighborhood of the Black Sea; they are consistent as to time; each reveals such suitable differences as proximity would indicate.

Thus, the Egyptian-Phoenician tradition calls for a rise of 35 feet and a period of twenty-four hours.

The Cimmerian tradition calls for an increase in level of the Black Sea of approximately 45 feet and a period of approximately twelve hours.

The Hebrew-Babylonian tradition must have a rise of 40 feet on the south-west coast of the Ocean of Atlantis and of sufficient rapid increment to carry a large vessel up the valley of the Arax into the great expanse at the foot of Mt. Ararat and flood this expanse over an area of approximately 50 miles square. The period would not exceed a few hours but the time taken to drain the expanse would be measured by weeks or even months. Taken as a whole the traditions require a tidal wave on the south-west shore of the Ocean of Atlantis, of a height of approximately 40 feet, lasting for approximately twelve hours and sufficiently rapid in its onset to produce bores up the river valleys of that shore.

That it had this tidal wave characteristic appears to be certain—the Babylonian tradition says specifically "Like a war engine it (the Deluge) comes upon the people."

The possible causes that could produce such an effect were next considered.

The Ocean of Atlantis was shoal over a great portion of its area but with considerable areas of much greater depth; the Caspian Sea, a present remnant of the old Ocean of Atlantis, is even now 3000 feet deep in places and the rivers flowing into it are notorious for carrying large amounts of sediment; therefore a possible, perhaps a probable cause, after several years of drought, followed by abnormal and long continued rain, may have been a great slippage of sedimentary deposit, which is one of the most common causes of tidal wave.

Writing to Professor Albert T. Clay of Yale whose book on the Babylonian version of the Deluge had cleared up some points for Fessenden, he said:—

> "I am attempting to show on geological evidence that the Deluge was an actual geological fact and occurred almost exactly or exactly as described.—What I have discovered is that the original ocean of Atlantis was the great Mid-Asian Sea, (the Asiatic Mediterranean) well known to geologists but hitherto over-looked by archeologists, though existing to 4000 B.C., stretching from the Caucasus to Tartary; that the Pillars of Hercules were at the entrance to the Sea of Azov; that there was water communication between the Sea of Azov and the Ocean of Atlantis (along the present Don and Manytch Lakes); that there was a real island of Atlantis, part still existing, (then not settled); that there was a real Deluge which really destroyed Atlantis and the Ionians of the shores of the Aegean Sea, but did not affect Egypt; how the straits of Gibraltar came to be wrongly identified with the Pillars of Hercules; that the original Iberia was what is now known as Georgia, in the Caucasus valley; that the original Libya was the country between the Sea of Azov and the Adriatic; that Mt. Atlas was Mt. Elbrus; what the 'Kirubi' were; that the old Greek traditions were not myths but actual voyages; that Hesperus was really the

'morning Star' and the Garden of the Hesperides in the Caucasus Valley;—

I would like to hold up publication for four or five years more. But the Russian Soviet Government is starting to colonize the remnant of the Island of Atlantis, and as the adjoining country is the place of origin (as I prove) of the Caucasian race, (country between the Manytch Lakes and Caucasus Mountains), *field work* on the problem must be done before the Russian peasant gets to work."

Here in rough outline is Fessenden's conception of the beginnings of Civilization.

Home Neanderthaliensis and Homo Sapiens had existed and disappeared.

The theory that mankind of today was a *slow development* of Homo Sapiens was not Fessenden's belief. Instead, he conceived that because of a given environment, a district of unique . . . characteristics, there occurred not a gradual but an abrupt change into mankind as of today.

Life had been pushed down by a glacial line on the North, had been hemmed in by the Mid-Asian Mediterranean (the Ocean of Atlantis) on the East, by a vast morass on the West and by (for a time) an insuperable barrier of the Caucasus Mountains on the South; pocketed so to speak, in a district possessed of physical characteristics extraordinarily favorable to development.

"It is," wrote Fessenden, "as if the Creator impatient of the futile Paleolithic developments had swept Man up into this corner and said; 'Here is everything you can possibly need.' For here in this unique location were fire, oil (the burning fields), metal ores, timber, alluvial soil, irrigating streams and useful animals, fruits and grains."

And here Civilization did arise, persist and prosper until the catastrophe of the Deluge when the great dispersion began.

Strand by strand Fessenden picked the revealing threads from the ancient writers and with them constructed his vivid tapestry of that drowning out of a great civilization. Thus he pictured it:—

"Tamischeira is not a high mountain (6000 ft.) but it is the outermost of the northern spur of the Ceraunian mountains, and from there it is possible to see far out over the plain; it is in the country of the Chalybes, and since it was the place where the women observed the rite of the "Wailing for Thammuz", there can be little doubt but that it was from this point that Queen Ashirta saw her husband and his forces drowning in the Deluge.—

We can see the slopes of Mount Tamischeira, covered with the women of the Chalybes, their queen among them, terrified by the earthquakes, looking out over the drowning plain through the storm of rain, as the great tidal wave sweeps past to the west. It is the last scene, when the light comes the shuddering spectators will leave that stage, the far dispersion has begun."

By the fall of 1923 Fessenden had his main thesis broadly outlined, much material collected and several chapters written—sufficient he believed to carry conviction.

Knowing however from experience how hopeless it was to expect a hearing in any publication devoted to such matters, he proceeded to publish the material himself. A limited edition was brought out, some on chart paper for utmost permanency, the rest on good stock and with most careful attention to type and form to ensure a dignified presentation of a matter of great import—nothing less than adding perhaps 10,000 years to the beginning of history.

The title of the Book was "The Deluged Civilization of the Caucasus Isthmus." Very careful lists were made so as to effect as international a distribution of this work as possible among the individuals, societies and libraries most interested in such research. The response on the whole was gratifying; leaders who had earned the best right to say, admitting that Fessenden had made out a strong case but warning that the concrete results of field work would be needed to arouse anything like public interest.

It will be impossible to convey the tremendous activity with which Fessenden pursued the enthralling problem of this vanished, reasoning people.

His reading was all embracing; from Strabo, Herodotus,

and Josephus he gathered every illuminating hint; from cyclopedias, biographical, mythological and geographical, of antiquity, he culled his data and stiffened it with a backbone of reality; the classics and the Old Testament were sieved through the meshes of his mind for every grain of truth about these people of the past; by means of maps and charts the country which they had inhabited became in thought his familiar camping ground; he steeped himself in the atmosphere of place and period, he foregathered with the spirits of its heroes; for one of Fessenden's rare qualities was an imagination that far outstripped the concrete.

The libraries of Boston and of Harvard were consulted and where prolonged consultation of rare volumes was necessary, as with 'Diodorus Siculus' for example, Fessenden had a page by page photostat made of the book.

For maps, in addition to the Times Atlas and Stieler's, he obtained through the great kindness and interest of British Governmental Departments, Divisional Staff Maps of the Caucasus. One known as the Petropolis map dated back to 1793, there were some of 1842 but the group that he found most valuable were the staff maps of 1847 which gave the old place names with remarkable fidelity. These 1847 maps Fessenden found so important for his work that full size glass negatives together with the prints of the series of twenty-five sheets were made for him through the courtesy of the Royal Geographical Society.

It was a quiet period for us; Fessenden had withdrawn from active contact with the Submarine Signal Company though patent work still continued in full force. Our son and his wife were no longer with us as he had been placed by his firm in charge of their New York office. So we were alone and it was a good deal as if we lived a dual existence— in a world of the 1920s and in another of B.C. 5 or 6 or 7000 —that is, Reg did, I only caught glimpses and reflections of this distant world at meal times or when he felt like talking and getting his data in clearer sequence.

Then to an uninitiated listener our topics would certainly savor of the fantastic. It might be of 'cherubim' ('kerubi') which instead of something mystic turned out to be a brilliant flying lizard, 'draco' by name, well known to present day museum field workers in the Malay Peninsula—now only about ten inches in length but then nearly three feet, having membranous wings of vivid blues, reds and yellows, so that they looked like huge, gorgeous butterflies. These in great numbers guarded the 'tree of life'—*Guarded it* because stretched along its branches they could most readily catch the insects on which they lived. The ancients feared them and thought them poisonous.

The 'tree of life' was believed to be the 'Citrus Medica. Through the kindness of the Agricultural Bureau in Washington a number of specimens of the fruit of this tree were sent to Fessenden.

Or talk might turn on the 'tree of the knowledge of good and evil,' believed to be the 'thorn apple' or 'datura' a tree or shrub still found growing in the Caucasus region and against which, warnings to settlers were issued by the Russian Government as recently as just before the war. A fruit of remarkable and dangerous qualities. A deadly poison, but taken in sublethal quantities, producing as a first effect, greatly increased mental acuity. In ceremonial observances as recorded, the habit obtained of throwing some of this fruit into the sacred fire around which the leaders were gathered, the fumes producing a sort of intoxication.

Fessenden cautiously considered the possibility whether some chance or unregulated use of this fruit may have been a contributing factor to the abrupt change to reasoning Man, through the increased cerebral circulation produced by it.

Or talk might turn to Noah and his sane preparations for an impending disaster. Then speculation as to probable human friction in the limited quarters of the Ark. A chance reference disclosed that after flood waters receded and land travel again became possible there was a quick dispersal. Fessenden much enjoyed the very human touch of Mr. and Mrs. Noah 'hot-footing it' as he said, back to their own district, leaving their companions of the Ark to shift for themselves.

Or it might be of Hercules, the great engineer and of the constructional and political significance of his engineering undertakings.

It might be of that mysterious, awesome Dariel Pass, the one passage way through—the Caucasus Mountain range—a narrow gorge barely affording passage for a rushing torrent and on either side cliffs rising abruptly to heights of more than 5000 feet. A passage dark and forbidding but, once traversed from North to South, giving access to the Garden of Eden as fair and fertile a land in reality as the Bible portrays. Here, in Fessenden's opinion, as Civilization developed, the great leaders, the men who controlled the technical trade secrets, of glass making, of ore reduction, of steel, of enamels, of trade routes, who were also the astronomers and the mathematicians of their time, made their home. They were the Kabiri, a great secret society, living in an earthly paradise, from which they sought to control the known world.

That these advanced workers, the leaders of civilization, made and preserved records cannot be doubted. Fessenden believed that these would have been stored in subterranean chambers and that quite possibly they may have withstood the ravages of time. In his various papers on the "Deluged Civilization" he noted several places where excavation should be undertaken in a search for such records. His idea was to explore first of all with his ore detecting apparatus and methods, which have been applied so successfully in the location of salt domes and oil wells. It is to be hoped that eventually this will be done. Though this vanished civilization had been swept out of existence yet echoes of it sounded faintly, mysteriously, down the corridors of Time and ages later when the tide of Empire had passed to Egypt and that first Civilization had become nothing but a myth, still the priestly records stressed as the great dogma of salvation, the return of the spirit to the 'home land,' and in the elaborate ritual of "The Book of the Dead" Fessenden uncovered directions which to the initiated plainly and unmistakeably pointed the way to that 'home land' of the Caucasus Isthmus.

Fessenden's publications on the subject were:

The Deluged Civilization of the Caucasus Isthmus, Privately printed and distributed, Massachusetts Bible Society. 1923.

Finding a Key to the Sacred Writings of the Egyptians, *Christian Science Monitor,* March 18, 1924.

How it was discovered that all so-called Myth-Lands were the Caucasus Isthmus, *Christian Science Monitor,* March 8, 1926.

Chapter XI of the Deluged Civilization, Privately printed and distributed, Massachusetts Bible Society. 1927.

A number of unpublished papers on the same subject were assembled and edited by our son R. K. Fessenden and brought out by him in 1933 in the same format as the two earlier publications of 1923 and 1927.

It is anticipated that in the next decade as field work discloses more and more signposts pointing to this first Civilization of the Caucasus Isthmus, that a literature on the subject as voluminous as that on Egypt and on Babylonia will arise, and then the extensive accumulation of data compiled by Fessenden which is carefully preserved, will doubtless find skilled and appreciative analysts.

Fessenden in all humility felt that his mental equipment to perceive, develop and launch this theory was such as might not occur again. The many-sidedness of his mind was unique. He was serenely certain of the correctness of his theory but he felt that time pressed and so he drove himself beyond reason, working all morning and at night until two or three o'clock and with only the afternoon intermission of a strenuous round of golf. It was all too strenuous and in 1925 the warning came—a slight stroke which he believed was the direct result of prolonged hours of handling heavy volumes weighing often ten pounds or more. Fortunately the condition soon cleared up but he realized that he must 'go slow' or at least slower; all the more was this driven home by news of the sudden death of Dr. Albert T. Clay the noted Assyriologist, in the full tide of accomplishment, whose work was such an inspiration to Fessenden.

Writing to Clay after reading his "Empire of the Amorites" he said "Please do not bother to answer this. I am just writing in the *mental thought shower-bath* of your book." One might almost venture to think the inspiration mutual, for in Clay's last letter to Fessenden he writes:—

"Your kind, interesting and instructive letter I have received. Your map I have before me on my table. You have introduced me to a new world which was not much better known than Mars. It seems so strange that a country adjoining my own should have so many important problems having a bearing on the lands to the South of it, and be so little recognized by Assyriologists. I have been crowded to my neck since my return with all kinds of reports, articles, lectures etc. etc. My desk is still full of unanswered letters but I begin to see the end. I am crazy to look up some of the maps to which you have referred. I hope the Yale Library has them. Why should not the home of the Sumerians be in that district?"

More and more archeological sign-posts point the way to the Caucasus and chance revelations affirm and encourage. In the spring of 1933 came word of the discovery of a sea-going vessel embedded 7500 feet above sea level in the Caucasus Mountains in the region where Fessenden assumed the Ark would have been carried and stranded. But first hand source is not at present available so this statement must await confirming details.

Fessenden appreciated to the full the necessity for field work but recognized at the same time his own physical unfitness for such an undertaking. With Dr. Edward Chiera he had several times discussed where and how exploration should start in the event that funds were forthcoming to finance the work, but it was not till 1928 that he himself was prepared to make some contribution. At that time he made a substantial offer to one of the American Archeological Departments, to cover the expense of a preliminary investigation at points indicated by his research, but this offer was not accepted, possibly for fear of causing interruption of consecutive work in other fields.

The utmost that Fessenden hoped and planned for himself was, sometime, with his friend Colonel Degen, to go as a traveler over that age-old route back to the 'home-land,' picking up one after another the timeless landmarks, till at last through the gloomy pass of the Caucasus, the land of the Kabiri, the Garden of the Hesperides, the Garden of Eden should be reached.

But for him, the sands of life ran out too soon.

CHAPTER XXIX

THE FESSENDEN FATHOMETER

As ALREADY STATED, at the beginning of 1921 Fessenden's engineering connection with the Submarine Signal Company ceased, since under new management a new policy was inaugurated, a policy which he believed to be inimical to the Company's future prosperity. The separation might have been permanent and complete but that his help was needed for patent applications then in the Office and for possible infringement suits.

Reg had not envisaged such a change in policy in 1917 when the offer of 4000 shares of Submarine Signal Company stock had been proposed and accepted in exchange for oscillator rights for other than submarine uses. These shares with 1050 more which we had previously purchased, made, for us, a large number of eggs in one basket. To continue the simile, if all these eggs were to be addled by a changed policy, the outlook was not very promising. However, majority decision ruled and all that could be done was to await results.

Reg did not need the slow clogging processes of Laboratory and Shop to aid him in invention, so now in the quiet of his study and in the storeroom of his mind, his "Jewels of Great worth" rolled and revolved, burnishing themselves to greater perfection, developing new possibilities.

As he lived over again the iceberg tests, to his vision "Soundings," in the word's most comprehensive meaning, sloughed off past difficulties, limitations and imperfections and the shining goal of a continuously dialing chart of the ocean's bottom revealed itself to him. The outcome of this was a patent application filed on March 28, 1921 for the "Rotating Scale Sounder" also called the "Echo Distance

Finder," "Singing Sounder" and finally issued under the title "Methods and Apparatus for determining Distance by Echo."

When nearly a year later this application had made such progress in the Patent Office that it was seen that valid patents would issue in due time, Fessenden formally called this invention to the notice of the Submarine Signal Company and offered them the option on it, on easy terms, stating that he preferred to work constructively with them, rather than to form a competing company. With his considerable stock interest in the Company, it was common sense to want to work with rather than against it.

He offered to disclose the invention fully to Company officials under the stipulation that it should be considered a confidential communication and that the Company would not infringe it. This offer was accepted and full disclosure and explanations made to the Company officials best qualified to pass on the proposition.

The option was not accepted and for a time nothing more was heard of the matter. This was in February, 1922.

Time passed and by September, 1924, Fessenden had learned that the stipulation binding the Company not to infringe the devices disclosed by him in 1922 had been disregarded and that the Company had built, experimented with, offered for sale and disclosed to others a "Chinese copy" of his Rotary Scale Sounding apparatus. Thereupon, in the phraseology of an old negro, Fessenden wrote the Company "some demandin' words."

The outcome was an agreement whereby the invention was assigned to the Submarine Signal Company for the sum of $50,000, payment to Fessenden to be spread out over a period of ten years; thus making terms which, extremely moderate at best, were still further favorable to the Company in its straitened circumstances. But again, it was to Fessenden's own interest to give if possible a constructive slant to the Company's policies. It will be necessary to refer once more to this contract.

Meantime danger threatened from other quarters as well.

In March, 1921 Fessenden communicated his invention of "Echo Sounding and continuous indication of same by rotating scale" to the U.S. Navy, by way of 'caveat.' Within six months someone in or working for the Navy filed an application to achieve the same results but with such ingenious differences as would satisfy the patent office and later serve to support the Navy's claim to a system of its own with all the consequent credit and without the expensive development charges of a commercial company.

In due course the Navy proceeded to use this infringing device and actively propagandized on its behalf, by inspired articles etc., notably "Telephoning beneath the Sea" in the Scientific American of March, 1926. The ghost writer of that article not only ascribing the invention incorrectly but defaming the Fessenden apparatus.

On account of the Navy's attitude, the Submarine Signal Company immediately on acquiring the rights to the Fessenden device, which for brevity may now be given its present familiar name of "Fathometer," brought suit against a certain firm using the Navy device as contributory infringers, suing on Patent 1217585, "Method for measuring Distance," which embodied the fundamental principle.

This was in 1924. In February 1926 the case was tried and in July of that year Judge Lowell of the Federal District Court of Massachusetts rendered a strong decision in favor of the Submarine Signal Company, ascribing invention to Fessenden.

"The apparatus," he said, "was quite different from anything known in the prior art.—The Method devised by Fessenden was new.—In my opinion the method discovered by Fessenden involved a new function which was not set forth in the prior art.—On the question of infringement, the defendants contended that their device does not measure time, but only the number of signals sent out each second by the oscillator after it has been synchronized with the echo in the manner before described. It is difficult to understand the argument, but whatever be the idea at its base, it is fundamentally unsound, since the art of determining depths by the echo method depends wholly on the lapse of time between the signal and the receipt of the answering echo.

"In my opinion, all the features of the plaintiff's claims are present in the defendant's apparatus. Identity of time.—Identity in character.—Identity in frequency.—Let a decree be entered for the plaintiff for an injunction."

The Submarine Signal Company has for its great objective the safety of "those who go down to the sea in ships." Harmonious co-operation with all Government Departments whose duties link them with the sea is therefore paramount and vital if the Company is to endure and its work go forward. With the Coast and Geodetic Survey such co-operation appears, from the 1927 and 1928 Annual Reports, to have been of great mutual benefit, which is as it should be.

But in Government Bureaus the urge for budget increase and added powers fosters a ceaseless policy of piracy and distortion. A very poignant memory of an occurrence on the 22nd of July, 1932, the day on which my husband died, is connected with this bureaucratic tendency.

Browsing through a recent copy of the New York Times, I had run across an illustrated article which opened with the words, "The name *Fathometer* has been given to a new instrument devised by Dr. Herbert G. Dorsey of the United States Coast and Geodetic Survey"—followed by a standard description of the great uses of the device and as caption for the illustration *The Fathometer and its Inventor.*

No mention whatsoever was made of the Submarine Signal Company or of Fessenden. The data ascribing the Fathometer to Dorsey was doubtless 'publicity' handed out by the Coast and Geodetic Survey and was merely a flagrant example of the lengths to which propaganda is carried and of the vast amount of mis-information foisted upon the public.

Going later to my husband's room for a morning chat I said "Did you see that Times Fathometer article?" "That Government Bureau chap?" he asked—"Yes, I did." "Isn't it the limit" I said, "one would think after Judge Lowell's opinion and the Medal award they would be ashamed to keep on trying to grab it."

"Oh, well," he said "it's the policy; haven't they always done it? You might clip it out however, as the Sub. Sig. may not have seen it," and we passed to other topics.

It is human to feel some disturbance at these things however used one may be to them. But I am thankful that he had already seen the article, thankful that there was a quiet nap following our talk and later pleasant steamer mail to enjoy before the fatal attack started, otherwise, in addition to my overwhelming loss there might have been a sense of blame for having stirred anew those troubled memories.

Perhaps it has not been made clear what the Fathometer is and does. Omitting all technical details of its component parts, the Fathometer, in operation on a ship's bridge, indicates at every instant of time, by means of a spot of light on a dial measured in fathoms, the exact depth of the water beneath the ship's keel.

Commercial installation of this apparatus proceeded rapidly and testimony to its high worth came from all sides. In the Company's booklet, "Submarine Signal Fathometer," several of these letters were reproduced.

Commodore H. A. Cunningham of the S.S. Leviathan wrote (1928) as follows:—

"The Fathometer installed on this ship by the Submarine Signal Company has been in use on the past two voyages and its operation has proved to be very successful and gratifying. It has been given a strenuous test since the installation and it has far exceeded our highest expectations; not only do I approve of it for this ship but I am of the opinion that it should be installed on all the ships of the U. S. Lines. So far as its usefulness in the matter of safety, it stands in a class by itself for there is nothing with which to compare it at the present time; it has brought the Mariner's dream of Paradise one step nearer."

Mr. William Perrot, Operating Manager of the United States Lines also wrote:—

"I regard the Fathometer as one of the greatest improvements in the science of navigation in recent years.—I have recommended to the American Committee of the International Conference on Safety at Sea, which meets in London next year (1929), that its adoption should be indorsed as standard equipment on every passenger vessel."

From the 1927 Annual Report of the Director, United States Coast and Geodetic Survey:—

"——By means of this echo-sounding apparatus known as the "fathometer," it is possible without stopping the vessel to take soundings in any depth from a few fathoms under the keel to at least 2,500 fathoms (15,000 feet), and probably to greater depths. The advantage of this apparatus for survey service is that soundings can be taken as rapidly as desired— as frequently as four per second—with the vessel steaming at full speed. It is, therefore, possible to survey more than twice as much area per day with this apparatus as would be possible by any other means.—"

The Gloucester fishermen now deem it a wise insurance for their costly nets, warning as it does of shoaling waters and of hidden banks which may tangle and rend and destroy their costly equipment. Its use for detecting Schools of Menhaden (small fish seined for fertilizer) has also been considered.

On October 16, 1929, at a meeting of the Committee on Award of the Scientific American Medal for Safety at Sea "by unanimous vote the Gold Medal was awarded to Professor Reginald A. Fessenden, inventor of the Fathometer and many other safety instruments for use at sea." This award Fessenden regarded as one of the greatest honors of his life, both by reason of the distinguished membership of the Committee as well as of the outstanding devices between which they were called upon to decide, in particular that of the Automatic Stability Indicator of Mr. J. Lyell Wilson.

That Fessenden was unable personally to receive this award was a matter of keen regret but already there was a recognized heart weakness which would have made such excitement dangerous. So on November 7, 1929, at a

THE FATHOMETER FOR DEPTH FINDING
Black Arrows Show Electrical Impulses
White Rings and Arrows Show Sound Waves

THE FESSENDEN FATHOMETER

luncheon at the Union League Club, our son, Major R. K. Fessenden, on behalf of his father, received the Medal and Citation from Mr. Arthur Williams President of the American Museum of Safety, through Miss Frances Perkins, State Industrial Commissioner.

To refer again to the agreement covering the sale of the Fathometer Invention to the Submarine Signal Company, the contract provided that the ten annual payments of $5000 covered not only payments on the Fathometer but a yearly retaining fee as well. Reg often said to me—"Remember if anything happens to me the Submarine Signal Company must pay you the $5000 annually up to the end of the ten-year period, i.e. from 1924 on.

The retaining fee angle seemed negligible since the contract also provided that any work which Fessenden might be called upon to perform was to be paid for at additional stated rates. But that there was a reason for the retaining fee clause was fully revealed in 1932 after Reg's death, when the Submarine Signal Company successfully maintained in Court that the contract was for retaining fee and therefore terminable with death.

By this Court ruling, the $10,000 still due on the Fathometer was 'wiped from the slate.'

In connection with Fessenden's Echo Sounding Methods and Devices it is a great pleasure to record their successful use in a totally different and very important field—that of locating salt domes, oil wells, sulphur beds, etc., broadly called "Ore Detection."

The Geophysical Research Corporation, a subsidiary of the Amerada Corporation engaged in the location and development of oil wells, tried out the Echo Method in 1925 with some success, using explosions of dynamite. In search of Patent Office records for references covering such uses, the Fessenden patents bearing on Echo Sounding in all its phases were noted. Negotiations between the Geophysical Research Corporation and Fessenden resulted in 1926 in an agreement which has been lived up to with meticulous rectitude and with, I believe, eminently satisfactory financial returns to the Corporation as well as to us.

CHAPTER XXX
OTHER DEVICES

The fathometer was not the only invention Reg made in the early years of the 1920's.

The flow of invention continued and to this period belong very important contributions to the artistic side of radio, that is, the devices and methods which made possible the use of musical instruments as Loud Speakers, whereby not only beauty of tone was immeasurably enhanced but static, that pest of radio, was largely controlled.

We began to use both a violin and a piano as Loud Speakers in our home in 1922 or 1923 and the quality of reception was at once lifted to another plane. It was freely shown to members of the Radio Corporation who disclaimed any interest. The Navy tested it out at the Boston Navy Yard for elimination of static in working with their Canal Stations and found it very efficient.

The Piano industry had fallen on lean years and Fessenden believed it could be very greatly stimulated by this combined function of musical instrument and super-excellent Loud Speaker, each operating without detriment to the other. So for a year or more we gave demonstrations to the various Piano Manufacturing concerns, of phonograph records and of Broadcasting as it came in over the aerial, reproduced on our violin and piano.

Everyone was extremely interested; every one admitted that it gave reception of a new order, but, though the Piano industry was dying on its feet, among them all there was not one with the initiative to grasp this new function as a life saver. Perhaps none of them were free to do so—that was Fessenden's belief.

That the patent applications were considered important

and valuable is clear enough for by 1927 no less than *eight claimants* had managed to get themselves put in interference with Fessenden. All of them had to be dealt with by process of hearings, taking testimony, briefs, etc. One by one they were eliminated, the last one in 1932 and then the patents issued to Fessenden. This one instance illuminates in a small way, the tribulations of an inventor.

The invention which Reg called "Tea Money" was another venture which consumed considerable time and funds from 1922 to 1926. He hoped that something so strictly practical and utilitarian as this form of individual tea container might find ready adoption, in which case it could be counted on to provide that safe competency for our old age, still so remote.

The first novel feature of the Tea Money was the escape from the cloth bag. In its place was an aluminum container about the size of a silver dollar and twice as thick, made of very thin foil from one to three-thousandths of an inch thick. Simple punches were made for stamping out and sealing these containers, with the proper amount of tea per cup enclosed; also a machine was designed for the automatic process of punching out, filling and sealing the containers in immediate connection with the ovens of tea plantations whether in Ceylon, Assam, or elsewhere. Thus hermetically sealed at the very instant of its final preparation, the tea would retain its full flavor and freshness until the moment of use when, with tongs provided with pricking points, each disc would be perforated, dropped into a cup and freshly boiling water poured on.

A good deal of calculation and care went to the size and arrangement of the punctures so as to ensure perfect diffusion. Tea tasters who gave the container the most exacting tests to determine whether the metal in any way affected the flavor of the tea, were unanimous in reporting that it did not. The added cost per pound of tea was considerably less than the cloth bag type. The slogan "Fresh from Oven to Cup" would have been a guarantee of an uncontaminated product and other advantages might be enumerated. Reg did not rely on his own salesmanship but entrusted it to men trained in such work, but without success.

Even now, considered dispassionately, it is not clear why no firm took it up, unless again human inertia—that ever-present factor which opposes change with drag-ropes of lead, must be reckoned with.

Sometimes echoes of his early work reached Reg. In 1925 or 26, a visiting German scientist, an expert on Latex, was lecturing in Boston and ascribed to Fessenden the theory that first disclosed the true structural nature of rubber. To his great surprise he was told that Fessenden was still alive and living in Boston, and a meeting was arranged. Later the wife of this German specialist, Dr. Hauser, told me how, as he mastered one detail after another of his chosen subject, she would hear again and again the phrase: "Na, da kommt diesar Kerl, Fessenden, wieder," as the trail led back to the theory propounded by Fessenden in 1889.

Reg's forecast of the properties of Beryllium, or as it is sometimes called Glucinum, in an article "Use of Glucinum in Electrical Instruments" which appeared in the Electrical World, July 16, 1892 was confirmed 40 years later. All the physical constants of this new metal were disclosed by him in the article, the method of extraction recommended, the approximate cost estimated and its uses specified. That he disclosed it widely is shown by an extract from a letter of Sir William Crookes, editor of Chemical News, June 27, 1893.

> "Your account of the properties of Beryllium (Glucinum) is very important and I await your further research which you propose to carry out this summer. If confirmed, Beryllium will become one of the most valuable of the metals from a theoretical point of view. It could be obtained in considerable quantities if there were any demand for it as there are large deposits in Ireland."

In the New York Times, December 7, 1932, appears a description of a new copper alloy, which:—

> "looks like gold, is as hard as iron, and stronger than steel,—

which resists abrasion and fatigue and can be made into tools which do not spark. For this reason oil refineries are expected to adopt it to remove one of the great fire hazards. As the alloy does not corrode and retains its set in superheated steam, it is recommended for valve springs in steam power transmission. Its high conductivity combined with high tensile strength mark it for electric power transmission.—All this the result of a small percentage of Beryllium which was only a laboratory exhibit a few years ago."

Compare the above with the last paragraph of Fessenden's 1892 Electrical World articles:—

"For these reasons then, its great lightness, its resistance to oxidation, its great rigidity, tensile strength and malleability, its excellent conductivity and comparatively moderate cost of production, we may expect to see this metal used in instrument work in the future."

So the mists lift and dimmer visions clear and a treasure is set to work for the world.

There was never anything hap-hazard about Fessenden's work. He approached a subject with an open mind, examining and if necessary discarding the findings of previous workers and with his own mind tensely alert for a wrong turn in reasoning. A problem received drastic treatment at his hands—it was turned upside down, hind part before, inside out. This I know to my own frequent discomfiture—not on scientific matters which were not my province, but on every day affairs. My carefully thought out plan would come up for discussion—in a flash its foundations were gone, its outlines and purposes changed and fresh methods suggested. Often because of my inhibitions the new plans were difficult ones for me to accept, but the soundness of them evoked, nevertheless, a grudging admiration.

Thus it was that his reputation for sound work gave him a very enviable standing in patent litigation. As one of his attorneys once wrote to him:—"Your opponents in suits are half whipped before the battle," and though, in Wireless work, patent interferences were constant, long drawn-out, irksome, very vexatious, exhausting and expensive, nevertheless as long as a case was fought out on its merits we were seldom apprehensive of the ultimate outcome, so *sound* was Fessenden's reasoning, so individual his conception of a problem.

Soon after settling in our new home, a full *grown* and very handsome tiger cat came miaowing to our front door, wisely choosing a time when the more vulnerable members of the family were present. I, who had butlered and valeted for 'Mikums' for a number of years, had misgivings. But I may as well not have had them, since adoption was a foregone conclusion, the only question requiring consideration being a suitable name. 'Cato,' the name of that stern old Roman was felt to give the antique flavor that fitted with the mood and atmosphere of the house. So 'Cato' our new pet was named, and for many years supported his title with unimpeachable dignity and with a national tolerance that his namesake never knew, for he was well content to be a citizen of two countries, being equally at home in Boston and Bermuda.

Another of the diversions which we at that time shared with a large percentage of our fellow countrymen was the making of 'home brew.' After a few small successes on my part in wine making Reg started to experiment with beer and at once it became a matter of research, with particular attention to the chemical analysis of the springs that in England had long been used in the brewing of notable beers and ales. These chemicals in proper proportion were added to our concoction, together with such niceties of detail as the use of maltose instead of sugar, utmost care in sterilization, aeration at the proper stages, etc., a very involved process and sometimes burdensome; but at least our transgressions against prohibition were limited strictly to our own products.

It was in 1924 that Mr. Gernsback, editor of Radio News and other technical magazines, inquired if Professor Fessenden would be willing to write a series of articles for Radio News. Various topics on which Fessenden's views would be important were under consideration when the broader plan of an autobiography came up and was decided upon.

Fessenden's one stipulation being that he must see proofs before printing and that no changes must be made without his O.K.

The title was "Inventions of Reginald A. Fessenden" and the first installment appeared in Radio News January 1925.

It was taken more or less for granted in the editorial rooms that this autobiography would proceed along the very usual lines of interviews, the actual writing being done by some capable young man on the editorial staff, in other words, by that well known but elusive creature, a ghost. But this was not Fessenden's idea, he must put *himself* into it, every word and phrase must be instinct with his own personality and mentality and designed to train, help and inspire young inventors, more especially those whom he called "the finest body of radio men in the world, our U.S. amateurs."

It was this band of youthful workers, aflame with enthusiasm, whom he sought to reach and in a comprehensive way to prepare for work and for difficulties. Sometimes the Staff of Radio News was not quite in sympathy with the form these articles took but Fessenden was convinced that he knew what was needed, and tried to convince Mr. Gernsback.

   (to Mr. Gernsback)   December 1924.
"I can of course see just how you feel, that I am too slow getting into the 'stride' of the story. But that will come at the proper time. If you come on the stage and say "Hamlet is dead and Ophelia drowned" at once, you have not got much of a story to tell, even if you kill off another Hamlet and Ophelia every act. It gets monotonous.

Now you are quite right in saying that people want to know how inventors go about their work, (in fact if you will remember it was I who originally proposed that that should be the important element featured.)

And it is quite easy to write something like what is given in novels, about how the inventor worked away for years and then suddenly smote himself on his pale brow and said "the discovery is made." But I want to give these young men not fakes, but the real thing. And the real thing is not in the moment of invention but in the preparation which led up to it. That is one thing, i.e. I want to give the facts so they will be useful. Another thing is that if you will analyze the desire of these young men you will find that what they really want is not simply to know *how the inventor did it*, but *how they can do* it. That is the real reason why they like to know how the inventor did it, so they can go out and do something themselves.

Now that, I am looking after, for I am already training them to invent as I go along, so that when I come to my own work they will understand it fully. In my second article I give them a little steer that way by telling them about the way new plants are invented, because that is the simplest kind of invention of all. I will bet a lot of them take it up, if too many mistakes are not made in the proofs, so they can understand it. And in the third article I start them good by showing them how they can invent something simple but yet immensely important, i.e. the automatically written speech and phonograph."

Again in March 1926 to Mr. Gernsback:—

"If you asked Strauss to write about composing music, or Sargent about painting, and one of your men headed the articles so that some kid thought that the articles were going to be about how to play the scales or how to paint fences, you would not expect Strauss or Sargent to change the whole series of articles to that kind of stuff. What I am giving them is the real thing. Mucking around with wires and batteries is not real inventing. I am telling them what real inventing is."

It is this unfinished autobiography that has been quoted so freely in the present work. Reg enjoyed writing it and enjoyed his reading public. As he wrote to Mr. Gernsback "You preach from a tall pulpit," for the circulation of the Gernsback publications was extensive and among a class of readers that Fessenden especially wanted to convince of his own fundamental article of faith, the importance to a nation of its inventions and of its inventors.

The series continued to appear till November 1925, then

an accumulation of mistakes and carelessnesses on the part of Radio News staff, of somewhat exacting stipulations on the part of Reg, as to proofs and corrections, plus continued criticism as to the scope and policy of the articles brought about a temporary halt till work could be resumed on a sounder and more clearly defined basis. The autobiography had reached the Pittsburgh period and was on the eve of wireless developments of just a quarter of a century ago.

Now, in December 1925 Fessenden was once more buckling on his armor to wage another fight for our wireless rights. The public knew it and Fessenden believed that publicity for himself would be discriminated against, and he believed that the staff of Radio News felt concern at the prospect of it. So the matter of continuing the autobiography was quietly dropped. Time and Chance were never again in conjunction for the completion of his own story of his life and the world is the poorer.

CHAPTER XXXI

"GOD ALMIGHTY HATES A QUITTER"

In 1916 a truce to hostilities in wireless litigation between Fessenden and the representatives of the National Electric Signaling Company had been called and for a time it seemed as if there might be a settlement.

Prior to this, in 1914 to be exact, the N.E.S. Co., in return for large royalties, had licensed the Marconi Company to use the Fessenden inventions and in order to carry out this contract it was necessary to secure from Fessenden proper assignment of foreign patents.

When approached by the legal representatives of the N.E.S. Co., Fessenden refused to execute the assignment for any of his wireless patents, either U.S. or foreign. But he said "If the N.E.S. Co. will give me a license to use my own inventions, I will sign whatever is required to effect a settlement.

He asked only for a license for his own inventions—not a license under the patents of Austin, of Boyle, of Cohen, of Hogan, of Lee, (all workers in connection with or under N.E.S. Co.) but for his own inventions only.

A somewhat similar suggestion had been made in March 1915 at a meeting in New York between Fessenden, Given and Walker. Fessenden had then proposed to swap patents —they to license him under the U.S. patents and he to license them under the foreign patents. Given and Walker said they would think this proposition over. But the pressure at that time was not heavy enough to force them to face the issue and nothing was done.

In 1916 however, the assignment of foreign patents had become a vital necessity to the company and they *had* to dicker. Fessenden's terms were a full, mutual release of all claims between the company and himself, assignment of foreign patents by him to the company, also release of his stock in the company in consideration of a license to use his own inventions.

This was clearly understood by the legal representatives, by the receivers and by the owners of the company. Indeed without this license to Fessenden there would have been no consideration and the agreement therefore invalid. The objection interposed to granting an immediate license when the settlement was signed was that the company was still in the hands of receivers and that such a license would greatly delay the process of getting the company out of the receivership—i.e. out of the New Jersey Court. Fessenden insisted that there should be some evidence of this specific agreement and to the clause in Fessenden's letter which referred to it, Kintner, before a witness, signed his O.K., his name, and below his name "receiver for the National Electric Signaling Company," and Kintner further agreed to bring before the Judge a petition for authority to issue to Fessenden a license under his own patents. This was on October 19, 1916.

When at the end of November 1916 no license had been received, Reg, believing that the settlement was still pending, wrote to Judge Rellstab of the New Jersey Court questioning the good faith of the N.E.S. Co. and stating that while he was aware that the granting of the right to use his own patents must be delayed until the Company was out of the hands of the receivers, all other parts of the settlement could be performed and as evidence of good faith should be performed.

A copy of this letter was sent to the negotiating attorneys who advised Reg that all matters had been closed up (with the exception of the license). Reg then requested to be informed as soon as the company was out of receivership. In April 1917 he was informed by Colonel Firth that it was the intention of the N.E.S. Co. to remain in the hands of the receivers for a further period. He thereupon wrote to the N.E.S. Co. as follows:

> "Under the circumstances (i.e. remaining in receivership) I think it only fair that the receivers should forward me a formal license as the only documentary evidence I have of our agreement is the Memorandum O.K.-ed by Mr. Kintner and it is now considerably past the three months' date at which I understood I would receive the formal license."

There was no reply to this.

Reg then consulted the negotiating attorneys as to whether in their opinion the Memorandum O.K-ed by Kintner was itself in effect a license. They did so believe and that under it, he might start to make, use and sell wireless apparatus covered by his patents. Reg communicated this to Mr. Albert G. Davis of the Patent Department of the General Electric Company, also to the U. S. Navy.

On November 28, 1917, the receivership came to an end. Full transfer of all N.E.S. Co. franchises, rights and effects was made to the International Signal Company later International Radio Telegraph Company, this corporation having been designated by Given and Walker to receive such conveyances, the receivers obtaining from Given and Walker jointly and severally, and from the International Signal Company, an agreement in writing faithfully, fully and promptly to pay all obligations and liabilities of this receivership.

At the close of the year Given, in reply to a formal communication from Fessenden, replied:—

> "I know of no agreement or understanding to license you under the Company's patents."

A similar communication from Fessenden to Kintner brought the followings:—

> "We assume that what you refer to as the "Kintner endorsed Memorandum" is the memorandum signed by Mr. Kintner on the Margin of your letter addressed to Messrs. Browne and Woodworth. This memorandum obviously only refers to the matter of photographs, drawings and memoranda of your note books and is not the basis of any agreement as to the use of your patents."

To this Fessenden replied:—

"I note that you now disclaim the agreement, verbally entered into and confirmed by the Kintner Memorandum and other papers, to the effect that I was to have the use of all my own wireless patents in exchange for signing the contract and that I was to receive a license to use all of said patents as soon as the company went out of the hands of the receiver.—You will realize that the obtaining of this license to use all of my own wireless patents was the only object I had in settling my claims against you and surrendering my stock, as there was no other consideration of any kind for the contract except this.—"

So, once more, stalemate.

1917 and War time and upheaval. Regimentation and Manipulation; everything and everybody came in for a share of it—Radio no less than other arts and activities. There were Committees and Hearings to Regulate Radio Communication; discussions of Government Monopoly of Wireless and Naval Valuation of all commercial wireless companies' coastal and high-powered stations.

On this point Mr. Kintner came valiantly to the defense of patent rights. Said he:—

"Commander Todd stated, as his opinion, that a fair valuation of all commercial wireless companies' coastal and high-powered stations would not be in excess of $5,000,000. Where does Commander Todd get his information? One would think that he valued only twisted wires, tables and steel masts in arriving at such a figure. Surely ideas as set forth in patent rights are worth something. Are the pioneers in this art who have devoted years of their lives and millions of dollars in bringing the art to where there is now some chance of securing some reward to be deprived of all opportunity of securing it? Is the greed for power of a few Navy officers, and I may add that this display of greed has not been confined to the present administration, to be allowed to stifle these developments?

It is developments of this kind that have made America great."

Fessenden, this time an onlooker, recalled the days of 1907 and 1908 following the first International Radio Convention, when he and the Marconi Company had fought to keep this new art out of the clutches of Government Departments.

He endorsed to the hilt these scathing words of Mr. Kintner in defense of patent values but meditated the while that words and deeds of the speaker could be so at variance.

It would be a natural assumption that if a man, for any reason, suddenly dropped out of a line of work on which popular interest was focussed at white heat so that stimulation, competition and progress in that line was phenomenal, that such a man would quickly fall behind.

Fessenden never fell behind. He was always ahead, whether in or out of the procession, so far ahead that often he was out of sight. An editorial of the New York Herald Tribune at the time of his death—"Fessenden against the World," said in part:—

> "——It sometimes happens, even in science, that one man can be right against the world. Professor Fessenden was that man. It is ironic that among the hundreds of thousands of young radio engineers whose commonplaces of theory rest on what Professor Fessenden fought for bitterly and alone only a handful realize that the battle ever happened. When the radio experiments of Rhigi and Marconi startled the world in the closing years of the last century, it already had been known for ninety years or so that electric sparks could cause some mysterious kind of 'action at a distance'. There already existed too, the classical experiments of Hertz with what he called "Electric waves" correctly identified as an invisible variety of light. It is one example of the epidemics of inexplicable blindness which occasionally afflict the scientific world that no one saw what now seems the transparently obvious relationship between these influences of sparks and the wave experiments of Hertz. No one, that is, except Professor Fessenden. It was he who insisted, against the stormy protests of every recognized authority, that what we now call radio was worked by 'continuous waves' of the kind discovered by Hertz, sent through the ether by the

transmitting station as light waves are sent out by a flame. Marconi and the others insisted, instead, that what was happening was the so-called 'whiplash' effect—a sudden etheric impulse created by the violence of the electric spark and shot out like the sharp sound of a whip cracked in the air.

It is probably not too much to say that the progress of radio was retarded a decade by this error, which Professor Fessenden, never a good persuader, could not root out of the engineering mind. As is the way of scientific battles, also, the fight never ended in a knock-out. The whip-lash theory faded gradually out of men's minds and was replaced by the continuous wave one with all too little credit to the man who had been right—"

Another confirmation of the pioneer quality of Fessenden's work comes from Mr. Madden President of the Submarine Signal Company. He writes:

"My mind reverts to a conversation I had with the late Mr. Jackson, of Hazeltime, Lake Company of London, along in 1910-1912. It seems that the Marconi Company was having a patent litigation with the British Admiralty and Mr. Jackson was called in by the Admiralty to make a complete study of the patent situation. Mr. Jackson informed me that after making this study he became convinced that had Professor Fessenden been ten years *later* with his work he would have controlled the entire radio patent situation, but that Professor Fessenden was so far ahead of the commercial development of the radio art that many of his important patents had already expired."

It has been shown that Fessenden was the first to discover the true laws of radio, the first to accomplish trans-Atlantic radio working, the first to invent and to demonstrate the wireless telephone, the first to accomplish trans-Atlantic voice transmission, the first to broadcast.

So also with his 'Sound Spectrum Apparatus for Secret Sending,' better known as the 'Secrecy Sender,' the basic method of obtaining secrecy in radio communication by breaking sound waves up into component parts so that they remain unintelligible during transmission and only become intelligible when reassembled at the receiving end.

It is fair to state that in interference on this application Fessenden was defeated by two engineers of the Western Electric Company but to the time of his death he was striving to overcome what he believed to be miscarriage of justice in this case. For to Fessenden was conceded without shadow of dispute priority of invention and reduction to practice by a period of nearly four years.

The ground on which the patent was denied him was delay in filing his specific application. But there was no delay as far as Fessenden was concerned.

In 1915 he had filed an 'omnibus' application covering sixteen different inventions, of which the Sound Spectrum was one, for the purpose of placing them on record in the Patent Office and of affording a full description of these inventions to the U. S. Navy (under which he was serving during the war), and to the Coast Defense Board. Naval orders placed all who engaged in such work as Fessenden's under strict oath of secrecy. On advice or request, certain applications might be proceeded with in the usual way —others still remained subject to the oath of secrecy.

It must be remembered too that all members of the Civilian War Boards had access to disclosures in the Patent Office.

As late as 1920 the Navy still required certain inventions to be kept absolutely secret, "among them the invention of interference," Fessenden believed this to be the case with his Sound Spectrum until December 1921 when he saw a magazine article describing a device or method similar to his 1915 application, and he realized the matter was no longer secret. At once he applied to be relieved of his oath of secrecy and filed an application which was a *verbatim* repetition of his 1915 application. In November 1921 the Western Electric patent, the earliest conception date of which was March 21, 1919 was cited as an anticipation. Fessenden asked to be placed in interference with it, with an ensuing struggle that lasted till 1932. Priority was Fessenden's, his 1915 date of invention had to be admitted, there was no getting round it, but *Delay* was the argument which the Western Electric Company hammered at through appeal after appeal and finally won on that argument.

These results emphasize, rather than diminish, the pioneer quality of Fessenden's work.

It was therefore a matter of course that Fessenden should have been the first to discover the remarkable qualities of what he calls "a very short so to speak, transparent band of wave length lying between fifty (50) meter wave length and one (1) meter wave length" now generally called the Short Wave.

It was a matter of course because at every stage of Radio development he had made his quantitative measurements of every component of wireless transmission. Recall the early days at Cobb Island when receivers were buried at different depths in the ground and immersed at different depths in sea water, and at different degrees of salinity, and, by means of ladders, at different distances and at different heights from the antennas to find out what happened to wireless waves.

Recall his tests and calculations for trans-atlantic working which showed that absorption increased slightly as the wave length increased up to a frequency of 70,000 and then fell off with extreme rapidity, for which reason the long wave length was adopted by Fessenden for trans-atlantic working in January 1906, which, immediately on being published, was adopted by everybody.

Recall the data secured while the Brant Rock and Machrihanish Towers were in operation, to find out about 'daylight fading'; this was obtained by measuring accurately and simultaneously at six different stations at distances of 200 yards, 30 miles, 170 miles, 270 miles, 400 miles and 3000 miles the difference in intensity between daytime and night time reception of signals.

Then followed the years when he was working in a different medium and under different conditions—with submarines and aeroplanes which barred high masts and long waves. Back once more to his old work, to check and elaborate his data on the lower wave lengths, between 300 meters and a few centimeters. Since wave lengths of a few centimeters were much worse than those of 300 meters, he explored the range between, tabulating and comparing the mass of results collected between 1899 and 1918. Out of this study and comparison emerged the surprising fact which Fessenden said he had not expected nor was he able entirely to explain, that there was this band of wave lengths "of the order of five (5) meters, i.e., of pitch, i.e., frequency, lying between sixty million (60,000,000) and three hundred million (300,000,000) which was abnormally favorable for transmission."

Fessenden's patent on this discovery was granted in 1927 the application having been filed in 1922. But already by 1924 knowledge of it had spread abroad and the radio world was agog with the wonderful results being obtained by this band of short waves.

One other outstanding example of Fessenden's pioneering ahead of his times is his Pherescope, Radio-telescope, Radioscope, as it has variously been called. Parenthetically Fessenden's habit of giving his inventions unusual, distinguishing names may be noted. The Barreter was the first of these, meaning a tiny bar or gap. Pelorus, a wireless direction finder, was so called because "it gives the direction of the source of electromagnetic waves relative to the lubber line of the ship and has no relation whatever to the points of the compass." Commander Lavender has been kind enough to note other examples of this nomenclature, he writes:—

> "Professor Fessenden was not only an inventor but he also was a profound student of languages. With most of his inventions he coined new English words taken mostly from Greek roots with which he was evidently so familiar. It was Professor Fessenden who first used the words heterodyne (beat frequency), anacysm (sound wave above audibility), cratophote (light controlling device), photocrat (light controlled device), and many others."

To return to the Pherescope—Fessenden referred to this

invention in a speech at a Radio Institute dinner January 19, 1925.

> "There are in existence today, fully developed and tested in all essential details, wireless methods for operating direct, without exchanges, by setting direct to the subscriber's number, bodies of subscribers as large as those comprising the New York Exchange. The wireless Pherescope has been developed from the first crude apparatus of 1906 to a device capable of putting vision into every house in the United States and was tendered to the U. S. Navy under guarantee in 1921. Its success depends upon two inventions, the multiple valued function method, as it is called, and the shutter, which has been operated by independent engineers to a frequency of 400,000 per second and is capable of more. I have pleasure in showing you the shutter and in presenting a photograph showing the general arrangement of the action, and a sample of the wire used, of which it takes 900 twisted together to make the size of a single human hair."

There was a verbal order from the Navy for two sets of the Pherescope guaranteed to work 500 miles. But on writing later for a confirmation of this order, a departmental reply at its best was received. It said nothing, evaded everything and omitted the order.

Linked with this experience was a general disinclination on the part of wireless manufacturing companies to undertake any construction work under these patents, until finally Fessenden was forced to believe that it was the decision of the Radio Trust to play a waiting game and prevent the introduction of these new devices until there had been appreciable returns on their present investment or until the Trust itself controlled similar patents.

Enough has been said to show that even after ten years of exile from the radio field, Fessenden was still a figure to be reckoned with, still a giant, still an independent, whose inventions controlled the fundamentals of present day radio.

As the world picked up the broken pieces after the war and as each industry strove to establish itself on a firm foundation, it was obvious that some modus vivendi must be found for this new science just coming of age—Radio. Its youth had been one of turmoil, of storm and stress, of gallant fights, of crashes from the heights, for most of the pioneers in the art, but always it grew to bigger stature. And now the 'cautious ones' feel that it is safe to enter the field.

In the "Education of Henry Adams" this aloof student makes the following reflection:—

> "Mr. McKinley brought to the problem of American Government a solution which lay very far outside Henry Adams' education. He undertook to pool interests in a general trust into which every interest should be taken, more or less at its own valuation, and whose mass should, under his management, create efficiency. He achieved very remarkable results. How much they cost is another matter; if the public is ever driven to its last resources and the usual remedies of chaos, the result will probably cost more."

This Government panacea quickly became one for general business and threatened to become a Frankenstein. Under Roosevelt, the Sherman Anti-Trust Act was launched to hold the tendency in check.

This Act has always met with head winds and heavy weather because it opposed a course of procedure which is very alluring. The arguments in favor of pooled interests are soothing; they offer support to the weak and opportunity to the strong. How plausible it sounds to say "Get together, stop foolish competition, decide among ourselves what each shall do, make ourselves strong enough to control the situation, and then (sotto voce) charge what the traffic will bear."

It was Reg's conviction that with the policy of Mergers, the dissolution of American vitality began; the stifling of its initiative; the loss of its individualism; in their stead, huge organisms were created whose internal cells quickly died or became sterile until dry rot invaded the whole. It was the policy of Merger that was to shape the destinies of Radio.

It was a progressive combination involving tremendous

detail, huge sums and accomplished with little publicity, but in the end the vast amalgamation which had been effected comprised the Radio Corporation of America, the General Electric Company, the Westinghouse Electric and Manufacturing Company, the American Telephone and Telegraph Company, the Western Electric Company, Incorporated, the United Fruit Company, the Wireless Specialty Company and the International Radio Telegraph Company.

Between the years 1920 to 1925 Reg had been aware of currents setting in from many directions: without attempting tedious particulars, the following were some of these forces:—

> The old National Electric Signaling Company in its various impersonations had lost its mainspring, Given, by death; Walker had in some mysterious way disappeared from partnership—possibly another freeze-out—and at some time either before or after Given's death the Company had passed into the hands of the Westinghouse Company.

Claims against the U. S. Government for inventions used by it during the war were made by all and sundry—Fessenden among the rest—and particularly he notified the Navy that in the event of any award to the N.E.S. Co. or to the Westinghouse Company representing it, he was entitled to half the amount. The Navy put itself on record as follows:—

> "I (Commander Hooper, Naval representative) remember also asking Mr. Kintner either directly or through a member of the patent board, whether Mr. Fessenden would receive his share of the award, if granted, and of being promptly assured that he would."

A later communication from the Navy stated:—

> "The Navy department has not paid the Westinghouse any sum in cash for the use of their patents, but has a cross-license agreement covering an exchange of patent rights."

In 1920 overtures from the General Electric Company were made to Reg in regard to co-operation in its wireless work, more especially with reference to patent suits. Reg indicated his willingness to do this and anticipated such connection by a Memorandum to the G.E. Co. listing his recent inventions. This was in the nature of a 'caveat,' as well as an indication of what he had to offer.

In 1921 as the Merger grew more defined, prosecution of patent interferences became apparently the province of the Radio Corporation and Fessenden's services were sought by this corporation, Mr. Sarnoff, Gen. Mgr. of R.C.A. and Mr. Adams of its patent department visiting Fessenden at his home for the double purpose of examining into the testimony that he could give in a certain interference and of discussing a suitable contract for such services between him and the Radio Corporation.

As representatives of the Radio Corporation, Reg took the occasion to bring fully to the attention of these gentlemen the matter of his unsatisfied claims against the N.E.S. Co. He notified them of his intention of pushing these claims and asked them to hold up merger negotiations with the Westinghouse Company until he had entered suit, or he offered to postpone suit until a thorough and real consideration of his claims had been made by lawyers of the standing of Mr Frederick P. Fish, with his own lawyers present to present his side. At the same time he disclosed certain of his important, recent patent applications as he had done by Memorandum to the General Electric Company, and asked that they be considered.

Both in interviews and in letters there was apparently marked friendliness on the part of the representatives of the Radio Corporation but, Mr. Adams reported to his chief that he believed Fessenden to be bound by the 1916 agreement and with no rights to use his own patents. If, however, the company, i.e. Radio Corporation wanted another opinion, they should consult Mr. Fish.

This was certainly a distorted version of the understanding with Fessenden. Why on earth should the Radio Corporation want another opinion? Here was one made to their order.

It was Fessenden who wanted an opinion, from corporation lawyers of probity and high standing, with both sides presented. That was what he had stipulated.

In reality the plan appears to have been to keep the troublesome independent soothed and quiet till the big merger was complete, when by its overwhelming mass there could be no chance for a David against its Goliath strength.

Two medals were awarded to Fessenden at this time—the Medal of Honor of the Institute of Radio Engineers, in 1921, and the John Scott Medal from the City of Philadelphia under the Will of John Scott of Edinburgh, in 1922.

Reg was no iconoclast—no breaker of idols. He was as humanly pleased at honors and recognition as any one and as anxious to accept them at their face value, but if the years had taught him 'timeo Danaos et dona ferentes' is it to be wondered at?

Concerning the Radio Institute Medal though awarded in 1921 it was not actually forwarded to him until 1924, owing to the Institute's desire to make the presentation a public function and to Reg's need to avoid such a nervous strain. Unfortunately in 1926 from a source unknown to me, the rumor reached him that the Medal presented to Marconi in 1920 had been of solid gold and that to him in 1921 a plated imitation. This led him to send the medal to Washington for official assay and valuation and as this was considerably below the announced estimated value, Reg returned the medal to the Institute with the request that his name be stricken from the list of recipients.

This affront was met with dignity and tolerance on the part of the committee and led of course to an investigation.

Dr. G. W. Pickard, a founder of the Institute, one of its past presidents, himself a medal recipient and a warm friend of Fessenden's, set himself personally to investigate this matter with great thoroughness. By his findings he convinced Fessenden that at no time had there been variation or discrimination in the quality of the medal and to quote Dr. Pickard—

"I have in the past six months interviewed eleven of the twelve surviving members of the 1921 Board of Directors, who have each asserted that the award was made on merit, with the sincere desire of honoring Professor Fessenden for his invaluable contributions to the art of radio communication, on the basis of votes cast for the candidate and their personal knowledge of his achievements. These men also deny emphatically that this award was suggested or in any way influenced by any group, organization or company, other than the membership of the Institute as a whole."

So the Medal came again into Fessenden's possession.

As regards the John Scott Medal and fund of $800, it was awarded in 1922 for a notable invention that made Radio practical—"Continuous Wave Reception." It was awarded to the man who invented it—Fessenden. One hopes that John Scott of long ago would have approved it.

But later, certain deductions were inevitable.

The award was made on the recommendation of a group the Westinghouse men. The Westinghouse Company had bought the patents of the N.E.S. Co. and in 1922 the deal was going through which transferred these patents to the Radio Corporation of America for several million dollars. Fessenden's claim against the N.E.S. Co. had never been satisfied.

The Medal cost them nothing and was a good 'sop to Cerberus.'

The depreciated worth of this John Scott Medal was even more keenly perceived in 1926 when it was awarded to Dr. Hayes for his work on Ocean Depth Sounding. Certainly Dr Hayes had worked on Ocean depth Sounding ever since 1921 when Fessenden had disclosed to the Navy his invention of "Echo Sounding and continuous indication of same by rotating scale" and the Navy had set its own men to work, to evade the patent. The more reason therefore, in 1926, by awards and publicity, to minimize the decision in Fessenden's favor of the suit against Hayes' infringing patent.

Medals should not be degraded from their high estate,

nor should they be kept like small change for tips in the pockets of Big Business.

The foregoing were the more important contacts that Fessenden had at this period with the various companies forming the Radio Trust. He was not anxious to fight; any move to satisfy his original claim would have been welcomed. But there was none. No question of right or justice to the individual existed in the corporate mind. So grimly we prepared for war.

First, legal representatives of unquestioned standing and ability must be found who on investigation were convinced of the validity of Fessenden's claims. Messrs. Hurlburt, Jones and Hall, in association with Mr. Sherman L. Whipple, all of Boston, became his attorneys.

Then began once more the trying task of preparing the case. As in 1911 and 1912 files were ransacked for every letter or document or clipping which might have a bearing or shed a ray of explanation. To Mr. Herbert U. Smith, a junior lawyer of the firm, was entrusted the work of constructing the case; it was like assembling a monster jig-saw puzzle, the pieces of which were scattered, some apparently missing. The sequence of events had to be built up logically and chronologically till the whole story was revealed to mental vision with the threads of motive, cause and effect, standing clearly forth.

This was an affair of many months. Each conference in connection with it took on the character of a minor engagement. Reg's habit at all times was to attend a conference armed cap-à-pie with all conceivable data. Knowing this I sought to anticipate preparation for each meeting with the standard inquiry—"Have you thought what you are going to need for the next conference?" so as to have ample time to dig out the required papers. But equally Reg hated to set his mind in turmoil before he had to, or to interrupt perhaps a totally different line of thought, so the answer usually was—"No, I don't want to think about it yet."

But face to face with the event, probably the night before, his mind would begin to function furiously and thereafter till he set forth the next morning there would be a hectic and sometimes fruitless search for needed data. The days when he could go off with an unexpected find or confirmation of some point were red-letter ones. Usually the strain was tense until he drove off with his case of papers, then I would find myself weeping into the breakfast dishes from sheer relief.

Home again at noon, all traces of tension would have vanished. A basket of luscious mangoes or avocado pears would appear on the dining table; items of gossip or news from club or office would float to the surface in talk and an afternoon round of golf would clear his mind for fresh effort along other lines.

When Mr. Smith's accumulated data had been boiled down to 120 odd typewritten pages of 'facts,' there followed the application of 'law' to these facts, with case after case cited in reference. All this was going on through 1924 and 1925 and as this careful and thorough preparation progressed, clear intimation was given the Radio Merger of intention to file suit.

Unofficial opinion of associated attorneys seemed to be that a settlement out of court was more probable than a court battle and some color was given to this view when at the close of November 1925 a meeting was arranged to take place in New York between legal representatives of the Radio Corporation of America and Fessenden and his legal representatives.

This meeting was abruptly called off by the Radio Corporation, and the immediate and logical consequence was the formal filing of Suit by Fessenden's attorneys on December 4, 1925, against every member of the Radio Merger.

The amount claimed and the Merger attacked were both of a size to excite newspaper interest, so for a few weeks there was considerable publicity. Following quickly on the heels of this a printed letter signed by Mr. Whipple and Mr. Boyd B. Jones was mailed to every Congressman calling attention to the danger of Radio Monopoly and on January 15, 1926 Whipple, Jones and Fessenden attended a hearing of the Senate Committee on the White Bill, Mr. Whipple speaking with such good effect as practically to reverse the Committee's opinion on the question of Monopoly.

The Suit was launched, it was true, but there was no inclination on either side to bring it into Court if negotiations could find a satisfactory solution. The expense for all would be heavy, the notoriety for the Radio Trust unpleasant, the physical strain for both Fessenden and Mr. Jones unwise. But as the months dragged slowly by with pitifully meager results to show for negotiations, the long-drawn-out strain seemed worse than a sharp struggle. A line of a sonnet that Reg once wrote seemed to express the quality of our tension:—

"The moments drip, as Time were building stalagmites."

In May, 1926 a letter from Mr. Owen D. Young asked for a conference with a view to settling this suit out of court. The conference took place on June 25, 1926, Mr. Young coming in person to Boston, to meet Fessenden's attorneys. Reg was not present at the interview but was presented to Mr. Young on his arrival and struck the key-note of the meeting by saying that he hoped this Reparations Commission would be as successful as the European one. The first step decided on was the investigation of certain Fessenden patents by or under the direction of Frederick P. Fish.

After a month had elapsed Mr. Jones, hoping to expedite matters, wrote to inquire if Professor Fessenden could be of any assistance to Mr. Fish and the reply was that they would not be ready to go into the matter until after August. By the end of September a second letter was received indicating what progress had been made and by December 8 the patent analysis was reported completed.

On December 21, 1926 another conference took place, Mr. Young and Mr. Fish representing the Radio Trust. The gist of the interview was that they were prepared to dicker but it must be for *granted* patents, not patent applications, and Mr. Young said in effect that the more valuable the patents were the better pleased he would be—the idea seeming to be that as he would have to go to his Directors to advocate a large disbursement, persuasion would be easier if he had something valuable to show for it.

It seemed however that Mr. Fish must have put on his darkest glasses to consider these matters and to write his report, for on December 22 when Fessenden read it, the disparagement of the inventions and patent applications under consideration was such that Fessenden questioned the underlying sincerity of the entire negotiations.

His attorneys thought differently and it was decided to act on Mr. Young's statement that they were prepared to dicker for granted patents, not patent applications, and with that in view Fessenden and Mr. Hall spent the week of January 2, to 9, 1927, in Washington in intensive patent work, getting the pending Fessenden applications in shape for allowance. It was a week of intense effort but as Reg said, it was also a week when things seemed to go almost uncannily well.

Ten Fessenden inventions were dealt with in this week's work—the 'Short Wave,' the 'Horizontal Wave,' the 'Combination of Piano with Wireless and Phonograph,' the 'Piano Case,' the 'Radio Telescope,' the 'Radio Telescope Accessory Inventions,' the 'Multiple valued Function,' 'Microphotographic Books,' 'Microphonographic Records' and 'High Tension Insulators.' All but two of these were allowed and the patents were fundamental and broad. The remaining two might meet with interference but not of a dangerous nature.

Meanwhile there had been no let-up of propaganda ascribing Fessenden inventions to others. On December 2, 1925 in the New York Sun, Secrecy Sending was attributed to John Hays Hammond,—the method which as already described had been first filed by Fessenden in 1915. In May, 1926 an article appeared in some Radio magazine headed "Fessenden Case Thrown Out of Court."

On November 28, 1926 the New York Times gave a column to a description of the Piano as Loud Speaker ascribing the invention to Roehm and Adsit and the financial backing of the inventors to Radio Corporation of America. In consequence of this Reg sent a notice of infringement of his Piano Loud Speaker to the Radio Corporation, on December 12, 1926.

On December 15, 1926 at the St. Louis section of the American Institute of Electrical Engineers, Dr. Alexanderson described a Television Projector on which he was working and on which he was hopeful of getting 300,000 brush strokes per second. This statement was given extensive press notice. Fessenden's speech at the Radio Institute dinner on January 19, 1926 will be recalled at which he described his 'pherescope' which had been worked by independent engineers up to a frequency of 400,000 per second.

Beyond filing several notices of infringement, the first half of 1927 was barren of progress in the suit. This was partly due to absence, first of Fessenden and later of Mr. Young. After his strenuous patent work Reg was glad to get away to Bermuda for two months and it was late March before we returned: Mr. Young was in Europe.

So it was not until September 29, 1927 that negotiations were resumed at a meeting in New York between Mr. Young and Mr. Jones. In preparation for this a comprehensive reply to the Fish patent report had been drawn up, Reg being in daily conference at the office of Hurlburt, Jones & Hall, for a week or ten days before the meeting. Mr. Jones was able to convince Mr. Young that much more remained to be said in support of these patents than was evidenced by the report and Mr. Young announced that he would call Sarnoff and Fish in conference.

1924, 1925, 1926 had crawled by and the closing months of 1927 were upon us and still delay. More and more Reg inclined to the belief that Mr. Jones' policy of negotiation was a wrong one. He showed his impatience and set January 1 as his limit for such tactics. No doubt this quiver of impatience vibrated along the whole line of communication, adding a touch of asperity to Mr. Jones' suave letters and conveying to our antagonists the impression that decisive action was looked for. Whatever the cause, the conference in New York on December 1 between Mr. Young and Mr. Jones had more concrete results—a tentative though inadequate sum in settlement of Fessenden's original claims and for calling off the suit was mentioned, and a secondary arrangement discussed looking to the purchase of Fessenden's recent radio inventions, on which point the American Telephone and Telegraph Company was to be consulted. Coincident with this, two other matters were in progress each with its bearing on the situation.

It will be recalled that the receivers for the N.E.S. Co. had made heavy claims against the Government for use of N.E.S. Co. or Fessenden patents. The Navy's stand on this matter has already been referred to. When the holdings of the International Radio Telegraph Company passed into the hands of the Westinghouse Company, these claims appear not to have been included and in the fall of 1927 Fessenden learned that they were being pressed very actively in the Court of Claims by the former receivers with some prospect of recovery. The amount of the claim was seven and one-half millions. Again he called the attention of the Department of Justice as well as of the Receivers to his right to a share of any amount recovered and demanded to be allowed to make his statement in Court. Later his deposition was taken.

The second matter was the comprehensive action taken by the Federal Trade Commission to prove combination in restraint of trade by the Radio Merger. Fessenden's testimony was required for this and began on December 7, 1927. The presence of about a dozen of the Trust lawyers at the hearing bore witness to the importance ascribed to it, but as Fessenden afterwards said "none of them were very anxious to get into a discussion for fear of getting into deeper technical waters than they could wade through."

By February 1928 it appeared certain that the Federal Radio Commission would declare the Radio Corporation a Trust in restraint of trade and the rumor was that in anticipation of this the Radio Corporation of America was already dissolving into several companies All the greater reason for pressing to a conclusion Fessenden's claims.

Perhaps it is not to be wondered at that the wheels of *Justice* functioned with such creaking slowness; they hadn't been used very much and few knew how they worked. Throughout the negotiations Mr. Owen D. Young personally appeared to range himself on the side of what was fair; if a wrong had been done it ought to be righted and Fessenden was glad to have so just an adversary. A year later when great international decisions were at stake, Fessenden, in hospital following a heart attack, sent Mr. Young the following message:—

"As the old Greeks would have put it, 'May Victory never cease from crowning you' ".

and in a day or two the reply came:—

"Many thanks for your fine message which is so characteristic of you".

Mr. Young outlined the policy for the Fessenden Reparations and then turned it over to the various attorneys of the Trust to work out mutually satisfactory details. Slowly through January and February 1928 the matter bumped and dragged and hitched along and even after March 8 when a formal notice was received that the representatives of the Trust expected to be in Boston the following week to settle up matters in accordance with Mr. Young's and Mr. Jones' letters, there were still vexatious delays. I find a diary record for March 26:—

"R.A.F. comes back very tired and evidently very upset but says nothing till about nine o'clock, after he has written a short note to Mr. Jones and asked me to mail it. Then he says that it has been a very vexatious day—that *those people,* meaning the New York crowd, make him feel as Cato does about the black cat—i.e. sick at the stomach. It seems that last Saturday when Mr. Hall went on to New York they made a lot of new, unreasonable demands—the Westinghouse people are making the most trouble—I suppose the money involved hits them hardest—hope it does anyway—All the other companies are in line with Mr. Young's policy, but now he has gone to Europe and can't be reached to speed things up."

Again—on March 27, my diary records:—

"Mr. Smith called me up to say that at last everything seems to be ironed out, I thanked him and said I knew they had all been under great strain the past few days. He said 'I wish you could have been here this morning—everybody exploded —Mr. Jones was a wreck'. When R.A.F. came home he went into more detail. Said he had exploded yesterday and Mr. Jones and Mr. Smith this morning, and got Mr. Hall (a negotiating attorney for the Radio Trust) so worked up that he came round to Mr. Smith as being the least exasperated of the Fessenden group and said 'You must help us to put this thing through.'"

Even on March 31, the day on which the agreement was to be signed and the certified check paid over, hour after hour of haggling went on before the conclusive act of signing. Finally, disgusted, Reg seized his hat and cloak and started to leave the office and then opposition ceased and the agreement was signed.

So, at long-last, some sort of a settlement had been won.

CHAPTER XXXII

SANCTUARY

When the option agreement was signed on March 31, 1928 and the certified check paid, Fessenden, like Drake the indomitable, could say "the voyage is made."

But though the voyage was made and the chief objective achieved it was still not ended and much remained to be accomplished.

The three patents selected for option by the Radio Corporation were required to run the further gauntlet of 'adjudication' before purchase. This was one more condition added to the 'granted patents' for which Mr. Young had stipulated; but it was not entirely unreasonable and Reg seldom felt concern for the ultimate validity of his patents. Doubtless too, such a clause in the agreement met with full approval of the legal fraternity on both sides, as a guarantee of additional legal work.

The patents involved were the 'Short Wave,' the 'Horizontal Wave,' and the 'Broad Diaphragm.'

But this was not a matter that pressed and the first essential thing was to relax, to realize that the burden was lifted, the vow accomplished. Reg at once proceeded to make a dream of many years come true and that was the purchase of a home in Bermuda—"Wistowe," the very place he had yearned for since that first glamorous visit of forty-four years ago. An unpretentious house but an ideal location between Flatts Inlet and Harrington Sound, with a stretch of shoreline altogether disproportionate to its acreage.

Thenceforth this place was to be one of his chief preoccupations. It was his first chance to play with stone and mortar, with sea walls and reclaimed land, with windbreaks and hedges, palms and fruit trees, with landscaping.

To all these new activities he applied his methods of inventing; the waste from one development satisfied the requirements of another, the excavations from his tennis court filled to the last barrow load the space reclaimed by the sea wall.

He planned for progressive beauty and usefulness and sought always for these two factors in combination. The bulk of the work was accomplished in the winter season 1928-1929 but seldom a month went by during the four winters that he was in residence that his inventive mind did not devise some new enhancement.

It was his joy to stroll forth at dawn, with Cato following, to make the rounds, glorying in the sheer beauty of sunrise on placid waters and on blossoming, dew-drenched gardens, and to absorb the peace of his sanctuary. These were not lonely hours but filled with rich imaginings of adventure of bygone ages and, often no doubt, of that lost people and the lost land which so occupied his thoughts. Then as the day stirred to action, enchantment faded and he returned to bed for another nap.

It is said of Bermuda as of a baker's dozen of other places scattered over the world, "wait long enough and sooner or later everyone you have ever known will turn up there."

Certainly to us it brought the pleasure of renewing old and making new acquaintances. Mr. Grigsby of "Majestic Radio" fame was one of our earliest visitors. Himself an inventor and an independent as well as an executive of high ability, ensured mutual interests; the problems of radio were many and needed a long perspective and Mr. Grigsby hoped for cooperation from Fessenden. Very pleasant relations and business connections resulted.

In 1930 Dr. Alexanderson was another welcome visitor, coming though he did from a rival camp. But his and Reg's acquaintance dated from the early years of the century, their minds had met on many matters and met always with pleasure and for them there was no enmity in the land of science. Television as I recall was the chief subject of discussion and Fessenden offered what he believed to be helpful suggestions on the matter.

In the spring of the same year we were touched by the courtesy of Zeh Bouck the intrepid radio flyer who with Yancey and Alexander made the flight to Bermuda. It will be remembered that they got within sixty miles of the islands by dusk of April 1, but with a scant supply of gasoline which forbade a lengthy search; so their big bird perched for the night "on the face of the waters." Luckily the night was calm and next morning they flew the few remaining miles, circling Harrington Sound on their way to Hamilton.

We counted it a fine tribute that Mr. Bouck devoted the better part of an afternoon of his short stay on the island to a call at "Wistowe" to pay his respects to the man who had done so much to advance radio. When this call revealed to us the fact of his great physical handicap, it revealed too that the courage which led him to choose his profession must be of a very high order.

But perhaps most prized of all these chance meetings was that with Professor and Mrs. Michelson who were our neighbors in Bermuda in 1930. They came seeking health for Professor Michelson who had been down to the very gates of death in a series of operations and illnesses. Convalescence was discouragingly slow—warmth and sunshine were his most urgent need and Bermuda can sometimes be grudging in that respect in winter. Mrs. Michelson would say in despair "If we leave him for a moment he crawls back into bed again." So the sunniest and most secluded nooks of "Wistowe" were placed at his disposal and once convinced that his acceptance of these small courtesies gave us real joy, he yielded to the healing magic of the place.

As strength returned there were many happy afternoons of talk in sunshine or fireshine as the day decreed, and friendship ripened. Their return to the States a month or so before our own departure left us regretting their absence but richer by many pleasant memories. Professor Michelson went back to California to resume with unflagging patience his experiments on the velocity of light and lived just long enough to know that he had carried them through to a successful completion.

Men meeting Reg were conscious to a very high degree of his stimulating mentality; new heights, new vistas spread before them at his touch. No doubt a potent cocktail or a very special mint julep often added to the effect, but the stimulation was independent of any such contributing factor. The young poet, Chard Smith, aflame with the idea of the "Deluged Civilization" as a subject for his next epic, said with whimsical seriousness after a two hour discussion with Fessenden, "I feel as if I have been talking with God."

It was these long, long thoughts back to the beginnings of reasoning beings that led him, following the steps of Eddington and Sir James Jeams, to try and formulate his conception of the supreme rule or order or intelligence governing the universe. Dimly comprehended and meagerly stated, this is my recollection:—

He conceived this supreme controlling force to be perfect yet not complete

To be capable of absorbing perfection whenever achieved

To have been progressive since the beginnings of time

To be still progressive by the slow aggregation of contributed perfection

That humanity becomes a part of that supreme force of perfection as it contributes to it.

As an argument, open no doubt at every angle to attack, but as a guide, a helpful and constructive philosophy by which to live.

From the habits of his childhood there persisted a strong religious loyalty to the Episcopal Church and in Bermuda the closer communal life brought church life to a more conscious place in his mind. Though a church goer only on rare occasions he enjoyed participation in the well remembered rites—also he enjoyed companionship with the distinguished and scholarly padre of our parish.

Fond as Reg was of his other home in the States it was always with reluctance that he faced the necessity of return to Boston, for once there, work bombarded him from many quarters. Response to office actions on patents must be attended to, interference policies decided on; the Mechanical Car Transfer (the Garage project already alluded to) made heavy demands on him for it was proving difficult to promote, though it presented such economically and commercially sound prospects. Already the chill fingers of the great depression were being laid on the arteries of trade, new undertakings such as this met with no encouragement and the men concerned looked to Fessenden for help.

Very important too to Fessenden was the matter of adjudication of the three patents under option, 'Short Wave,' Horizontal Wave' and 'broad Diaphragm.'

Reg felt as did the Duke of Wellington towards the close of his career—"I have not time not to do what is right." He must not make a mistake and by plunging into prolonged patent litigation forsake perhaps his present safe vantage point. His attorney must be a man of brilliant mind and of unimpeachable record. Mr. Boyd B. Jones was dead; Mr. Sherman Whipple was the man of his confident choice; but he too passed, stricken in mid-career by the pressure of the times, and Reg knew that his own physical endurance had lessened. Ever and anon a warning sign.

In the summer of 1929 symptoms of angina, and in 1930 heart block. Quiet and a most rigid diet regimen were imposed by his physcians and faithfully followed for many months until his own reasoning supplied another line of treatment. The order to rest and reduce weight by diet was too sweeping, it lacked discrimination. Here, said Fessenden, is the heart already strained by overwork and obliged to keep on working, however much the other organs of the body may rest; yet it has to suffer the same reducing effects as all these other organs whereas logically, it ought to be built up at the expense of them. So he turned for information to that remarkable laboratory experiment, at the Rockefeller Institute I think, in which a section of chicken heart has been kept alive, pulsating, in a suitable medium, for several years. It was an article in 'Nature' which gave the analysis of this medium, a broth, before and after use, from which it became apparent that the protein content up to 90% (I am writing from memory) was what was withdrawn by this pulsating heart section in its business of keeping alive and working.

Thus, said Fessenden, reduce, but let the food used be a food rich in protein content and give the heart a chance to get what it needs.

Something helped, for the frequent cardiographs made in the fall of 1930 showed much improvement and the outlook was, after a year or so of going slow, for a restored and smoothly functioning organ.

But by the spring of 1931 a gland enlargement on one side of the throat became apparent and on examination by a Boston throat specialist a diseased tonsil was disclosed which might or might not be the cause of the enlargement but which in itself was serious enough to demand operation with grave uncertainty as to its outcome. All the old alarms for the heart flared up—could it stand an anesthetic?—could Reg stand local anesthesia? Hard questions to decide, knowing all the time that we were choosing blindly, in the dark. But Reg could always stand what had to be and he faced local anesthesia with fine pluck though we both knew that the outcome hung in the balance.

To break the strain we decided on the last afternoon before entering hospital, on a drive to Brant Rock. Old memories were thronging so thick about us, of all that had been attempted and achieved and endured that it seemed the pilgrimage most suited to our need.

The chauffeur, not a man who usually drove us, said he knew the way, but became hopelessly muddled beyond Cohasset and lost so much time that the trip had to be abandoned. We found a gleam of humor recalling the days of 1908 and occasional emergency trips from Brant Rock to Boston for some special gadget. On one such trip returning long after dark, we too lost our way and had to depend on infrequent sign-posts. One had borne the legend "8 miles to Marshfield," encouraged we pursued our way for a half hour or so without recognizing landmarks, then halted again beside a sign-post. Mr. Stein who was with us, got out, climbed the sign-post and flashed his torch. "Well," said Mr. Stein with fine philosophy, "we're holding our own," the same sign or another still read "8 miles to Marshfield."

The operation went perfectly. Reg's courage was magnificent and he was in the hands of a surgeon of unsurpassed skill; convalescence was rapid, and once more busy fruitful years seemed to stretch before us.

Later in the summer, with a group of friends our frustrated trip to Brant Rock was accomplished. Western Tower had been dismantled and abandoned by the National Electric Signaling Company in 1912 or 1913. We knew that a Newsreel event had been made of the fall of the Tower—guy ropes severed and at a given signal a pistol shot and the crashing fall of the 420 foot steel tube. Thank goodness we escaped seeing it, but now, standing beside the poor ruins of our Tower of Dreams and of Deeds, it was as if a soldier sorely maimed in service of his country had been deserted and forgotten. Nothing remained but the concrete foundation, the cement and insulator base and the socket in which the tube had rested.

Shards of the insulators strewed the ground, evidence of the small boy at play; we picked up a few pieces in memory; we went to the guy anchor beside which Mikums was buried; bayberries grew thick around it and we gathered a bunch of them, in his memory, and then we bade farewell to a spot where Reg had given the most and the best that was in him.

Writing at this time to Mr. Hadfield, our Brant Rock engineer, to thank him for a stirring protest in print against persistent newspaper mis-statements in regard to Radio history, I described our Brant Rock visit. So moved was he at thought of the pending destruction of even this poor remnant of our once famous station, that he appealed to such powers as he had once known in Massachusetts to see if something couldn't be done. Said he in part:—

"Because I know so well what important radio history was made there—I am deeply stirred by the prospect of the last physical remnant of our efforts going into the limbo of forgotten servants. The historic value of the old base is too great for Massachusetts to allow its loss.—An appropriation of a few hundred dollars would suffice to build a modest structure over it to protect it from vandalage. This should be a monument to Professor R. A. Fessenden whose work in the development of radio far transcends all others; but because he was interested in radio from a scientific instead of a publicity angle, the public have not heard so much about him or his work as it has of others of far less magnitude."

This was 1932. The protective structure most in vogue then was something designed to keep the wolf from the door and such a remote cause as radio history of the first decade of the century evoked little response.

Though we did not know, the sands were running swiftly out.

There is need to linger over 'last things'—the last Christmas, Reg's preparation for it as always was supervising the lighting. The whole front of "Wistowe" must be ablaze with festoons of Christmas lights—every connection carefully tested and plenty of reserve bulbs so that there need be no break in illumination. Promptly at dusk on Christmas Eve the lights went on and every night until after the New Year.

As a giver he was lavish beyond reason and his gifts had character and distinction. Christmas and birthdays were his best excuses but almost any reason served and I often bewailed the fact that his generosity in giving was beyond my power to assimilate. A gift must also live up to what was expected of it. On this last Christmas among my presents stood an unnoticed glass of water. "Did you see this?" asked Reg, lifting the glass, and there at the bottom was a Rolex oyster wrist watch with its watertight construction, and given in this way to head off my standard plea against a wrist watch—that my hands were always busy with household tasks which a wrist watch couldn't survive.

He was instinct with hospitality and nothing pleased him more than to welcome the members of our large family circle whether as expected or unexpected guests. He wanted life and activity around him and tried to provide sport and amusement for every age, even to swim toys of most intriguing character for the youngsters. Indeed his zest for life was in keeping with the extraordinary gamut of his being.

Ken spent three months with us in 1932 and undertook the transcription of his father's archeological notes which lifted a very real burden from Reg's mind, for their voluminousness and their very great importance had aggravated his regret at being unequal to the task himself and as he said, Ken made a far better job of deciphering his writing than he could have done.

But in February came another heart attack and two weeks in hospital—in May influenza followed by laryngitis and a prolonged low temperature. With infinite care once more the danger corner was turned and we could begin to look ahead hopefully, but the resolve was made to remain in Bermuda for the summer, not to attempt a trip to the States.

Frequently he approved this decision. "We could not find a pleasanter, more comfortable spot," said he. On a July afternoon, the last before the fatal attack, we had enjoyed with friends a run in the boat followed by afternoon tea on the veranda at "Wistowe." Later he said:—"That was a nice little party" and in a musing way, "I'm sure this summer is helping me, with all this rest and sunshine and the sunshine lamps—I ought to be able to find out something that will be helpful not only to me, but to others."

Next day his great spirit had passed, merged, as it seems to me it must be, in the vast controlling force of the universe.

THE END

ADDENDA

I
THE SCIENTIFIC WORK OF REGINALD A. FESSENDEN

Chief chemist for Edison, 1887-1889.
Professor of Electrical Engineering at Purdue, 1892-1893 and at Western University of Pennsylvania. (Univ. of Pittsburgh) 1893-1900.

Developed an entirely new system of wireless transmission distinct from and based on a different principle from that of Lodge, Marconi and all other workers—which principle was eventually proved to be the correct one.

Had over 500 patents issued in varied fields, especially in the transmission of light, sound and electrical waves.

Effected the first two-way, trans-Atlantic wireless telegraphic service, in 1906 between Brant Rock, Mass. and Machrihanish, Scotland.

Was the first to transmit wireless telegraphic messages over land a distance of 1600 miles, Massachusetts to New Orleans—in 1910.

Invented the wireless telephone and first tested it in crude form at Cobb Island, Md., at the close of 1900.

Made the first Radio Broadcast from the Brant Rock Station on Christmas Eve and New Year's Eve of 1906, which was heard by ships all along the coast as far south as Guantanamo Bay.

The Fessenden Radio patents, which were lost in the struggle with the National Electric Signaling Company, were acquired by the R.C.A. for $3,000,000.00.

He invented the Oscillator, the Fathometer (sometimes called the Sonic Depth Finder), the Wireless Compass and other submarine signaling devices.

He originated the Turbo-electric Drive for battleships.

He was given the Medal of Honor by the Institute of Radio Engineers in 1921, the John Scott Medal by the Advisory Committee of the City of Philadelphia in 1922 for his invention in "Continuous Wave Telegraphy and Telephony" and the Scientific American Medal in 1929 for his numerous inventions relating to safety at sea.

II

FESSENDEN'S DISCOVERY OF THE ELECTROSTATIC DOUBLET THEORY AND OF THE NATURE OF COHESION AND ELASTICITY.—as told by himself.

"I have referred previously to a job set me by Edison, to make a non-inflammable insulation which should be as elastic as rubber. How the compounds were made non-inflammable, by chlorine substitution, has been told, and was not difficult. But the "as elastic as rubber" clause was "anything but". After studying it a bit I concluded I did not know enough about the theory of elasticity, so got out Todhunter and Ibbotson's mathematical theory of elasticity from the Orange library and went carefully through it.

The original memoirs referred to by them were all in the Edison Library. Of course it was not possible to read them all through, but fortunately I had formed the habit of always translating into words all mathematical formulae as I went along (a habit which cannot be too strongly recommended to all students of mathematical physics, as helping to visualize the processes and as a great safeguard against mistakes in limits of integration, series, etc.), and so was able to get all that was necessary to give a clear idea of the subject in a few months. It was then apparent that the mathematical theory was not sufficiently advanced to give a solution and, so far as the immediate problem was concerned, was on the wrong trail.

But what was the right one?

The two great authorities on elasticity and cohesion were Kelvin and Sutherland, the latter of whom had made the subject peculiarly his own. Both of them, and all other physicists at that time, held that cohesion could not possibly be an electrical phenomenon because conductors such as copper and silver had cohesion, and electrical charges could not exist inside of conductors. Both of them were agreed that cohesion was a gravitational phenomenon; Sutherland had published a score of papers in the Philosophical Magazine to prove this, and

Kelvin had published in the same journal a paper demonstrating that the elasticity of rubber and similar substances was due to the gravitational attraction between very long and attenuated forms of atoms.

I saw that the behavior of these substances would not fit in with any gravitational theory. For example, the fact that if one stretched rubber and then heated it, it would contract, when according to the gravitational theory it should expand. By this time I was "indoctrinated" with the Edison methods, and decided that the thing to do was to get "more tumblers". So slips of paper, a lot of them, were taken and the first filled out with the names of all the chemical elements in alphabetical order. On the second slip were the atomic weights, so that when the slips were laid side by side the atomic weights would be opposite the proper elements. On the third the specific heats. On the fourth the electric conductivities. On the fifth the atomic diameters. On the sixth the atomic areas. On the seventh the atomic volumes. On the eighth the heats of fusion, etc. etc., until every known property of every known element was tabulated on those slips. Of course many of the slips contained very few entries, as the data were not known, and only a few were complete.

Then these slips were laid side by side, in all possible combinations and compared to see if there were any relation detectable between say heat of fusion and electric conductivity. If there appeared to be any possibility of relationship, curves were drawn. Finally it was found that there was definitely a relationship between the rigidity and the Young's modulus of the elements and the square of their atomic volume. Also between the tensile strength, i.e. cohesion, and the atomic volume and the fusion point, and a table was prepared. (See "The Laws and Nature of Cohesion". Science, N. Y. July 22, 1892, also Chemical News, lxvi, 206).

The square law suggested either gravitation or electric force.

Gravitation was tried but came out only a minute fraction of the observed value. Electrical attraction, on the other hand, gave a figure not so far out. So the force was probably electrical, but depended upon some configuration other than the simple attraction between positive and negative charges, located (mathematically) at the centers of the atom.

It was finally found that if the atoms were considered as electrostatic doublets, with a positive charge at their centers and a negative charge on their surfaces, the cohesion, rigidity and Young's modulus came out just right.

There was another vital condition which must be met. Clerk Maxwell had proved that any theory of cohesion must satisfy a certain fifth power law. The electrostatic doublet theory was tested by this and satisfied the law. But this was contrary to the the accepted ideas of the distance between atoms. They had to be substantially touching each other in order that the electrostatic doublet theory should give correct values, and all the text books made them far apart—some even taking them as mathematical points without any real size. Other theories made them variable in size; and there was one fact which seemed to prove definitely that they could not be touching. If one took 45.5 cubic inches of potassium and added to it chlorine atoms equal in number to the potassium, the resultant potassium chloride occupied a space of only 37.4 cubic inches.

More tumblers. A long strip of a compound of asphalt and paraffin was cut up into 64 equal parts, such that when each part was rolled into a sphere, and they were all stacked together evenly in four layers, and four balls to a side, they occupied a space of 45.5 cubic inches. Then 64 smaller balls were made, so that when they were stacked evenly they occupied a space of 15 cubic inches. The former stack of balls represented potassium, the latter stack represented chlorine. Then, the balls from the two stacks were used to build up a new stack, one ball from one stack next a ball from the other stack. This made a sloping stack.

It was found that the new stack, instead of occuping a volume of 60.5 cubic inches, occupied only 37.4 inches, owing to the smaller balls to some extent fitting into the vacant spaces between the larger balls. It was also found that the angle of slope of the new stack was very closely that of the crystals of the chemical compound formed.

Other combinations of elements were tried and the results showed conclusively that the atoms in a solid state were close together, almost touching, and therefore the electrostatic doublet theory was probably true. The theory was then applied to many other phenomena, to correct Van der Waal's formula for gases; to substitute for the then authoritative theory of osmotic pressure a new concept,—that of osmotic suction; to show that electric conductivity was a function of sound through metals, etc. etc. (*Electrical World,* Aug. 8th and 22, 1891; *Electrical Review,* London, November 27th, 1891; *Science,* July 22nd, 1892 and March 3rd, 1893.)

This explained the elasticity and cohesion of the elements. But no elements are nearly as elastic as India Rubber. So the elasticity of rubber must be due to some other cause. It could not be a direct effect of electrostatic doublets. Therefore it must be due to some configuration.

Still More Tumblers. First, rubber was examined very carefully under the microscope, and found to consist of two or even three differently appearing substances. Tested by solvents it was found that some solvents would dissolve it all, but others would dissolve only one part, swelling up the rest, but not dissolving it. The configuration giving rubber its great elasticity must probably be one, then, depending upon the mechanical mixture of two or more substances.

A simple type of double configuration was examined, that of a three-walled sphere of copper, filled with water. Such a body when compressed between two flat surfaces until it was shortened, say, 10 per cent, was found to have elastically strained the copper only a fraction of 1 per cent, and the volume of water had been changed still less. In other words, a body made up in this type of configuration, irrespective of the size of the elementary particles, for example a car bumper spring made of a large number of such water-filled copper balls, soldered at their points of contact, would compress or lengthen as a whole very greatly and with only a minute lengthening of any of its constituent parts, so resembling rubber. It would also resemble rubber in other ways. The metals follow Poisson's law, i.e. a rod of copper increases in volume when stretched and diminishes in volume when its ends are compressed, to a quite large amount. But rubber does not, nor would a rod made of water-filled copper balls.

Rubber heats when stretched, instead of cooling, and so would the rod of water-filled copper balls, because the water in the balls is really compressed when the rod is stretched. Also if a stretched rod of rubber is heated it contracts instead of expanding as a rod of copper would. And so would the rod of water-filled copper balls, because the water would, in expanding, try to make the balls return to their original round shape.

So all the different peculiar actions of India Rubber were gone through, one by one, and all found to be explainable as due to a configuration in which an A type of substance, such as the water, is contained in or surrounded by a B type of substance such as the copper sphere; like for example, a skein of silk embedded in gelatine, and when a rod of the compound is stretched the A substance is compressed and the B substance is stretched.

Artificially elastic substances were made up from various soaps which behaved exactly like rubber, even as to light polarization, but which could be squeezed in the hand to expel the A substance and then behaved like the metals. Having found out, in this way, why rubber is elastic, it was a simple job to make the compound, already non-inflammable, also elastic.

As will be seen later, this discovery resulted in a number of inventions. For example, the question at once suggested itself: If tensile strength and rigidity are a function of the atomic volume, may there not be some other metals which are better electrical conductors than copper or silver? It was found that there should be such a metal, *beryllium,* or as it is sometimes called, *glucinum.*"

III
BIBLIOGRAPHY

SECTION I
WIRELESS TELEGRAPHY, TELEPHONY AND TELEPHOTOGRAPHY

Lodge Wave Telegraphy, *Electrical World and Engineer,* July 29, 1899.

Lodge Wave Telegraphy, *Electrical World and Engineer,* Aug. 12, 1899.

Wireless Telegraphy, *Electrical World and Engineer,* Sept. 16, 1899.

The Possibilities of Wireless Telegraphy, *American Institute of Electrical Engineering,* Nov. 22, 1899.

Wireless Telegraphy over Frozen Ground, *Electrical World and Engineer,* Jan. 26, 1901.

Wireless Telegraphy, *Electrical World and Engineer,* June 27, 1901.

The Relative Reliability of Wireless and Wire Telegraph Systems, *Electrical World and Engineer,* Nov. 14, 1903.

Collins Articles, *Electrical World and Engineer,* Aug. 23, 1902.

Collins Articles, *Electrical World and Engineer,* Sept. 19, 1903.

Theories in Wireless Telegraphy, *Electrical World and Engineer,* Jan. 13, 1904.

The Government Use of Wireless Telegraphy, *Electrical World and Engineer,* Aug. 20, 1904.

Wireless Telegraphy, *The Electrician,* Sept. 16, 1904.

Wireless Telegraphy, *The Electrician,* Feb. 3, 1905.

Water-Stream Antenna, *Electrotechnischen Zeitschrift,* Nov. 6, 1905.

Water-Stream Antenna, *Electrotechnischen Zeitschrift,* Feb. 6, 1906.

Water-Stream Antenna, *Electrotechnischen Zeitschrift,* July 19, 1906.

Wireless Telegraphy, *Electrical Review*, May 11, 1906.
Wireless Telegraphy, *Electrical Review*, May 18, 1906.
Interference in Wireless Telegraphy and the International Telegraph Conference, *Electrical Review*, July 6, 13, 20, 27, 1906.
Austin Thermo-Electric Wave Detector, *Electrical World*, Nov. 10, 1906.
The Wireless Telegraph Situation, *Scientific American*, Jan. 19, 1907.
Recent Progress in Wireless Telephony, *Scientific American*, Jan. 19, 1907.
The Continuous Production of High Frequency Oscillations, *The Electrician*, Feb. 15, 22, 1907.
Wireless Telephony, *Electrical Review*, Feb. 15, 22 and March 1, 1907.
The Principles of Electric Wave Telegraphy, *The Electrician*, July 5, 1907.
The Principles of Electric Wave Telegraphy, *The Electrician*, Sept. 13, 1907.
Wireless Telegraphy During Daylight, *The Electrician*, July 26, 1907.
Atmospheric Absorption of Wireless Signals, *Electrical Review*, Sept. 6, 1907.
Wireless Telegraphy, *Scientific American*, Sept. 28, 1907.
Long Distance Wireless Telephony, *The Electrician*, Oct. 4, 1907.
A Regular Wireless Telegraph Service between America and Europe, *Scientific American*, Nov. 16, 1907; *The Electrician*, Nov. 22, 1907; *Electrical Review*, Nov. 22, 1907.
Trans-Atlantic Wireless Telegraphy, *Engineering*, Jan. 18, 1907.
Trans-Atlantic Wireless Telegraphy, *Engineering*, Jan. 25, 1907.
Trans-Atlantic Wireless Telegraphy, *The Electrician*, Jan. 3, 1908.
Wireless Telegraphy, *Electrical Review*, Jan. 17, 1908.
The International Radio-telegraph Convention, *The Electrician*, Apr. 3, 1908.
Wireless Telephony, *American Institute of Electrical Engineering*, June 29 and July 2, 1908.
Portable Type of High-Frequency Alternator, *The Electrician*, July 3, 1908.
The Predetermination of the Radiation Resistance of Antennae, *The Electrician*, Aug. 7, 1908.
Wireless Telephony, *The Electrician*, Nov. 27, 1908.

Tantalum Wave Detectors and Lamps, *The Electrician,* Feb. 5, 1909.
Correspondence with Reference to Obtaining Permit from Colonial Office to Provide the West Indies and Canada with Cheaper Telegraphic Communication, *British Blue Book,* July, 1910.
Statement Submitted, *British Blue Book,* July, 1910.
Memorandum, Proposals, Etc., *British Blue Book,* July, 1910.
Memorandum on the Advisability, etc., *British Blue Book,* July, 1910.
How Ether Waves Really Move, *Popular Radio,* November, 1923.

SECTION II
SUBMARINE TELEGRAPHY AND TELEPHONY

Long-Distance Submarine Signalling by Dynamo-Electric Machinery, *American Academy of Arts* and the *Lawrence Scientific Association* in joint session: Boston, Feb. 25, 1914.
The Fessenden Pelorus (Wireless Compass), A caution as to its use, *Electrician,* Dec. 19, 1919.

SECTION III
WIRE TELEGRAPHY, TELEPHONY AND CABLES

Sine Form of Curves of Alternating E. M. F., *Electrical World:* New York, Sept. 15, 1894.
Sine Form of Curves of Alternating E. M. F., *Electrical World:* New York, Sept. 29, 1894.
The Cause of Change of Microphone Resistance, *American Electrician,* Feb., 1897.
Microphonic Telephonic Action, *American Electrician,* May, 1897.
Electromagnetic Mechanism, with Reference to Telegraphic Work, *Journal of the Franklin Institute,* June, 1900.

SECTION IV
PHOTO-BOOK

Use of Photography in Data Collections, *Electrical World:* New York, Aug. 22, 1896.

SECTION V
ELECTRICAL ENGINEERING

Non-Arcing Metals, *Electrical Engineer:* New York, Apr. 6, 1892.
Vacuum Tube Lightning Arresters, *Electrical Engineer:* New York, Aug. 17, 1892.
Fireproof Insulation, *Electrical World:* New York, Sept. 3, 1892.
Conductors and Insulators, *Electrical World,* New York, Mar. 4, 1893.
Conductors and Insulators—II, *Electrical World:* New York, Mar. 18, 1893.
Conductors and Insulators—III, *Electrical World:* New York, Mar. 26, 1893.
Conductors and Insulators—IV, *Electrical World:* New York, May 6, 1893.
Conductors and Insulators—V, *Electrical World:* New York, May 13, 1893.
Conductors and Insulators—VI, *Electrical World:* New York, May 20, 1893.
Boilers for Small Central Stations, *Electrical World:* New York, Mar. 3, 1894.
Steam Boilers for Central Stations, *Electrical World:* New York, Mar. 10, 1894.
Anthony on the Incandescent Lamp. *Transactions of the American Institute of Electrical Engineers,* Vol. XI, March, 1894.
Definition of a Polyphase System, *Electrical World:* New York, Mar. 30, 1895.
On the Relation between Maximum Induction and Remanance, *Electrical World:* New York, Aug. 3, 1895.
The Loss of Energy in Changing from a Single Alternating Current to Polyphase Currents, *Electrical World:* New York, Dec. 7, 1895.
Probable Development in Electricity and Electrical Engineering, *Electrical World:* New York, Mar. 7, 1896.
Economic Use of Electric Power for Driving Tools, *Engineers' Society of Western Pennsylvania,* Sept., 1896.
Some New Electrical Apparatus, *Electrical World:* New York, Dec. 5, 1896.
The Evolution of the Rail Bond, *Electrical World:* New York, Feb. 5, 1898.
The Evolution of the Rail Bond, *Electrical World:* New York, Mar. 19, 1898.

The Evolution of the Rail Bond, *Electrical World:* New York, Mar. 23, 1898.
Insulation and Conduction, *American Institute of Electrical Engineering:* New York, Mar. 23, 1898.
The Relation between Mean Spherical and Mean Horizontal Candle Power of Incandescent Lamps, *Electrical World:* New York, Feb. 25, 1899.
Frequency Meters, *Electrical World:* New York, Nov. 11, 1899.
The Method of Insulation by Freezing, *Electrical World:* New York, Sept. 8, 1900.
Magnetic Observations and Traction Disturbances, *The Electrician:* London, Jan. 11, 1901.
Electrolytic Rectifiers, *Electrical World and Engineer,* June 1, 1901.
Recent Progress in Practical and Experimental Electricity, *The Philosophical Society,* Oct. 12, 1901.
Discussion of D. McFarlan Moore's Paper, *Transactions American Institute of Electrical Engineering,* Apr. 26, 1907.

SECTION VI

GENERATION AND STORAGE OF POWER

A Sun Storage Battery, *American Electrician,* May, 1898.
Official Report of the Ontario Power Commission, Mar. 28, 1906.
The Commercial Solution of the Problem of Utilizing, for the Production of Power, the Energy of Solar Radiation, the Wind and other Intermittent Natural Sources, *The Times:* London, Sept. 8, 1910.
"Banking" Electricity for Universal Use, *Scientific American,* April 30, 1921.
Boston May Revolutionize Heating Problem, *Boston Evening Transcript,* Nov. 29, 1922.
Cheaper Electric Heat is Demonstrated Possibility, *Boston Evening Transcript,* Jan. 27, 1926.

SECTION VII

GENERAL PHYSICS AND CHEMISTRY

An Electrically Driven Gyrostat, *Electrical Engineer,* May 19, 1889.

Electricity in Chemical Manipulations, *Chemical News:* London, Jan. 3, 1890.
The Volumetric Analysis of Copper, *Chemical News:* London, Apr. 18, 1890.
The Volumetric Analysis of Copper, *Chemical News:* London, May 23, 1890.
The Setting up of Clark Standard Cells, *Electrical World:* New York, June 7, 1890.
Action of Nitric Acid on Asphalt and Cellulose, *Chemical News:* London, Mar. 18, 1892.
Electrical Discharge through a Geissler Tube, *Science:* New York, Apr. 21, 1893.
Effect of a Gaseous Envelope on the Resistance of a Metal, *The Electrician:* London, June 30, 1893.
Some Measurements of the Temperature Variation in the Electrical Resistance of a Sample of Copper, *International Electrical Congress:* Chicago, 1893.
A New Method of Preventing Heat Radiation, *Electrical World:* New York, Jan. 13, 1894.
Standards of Illumination, *Transactions of the American Institute of Electrical Engineering*, Feb. 23, 1894.
Standards of Illumination, *Transactions of the American Institute of Electrical Engineering*, May 21, 1895.
Standards of Illumination, *Transactions of the American Institute of Electrical Engineering*, May 20, 1896.
Standards of Illumination, *Transactions of the American Institute of Electrical Engineering*, June 28, 1899.
Variations in Resistance,
On a Proposed Modification of the Generally Accepted Temperature Co-efficient of Resistance for Copper Wires, *Electrical World:* New York, Feb. 16, 1895.
On the Electrolysis of Gases, *Astrophysical Journal:* Chicago, Dec., 1895.
A New Method of Measuring Temperature, *Nature:* London, Jan. 16, 1896.
Outline of an Electrical Theory of Comets' Tails, *Astrophysical Journal*, Dec., 1896.
The Movement of Encke's Comet, *Nature:* London, Sept. 29, 1898.
On the Use of the Methven Standard with Blackened Chimney, *Electrical World*: New York, Feb. 28, 1899.

Absolute Determination of the Ohm, *Nature:* London, Apr. 27, 1899.
Nature of the Lightning Discharge, *Electrical World* and *Electrical Engineer,* Apr. 29, 1899.
A Multiple Lightning Flash, *Electrical World and Engineer,* Nov. 4, 1899.
The True Explanation of Dark Lightning Flashes, *Electrical World and Engineer,* Jan. 6, 1900.
Physics at the American Association, *Science:* New York, July 20, 1900.
Light Without Heat, *Electrical World and Engineer,* Jan. 5, 1901.
India Rubber, *The Electrician:* London, Nov. 6, 1903.
On Thermo-Galvanometers, *The Electrician:* London, June 24, 1904.
On Thermo-Galvanometers (Corrections), *The Electrician:* London, July 15, 1904.
The High-Pressure Electric Condenser, *The Electrician:* London, Nov. 3, 1905.
On the Magnetic Properties of Electrolytic Iron, *Transactions of the American Institute of Electrical Engineering,* May 30, 1906.
Wireless Telegraphy and the Ether, *Eastern Association of Physics Teachers,* Nov. 23, 1912.
A Safe Method of Using Mercury Bichloride for the Antisepsis of Wounds of Large Surface, *Science:* New York, June 18, 1915.

SECTION VIII

MATHEMATICS

The Centimetre Gramme Second and the Centimetre Dyne Second Systems of Units and a New Gravitational Experiment, *Science:* New York, Dec. 22, 1893.
A Formula for the Area of the Hysteresis Curve, *Electrical World:* New York, June 9, 1894.
Magnetic Formulae, *Electrical World:* New York, June 23, 1894.
On the True Dimensions of the Electrostatic and Electromagnetic Units, and on the Right Use of the Terms Intensity, Strength, Force and H, *Electrical World:* New York, May 4, 1895.
The Quantity upon which a Knowledge of the Nature of Electricity and Magnetism Depends, *Electrical World:* New York, May 18, 1895.

Dimensional Formulae and the Theory of Units, *Electrical World:* New York, June 29, 1895.
On the Use of Magnetic Formulae in Electrical Design, *Electrical World:* New York, Aug. 24, 1895.
Qualitative Mathematics, *Electrical World:* New York, Feb. 6, 1897.
How to get rid of "4" Eruption without changing any of the Legal Units, *Electrical World and Engineer,* Dec. 9, 1899; *Electrician:* London, Dec. 29, 1899.
A Proposed System of Units, *The Electrician,* Dec. 29, 1899.
Motion of Committee on Units and Standards, *Proceedings of American Institute of Electrical Engineering,* Mar. 28, 1900.
On a System of Units, *The Electrician,* May 20, 1904.

SECTION IX
ECONOMICS

On Professional Degrees, *Electrical World and Engineer:* New York, Nov. 11, 1899.
Colonial Telegraphic Communication, *Times:* London, Oct. 26, 1910.

SECTION X
AGRICULTURAL ENGINEERING

Fessenden Patent, No. 1121722, Dec. 22, 1914.
Fessenden Patent, No. 1268949, June 11, 1918.

SECTION XI
COHESION AND MOLECULAR PHYSICS

Note on the Volume Force of Solids, *Electrical World,* Aug. 8, 1891.
Atomic Volume and Tensile Strength, *Electrical World,* Aug. 22, 1891.
Theory of Solution, *Electrical Review:* London, Nov. 27, 1891.
Use of Glucinum in Electrical Instruments, *Electrical World:* New York, July 16, 1892.
The Laws and Nature of Cohesion, *Science:* New York, July 22, 1892, March 3, 1893; *Chemical News,* Oct. 21, 28, 1892, Oct. 27, 1893.

Some Recent Work on Molecular Physics, *Journal of the Franklin Institute,* Sept., 1896.

SECTION XII
NATURE OF ELECTRICITY, MAGNETISM AND GRAVITATION

On the Prospective Development of Ether Theories, *Electrical World:* New York, Jan. 2, 1897.
On the Prospective Development of Ether Theories, *Electrical World:* New York, Jan. 30, 1897.
A Determination of the Nature of the Electric and Magnetic Quantities and of the Density and Elasticity of the Ether, *Physical Review:* Cornell, Jan., 1900.
An Explanation of Inertia, *Electrical World and Engineer,* April 7, 1900.
Inertia and Gravitation, *Science:* New York, Aug. 31, 1900.
As to the Nature of Inertia and Gravitation, *Transactions of the Toronto Astronomical Society,* 1901.
An Explanation of Gravitation, *Electrical World and Engineer:* New York, Sept. 29, 1900.
Theories of Gravitation, *Electrical World and Engineer:* New York, Oct. 13, 1900.
A Determination of the Nature and Velocity of Gravitation, *Science:* New York, Nov. 16, 1900.
Cohesion, Electricity, Magnetism and Gravitation, Unpublished, Written June, 1909.
Transformation of Gravitational Waves into Ether Vortices, *Science:* New York, Oct. 17, 1913.
Gyroscopic Quanta, *Science:* New York, April 10, 1914.
Quantum Radiation a Gyroscopic Phenomenon, Unpublished, Written July 26, 1914.

SECTION XIII
HISTORICAL

The Deluged Civilization of the Caucasus Isthmus, Privately printed and distributed; also, through Massachusetts Bible Society, 1923.
Finding a Key to the Sacred Writings of the Egyptians, *Christian Science Monitor,* March 18, 1924.

How it was discovered that all so-called Myth-Lands were the Caucasus Isthmus, *Christian Science Monitor,* March 8, 1926.

Chapter XI—of the Deluged Civilization, Privately printed and distributed; also through Massachusetts Bible Society, 1927.

The Founding of Empire Day, Privately printed and distributed, 1930.

An apparently definite Identification of Masons with the Egyptian M-S-N, *Merseyside* Association for Masonic Research, 1932.

The Deluged Civilization of the Caucasus Isthmus (unpublished and reprinted papers), Posthumously Published, Privately printed and distributed, 1933.

INDEX

INDEX

Abbe, Prof. Cleveland, 76
abeam, 227
above, 201
abrasion, 307
abroad, 280
abrupt change, 289
absorption coils, 250, 251, 257
abstruse, 102
accident, 214
A.C. current, 50, 53, 55, 59
achievement, 215
Achilles tendon, 200
activity, 290
acyclic generators, 208
Adams, Mr., 324
adjudication, 335
administration, 160
administrators, 261
Admiral Taylor, 204
Admirality, 179, 224, 225, 226, 227, 228, 236
admiration, 307
Adriatic S.S., 171
Adsit, Mr., 331
advantages, 205
adverse report, 205
advice, 228
Advisory Inventor's Board, 241
Aegean Sea, 288
aeroplane, 319
aeroplane engines, 229, 230
aeroplane motors, 210, 211
affront, 325
agreement, 98, 100, 105, 106, 109, 111, 110, 112, 303, 313, 314, 315, 334
agricultural dept., 100
ahead, 227
ailments, 239
Ailesworth, Mr., 32, 35
aircraft, 229
aircraft in mass, 229
airman, 232
airplanes, 209
Alaska, 272
Albemarle Sound, 86
Aldrich, Judge, 191
ales, 308
Alexander, Mr., 337
Alexanderson, Mr., 149, 150, 331, 336
Alexandria, city of, 78, 275, 276
Allegheny City, 63, 64
Allegheny Observatory, 64, 78
allied art, 192

allied submarines, 255
Allies, 236, 241
alloy, 307
alphabet, 264
alternator, 134, 273
Altoona, city of, 57
aluminum, 51, 133, 305
aluminum discs, 143
amateurs, 309
Amazon, 123
Amerada Corp., 303
America, 241, 254, 315
American, 24, 88, 108, 322
American Academy of Arts and Sciences, 217
American Archeological Depts., 295
American Committee World Power Conf., 201
American Co., 169
American Electrician, 194
American Indian, 175
American Inst. of Electrical Engineers, 76, 331
American Museum of Safety, 303
American rights, 204
American systems, 123
American Telephone Journal of New York, 152
American T&T, 143, 155, 156, 323, 332
Amplifiers, 259
Amorities, 295
anacysm, 32
analysts, 294
anaesthetic, 340
Andover, 175
angina, 339
annealing, 71
animals, 289
antagonists, 331
antenna, 122, 126, 148, 319
antenna, horizontal, 169
anticipated, 294
antidote, 208
antiquated, 276
Anti-submarine development work, 241
Antimony trichloride, 33
anxiety, 191
apostolic, 285
Apparatus, 121, 123, 131, 133, 134, 135, 146, 147, 153, 161, 164, 165, 197, 198, 215, 216, 217, 227, 229, 241, 244, 248, 249, 252, 253, 268, 269, 271, 278, 279, 299, 300, 301, 302

applicant, 196
application, 298, 318, 320
applications, 170, 189
Appolonius, 276
apprentices, 243
apprenticeship, 246
appropriations, 282
approval, 281
Arax, 287
arbitrator, 167, 168
arc, 154
arc detecting apparatus, 293
archeological, 295, 343
archeologists, 288
Argentinians, 223
Argonautica, 276
Argonauts, 286
arguments, 322
aridity, 274
arise, 289
Aristotle, 275
Ark, 292
Arlington, City of, 80
armature, 246
armistice, 246, 251, 260
armiture, 149
Armor, Mr. James C., 133, 135, 136, 137, 139
Army and Navy officials, 163
art, the, 157, 162, 215, 277, 285
arterial pressure, 170
article, 180
articles, 295, 308, 311
artillery batteries, 229
artistic side, 304
asleep, 209
asphalt, 350
astern, 227
Astor Hotel, 182
Assam, 305
assay, 325
assets, 165
assignment, 192, 312, 313
Assistant Secretary of the Navy, 205
Associated Press, 143
Associates, 117, 212
Assyrologist, 294, 295
athwartship screens, 253
Atlantic, 95, 126, 286, 287
Atlantic Monthly, 274
Atlantic Union, 172, 175, 261
Atlantis, 287, 288, 289
atomic, 349, 352
atoms, 44, 54
A.T.&T., 162
attachment, 186, 188
attorney, 191, 339
attorneys, 307

attractive, 214
audio oscillator, 278
Austin, Dr. Louis, 182, 310
Australia, 179
Australian Postal Department, 120
author, 276
authority, 241
authorize, 226
autobiography, 272, 274, 275-285, 310
 *275-285 inclusive are from that portion of his autobiography as published in "Radio News" July, 1925
automatic stability indicator, 302
automatic transmission, 152
automobile, 89
automobiles, 208, 210
auxiliary, 205, 207, 273
"Aylwin", O.S.S., 249, 250, 251, 252, 253, 254
Azov, Sea of, 288

Babylonia, 294
Babylonian, 298
Baldwin Locomotive Works, 45, 52, 53
ball, 126
Balliol, 234
Balliol School, 21
balls, 350
bank, 113, 187
Bank, Newark, 49
bankers, 260
banking, 208
bankruptcy, 159
banquets, 172
Barreter, 320
Barreters, hot wire, 80
Batchelor, Mr., 32, 35, 271
Batley, Mr., 233
Battleships, 205, 347
Bausch and Lomb, 19
Bayberries, 341
Bay of Fundy, 126, 136
Beaches, the, 234
Blakes, Mr., 136
beat system, 132
Beck, A., 195
bed, 336
Beddersley, Mr., 172
beer, 308
bell, 215, 250
Bell, Dr. Louis, 143
Bell Laboratories, 214
below, 201
Bennet, Mr., 75
Bennett, Mr. Charles, 251, 258
Bennett, Mr. Edward, 119, 133, 137, 138, 141

INDEX

Benson, Admiral, 241, 243
Bent, Miss (Fess.' secretary), 136, 171
Berkshires, 56
Bermuda, 308, 331, 335, 336, 337, 338, 343
Bermuda, Islands of, 13, 14, 15, 16, 17, 18, 19, 20, 21, 22, 23, 24, 25, 34, 36, 47, 48, 69, 81, 86, 105, 108, 175
Beryllium (Glucinium), 306, 352
Bethune, Dr., Headmaster at Port Hope, 18
Bible, 293
big business, 202, 243, 273, 274, 326
Bill No. 184, 160, 174
Birmingham, Cruiser, 183
birthdays, 342
Bishop of Norwich, 175
Bishop's College School, 20, 21, 22, 25, 26
Black Sea, 287
Black-jacked, 282
blackmail, 101
Blackman, Mr., 186
Blake, Mr., 218, 219, 221, 240, 241
blindness, 316
blue print, 209, 210
bluff, 180
Boarding House (Pittsfield on South St.), 56
Board of Directors, 224
boards, 283
Boil, 198
bolometer, 65
Bolton Centre, Village of, 9
bombing, 250
bombshell, 271
Borden, Sir Frederick, 169
bores, 287
Boston, city of, 19, 127, 152, 186, 187, 207, 211, 212, 214, 217, 218, 219, 224, 235, 238, 241, 242, 252, 253, 254, 256, 258, 291, 306, 308, 329, 333, 339, 340
Boston Harbor, 223, 224, 240, 243, 254, 256
Boston office, 233
Boston Transcript, April 6, 1925, 281
Bouch, Mr. Zeh, 337
Bournemouth, city of, 250
Boyle, Mr., 125, 312
Bradshaw, Mr., 75
brain, 209
branch, 282
Brant Rock, 126, 127, 128, 131, 134, 136, 137, 139, 140, 141, 143, 146, 148, 151, 152, 154, 155, 161, 168, 169, 171, 182, 183, 184, 186, 187, 188, 214, 226, 227, 319, 340, 341, 347

Brant Rock Station, 268, 269
Brashear, Mr., 147
Brashear, Mr. and Mrs., 65, 66, 69, 81
Brashear Optical Co., 280
Brashear Optical Works, 65
Brauker, Colonel, 228, 232
Braun, Mr. A.E., 184, 190
Brazilian Govt., 123
breach of contract, 187
brewing, 308
brief, colonial office, 178
British Admiralty, 317
British agent, 170
British Assn. 69, 177, 197
British Embassy, 241
British Empire, 259
British Govt., 92, 108, 126, 169, 228, 238, 291
British Marconi Co., 151
British Naval Attache, 205
British officialdom, 171
British Postmaster-General, 169
British Post Office, 42
British trade, 232
British War Office, 210, 224
broadcast, 153, 317
broadcasting, 116, 304
broad diaphragm, 335, 339
Brooklyn Bridge, 145
Browne, Mr., 314
Brown Hoisting Machinery Co., 126, 127, 145, 146
Brown, Judge, 191
Bryan, Mr., 131
Buffington, Judge, 84
Burdett and Coutts, 225
Bureau, 157
Bureaus, 281, 300
Bureau of Equipment, 122
Bureau of Standards, 182
Bureau of Steam Engineering, 243
buried, 188
Burr, Theodosia (an early colonist), 89
Bushey Hall, 225, 233, 234
Business, 273
business connections, 336
business ventures, Fessenden's, 70, 71
Buxton, Mr. Sidney, 172, 179
By-Products of History, from Deluged Civilization, 270

cable, 272
cable companies, 176
cable monopoly, 108
cable systems, 151
cabling, 137
calculations, 209, 319

INDEX

Calhoun, U.S.S., 251
California, 338
Cambridge (England), 59
Cambridge Instrument Co., 172, 176
Campbell, Mr., 130
Campbellton, 126, 136
Canada, 9, 12, 69, 169, 180, 231, 238, 259
Canadian agency, 225, 234
Canadian engineers, 178
Canadian navy, 179
Canadian Postmaster General, 176, 179
Canal stations, 304
cancelling, 252
cancer, 280
cancerous growth, 203
Canterbury, 177
Cape, 223
Cape Charles, 95, 105
Cape Henry, 86, 90
carelessness, 317
Carnegie, 280, 281, 283
Carnegie Co., 45, 71
Carnegie Institute, 265
Carrel, Dr. Alexis, 43
cars, 208, 209
cardiographs, 340
cartridges, 255
case, 308
Caspian Sea, 288
catastrophe, 287, 289
cathode, 268
Cato, 303
Caucasian Race, 289
Caucasus, 288, 289, 293, 295, 296
Caucasus Isthmus, 294
caveat, 299, 324
Cavendish Laboratory, 59
cement, 267
centre of force, 274
centuries, 285
Cerarinian, 290
certified cheque, 334, 335
Ceylon, 305
Chairman, naval committee, 205
Chalybes, 290
Chambers Journal, 197
chart paper, 290
charts, 291, 297
chase (between U.S.S. Aylwin & submarine), 249
chauffeur, 232, 340
cheap power, 196
cheese, limburger, 6
Chemical News, 306
Chemist & Chemistry, 32, 36
Chesapeake Bay, 95

Chesney, Mr., 55, 56
Chestnut Hill, 260
Chevy Chase, 120, 226
Chicago, 42, 54, 63
Chicago Inter-Ocean Newspaper, 69
chicken heart, 339
chief (Bureau of Steam Engineering), 243
Chierce, Dr. Edward, 295
China mug, 201
Chinese copy, 202, 298
Chinese pigtails, 120
Chippewa Rectory, 47, 48
Chiseltine, Captain, 80, 86
Chlorine, 33, 350
Christian Science Monitor, 294
Christmas, 120, 135, 190, 342
Christmas Eve, 153, 347
Christy, 111, 112
chronological abstract, 204
churchmen, 274
Churchill, Winston, 226
Cimmerian, 287
circuit, for interference preventor, 122
citadels, 201
Civilian Advisory Committee, 243
Civilian Boards, 242
Civilian Committees, 242
Civilian War Boards, 318
Civilization, 260, 262, 264, 275, 284, 285, 286, 286-296, 289, 293
claimants, 305
claims, 315, 327, 332, 333
Claridge's Hotel, 171
Clark Hill Islands, 48
Clarke University, 280
classics, 291
Clay, Prof. Albert, 288, 294, 295
Clay, Mr. F.W.H., 142, 184
Cleveland, city of, 126
cliffs, 293
cloth bag type, 305
club house, 106
clublife, 217
coal, 115
coal dust, 200
Coast Defense Board, 318
Coast Station, 158
Cobb Island, 78, 79, 80, 81, 86, 94, 147, 319, 347
Cockshutt, Mr. W.F., 195
cocktail, 338
code, 135
code wheel, 255
Coffin, Mr., 96, 210
Cohasset, town of, 340
Cohen, Dr., 182

INDEX

Cohen, Mr., 312
cohesion, 340
cohesion and elasticity, 43, 51, 54
coherer, 81, 84, 85, 90, 93
coil, 102, 103
Cole, Colonel F. Minder, 169, 170
Collier's Magazine, 234
Collingswood, N.J., city of (sometimes known as Philadelphia Station), 110, 114, 120
Collins, Mr. Dan, 121
Colonel Firth, 161, 162, 164, 166, 167, 168, 190
colonial office, 172, 175, 176, 178, 180
colonial permits, 172, 175
Colonial Premiers, 169
colonies, 180
color, 262
Columbia Exposition, 54, 62
Columbia Univ., 234
Combines, 284
Combustion engines, 209
comfort, 277
Commander Hooper, 323
Commander Lavender, 320
Commander Simpson, 172
Commence, 259
commercial, 269, 317
commercial licences, 169
commercial messages, 133
commercial stations, 105
commercial success, 207
commercial wireless telephone, 155
commercial work, 139
committee, 177
committee on sound, 243
committees, 315
Committee on Standards of Electrical Resistance, 63
commission, 194
commissioner, 197
commissioner's report, 195
common good, 285
commutator, 53, 218, 253, 254
companies, 273
company, 187
company policy, 184, 228
compass, 249, 264
competition, 316
component, 319
composing, 310
compressed neon oscillators, 148
compressed nitrogen oscillators, 148
compressor, 213
concealed artillery, 229
concentric mains, 58
conception, 202, 308

condenser, 267
condensers, 55, 138
condensers, compressed air, 133, 134, 154
condensers, oil insulated, 134
condensite, 32
conductors, 348
conductivity, 34
conference, 226
confidential report, 284
confiscation, 160
Congress, 160, 254
Congressman, 92
Congressmen, 328
Conservation, 261
conservative, 180
consternation, 227
consulting engineer, 100, 204
contact breaker, 69
Continuous Wave Reception, 326
continuous waves, 148, 316, 317
contract, 98, 99, 117, 165, 167, 190, 315, 324
contribution, 295
control, 158
controlling force, 343
controls, 282
conveyances, 314
cooperation, relating to Submarine Board, 244, 245
copper, 36, 41, 348, 352
copper alloy, 306
copper b. lls, 351
copper tube, 216
copying press, 267
Corey, William, 225
corporations, 282, 283
corrections, 311
corrode, 307
cottages, 127, 129
cotton gin, 277
county sheriff, 186
court, 332
court martial, 238
court of claims, 332
court ruling, 303
courts, 284
Cowell, Mr., 176
cratophote, 320
Creator, 289
Creusot, 212
Crewe, Lord, 172, 175
cricket, 129
Crimmins, Mr., 28
Crisis, 169
criticisms, 311
Crookes, Sir William, 306

INDEX

cross-license agreement, 323
crucifies, 188
C tube, 250
Cunningham, Commodore H.A., 301
current operated wave responsive receiver, 84
cut off, 280
Cuxhaven, 119
cycle, 133, 211
cycles, 273
cylinder, 230

Dallin, Mr. Cyrus, 130
Dalzell, John, 93
damped wave, 83
dangerous, 302
Daniels, Secretary, 241, 248
Dare County, 89
Dare, Virginia, 88
Dariel Pass, 293
Darwin, Mr., 172
dashes, 215
data, 225, 241, 291, 294, 319, 320, 328
Davenport, Dr. Charles, 265
David, 325
Davis, Mr. Albert G., 150, 207, 314
Davis, Mr. LeConte, 119
dawn stroll, 336
daylight absorption, 157
daylight fading, 319
D.C. current, 46, 50
dead man, 285
debt, 164, 168
De Chair, Admiral, 241
decision, 285
deeds, 316
defaming, 299
defense, 284, 285
DeForest, Dr. Lee, 95, 119, 121, 122, 123, 132, 133, 278, 279, 284
Degen, Colonel, 296
Diesel engine, 212
delay, 226, 318, 319
delayed invention, 204
delegated, 241
Deluge, 287, 288, 289, 290
Deluged Civilization, 229, 261, 286-296, 338
demand, 269
demand notes, 162
Democratic party, 160
demonstration, 148, 223, 226, 277, 304
Dempster, Mr., 149
Dept. of Justice, 332
deposition, 332
depression, 339
Deptford, electrical station of, 58

designing, 209
design, 269
designs, 164
desk, 270
despaired, 190
despotism, 281
destroyer, 248, 252, 253
destroying, 213
detail, 202, 267
detecting, 215
detecting apparatus, 241, 245, 250, 251
detection, 243
detectives, 184
detector, 85
Deutschland, 119
DeVeaux, Military College, 13, 14
develop, 294
development, 202, 212
developments, 260
Devereaux, 223
devices, submarine signalling & receiving, 216, 244, 303
Dexter, Gordon, 237
dial, 301
diaphragm, 271
diary, 217
dictaphone, 257
died, 260
Diesel electric, 273
diet, 339
differential equations, 60
difficult, 245
difficulties, 183
dignitaries, 173
Diogenes, 275
direction, 275
directorate, 169, 170
Director of Laboratory, 243
disappointment, 197
disaster, 194, 292
disbursement, 330
disclosure, 144, 298
discontinue, 183
discourage, 275
Discoverers, 261
discoveries, 277
Discovery, 268
discredit, 245
discredited, 276
dismantled, 250
dismissal, 187
disparagement, 330
dispersal, 292
dispersion, 289, 290
disregarded, 234
dividends, 97
doctor, 170

INDEX

domestic, 121
Dominion Day Dinner, 175
Don River, 285
Door, Mr. John, 36, 41
Dorman, Mr., 103
Dorsey, Dr. Herbert, 300
dots, 215
downfall, 274
down payments, 202
drain, 284
drawings, 314
dreaming, 267
drought, 288
drowning, 289, 290
Dudley, Dr., 57
Duhamel, 271
Duke of Wellington, 339
dull, 219
Dunlop Tire Co., 173
duplicates, 278
dynamo, 32, 41, 51, 52, 53, 218, 236
dynamos, 198

earthquakes, 290
earth tremor range finder, 230
East Bolton, Village of, 9
Eastman, 281
echo, 144, 216, 217, 221, 222, 299, 300
echoes, 293
echo method, 239, 240, 244
echo sounding, 302, 326
echo sounding methods, 303
eclipse, 90
economics, 261
Eden, 253, 296
Edison, Thomas, 26, 27, 28, 30, 31, 32, 33, 34, 35, 36, 37, 38, 39, 40, 45, 63, 67, 75, 106, 201, 241, 248, 265, 266, 267, 270, 271, 276, 279, 282, 285, 347, 348, 349
Edison boys, 92
Edison Electric Co. of Boston, 200, 201
edition, 290
editor, 142
efficiency, 204
eggs, 297
Egypt, 276, 288, 293, 294
Egyptian Phoenician, 287
elastic, 348, 352
elasticity, 349
electrical current, 198
Electrical Engineering, 59, 66, 100, 189, 347
Electrical Engineer Mag., 44
Electrical Review, 122
electrical storage, 198
electrical waves, 347

Electrical World articles, 307
Electrical World Mag., 61, 67
 July 16, 1892, an article by R.A.F. on *Use of Glucinium in Electrical Instruments*, 306, 351
electric beats, 132
electric companies, 204, 205, 206
electric conductivity, 350
electric force, 349
electric forces, 216
electricity, 102, 273
Electricity, science of, 26, 44
electric motors, 204
electric power, 277
electric spark, 317
electric sparks, 316
electric wave radiation, 149
electric waves, 316
electric wires, 257
electric work, 200
electrodes, 131
electrolyte detector, 122
electromagnetic, 320
Electro-Magnetic Mechanism, 57
Electrostatic Doublet Theory, 43, 51, 54, 55, 348, 349, 350
elevator, 140
Elihu Thompson Oscillating-current galvanometer, 147
eliminated, 282
Ellis, Mr. P.W., 195
Emmet, Mr., 205, 206
Empire, 293
Empire Day, 259
Empire of the Air (a story by the Ventura Free Press, Ventura, Calif.), 51
empirical, 275
employees, 179, 284
enamels, 293
encircle, 216
endowed, 276
endowments, 284
endowment shares, 283
enemy, 231
engine, 200, 210, 212, 213, 237
engine construction, 238
engineering, 207, 217, 269, 293, 297, 317
engineering rivalries, 228
engineers, 122, 123, 173, 199, 211, 214, 215, 283, 318, 321
engines, 209
England, 125, 197, 224, 227, 229, 235, 246, 299, 308
English, 93
English Company, 171, 173
English Optical Works, 280
English Patent Attorneys, 139

INDEX

English Postmaster General, 176
English Technical Publication, 142
English trip, 171
enlisted man, 256
entrenched business, 272
environment, 289
Episcopal Church, 338
equipment, 199, 282
erroneous, 246
error, 317
estate, 226
ether, 316
etheric impulse, 317
ether waves, 80
Ethiopians, 264
Europe, 252, 331, 334
European power, 256
European waters, 250, 253, 254
Euston, 234
evade, 326
evaded, 282
Evans, Dr. & Mrs., 24
Evening Post, New York, 67
Ewing, Mr. (patent commissioner), 53, 59, 237
excavation, 293
excluded, 245
exhaust ports, 211
exhibition, 211
Expenditure, 278
expenditures, 190
experience, 199
experiment, 215
experimental, 162
experimental dept., 133
experimenting, 277
experiments, 316
Experiments, Fessenden, 80, 81, 102, 200
expired, 317
exploded, 334
explorers, 274
explosive mixture, 211
exterpolating, 275
eye strain, 19

facilities, 271
facts, 328
Fagin, 203
failures, 208, 278
fall docket, 190
false stories, 268
families, 264
family, 177
family exchequer, 161
farewell, 188, 341

Farmer's Deposit Bank, 108, 115
Farmer's National Bank, 184
fatal attack, 343
fate, 118
father, 343
Fathometer, 297, 300, 301, 302, 303, 304, 347
fathoms, 301
faulty conception, 236
Fay, Mr. Harold, 214, 215, 216, 242
feasible, 205
Federal District Court of Mass., 299
Federal Radio Commission, 332
Federal Telegraph Co., 128
Federal Trade Commission, 150, 332
Ferranti, Mr., 58
ferry, 89
Fessenden apparatus, 243, 246, 249
Fessenden, Reginald Aubrey, 3, 9, 10, 11, to end.
Fessenden, Clementina, 259
Fessenden Combustion Engine, 204
Fessenden, Cortez Ridley Trenholme, 9, 16
Fessenden devices, 224
Fessenden, Ebenezer, 5
Fessenden, Elisha Joseph, 5, 14, 18, 26
Fessenden, Elisha Moss, 5
Fessenden equip., 129
Fessenden, John, 3
Fessenden, Ken (born in May, 1892, at Lafayette), 60, 63, 64, 78, 79, 81, 88, 90, 106, 120, 129, 140, 161, 175, 176, 188, 190, 234, 343
Fessenden, Kenneth Harcourt, 9, 16
Fessenden Laboratories, 189
Fessenden Long Wave Method, 227
Fessenden, Major R.K. (Ken), 303
Fessenden, Nicholas, 3, 4
Fessenden, Peter, 4
Fessenden Radio Patents, 347
Fessenden, R.K. (Ken), 294
Fessenden, Rev. Mr., 9
Fessenden's Law, 202
Fessenden's Philosohpy, 261, 272
Fessenden's Report, 195
Fessenden System, 95, 96, 97, 98, 100, 101, 102, 107, 108, 120, 121, 136, 138, 161, 163, 165, 176, 183
Fessenden, William Pitt, 4
Fessenden Wireless Co., 169
field, 255
Fielding, Mr., 176, 178
field work, 290
fifty, 215
fight, 188

fight (Fessenden and Chisetine), 86
figures, 178, 206
filament, 34
filament galvanometer, 61
files, 185, 186, 189, 327
files shelves, 184
film, 279
financial, 105
financial reward, 269
fire, 141, 289
fire hazards, 307
first class, 225
first earnings, 162, 163
First Lord of Admiralty, 172
First Secretary, 172
Firth, Colonel, 313
Fish, Frederick P., 156, 324, 329, 330, 331
fishing schooner, 151
Fitzgerald, Mr., 55
five thousand years, 276
five years, 270
fizzle, 177
flame, 317
Flatts Inlet, 335
flavor, 305
Fleet Officer, 227
flier, 162
flood, 287
flood waters, 292
fluid piston engine, 200
fluids, 211
fly casting, 238
flying field, 199
fog, 215
foodstuffs, 115
football, 61
force, 185
forced, 272
Ford, 276, 279, 282, 285
Foreign, 105, 108, 113, 114, 115, 120, 121, 312, 313
Fore River, 238
Fore River Co., 206
Fore River Shipyard, 211
forgings, 127, 145
formal letter, 179
Fort Huger, 89
Fort Monroe, 258
Fort Pitt Hotel, 167
Fortress Monroe, 106, 107
foundation, 276, 284, 285
founder, 259
founders, 284
four oscillator apparatus, 254
four sets only, 227
France, 93, 212

franchises, 314
Frankenstein, 322
Franklin Institute, Journal of the, 57
Frascati (boarding house called), 23, 24
freedom, 275
French, 120
Frequency, 236
Frequency, Electrical, 4
freshness, 305
friendly giant, 217
fruit, 171
fruits, 289, 292
fuel alcohol, 199, 200, 211, 262
fundamentals, 321
funds, 305
fusion, 349
futile, 245

gale, 219
galvanometer, 42, 59
gang, 185
garages, 208
gas companies, 272
gases, 350
gasoline, 213
gates, 202
Gaunt, Admiral, 237, 241
Gaunt, Captain, 224, 225
Gawler, Mr., 128
Gear, Mr., 169
gelatine, 352
general conference, 195
General Electric Co., 139, 143, 149, 150, 151, 200, 204, 205, 206, 207, 210, 236, 237, 239, 242, 243, 252, 314, 323, 324
General Electric Patent Dept., 150
general manager, 191
General Motors, 210
generating, 273
generation, 196, 276, 284
generator, 134
generosity, 342
generous, 117 (Fessenden's habits and character are explained on p. 117)
genesis, 67, 208
genetical factors, 266
genetics, 265
geological, 288
geologists, 288
Geophysical Research Corp., 303
George, Henry (publications), 27
Georgia, 288
German, 35, 40, 65, 236, 253, 255, 256, 257, 306
German engineers, 201
Germans, 215, 229

INDEX

Germany, 93, 119, 176, 235
Gernsback, Mr., 308, 309, 310
ghost, 309
Gibbon, Mr. C.O., 68 (in reference to Fess. micro phot. patents, letter in *N.Y. Post,* Oct. 9, 1930)
Gibralter, 288
gifts, 342
Given, Mr., 105, 106, 107, 110, 111, 113, 114, 115, 116, 124, 125, 136, 138, 141, 146, 155, 161, 162, 163, 165, 167, 168, 170, 171, 186, 190, 191, 312, 314, 323
gland enlargement, 340
Glaublitz, Mr., 127
glimpses, 291
Gloucester, 302
glucinium (beryllium), 44, 352
gnomic projections, 125
God, 338
Godfrey-Fausset, 229
gold, 306, 325
Gold Medal, 302, 303
golf, 217, 233, 294
Goliath, 325
Goss, Dr., 6
government, 178, 179, 180, 242, 248
government bureau, 281
Government Depts., 202
Government funds, 251
Government monopolies, 181
Government Monopoly, 123, 169, 170, 315
Government officials, 181
grain cooler, invention of, 6
grain elevator, invention of, 6
grains, 289
Grand Banks, 217
Grant, Admiral, 239, 244, 247
gratifying, 290
gravitation, 349
Great Ages, 275, 285
Great Britain, 126
greed, 315
Greek, 287
Greek myths, 286, 287
Greeks, 264
Greely, General, 95
Grenfell, Hon. Mr. E.C., 171
Grey, Mr., 96, 97
Griffin, Admiral, 241
Grigsby, 336
grim, 187
ground, 319
groups, 281
Grubb, Sir Howard, 280
guarantee, 321

guess, 245
Gunn, Mr., 218, 220
guy ropes, 145
guy-wire, rope, 126, 127
gymnasium, 41
gyro-compass, 44
Gyroscopic compass, 273

Hadfield, Mr., 128, 141, 341
Hale, Judge, 83, U.S.C.C.—Maine, 83, 84, 191
Halifax, 218, 219
Hall, Mr., 327, 330, 331, 333, 334
Hamilton, Bermuda, city of, 23, 33
Hammond, John Hayes, 330
harmonizing, 257
Harrington Sound, 335, 337
Harry, 213
Harvard, 217, 259, 291
Hatteras, Cape, 93, 94, 95, 97, 102, 104, 107
Hauser, Dr., 306
hay-stuffed, 176
Hay, Walker Jr. M., 108
Hayes, Dr., 326
Hayes, Mr. Hammond V., 143
hazards, 188
Hazeltine Lake Co., 317
he (Ken), 259
head phones, 133
hearings, 315
heart, 339
heart attack, 333, 343
heart block, 302
heart weakness, 302
heat, 198
heat measuring device, 71
Heavenly Rest, Church of, 47
Hebrew-Babylonian, 287
Helmholtz, Mr., 63, 271
Hepborn, 93
Herald, New York, 34 (sketch of Edison and Fessenden), 75
Herbert, Victor (composer), 69
Hercules, 286, 288, 293
heredity, 264, 265
Herodotus, 290
Hertz, Mr., 38, 55, 60, 75, 316
Hesperides, 289, 296
Heterodyne, 268, 320
Heterodyne Receiver, 132 (patent no. 766, 740 applied for Sept. 28/01 and granted Aug. 13/02)
Heterodyne Suit, 133
Higginson, Major, 223
high frequency, 273
high frequency alternator, 132, 148, 149, 150, 151

INDEX 375

high frequency dynamo, 147, 151, 154
Highlands, 122
high-powered land stations, 161
high speed telegraphy, 57, 58
high tension insulators, 330
Hill, Captain, 149
Hines, Mr., 57
Hiscox tables, 209
historians, 248
history, 286
hitch, 211
Hobart, Mr., 200
Hodge, Mr., 97
Hogan, Mr., 312
holdings, 167
Holland, Dr., 62
holocaust, 258
home brew, 308
homeland, 293, 294
Homo Sapiens, 289
Hood, Rear Admiral, 226, 227
Horizontal Wave, 330, 335, 339
Horse Power ("H.P."), 210, 211
House of Representatives, 160
Hudson Bay Territory, 175
Hughes, Sir Sam, 224, 225, 228
human hair, 321
human inertia, 306
humanity, 338
Hurlburt, Wm., 327, 331
hybrid, 211
Hydrographic Office Bulletin, 221
hydraulic head, 196
hydrogen, 33
Hygeia, 225
Hyperboreans, 263

Iberia, 288
ice, 218
iceberg, 214, 215
icebergs, 216, 218, 221, 222
iceberg test, 217
iceberg tests, 297
illustrated article, 300
Illustrated London News (Sept. 6, 1910), 197 (May 30, 1931), 232
imagination, 291
imitation, 325
Imperial Bank, 20
Imperial Institute of Journalists, 169
impersonal appropriation, 158
impossible feat, 183
imprisonment, 159
improvement, 215, 282
improvements, 268, 269
inadequate sum, 332
incorporated, 208

increment, 287
independent, 275, 282, 284, 285
independent scientist, 28
India, 178
Indiana, 60
India Rubber, 351
indigestion, 239
indigo, 261
indifference, 206
individual initiative, 160
individuality, 274
inductance, 102, 103
inductance roller, 137
induction coil, 147
inductor compass, 273, 278
Industrial Organizations, 202, 203
industries, 281
industry, 282
influenza, 343
infringe, 298
infringement, 228, 331
infringement suits, 297
infringing, 326
infringing device, 299
inherited aptitude, 267
inhibitions, 307
initialled, 184
initiative, 274
injunction, 84, 187, 191
installation, 227, 234, 249
Institute of Radio Engineers, 325
instruments, 110, 307
insulation, 50, 51
Insulation Compound, 43
insulator base, 341
insulators, 127, 128, 146, 341
insurance cos., 170
intake ports, 211
integrating detector, 85
intense, 216
intentional, 243
interest, 162, 165, 167
interests, 165
interference, 121, 122, 123, 159, 305, 318
interference preventers, 121
internal combustion engine, 208, 211, 273
international, 281
International Conference on Safety at Sea, 302
international distribution, 290
International Electrical Congress, 42
International Radio Convention, 157, 316
International Radio Telegraph Co., 314, 323, 332
international regulation of wireless, 92

INDEX

International Signal Co., 314
interpretation, 246
interupter, 81
invent, 215
invented, 276
inventing, 277, 285
inventing work, 160
invention, 132, 133, 150, 151, 152, 215, 261, 266, 267, 268, 269, 282, 285, 297, 298, 310, 318
inventions, 165, 202, 244, 262, 263, 270 272, 276, 278, 312, 320, 321, 324, 330, 331
Inventions of Fessenden, 22 (tractor)
Inventions of Reginald A. Fessenden (This was the title of Fessenden's autobiography as it appeared in *Radio News* beginning January, 1925), 309
inventor, 160, 162, 200, 202, 210, 266, 273, 276, 279, 281, 282, 283, 284, 305, 310
inventors, 264, 270, 309
inventors, phony and pirate, 73, 74
iron, 115, 306
iron rod, 281
Issacs, Rufus, 92
Isbell, 122
Isthmus of Chignecto, 126
Ithaca, city of, 91

Jackson, Mr., 317
Jamaica (Long Island), 155, 169
Japanese, 223
Jason, 286
jealousies, 182
jealousy, 228
Jeams, James, 338
Jefferson, Joe (an actor), 66
Jeremiah, 203
Jersey City, 108 (sometimes known as N.Y. station), 109, 110, 114
Johns Hopkins Medical School, 236
John Scott Medal, 325, 326, 347
Johnson, Captain, 87, 91
Johnson, Mr., 172, 175
Johnson, President, 4
Jones, Mr., 331, 332, 327, 328, 329, 333, 354
Jones, Mr. Boyd, 339
Josephus, 291
judge, 313
Judge Lowell, 299, 300
judgement, 191
jury, 190
justice, 318, 333

Kabiri, 293, 296
Keel, 301
Keeler, Dr., 64, 65, 69, 70, 72
Keller, Helen, 257
Kelley, J.D., 46, 49
Kelman, Mr. John, 182, 183, 184, 185, 186
Kelvin, 348, 349
Ken, 260, 258
Kennely, Dr. A.E., 143, 152
Kennelly, Mr., 38, 41, 42, 53, 63
Kennelly, Prof., 217
kindergarten teacher, 56, 57
King Edward, 172
King Edward Method, 229
Kings, 276
Kintner, Mr. S.M., 115, 116, 148, 149, 189, 191, 193, 323
Kintner, Prof., 78, 81, 82, 313, 314, 315, 316
Kitchener, Lord, 232, 233
Kitten (Mikums), 107, 108
Kitty Hawk, 89
Knocker, 203
knowledge, 271
Koenig, 271
Kreussi, Mr., 28, 200

laboratories, 281
laboratory, 30, 297
laboratory activities, 235
Lafayette, City of, 60, 62, 63, 106
Lambert, Schmidt Telephone, 137
lamps, incandescent, 28, 36, 37, 62
lamp shade, 155
land of birth, 194
Langley, 64, 78
Lake Torpedo Boat Co., 237
landmarks, 296
land, 262
Largo, Handel's, 153
laryngitis, 343
latex, 306
lavish, 190, 342
Law, 158, 160, 188, 191, 272, 257, 317, 328
Lawrence Scientific Assn., 217
lawyer, 186, 207
leaders, 293
lectures, 217, 295
Lee, Mr., 129, 312
Lennoxville, P.Q., 20
legal, 105, 118
legislative remedy, 160
Lemieux, Mr., 176, 178, 179
Lenard, 268, 269

letters, 14, 15, 16, 17, 18, 19, 25, 26, 27, 28, 29, 34, 39, 40, 41, 53, 182, 205, 206, 218, 219, 220, 224, 295, 313
letters of intro, 225
lenses, 280
liabilities, 314
liberty, 283
libraries, 290, 291
library, 275, 276
Libya, 288
license, 170, 192, 312, 313, 314, 315
Lick Observatory, 65, 69, 72
life insurance, 190
life preservers, 176
light waves, 317
Lincoln, Abraham, 4, 6
linoleum, 48, 129
liquid air, 76
liquid barreter, 107, 154, 132
literature, 259, 275, 277, 294
litigation, 192, 339
Little, Admiral, 238
Liverpool, 225, 234
loans, 190
locating, 229
Lobley, Mr., 21
Locke, Insulation Co., 126
Lodge, Mr., 83
Lodge, 347
loop direction finding antenna, 229
London Banks, 174

Macaulay, 262
Macbeth Lamp Chimney Co., 71
machinations, 158
machine, 305
machine guns, 230
machinery, 239
machine shop, 133
machinist, 102
Macrihanish, 126, 127, 133, 134, 135, 136, 137, 138, 144, 145, 152, 154, 155, 169, 176
Macrihanish towers, 319
Mackey, 97
Macklem, Mr. Sutherland, 171
Madden, Mr., 317
Madden, Mr. & Mrs., 225, 233
Madden, T.R., 224, 225, 226, 230
mad house, 224, 254
magnetic, 148
magnetic compass, 44
magnetism, 53
magnetometer, Kew, 42
maid, J 20
main drive, 205
Maine Carlos, schooner, 87

Majestic Radio, 336
maleability, 307
maltose, 308
manager, 115
manaos, 123
manganium (an alloy), 50
manifestations, 257
manipulation, 315
Mann, Mr., 50
Mann's Harbor, 89
Manshendel, Mr., 133
Manteo, 86, 87, 89, 90, 91, 92, 93, 95, 97, 99, 100, 101, 103, 104, 107
manufacturer, 281, 282, 283, 284
Manytch Lakes, 288, 289
maps, 291
Marconi, 75, 83, 84, 92, 119, 312, 316, 317, 325, 347
Marconi Co., 157, 192
Marconi System, 100
Marconi Wireless Telegraph Co., 83
Margaret (a yacht), 241
marine, 207
marine propulsion, 204
Mars, 295
Marshfield, 340
Marvin, Prof., 80
Maryland, State of, 78
Mascart, Mr., 63
Masonic degrees, 259
Massachusetts, 126, 151, 152, 341, 342, 347
Massachusetts Bar, 259
Massachusetts Bay, 129
Massachusetts Bible Society, 294
Massachusetts Courts, 190
Massachusetts Institute of Technology, 127, 145
Mass production, 231
mast, 155
masts, fifty ft. wooden, 80, 81, 84
mathematical, 218
Mathematical Monograph, 246
mathematical solution, 216
Maxim Co., 173
Maxim, Mr., 50, 96
Maxim, Hiram, 96
Makins, 265
Maxwell, Mr., 59
Mayer, Judge, 132, 133
McCargo, Grant, 70
McDowell, Mr., 66, 280
McGill, University of, 6
McNab, Mr., 169, 170
Meadowcroft, Mr., 248
Meaness, 117
mechanical, 275

INDEX

Mechanical Car Transfer, 339
mechanical movement, 209
mechanics, 158
medal, 301
Medal of Honor, 325, 347
medals, 325, 326
mediator, 166
Mellon, Mr., 96
Member of Parliament, 180
memoirs, 212
memoranda, 205, 228, 229, 230, 314, 315
memorandum, 98, 172, 210, 314, 324
memories, 340
memos, 128, 129
Mendalian Law, 264
Menlo Park, 39
mental acuity, 292
mental equipment, 294
Mentality, Fessenden's, 338
merchant marine, 123
merger, 325
mergers, 322, 324
messengers, 263
metals, 350
meteorological, 99
Mexico, 95
Michelson, Prof. & Mrs., 337
microphone, 215, 257
microphonic contact, 97
Microphonographic Records, 330
microphotographic, 279
Microphotographic Books, 330
microphotography, 67
microscope, 142
Mid-Asian Sea, 288
Mike The Cat, 127, 129
Mikums The Cat, 155, 171, 188, 308, 341
miles, 287
milk, 107, 118
Miller, Prof., 127
mill-stone, 162
mimeograph, 267
mind, 294
mint julep, 338
miracle, 211, 228, 231
miscarriage, 318
misconception, 206
mission, 171, 224, 259
Missionary American, 24
mistakes, 311
model engine, 210
modern, 211
modern physics, 102
modification, 165
modifications, 99
molds, 236
molecule, 55

money, 162, 167, 190
Mongols, 264
monkeys, 120
monopoly, 37, 275, 276
Montreal Board of Trade, 169
Montreal, City of, 6, 169, 172
Montreal Harbor Commission, 169
Montreal Star, 170
monument, 342
Moore, Willis L., 76, 77, 78, 80, 91, 99, 100, 101, 103
morale, 284
morass, 289
Morgan, J.P., 29
Morgan, J.P. & Son, 171
Morgan, Rev. Dr., 47
moribund, 228
Morning Post, 175
Morse Recorder, 97
mortar, 335
mortification, 276
mosquitoes, 88
Mother Country, 259
motor, 255
motor generator, 247
mountains, 289, 290
Mount Hope, 23, 24
Mt. Whitney Observatory, 280
Mt. Ararat, 287
moving pictures, 37
Muldoon's, 170
Mull of Kintyre, 126
Multiple valued function method, 321, 330
multiplex resonant telegraphy, 60, 61
municipal activity, 196
municipalities, 181
municipality, 196
munitions, 238
museum, 275
Musgrave, Mr., 161
music, 153
musicians, 257
myths, 288, 293

Nag's Head, 89
Nahant, 242, 244
nap, 336
narrowly educated, 275
Nassay, Mr., 49
Nathan, Sir Matthew, 179, 180, 181
national decadence, 160
National development, 203

INDEX 379

National Electric Signaling Co., 82, 83, 105, 106, 107, 113, 114, 115, 116, 120, 123, 126, 133, 142, 152, 155, 157, 159, 161, 163, 167, 180, 189, 191, 192, 193, 312, 313, 323, 324, 332, 341, 347
National Guard, 259
natural resources, 175, 261
"Nature", 280, 281
Nature Magazine, 340
naval architecture, 211
naval attache, 172, 226
naval committee, 205
naval men, 249
naval offices, 239, 240, 250, 315
naval valuation, 315
Navesink, New Jersey, 122
navy, 182, 212, 237, 323, 326, 332
Navay (Navy) Consulting Board, 242, 247
navy department, 239, 254
navy operator, 159
Navy Special Problems Committee, 242
navy station, 121, 159
neanderthaliensis, 289
negative charge, 350
negotiating attorneys, 313, 314
negotiations, 172, 228, 329, 331
negro, 283
Nernst Lamp, 70
nerve strain, 260
nets, 302
neutrality, 235
neutralized, 284
Newark, City of, 46, 48, 49, 56, 57
Newark Electrical Society, 55
New Brunswick, 238
Newcastle, City of, 59
New England, 129
New England Conservatory of Music, 257
"New Fish Story", 151
Newfoundland, 126, 136, 170
New Jersey Court, 119, 313
New Jersey District, 119
New Jersey Station, 120
New London, 227, 239, 243, 244, 251, 255
New London Ship and Engine Co., 211
New Orleans, 183, 185, 347
New Orleans Station, 183
Newport, 223
News, 179, 180, 233
Newsreel, 341
New Type of Vehicle, 211
New Year, 342
New Year's Eve, 153, 347
"New York", 234

New York, City of, 26, 27, 28, 34, 35, 47, 166, 182, 224, 237, 291, 321, 331, 332
New York Crowd, 333
New York Herald Tribune (editorial re. Fessenden's death), 316
New York newspaper, 268
New York Sun, 330
New York Times, 276, 278, 300, 306, 330
Niagara Falls, City of, 13, 171, 194, 196
Niagara Falls Power, 178
Nichols, William, 274
niece, 282
nightmare, 189
nine, 282
nitrates, 262
nitrogen lamp, 279
Noah, 292
Norfolk, 87, 90, 95, 97, 154, 223
North Caucasus, 264
North Station, 218
note books, 314
nothing, 283
Nullified, 242
nuts, 262

obligations, 314
obstruction, 248
Ocean Depth Sounding, 326
Ocean's Bottom, 297
Ocean's View, 106
official order, 235
Official Report of Naval Consulting Board, 246
officer, 256
officers, 222
Ohio, 126
ohm, 103
ohm shunt, 136, 137, 138
oil, 289
oil magnets, 199
oil refineries, 307
oil wells, 293, 303
"O.K.", 309
old love, 194
Old Point Comfort, 95, 105, 106, 217
Old Testament, 291
"Olympic" (a ship), 225
omission, 243
O'Meara, Major, 179
Omanney, Sir Montague, 174
Omnibus application, 318
only son (Ken), 258
Ontario Power Commission, 194
operation, 341
Operations Bureau, 253

operator, 121, 123, 136, 137, 152, 154, 252
optical, 218
option, 106, 109, 110, 114, 298
option agreement, 335
Orange Library, 348
ore detector, 303
ores, 289
organization, 272
organized research, 277
Organizers, 261
original, 276
originator, 207
Oscillations, 94, 128, 217
Oscillator, 215, 216, 217, 218, 219, 221, 222, 223, 224, 225, 226, 227, 228, 234, 297
Oscillators, 235, 236, 243, 246, 252
oscillatory arc, 148
oscillograms, 244
oscillograph, 244
Osler, Sir William, 234, 265
osmotic, 350
Ottawa, 172, 224
out of business, 282
outside competition, 282
overboard, 219
over organization, 275
Oxford, 234
oxidation, 307

Pacific, 95
Pacific Cable Co., 97
padre, 338
painting, 310
paleolithic, 289
Palmer, Mr., 234
Panama, 176
Pannill, Mr., 106, 109, 121, 122, 128 137, 140, 144
pantograph, 267
paper, 197, 270
papers, 184, 187, 315
papers (Fessenden), 80
papers (verbal), 63
Papyrus, 275
para, 123
parade ground, 258
paradise, 293
paraffin, 350
paralysis, business, 208
parchment, 276
Paris, city of, 24, 38, 225
Parker, Mr. Frederick, 237, 260
Parker, Mr. M.G. (of New England Telephone Co.), 96

parking, 208
parsons, 265
Parsons, 59
Parsons steam turbine, 204
partnership, 117
patent, 213, 282, 316, 317, 318, 320
patent, #706, 736, 83
Patent Agents, Chartered Institute of, 172
patent analysis, 329
patent application, 142, 297, 304
patent attorney, 144
patent complications, 189
patent department, 210, 314
patent interferences, 307
patent, issued Jan. 14, 1907, 229
patent litigation, 307, 317
patent office, 143, 268, 270, 282, 283, 284, 285, 298, 299, 303, 318
patent pooling, 254
patent rights, 315, 323
patents, 96, 100, 105, 108, 113, 116, 119, 123, 124, 126, 132, 141, 160, 162, 163, 164, 165, 183, 208, 225, 237, 238, 298, 305, 312, 313, 314, 321, 324, 326, 329, 330, 332, 335, 339, 347
patents (Fessenden's), 54 (Nos. 452, 494, &453, 742 applied for or granted Feb. 18, 1891 & Feb. 18, 1891 (?) re alloys of silicon and method of keeping a joint clean by sealing it in a vacuum), 62, 192, 196
patents (Fessenden's), 67 (Nos. 1, 616, 848, &1, 732, 302 were reported in *N.Y. Post*, Oct. 13, 1930), 70, 77
patents, foreign, 192
patents granted
  (No. 1, 246, 520), 197
  (No. 1, 217, 165), 197
  (No. 1, 191, 072), 200
  (No. 1, 214, 531), 200
  (No. 1, 114, 975 & No. 1, 132, 465), 208
patent situation, 176
patent solicitors, 172
patent suits, 323
patent work, 170, 291
patriotic, 243
patriotism, 242
Patterson, principal of DeVeaux, 14
payments, 303
peak loads, 199
Pearman, Scott, 23, 24, 25
Pelorus, 320
Pennsylvania Avenue, 138
pension funds, 283

INDEX 381

people, 290
perceive, 294
perfection, 203, 338
perfumes, 115
Pergamus, 275
perils, 214
periscope, 250
Perkins, Miss Frances, 303
Perkins, Mr., 216, 226
permanent cure, 280
permission, 205
perpetual trundling, 199
Perrine, Mr., 54
Perrot, Mr. William, 301
Persian Minister (Mr. Khan), 120
persist, 289
personality, 117
persuader, 317
Petropolis, 291
pherescope, 172, 320, 321, 331
Philadelphia, City of, 111, 325
Philadelphia Newspaperman, 79
Philips Andover, 161
Phillips, Mr., 172
philosophical magazine, 55
philosophy, 260
philosophy, Fessenden's, 27, 338
Phipps, Mr. Henry, 96
Phipps, Mr. Lawrence, 96
Phoenician, 264
phones, 137
phonetics, 234
phonograph, 47, 270, 310
photocrat, 320
photograph, 279, 321
photographic doublet, 66
photographic plate, 268, 280
photographs, 314
photography, 67
Phrygian, 287
physicians, 339
physicists, 271
piano, 304, 330
piano case, 330
Piano Loud Speaker, 331
piano manufacturer, 282
Piano Manufacturing Concerns, 304
piano with wireless & phonograph, 330
Pickard, 278
Pickard, Dr. G.W., 143, 325
Pickles, Mr., 103
pickpockets, 203
Pierce, Prof., 143
pilgrimage, 340
pillars, 288, 340
pine cones, 262
pioneer, 317, 319

pioneering, 274, 320
pipe, Indian, 130
piracy, 300
piston, 209, 210, 230
piston rings, 209
piston sleeve, 209
Pittsburgh Academy of Science and Art, 69
Pittsburgh, city of, 48, 64, 80, 82, 108, 109, 114, 115, 163, 166, 167, 183, 184, 185, 187, 311
"Pittsburgh's Contribution To Radio", 149
Pittsburgh, University of (formerly Western U.), 62, 64, 65, 66, 67, 68, 75, 217
Pittsfield, City of, 47, 55, 56, 59, 60, 182
Plain, 290
plaintiff, 300
plantation owner, 283
platinum, 54, 132
Plato, 275
play, 217
plea, 172
pleased, 195
Plymouth, 151, 152, 154, 169
pocket money, 258
poets, 276
poison, 292
Poisson's Law, 351
police, 186
policies, 202
policy, 297
political power, 188
pooled interests, 322
popular radio, 80
Portsmouth, 227
Poser, Dr. Man, 19
position, 283
positions, 283
positive charge, 349
possession, 279
postal telegraph, 95
Postal Telegraph Co., 155
Postmaster General, 172, 180
post office, 179, 180
potassium, 350
Potomac River, 78, 79
power, 208, 230, 241
power banks, 198, 201
power clearing house, 199
power commission, 178
power plant behind, 211
power producers, 200
Power Storage Group, 197
Pratt, Lambert, & Co., 44, 45
Pratt, Mr., 44, 45

INDEX

Preece, Mr., 63
premiums, 190
prep school, 161
presentation, 290
preservation, 285
preserved, 266
president, 166, 185, 243
President Hoover, 202
press, 223, 259
press notice, 197
pressure, 239, 275
preventer, 122
Price, Mr., 218, 219, 226, 234, 244
principle, 179
priority, 318, 319
problem, 216, 290
procession, 316
producing, 231
professor, 283, 347
profitable, 283
profits, 167
"pro" (golf), 223
progress, 199, 262, 285, 316, 317
prohibition, 308
project, 208
projects, 202
promise, 202
prompt action, 231
promptness, 214
proofs, 309, 311
propaganda, 245, 256, 278
proposal, 224, 243
proposition, 165, 166
prosper, 209
prosperity, 282
protein, 340
Ptolemy, 275
public, 202, 258
publication, 284, 290
publications, 281, 294
publicity, 82, 342
public utilities, 195
publish, 290
pulverulent matter, 200
pumped, 198
pumps, 198
punctures, 305
Purdue, Univ. of, 47, 59, 60, 61, 75, 347
pyrene, 34

quantitative measurements, 131
quartz discs, 279
Queen and Co., 96 (Insts. Philadelphia), 97, 98, 105
Queen Ashirta, 290
Queen Hotel, 218
Quinan, Captain, 218, 221
quondam, 237

Races, 264
Radiation, 139
Radio, 82, 115, 116, 132, 304, 315, 316, 317, 319, 321, 322, 342, 336
radio art, 317
Radio Broadcast, 347
radio communications, 317, 326
Radio Corporation, 304
Radio Corporation of America, 323, 324, 328, 331, 332, 335
radio engineers, 316
radio history, 341, 342
radio institute, 153
radio institute dinner, 321
radio institute library, 153
radio marine corporation, 121
radio merger, 328
"Radio News"
 (Jan. 1925), 202, 308, 311
 1925), 262
Radio News Magazine, 11
"Radio Octopus", a story in *American Mercury*, Aug. 1931, 150
radio patent situation, 317
radio scope, 320
radio station, 121
radio supplement, 268
radio-telephony, 214
radio telescope, 320, 330
radio trust, 150, 321, 326, 329
radio, two way trans-Atlantic, 83
rain, 288, 290
range, 155, 169, 215
rapid, 287
rats, 285
Rayleigh, Lord, 218
R.C.A., 347
real inventing, 310
reality, 291
reasonableness, 286
reasoning, 292, 307, 308
receipt, 279
receiver, 93, 94, 107, 119, 147, 315
Receiver, financial, 115
receivers, 121, 222, 232, 313, 314, 319
receiver's hands, 166
receivers, legal, 192, 193
receivers, ring, 80
receivership, 191, 313, 314
receiving, 152, 318
receiving apparatus, 215
receiving circuit, 147
receiving room, 129
receiving submarine, 245
reception, 242
recognition, 207
recognition signal, 255

ID# INDEX 383

recommend, 226
recommendations, 159
records, 184
Rectory, 9
red tape, 226
reduce, 340
reflections, 291
refractions, 218
refusing facilities, 255
Regenerative Mercury Tube, 148
regeñerator, 284
regulations, 157, 158, 159
regimentation, 315
Reid, Sir George, 175
reimburse, 160
relationship, 226
relax, 335
Rellstab, Judge, 313
remarkable, 232
rental, 208
reparations, 333
reparations commission, 329
report, 178
Republican party, 160
reputation, 307
request, 205, 234
research, 182, 267, 268, 286, 308
Research Cabiri, 281, 283
Research Council, 276, 277, 278, 279, 280, 282, 283, 284, 285
researches, 280
research staff, 281
reservoir, 197, 198
resistance, 211
resolutions, 254
resonance, 102, 148
resonator, 94
resources, 280, 284
response, 290
rest, 339
restraint of trade, 332
restrictions, 158, 159
retaining fee, 303
retrogression, 285
Revenue Cutter Service, 217
reversible meter, 199
revolutionized, 215
reward, 315
Rhigi, 316
Rhodes, 276
Rhonda, Lord, 238
Rice, Mr., 96, General Electric, 200, 207, 210
Ridley, 3
Ridley, Marion, 5, 8
Ridley, Mr., 9
rifles, 185, 250

riggers, 140
Riggs Place, 106, 120 (their Washington address in 1903, #1677), 125
rights, 314
rise, 237
risk, 170, 176 (prophetic), 223
rites, 338
rivalries, 182
rivers, 288
Rivett, Mr., 209, 210
Rivett Precision Lathe Works, 209
Roanoke Island, 86, 87, 88, 89, 93
Roberts, Mr., 106, 109
rock, 214
Rockefeller, 281
Rockefeller Institute, 339
Rockmore, 23
Rock Point, 94
Rocky Point, 78
Roeblings Works, 54, 145
Roehm, Mr., 331
Roentgen, Mr., 69, 268
Rogers, 278, 284
Roosevelt, 131, 322
Roosevelt, President Theodore, 160, 174
roses, 171
Roses and Holgate, 195
Rosse, Lord, 265
rotary gap, 154
Rotating Scale Sounder (patent applied for March 28, 1921), 297, 299 Better known as Fathometer, patent No. 1217585 (also called "Echo Distance Finder")
Route 90, 89
Rowland, 63, 266
Royal Commission, 172, 175, 176, 178, 179, 180
Royal Geographical Society, 291
royalties, 202, 237, 312
Royalty, 171
rubber, 306, 348, 349, 351
Rugby, 227
Ruhl, Arthur, 234
rumors, 227
Russell ("Nature" Nov. 1, 1924), 277
Russia, 272
Russian Govt., 289
Russian legation, 120

safe, 184
safeguarded, 266
sailing, 176, 234
salary, 163, 166, 167, 281
sale, 268
Salem cruiser, 183
salesmanship, 306

INDEX

salinity, 319
Sally Ann (a dinghy owned by Pearman, nephew of Helen May), 25
salt domes, 293, 303
salvation, 293
Samuels, Mr., 180
sands, 342
Sandy Hook, 121
sarcasm, 238
sargent, 310
Sarnoff, Mr., 324, 331
saturated market, 273
"Saturday Review", 234
Sawyer, Mr., 50
Scaife, Mr. W.L., 69
Scanlin, Mr., 121
scavenging, 212, 213
schemes, 279
Schenectady, 30, 45, 200, 205, 206, 236
scholars, 276
school inspector (Bermuda), 24
schooner, 86, 87
science, 285, 316, 336
scientific, 103, 281, 317, 342
Scientific American Magazine, 22
Scientific American Medal, 347
Scientific American Medal For Safety At Sea, 302
scientific body, 177
scientific knowledge, 228
scientific training, 213
Scotland, 347
screw propellors, 204
scrub woman, 115
sculpture, 262
sealed, 184
sea water, 319
secondary spark, 85
secrecy, 318
"Secrecy", 247
secrecy sender, 317
secrecy sending, 330
secretary, 226
Secretary Knox, 160
Secretary of Agriculture, 101, 102, 104
Secretary of Navy, 131, 159
Secretary of War, 237
Secretary Straus of Dept. of Comm. and Labor, 159, 160
Secretary Taft, 160
secret international reports, 281
secret reports, 284
secrets, 281, 282
Secret Sending, 317
secret sending method, 254
Secret Service, 256
secret society, 293

sediment, 288
Seeley, Mr., 70
seize, 284
seized, 276
selector, 138
self-tightening, 209
Semites, 264
"Senaca" (a ship), 221
Senate, 177
Senate Committee, 329
sender, 85
sending power, 139
sensitiveness, 94
sensitivity, 108
seven and one half millions, 332
severed, 235
sewing machine, 277
shade imperceptibility, 269
shaft, 198, 199
shareholders, 283
shares, 297
Shaw, George Bernard, 234
Sheffield, 177, 197
Sherbrooke, city of, 7
Sherman Anti-Trust Act, 322
Shields, Mr., 139
ship, 154
ship-building, 273
Shipping Federation of Canada, 169
ships, 158
ship's bridge, 301
shoal, 214, 288
shoemaker, 119
shou, 287
short wave, 319, 320, 330, 335, 339
shutter, 321
sick, 333
sighting, 230
signal, 222
signalling, 215, 216, 223
signals, 136, 137, 139, 319
signature, 128
signing, 334
Silicon, 54, 57
silk, 273, 352
silver, 348, 352
sine waves, 61
singing, 153, 257
sinister, 274
Sister of Helen May, 23
skin, 245
skirmish, 186
Slaby, Prof., 102
slave, 283
sleep, 118
slow, 289
small diaphragm, 279

INDEX

small oscillator, 254
Smart, Dr., 60, 61
Smith, 234
Smith, A.L., 21
Smith, Chard, 338
Smith, Donald, 175
Smith, Herbert, 327, 328
Smith, Mr., 334
smoke stack, 126
snowplough, invention of, 6
soaps, 115, 352
Social Science (a magazine), 28
societtes, 290
socket, 126
soldiers, 274
solution, 201
solvency, 161
solvents, 351
something new, 273
son, 290, 291
sonic depth finder, 278, 347
sound, 215, 218, 222, 257, 279, 350
sounder, 97
soundings, 221, 302
"Soundings" (S.S. Company Magazine), 214
sound screens, 252
Sound Spectrum, 317, 318
sound standards, 218
sound waves, 230, 271, 317
South Africa, 176, 178
Southampton, 171
South Frainingham, 217
South Shore Fishermen, 152
South Station, 214
spark, 122, 274
spark gap, 131, 132, 148
spark gap, compressed gas, 131
spark gap, rotary, 131, 134
spark plugs, 213
Spartan, 115
Special Board on Submarine Devices, 254
specialist's opinion, 244
specific application, 318
specification, 196, 207
speech (made by Fess. to Radio Institute on inventing the wireless telephone and the future), 147, 152, 153
speed, 208
Sperry, 44
sphere, 350, 351
spirit, 343
springs, 308
spying, 141
S.S. Leviathan, 301
stabilizer, 232

stagnation, 282
stalemate, 191
Stanley Company, 182
Stanley, Mr., 55, 56, 57, 58, 59, 210
Stanley Steam Car Co., 210
State Commissioner, 190
State Department, 171
States, 234, 337, 338
static, 148, 304
statical, 275
station, 133, 134, 135, 154, 183, 185, 243
stations, 105, 108, 114, 123, 125, 128, 146, 164
St. Botolph Club, 257
steam, 198
steam boat, 277
steam engine, 133, 273
steam power, 307
steam turbine, 204, 265, 273
steam turbine generators, 204
steel, 115, 293, 306
Stein, Mr. Adam (D.B.&S. were all technical men), 149, 154, 189, 341
Steinmetz, Mr., 149
Stephen, Mr. G.W., 169
Stephenson, 265
St. Francis River, 5, 20
Stielers, 291
stimulation, 316
stipulations, 311
St. Louis, 331
St. Martin's Church, 177
stock, 105, 106, 109, 110, 111, 112, 116, 117, 162, 163, 164, 168, 237, 313, 315
stock jobbing, 96
stone, 335
Stone and Webster, 210
Stone, Mr., 200
storage, 196, 198, 199, 200
storage battery, 147
"Storage of Power", 177
stormy interludes, 258
Strabo, 290
strain, 170, 266
strangers, 184
Strauss, 310
stream-lined, 211
stress, 117
stroke, 294
stronghold, 284
student, 275, 283, 286
sub-conscious, 118
submarine, 240, 255, 256
submarine base, 239
Submarine Board, 242, 244, 245, 246, 247, 248, 249, 250, 251, 252, 253
Submarine Defense Assn., 247

INDEX

submarine detection, 239
Submarine Detection by Sound, 242
submarine detector, 227, 235, 236, 245
Submarine Electric Oscillator, 221
submarine matters, 244
submarine motors, 212
submarine problems, 214
submarines, 211, 213, 243, 246, 247, 249, 250, 252, 253, 319
Submarine Signal Co., 211, 214, 215, 217, 221, 224, 225, 226, 227, 228, 230, 235, 236, 237, 239, 241, 242, 243, 245, 247, 248, 249, 250, 252, 256, 260, 291, 297, 298, 299, 300, 301, 303, 317
Submarine Signal Co. Report, No. 87, May 9, 1917, 254
"Submarine Signal Fathometer" (a booklet put out by Sub. Sig. Co.), 301
Submarine Signalling, 214, 215, 228, 235, 243
submarine signalling apparatus, 227
Submarine Telegraph, 223
submarine telegraph apparatus, 215
submarine telephone, 223
subsidiary companies, 167
substitution, 269
subterranean, 199
success, 180, 202, 213
successful, 227, 240
Sudbury, city of, 36
sugar, 262, 308
suicides, 280
suit, 187, 328
Suite, Louis Seige, 225
suits, 307
suits, legal, 107
sulphur beds, 303
summer, 161, 182, 195
summer cottage, 106
sun, 198
sunshine lamps, 343
sun's rays, 197
super-centre of force, 274
superior, 251
surgeon, 341
Sutherland, 348
synchronous generator, 199
syntonized circuits, 199
system, 208, 274

Tabusintac River, 238
tactical, 240
Tamischeira, 290

tank type, 228
tantalum, 132
Tantalus vision, 199
tapestry, 289
Tartary, 288
Tasimeter, 36
taxation, 284
taxes, 285
taxpayer, 281, 284
tea money, 305
teamwork, 277
technical grounds, 245
technical journal, 151 (a story of Nov. 10 calling Fess.' radio telephoning to the fishing schooner a "Fishy fish story")
technical journals, 142
technical waters, 332
telegrams, 158
telegraph, 99, 253, 272, 277
telegrapher, 102
telegraphic, 106
telegraphic apparatus, 57
telegraphic signals, 215
telephone, 95, 97, 272
telephoned, 243
Telephone Journal, 152, 153 (mentions report of tests in issues of Jan. 26, and Feb. ", 1907)
telephone sets, 148
telephone transmitter, 214
telephonic transmission, 149
"Telephoning Beneath The Sea" (an article in the *Scientific American*, March, 1926), 299
telephony, 347
telescope, 65
telescopes, 265
television, 336
television projector, 331
temple shrines, 263
ten billion dollars, 281
ten miles, 240
tennis court, 336
tensile strength, 307
tension, 161, 328
ten thousand airplanes, 231
test, 251, 252
testimony, 324, 332
tests, 183, 217, 218, 223, 227, 238, 239, 240, 243, 244, 319
Thaw, William, 64, 66
The Board, 254
theft, 186
Theodore, Mr., (ran boarding house in Pittsfield), 56
theory, 294

INDEX

"The Paper", 178
thesis, 290
Thiessen, 86, 103
Thiessen, Mr. Alfred (Weather Bureau man assisting Fess. at Cobb Island), 78, 79, 81
Thomas, Mr., 238
Thompson, J.J., 38, 59, 172, 176, 177
Thompson, Prof. Elihu, 152, 200, 210
Thomson-Houston Co., 227
thorn apple, 292
thoroughness, 286
three miles, 240
thwarted, 255
Tibbits, 3, 5
tidal wave, 287, 288
tiger cat, 308
Tillman, Senator, 237
timber, 289
Time, 293, 305
time-constant, 117, 216
"Times" (a newspaper), 291
Times (London) Engineering Supplement (Sept. 14, 1910), 197
Timon, 276
Titanic, 214, 216, 217
Todd, Commander, 315
Todhunter & Ibbotson, 348
tonsil, diseased, 340
tools, 307
Topeka, U.S.S., 121
Toronto, 69, 195
torpedo tube, 256
total ignorance, 178
tower, 126, 127, 130, 131, 133, 140, 141, 147, 155
Tower of Dreams, 341
trade, 293
trade secrets, 284, 285
tradition, 287, 288
training, 170
train, special, 120
Trans-Atlantic, 169, 317, 319, 347
Trans-Atlantic permit, 178, 179
Trans-Atlantic Radio, 83, 124, 125, 126, 155
Trans-Atlantic Telephone, 128, 133, 143
Trans-Atlantic Wireless, 180
transcription, 343
transformers, 134
transformers, insulation of, 57
trans-Pacific, 169
trans oceanic wireless telegraphy, 169
transmission, 98, 107, 124, 158, 242, 318
transmission of music, 152
transmission of ordinary phonographic talking, 152

transmission of ordinary speed, 152
transmitter, 121
transmitting, 152, 163, 215
transmitting station, 317
traveller, 296
treaty, 159
trebling, 215
Trenholme, 3
Trenholme, Ann Winn, 5
Trenholme, Clementina, 7, 14, 15, 16, 17, 45
Trenholme, Edward, 5, 6, 7, 8
Trenholme, Mrs. Edward (Marion), 7, 9
Trenholme, Village of, 51
Trenholme, William, 5
trial, 190
tribulations, 305
trigger acting receivers, 83
Trinity College School, 14, 15, 16, 17, 18, 19
troop ships, 235
trouble, 213
Trowbridge, Dr. John, 217
truce, 312
trucks, 186
trust, 285, 332, 333
trusts, 281, 282, 284
Tube, 420 foot steel, 341
tube, steel, 126
tumblers, 350, 351
tuned circuit, 102
tuners, 121
"Tunes", 135, 158
tungsten filaments, 279
tuning, 103
tuning circuits, 83
tuning devices, 106
turbine, steam, 59
turbo-electric drive, 204, 205, 206, 207, 347
turbo-electronic, 273
Turner, Mr. Christopher, 171
Turner, Mr. Eben T, 91
"Tuscania", a ship, 253
Tutankamen, 271
typewriter, 277
twenty-year license, 181
two-phase drive, 208

U-boat, 241, 242, 245
U-boat danger, 239
U-boat detection, 255
Ultra-violet signalling, 278
umbrella capacity, 126, 135
undertaxing, 196
underwater sounds, 242
underwater wireless, 278, 284

unintelligible, 318
Union Boat Club, 239
Union League Club, 303
United Fruit Co., 153, 161, 162, 167, 183, 247, 323
United States, 84, 85, 93, 96, 100, 157, 177, 224, 227, 238, 239, 259, 277, 281, 282, 283
United States Ambassador Reid, 172
United States Army, 143
United States Coast and Geodetic Survey, 300
United States Dept. of Agri. (Weather Bureau), 76, 77, 81
United States Engineers, 178
United States Government, 120, 123, 160, 162, 247, 323
United States Lines, 301
United States Merchant Marine, 247
United States Navy, 120, 122, 123, 143, 153, 157, 161, 204, 205, 207, 240, 299, 314, 318, 319, 321
United States Patents, 192
United States Senate Committee on Foreign Relations, 158, 159
universe, 343
universities, 283, 285
unpublished papers, 294
unsatisfied claims, 324
unsuccessful, 227
urgent, 226
usefulness, 336
U.S.R.C. Miami, 218, 219, 221, 222
U.S.S. Aylwin, 227
U.S.S. Delaware, 227
U.S.S. Utah, 227

vacuum, 94
Vail, Mr., 156
validity, 335
valuation, 315
vandalage, 342
Van der Waal's formula, 350
Vauclain, Mr., 52, 53
Vaux, Mr., 226
velocity, 222
venture, 305
veranda, 343
verbal order, 321
verdict, 191
"Vernon" (a ship), 227
Very, Mr., (assistant to Langley), 78, 79, 91
vessels, 228
vested, 285
vibrations, 230, 257, 271
vibrator, 236

vibrograph, 271
Vice-President, 207
Victor, town of, 126
Viking, 117
violin, 153, 257, 304
vision, 321
vital, 286
voice handicap, 257
voice transmission, 317
volcano, 109, 115
volt, 103
voltage, 148
voltage gap, 134
Voltmeter, Weston, 97
volts, 127
volumes, 275
voluminous, 294
Von-Turpitz, 212
Vreeland, Mr. Frederick, 106, 107, 119

Wadsworth, 280
Wakefield Estate, 79
Walker, 105, 106, 107, 109, 110, 111, 113, 114, 116, 124, 125, 136, 138, 141, 146, 155, 161, 162, 163, 166, 167, 168, 170, 171, 182, 183, 186, 190, 191, 312, 314, 323
"Wall of Sound", 216
war, 241, 286, 315, 318, 326
warning, 274
warning sign, 339
war office, 228, 229, 230, 238
war trends, 213
Washington, 119, 120, 172, 204, 205, 217, 237, 238, 240, 325, 330,
Washington, city of, 6, 78, 91, 100, 102, 103, 106, 108, 125, 127, 133, 138, 161, 169, 171, 265
Washington, George, 79
Washington House, 161
Washington Shop, 149, 154
Washington Station, 131
wasteful, 200
watchman, 141
water, 129, 201, 215, 222, 301
Waterbury, Mr. John I., 156
water, glass of, 342
water noise cut-out screens, 254
water noises, 215
water storage, 198
water turbine, 198
Watt, 266, 267
Watt's dictionary, 32, 35, 67
wave lengths, 134, 157, 159
waves, 94, 319
wealth, 188, 283
weapon, 235

INDEX

Weather Bureau, 86, 91, 99, 100, 102, 103, 104
Weaver, Colonel Erasmus, 106
Weaver, General, 237
Weaver, Judge and Mrs., 60
Weaverson, Mr., 28
Webster, 28
Webster, Prof., 143
wedding, 45, 47
weeping, 328
Wehnelt interrupter, 147
weight, 213
weights, 206
Wells, H.G., 233
Welsbach, Mr., 58
Wescoe, Mr., 137
Western Electric Co., 243, 252, 318, 319, 323
Weatern Tower, 188, 341
Western Union, 156
Western University (University of Pittsburgh), 100, 114, 189, 347
West Indian License, 180
West Indies, 154, 180, 199
Westinghouse, 46, 54, 62, 82, 115, 189, 333
Westinghouse Co., 205, 332
Westinghouse Electric, 323
Westinghouse, George, 204, 205
Weston, 265
Weston, Mr., 50
Wheatstone Bridge, 94
wheeled vehicles, 208
whip, 317
Whipple, Sherman, 207, 327, 328, 329, 339
whirlwind, 187
White Bill, 329
Whitehall, 172
White, Mr. Charles, 257
White Plains, 170
White, Sir William, 178
Whitney, Dr. W.R., 242, 243, 247
Whitney Institute, 22, 23, 24
Whittlesey, Mr., 57
widows, 115
Wien, Dr. Willy, 65
wife, 164
Williams, Mr. Arthur, 303
Williams, Senator John Sharp, 237
Wilson, Dr., 246
Wilson, Mr., 68
Wilson, President, 151, 283
windmills, 198
wine, 308
winters, 336
wire, 321
wireless, 86, 89, 107, 119, 123, 136, 161, 214, 221, 307, 311, 312, 315

wireless apparatus, 315
wireless circuit, 103
wireless companies, 157, 158, 159, 161
wireless compass, 273, 278, 347
wireless key, 93
wireless license, 175
wireless litigation, 312
wireless moving picture transmitter, 61
wireless patents, 315
wireless partners, 237
wireless picture transmission, 278
wireless room, 222
wireless situation, 176
Wireless Specialty Co., 323
wireless station, 87, 88, 99, 126, 169, 179
wireless telegraph, 226
wireless telegraphic messages, 347
wireless telegraphy, 75, 76, 80, 81, 82, 83, 84, 100, 102, 105, 123, 145
wireless telephone, 147, 152, 153, 155, 169, 226, 272, 347
wireless telephonic transmission, 151, 152
wireless telephony (radio), 81, 82
wireless transmission, 183, 319, 347
wireless treaty, 161
wireless waves, 319
wireless work, 172
Wistowe, 335, 337, 342, 343
Withington, Dr. & Mrs., 56, 57, 60
Wolcott, Mr. Darwin S. (Pittsburgh) (of the law firm of Christy and Christy, Reg's patent attorney), 82, 93, 95, 96, 99, 101, 105, 106, 107, 109, 110, 111, 112, 119, 163, 190, 191
Wolf, Mr., 19
Wood, Mr., 172
wonders, 144
Woodstock, city of, 20
Woodsworth, Mr., 314
words, 316
workers, 293
working drawings, 164
working model, 210, 215
works, 275, 276
world, 293
World's Fair Electrical Congress, 63
World War I, 224
world-wide power, 199
Wright Brothers, 210
Wrights, 266, 285
writers, 275, 289
writing, Fessenden's (*Electrical World*, Aug. 22, 1896), 67
written order, 183
wrong hands, 235
wrong turn, 286, 307

X-rays, 69, 70

Yale, 175, 188, 288
Yale Library, 295
Yancey, Mr., 337
Yankee, 35
Yankee Boy, 201
Yellow Maria (a cat), 88
Yorke, Dane, 150
Young, Hon. John (Montreal financier), 6

Young, Owen D., 151, 329, 330, 331, 332, 333

Z—the letter, 128
Zenith, 263
Zeppelin, 229
zest, 343
Zimmerman, 49
zinc, 146

TELECOMMUNICATIONS
An Arno Press Collection

Abramson, Albert. **Electronic Motion Pictures:** A History of the Television Camera. 1955

[Bell, Alexander Graham]. **The Bell Telephone:** The Deposition of Alexander Graham Bell in the Suit Brought By the United States to Annul the Bell Patents. 1908

Bennett, A. R. **The Telephone Systems of the Continent of Europe** and Webb, Herbert Laws, **The Development of the Telephone in Europe.** 1895/1910. Two vols. in one

Blake, George G. **History of Radio Telegraphy and Telephony.** 1928

Bright, Charles. **Submarine Telegraphs:** Their History, Construction and Working. 1898

Brown, J. Willard. **The Signal Corps U. S. A. in the War of the Rebellion.** With an Introduction by Paul J. Scheips. 1896

Chief Signal Officer, U. S. Signal Corps. **Report of the Chief Signal Officer: 1919.** 1920

Danielian, N[oobar] R. **A. T. & T.:** The Story of Industrial Conquest. 1939

Du Moncel, Count [Theodore A. L.] **The Telephone, the Microphone, and the Phonograph.** 1879

Eckhardt, George H. **Electronic Television.** 1936

Eoyang, Thomas T. **An Economic Study of the Radio Industry in the United States of America.** 1936

Everson, George. **The Story of Television:** The Life of Philo T. Farnsworth. 1949

Eyewitness to Early American Telegraphy. 1974

Fahie, J[ohn] J. **A History of Electric Telegraphy to the Year 1837.** 1884

Federal Communications Commission. **Investigation of the Telephone Industry in the United States.** 1939

Federal Communications Commission. **Public Service Responsibility of Broadcast Licensees.** 1946

Federal Trade Commission. **Report of the Federal Trade Commission on the Radio Industry.** 1924

Fessenden, Helen M. **Fessenden:** Builder of Tomorrows. 1940

Hancock, Harry E. **Wireless at Sea:** The First Fifty Years. 1950

Hawks, Ellison. **Pioneers of Wireless.** 1927

Herring, James M. and Gerald C. Gross. **Telecommunications:** Economics and Regulations. 1936

Lodge, Oliver J. **Signalling Through Space Without Wires:** Being a Description of the Work of Hertz and His Successors. [1900]

McNicol, Donald. **Radio's Conquest of Space:** The Experimental Rise in Radio Communication. 1946

Plum, William R[attle]. **The Military Telegraph During the Civil War in the United States.** With an Introduction by Paul J. Scheips. Two vols. 1882

Prime, Samuel Irenaeus. **The Life of Samuel F. B. Morse,** L.L. D., Inventor of the Electro-Magnetic Recording Telegraph. 1875

The Radio Industry: The Story of Its Development. By Leaders of the Radio Industry. 1928

Reid, James D. **The Telegraph in America:** Its Founders, Promoters and Noted Men. 1879

Rhodes, Frederick Leland. **Beginnings of Telephony.** 1929

Smith, Willoughby. **The Rise and Extension of Submarine Telegraphy.** 1891

Special Reports on American Broadcasting: 1932-1947. 1974

Thompson, Silvanus P., **Philipp Reis:** Inventor of the Telephone; A Biographical Sketch. 1883

Tiltman, Ronald F., **Baird of Television:** The Life Story of John Logie Baird. 1933

Wile, Frederic William. **Emile Berliner:** Maker of the Microphone. 1926

Woods, David L., **A History of Tactical Communication Techniques.** 1965